THE WATERS AROUND THE BRITISH ISLES

THE WATERS AROUND THE BRITISH ISLES

Their Conflicting Uses

Report of a Study Group of the David Davies Memorial Institute of International Studies

R. B. CLARK

CLARENDON PRESS · OXFORD
1987

Oxford University Press, Walton Street, Oxford OX2 6DP

Oxford New York Toronto
Delhi Bombay Calcutta Madras Karachi
Petaling Jaya Singapore Hong Kong Tokyo
Nairobi Dar es Salaam Cape Town
Melbourne Auckland
and associated companies in
Beirut Berlin Ibadan Nicosia

Oxford is a trade mark of Oxford University Press

Published in the United States
by Oxford University Press, New York

British Library Cataloguing in Publication Data
Clark, R. B.
The waters around the British Isles: their conflicting uses: report of a study group of the David
Davies Memorial Institute of International Studies.
1. Coastal zone management—Law and legislation—Great Britain.
2. Territorial waters—Great Britain
I. Title II. David Davies Memorial Institute of
International Studies
344.1064'69164   KD1098
ISBN 0-19-828492-6

Library of Congress Cataloging in Publication Data
Clark, R. B. (Robert Bernard), 1923–
The waters around the British Isles.
Bibliography: p.   Includes index
1. Maritime law—Great Britain.
2. Marine resources conservation—Law and legislation—Great Britain.
3. Maritime law.   4. Marine resources conservation
—Law and legislation.
I. David Davies Memorial Institute of International Studies.
II. Title.
JX4422.G7C54 1986   333.91'64   86-23497
ISBN 0-19-828492-6

Set by Spire Print Services Ltd, Salisbury, Wilts
Printed and bound in Great Britain by Biddles Ltd,
Guildford and Kings Lynn

Preface

This volume is the last of three enquiries conducted by the David Davies Memorial Institute of International Studies into the rational management of the seas around the British Isles and the national and international legal regimes designed to achieve this. The first of these enquiries dealt with the North Sea[1] and the second with the Celtic Sea and Western Approaches[2]. It was originally envisaged that the final report would provide a brief synopsis embracing and supplementing the two earlier studies, but in the decade since the publication of the North Sea report there has been a sufficient advance in technical knowledge and change in the legal instruments that a major new review of the situation has proved necessary.

As with the North Sea study, this report is the product of a Study Group, in this case consisting of Mr Ray Beverton, Dr Patricia Birnie, Mr Tom Busha, Professor R. B. Clark (chairman), Professor James Fawcett, Dr David Greenwood, Vice-Admiral Sir Ian McGeoch, Professor Alasdair McIntyre, and Miss Mary Sibthorp (then Director of the Institute). Mr Jack O'Sullivan was rapporteur.

Consultation and data collection by the Study Group was completed in mid-1983, and the final form of the report was approved towards the end of that year. Editing and publishing the report has taken a further three years and as a result, some of the data, though as up-to-date as we could make it in 1983, now appears more appropriate to the start of the decade than to its final years. We are satisfied, however, that the situation has changed little in the interval. Indeed, as we show in the final chapter, the problems revealed in our North Sea report in 1975 still await a solution even if the technical details have changed in the meantime.

The North Sea report noted the decline of herring catches but did not forsee their total collapse, nor the subsequent recovery of the stocks of fish, but the need for a rational, internationally enforced fishery policy still remains. The discussion of shipping in the present volume (chapter VI) did not forsee the collapse of world oil prices in early 1986 and the economic consequences of it during the following months, but the underlying problem of regulating shipping in the heavily trafficked sealanes of the English Channel and southern North Sea is unaffected by these events. Technical details change, often radically, and economic factors can be revolutionized in a few months, but the conflicts of interests in the use of the waters around the British Isles are basically unchanged by these perturbations and the need remains for an adequate legal regime to resolve them. Indeed, as we point out, such is the difficulty of negotiating international conventions and such the delay in bringing them into effect once the agreement has been reached, that the time-scale for these remedial actions is measured in decades, not in months or a few years.

Nevertheless, the involvement of the European Community in environmental affairs and the inter-ministerial discussions of the pollution of the North Sea, the first in Bremen in 1984 and the next scheduled to be held in London in November 1987, add fresh urgency to considerations of the management of the regional seas which this book addresses. We hope our analysis of the problems will help clarify the issues that need to be resolved.

R. B. Clark
Newcastle upon Tyne
September 1986

1 Sibthorp, M. M. (ed.) *The North Sea: challenge and opportunity*. Europa Publications, London, 1975.
2 Sibthorp, M. M. and Unwin, M. (eds.) *Oceanic Management: conflicting uses of the Celtic Sea and other western U.K. waters*. Europa Publications, London, 1977.

Acknowledgements

The Study Group are very grateful to the following who contributed papers, or gave general advice and guidance: Mr Paul Adams, OECD; Mr Alan Archer; Dr John Barrett; Dr Michael Barry, SW Regional Fisheries Board; Professor B. McKay Bary, University College, Galway; Dr R. W. Blacker, MAFF; Professor Sir Hermann Bondi; Professor K. F. Bowden, Liverpool University; Dr W. M. Brancker; Dr Robert Buchanan; Professor Brian Clark, Aberdeen University; Mr A. J. Cluness, Shetland; Dr H. A. Cole; Dr R. M. Crockett, Institute of Geological Sciences; Captain John Crosbie, Maritime Institute of Ireland; Dr R. I. Currie, Scottish Marine Biological Association; Mr Tim Dixon; Mr Trevor Dixon, Buckinghamshire College of Further Education; Dr Eric Edwards, Shellfish Association of Great Britain; Mr J. L. Edwards, Crown Estate Commissioners; Mr R. T. Edwards, Bank of Scotland; Dr Michael Flood, Friends of the Earth; Dr Peter Fotheringham, Glasgow University; Mr Eamonn Gallagher, Commission of the European Communities; Dr D. J. Garrod, MAFF; Dr Ian T. Gault, Canadian Institute of Resources; Mr Henry George; Dr Alec Gibson, Department of Fisheries, Dublin; Dr John Gibson, UWIST; Dr Sydney Gilman, Liverpool University; Dr Clive Grove-Palmer, Energy Technology Support Unit; Dr E. I. Hamilton, Institute of Marine Environmental Resources; Mr Bob Hanna, National Board for Science & Technology, Dublin; Mr E. R. Hargreaves; Rear-Admiral J. B. Haslam, Hydrographer of the Navy; Dr Peter C. Head, NW Water Authority; Mr A. Hill, MAFF; Dr H. W. Hill, MAFF; Rear-Admiral J. R. Hill; Dr Martin Holdgate, Department of the Environment; Mr David Hugh-Jones, Atlantic Shellfish Ltd.; Dr John de Courcy Ireland, Maritime Institute of Ireland; Rear-Admiral Sir Edmund Irving; Dr Ray Keary, Geological Survey of Ireland; Sir Peter Kent; Mr Eamonn Kinsella, National Board for Science & Technology, Dublin; Dr A. S. Lawton, Institute of Oceanographic Sciences; Dr Arthur Lee, MAFF; Ms B. T. Lees, Institute of Oceanographic Sciences; Mr J. K. Lindsay, Highlands & Islands Development Board; Mr C. C. Lucas, Newtown Oyster Fishery; Dr Nigel Lucas, Imperial College of Science & Technology; Mr Neil McKellar, Sea Fish Industry Authority; Mr W. D. McKenzie, Highlands & Islands Development Board; Mr Neil MacPherson, Fisheries Development Office, Benbecula; Mrs Julie Martin, University of Aberdeen; Mr George Mason, Department of Trade; Dr Roger Mitchell, Nature Conservancy Council; Mr N. T. Mitchell, MAFF; Dr G. Musgrave, Reading University; Mr R. M. O'Flaherty, Electricity Supply Board, Dublin; Dr Michael O'Toole, National Board for Science &

Technology, Dublin; Mr G. R. Patterson, Oil Industry Exploration & Production Forum; Dr R. D. Pingree, Marine Biological Association, Plymouth; Dr John Ramster, MAFF; Mr A. D. Read, Department of Energy; Mr Ian Richardson; Dr Keith Robinson, National Board for Science & Technology, Dublin; Dr Stephen Salter, Edinburgh University; Mr J. L. Sanderson, Alginate Industries Ltd.; Mr I. A. Scott, Sea Fish Industry Authority; Mr Allan Scott, Highlands & Islands Development Board; Dr T. Shaw, McAlpines; Dr T. L. Shaw, Liverpool University; Mr J. M. Slater, BP Coal; Professor J. A. Steers, Cambridge; Dr A. H. Stride, Institute of Oceanographic Sciences; Dr D. T. Swift-Hook, Central Electricity Generating Board; Mr Clive Symmons, Bristol University; Mr Roland Tarr, Devon County Council; Mrs B. A. Taylor, MAFF; Mr R. L. Tollenaar, Commission of the European Communities; Mr M. J. Tucker, Institute of Oceanographic Sciences; Ms Sarah Welton, Devon County Council; Mr J. Wilson; Mr J. B. Wright, Board Iascaigh Mhara.

The Study Group would also be remiss if it failed to acknowledge the enormous help it received in the production of this volume through the efforts of Mary Unwin and Esme Allen, both members of the Institute staff.

Contents

Abbreviations

ACFM	Advisory Committee on Fisheries Management (ICES)
ACMP	Advisory Committee on Marine Pollution (ICES)
ACMRR	Advisory Committee of Experts on Marine Resource Research (FAO)
ACOPS	Advisory Committee on Oil Pollution of the Sea
ACR	Annual Catch Rate
AERE	Atomic Energy Research Establishment (UK)
ASIFIS	Aquatic Science and Fisheries Information System (IOC)
ASW	Anti-submarine Warfare
BOD	Biochemical Oxygen Demand
BTDB	British Transport Docks Board
CBT	Clean Ballast Tanks
CCMS	Committee on the Challenges of Modern Society (NATO)
CEPS	Environment and Consumer Protection Service of the European Commission
CFP	Common Fisheries Policy (of the European Community)
CLC	International Convention on Civil Liability for Oil Pollution Damage
COFI	Committee on Fisheries (FAO)
COST	Coopération Scientifique et Technique
COW	Crude Oil Washing
CRISTAL	Contract Regarding an Interim Supplement to Tanker Liability for Oil Pollution
DAFS	Department of Agriculture and Fisheries for Scotland
DDE	Dichloro-diphenyl-dichloroethylene
DDT	Dichloro-diphenyl-trichlorethane
d.w.t.	dead-weight tonnes
E & P Forum	Oil Industry Exploration and Production Forum (UK)
EC	European Community
EEB	European Environmental Bureau
EEZ	Exclusive Economic Zone
EIA	Environmental Impact Assessment
FAO	Food and Agricultural Organization
FOOCG	Fisheries and Offshore Consultative Group (UK)
FPS	Fishery Protection Squadron
FZ	Fishing Zone

GEMS	Global Environmental Monitoring Service (UNEP)
GESAMP	Group of Experts on the Scientific Aspects of Marine Pollution (UNEP)
GIPME	Global Investigation of Pollution of the Marine Environment (IOC)
GRT	Gross Registered Tonnes
HRS	Hydraulics Research Station (UK)
IAEA	International Atomic Energy Agency
IALA	International Association of Lighthouse Authorities
ICES	International Council for the Exploration of the Sea
ICNAF	International Council for North-West Atlantic Fisheries (now NAFO)
ICS	International Chamber of Shipping
IDP	Integrated Development Programme
IEA	International Energy Agency
IGOSS	Integrated Global Ocean Station System (IOC)
IHO	International Hydrographic Organization
IIED	Institute of International Environment and Development
ILO	International Labour Office
IMF	International Monetary Fund
IMO	International Maritime Organization (formerly IMCO)
Infoterra	Information retrieval system (UNEP)
INMARSAT	International Maritime Satellite Organization
INTERTANKO	International Association of Independent Tanker Owners
IOC	International Oceanographic Commission
IP	Institute of Petroleum
IPIECA	International Petroleum Industry Environmental Conservation Association
IRPCS	International Regulations for the Prevention of Collisions at Sea
ISA	International Sea-bed Authority
IWC	International Whaling Commission
JMC	Joint Maritime Commission (ILO)
LDC	London Dumping Convention
LEPOR	Long-term and Expanded Programme of Oceanic Exploration and Research
LLGDS	Land-locked and Geographically Disadvantaged States
lo-lo	load-on/load-off
LOT	Load on Top
LNG	Liquefied Natural Gas
LPG	Liquefied Petroleum Gas

MAFF	Ministry of Agriculture, Fisheries and Food (UK)
MARPOL	International Convention for the Prevention of Pollution from Ships
MEDI	Marine Environment Data Information referral system (IOC/UNEP)
MEPC	Maritime Environment Protection Committee (IMO)
MRCC	Maritime Rescue Co-ordination Centre
MSC	Maritime Safety Committee (IMO)
MSY	Maximum Sustainable Yield
NAFO	North-West Atlantic Fisheries Organization
NASCO	North Atlantic Salmon Conservation Organization
NATO	North Atlantic Treaty Organization
NBST	National Board for Science and Technology (Ireland)
NEAFC	North-East Atlantic Fisheries Commission (or Convention)
NGO	Non-Governmental Organization
NHSC	North Sea Hydrographic Commission
NM	Notice to Mariners
NNR	National Nature Reserve
OCIMF	Oil Companies International Marine Forum
OECD	Organization for Economic Co-operation and Development
OPOL	Offshore Pollution Liability Agreement
OSCOM	Oslo Commission of the Convention on the Prevention of Marine Pollution from ships and aircraft
OSPARCOM	The Oslo and Paris Commissions of the Conventions on Pollution (see OSCOM and PARCOM)
PAH	Polynuclear aromatic hydrocarbon
PARCOM	Paris Commission of the Convention on the Prevention of Pollution from land-based sources
PCB	Polychlorinated biphenyl
PEXA	Practice and Exercise Area
PPP	Polluter Pays Principle
Prep Com	UN Law of the Sea Preparatory Committee
ro-ro	roll-on/roll-off
RSPB	Royal Society for the Protection of Birds
SACSA	Standing Advisory Committee for Scientific Advice (OSCOM)
SAR	Search and Rescue
SBT	Segregated Ballast Tank
SCOP	Steering Committee on Pilotage
SCOR	Scientific Committee for Oceanographic Research
SDR	Special Drawing Rights
SHOM	Service Hydrographique de la Marine

SOLAS   Safety of Life at Sea Convention
SSSI   Site of Special Scientific Interest
STCW   International Convention on Standards of Training, Certification and Watchkeeping for Seafarers
TAC   Total Allowable Catch
TOVALOP   Tanker Owners Voluntary Agreement concerning Liability for Oil Pollution
UKPIA   United Kingdom Petroleum Industry Association
UKOOA   United Kingdom Offshore Operators Association
ULCC   Ultra Large Crude Carrier
UNCHE   United Nations Conference on the Human Environment
UNCLOS   United Nations Conference on the Law of the Sea
UNCTAD   United Nations Conference on Trade and Development
UNDP   United Nations Development Programme
UNECE   United Nations Economic Commission for Europe
UNEP   United Nations Environment Programme
UNESCO   United Nations Educational Scientific and Cultural Organization
VLCC   Very Large Crude Carrier
WGs   Working Groups
WHO   World Health Organization
WMO   World Meteorological Organization

Introduction: Conflicts and their Resolution

The law is concerned not only with the resolution of conflicts of interest by regulation of activities, but also with the distribution of resources. In the former role it can attempt, for example, to control and contain disputes that might arise from competing uses of the seas or sea areas—such as those between the waste disposers and the fishermen or the oil exploiters and the navigators; in the latter role, it is designed to determine not only who shall have access to resources such as minerals and fish, but on what terms: laying down the resources and areas to be exploited, the rate of exploitation, the taxes and surcharges, the safety and pollution-control measures. Many preliminary vital scientific, social, economic and political decisions have, of course, first to be taken at the national and, with increasing frequency, at the international and regional levels, especially on environmental issues involving complex ecological relationships, before the legal rules can be promulgated, applied or enforced. However, establishment of the legal regime is the key to the solution of conflict problems, opening the way to orderly and profitable development and use of the shared resource represented by the seas overlying the continental shelf of north-west Europe.

Lack of a legal regime, or undue delay in establishing it, leads, as evidenced in our chapter V on fisheries, to a wasteful competitive scramble for open-access common property, which can and often does result in its damage, depletion or even destruction. In semi-enclosed seas such as those scrutinized in this study, surrounded by developed and industrialized states and navigated also by others, shared resources, unless they exist in great abundance, are highly vulnerable to adverse effects and a lack of co-operative management. Here again the law, especially international law, fulfils a vital role in its constitutional aspect, since it provides the charter and framework for the required management or administrative bodies, establishing their organs and powers and regulatory scope.

For the seas around the British Isles, we are concerned with nothing less than the management of a large, complex natural resource extending over a wide geographical area, with different international interactions in different parts of it. The interests represented are enormously varied: shipping, fisheries, tourism and recreation, mineral and oil extraction, energy generation, the management of waste disposal and pollution, land reclamation, sea defences . . . the list can be extended in detail almost indefinitely. The requirements for each activity differ and are in potential conflict with others, both internally, and externally, nationally and internationally.

The conflicts are internal when the practices of an industry are ultimately destructive of its own self-interest, as is only too evident in commercial fisheries and some aspects of tourism. External ones arise when the consequences of one activity are inimical to another, as when the needs of industry conflict with conservation, or energy generation with shipping. Some of these conflicts are capable of resolution at a purely national level, though in north-west Europe the needs for harmonization of legislation within the European Community increasingly introduces an extra dimension to the regulation of the national affairs of its member states. International agreement is necessary when there is competition for a common resource, or when one coastal state's activities come into conflict with the interests of neighbouring states, or for practices affecting international waters. The consequence is a web of interacting activities, and although any may be treated in isolation, such treatment has inevitable repercussions on others, and these cannot be ignored.

A substantial fraction of the waste products of north-western Europe finds its way into the North Sea by direct discharges and offshore dumping, via rivers and by deposition or rain-out from the atmosphere. Other waters of the continental shelf are similarly affected, though for the most part on a less dramatic scale. Much of this discharge is deliberate, but in addition to accidental losses from shipping or mishaps at shore-based facilities, unplanned inputs to the sea also include agricultural pesticides washed off the land and entering water-courses, and atmospheric pollutants derived from coal burning, petrol-engine exhausts, industrial emissions, and so forth, which eventually return to earth in particulate form or dissolved in rain. Ultimately they find their way into coastal waters.

These wastes can be toxic. Fears that the discharges threaten public health and may cause unacceptable damage to commercial fisheries— or, worse, lead to a serious and general decline in the marine environment—have already resulted in some international regulation of waste-disposal practices. The Convention for the Prevention of Pollution of the Sea by Oil, 1954, and the International Convention for the Prevention of Pollution from Ships (MARPOL) 1973, control legal discharges of oily water from crude-oil carriers, the Oslo and London conventions regulate dumping at sea, the Paris convention sets limits to what may be discharged from the shore and from man-made structures, and the Transboundary Air Pollution convention establishes a framework for the control of air-borne pollution. Within the European Community there are common bacteriological standards for bathing beaches. There remains, however, the fear that these measures deal only with the tip of an iceberg, which leads to the view that as a matter of principle, prudence dictates that waste products should not be discharged into the marine environment. This view is reinforced by the fact that some conventions and regulations are either not in force or enter into force only for a few states;

many also have specific limitations and are open to political compromises, which in many cases ignore scientific advice, in order to obtain the global or regional consensus necessary for their operation.

However, it should be remembered that the sea has the capacity to accept many wastes and break them down to their basic constituents without harm and sometimes even with a beneficial fertilizing effect. Other materials, particularly heavy metals, are already present at a low level as natural constituents of sea-water. Yet others, like hot water, rapidly lose their damaging properties after they have been discharged and any effect they may have is very localized. Furthermore, it is also important to consider the consequences of not discharging the wastes into the sea: a blinkered concern to preserve one environment from damaging influences may easily result in transferring the problem elsewhere rather than solving it.

Clearly, waste discharges must be treated selectively and it is also essential to have a clear idea of what constitutes pollution. From the outset of its deliberation, the UN Group of Experts on the Scientific Aspects of Marine Pollution (GESAMP) has made a sharp distinction between contamination and pollution. Contamination is the presence, in seawater, sediments or marine organisms, of a substance in concentrations above local background levels. Pollution is 'the introduction by man, directly or indirectly, of substances or energy to the marine environment which results in such deleterious effects as harm to living resources, hazards to human health, hindrance of marine activities including fishing, impairment of quality for the use of seawater, and reduction of amenities'.[1] This is a broad definition, though it may be observed that contamination, which is most readily detected in surveys and monitoring programmes, may provide warning of, but does not itself constitute, pollution. The contamination must be caused by human activities and, secondly, it must have, or threaten, some damaging effect. Assessment of pollution by a particular substance or discharge therefore raises the important question of whose interests suffer as a result of pollution damage, by how much, and whether the polluter or the sufferer has a greater claim to the local marine resources and on what grounds. Problems arise, however, in applying the references and definitions of terms such as 'pollution' and 'contamination'. Ambiguities remain in the terms used and there is scope for considerable political argument deriving from the economic implications of controlling or eradicating particular adverse effects from substances that allegedly pollute or contaminate; it is difficult to determine the relevant 'concentrations', 'likely results' and 'deleterious effects' which bring the definitions into legal operations, as our chapter VIII on pollution illustrates.

Part of the debate about the disposal of waste into the sea is not connected with local and specific conflicts of interest, but with a more fundamental concern that the toxic materials introduced into coastal waters are inflicting irreparable damage on marine ecosystems. This is not a 'deleterious effect' in the terms of the GESAMP definition of pollution, but a threat, the consequences of which, if they materialized, would be of the utmost gravity. The commercial interest with most at stake in such an eventuality is fisheries, though tourism and ultimately nature conservation have a general interest in preserving the marine environment in a healthy condition.

The size of the various fish stocks on the north-west European continental shelf, as well as the annual recruitment to them, has been monitored and estimated regularly from the beginning of this century by the International Council for the Exploration of the Seas. These estimates are far from perfect, but they give a far clearer impression of the fluctuating success of the populations of these commercial species than is known for any other organisms in the sea. This does not mean, however, that the size of fish stocks or success of recruitment are, of themselves, a sufficient guide to the health of the seas or to the growing damage that might be being caused by pollution. Fish stocks are, in fact, completely dominated by arbitrary fishery practices and whatever effect toxic wastes in the sea may have is largely obscured by the pressure of fishing. Indeed, even substantial pollution abatement would bring no detectable improvement in fish catches or the strength of fish populations. As we observe later, half or more of the money, time and resource at present expended by fishing fleets is not just wasted, but is actually depressing the yield which could be achieved with much less fishing effort.

The fishing industry has always been in need of international regulation, which has until recently been supplied by the North-East Atlantic Fisheries Commission. This has been only a partial success as can be seen from the depletion of a number of fish stocks by overfishing, but the declaration of national jurisdiction over fisheries has struck at the roots of NEAFC. Although fishery authorities are rightly concerned with the possibly catastrophic consequences of pollution, it is evident that the chief threat to the well-being of fisheries at present in all north-west European states is the fishing industry itself.

The difficulties in which the catching industry has found itself over the years have encouraged the development of mariculture. The culture of molluscs and some freshwater fish like the carp on a small scale has been established for centuries, but these activities are being greatly extended and other fin-fish (particularly salmonids) and crustaceans are now included. The newer species that have been introduced to mariculture have special requirements for clean water and are vulnerable to exposure to toxic materials in a way that the wild population is not, since it generally moves away from a contaminated area. While European mariculture has far to go to equal the variety of Japanese practices there is certainly the promise of further developments, though perhaps not on the scale that is sometimes claimed.

Conservation organizations have a concern not simply with the well-being of exploitable plant and animal stocks, but with wildlife in general and, indeed, the preservation of all features of the natural environment. Practical measures may include the establishment of nature reserves or 'marine parks' in areas of particular scientific or natural interest; or, in order to conserve representative samples of natural types of habitat, protection in law may be given to scarce or endangered species. More generally, conservationists are anxious to inculcate an appropriate attitude in other users of the marine or maritime environment so that their activities are carried on, so far as possible, non-destructively. Unfortunately this is often not possible, and conservation interests find themselves at odds with a wide range of other activities in the sea.

Like fisheries, conservation areas are at risk from pollution damage, but fishery practices are themselves inimical to the conservation interest, not particularly because of the pressure they exert on the commercial fish species (with which conservationists do not concern themselves) but because trawling and other benthic fishing methods can be extremely destructive of organisms living on or in the sea-bed. A more important threat to conservation interests is the reclamation of coastal wetlands which is proceeding around the North Sea and which has already destroyed significant areas of feeding grounds for the enormous number of arctic and subarctic ducks and shore birds which winter there. The construction of harbours and sea defences and industrial development on the coast are almost equally detrimental to wildlife. The tourist and recreation industry is often attracted to areas of great conservation interest because of the natural beauty and scientific interest of the fauna and flora or coastal landscape, but it only too easily becomes destructive, through pressure of people, of the features that draw them there in the first place. Unexpectedly, coastal military reservations often prove prime conservation areas because the general public is excluded from them.

Many essential activities in the maritime zone are inevitably destructive and conservation interests often appear to be fighting rearguard battles in opposition to all new coastal development and to many other activities in the sea. Here the problems created by taking too selective an environmental perspective became apparent. Concern with safeguarding marine wildlife rarely takes account of the consequences for non-marine environments of reducing man-made pressures on marine or maritime ecosystems. Shifting a problem from one place to another is no solution, as the recent UN Convention on the Law of the Sea recognizes (see chapter X). Nor can these problems be resolved on a purely national scale. Winter feeding grounds for shore-birds are lost through land reclamation on both sides of the North Sea, and it is assumed that birds displaced from one area of reclamation will 'go elsewhere' although the steady attrition of winter feeding grounds cannot continue indefinitely without a serious impact on populations. Oil floating on the North Sea will affect birds on the Dutch or British coasts during periods of easterly or westerly winds respectively, when both the birds on the surface of the sea and the oil are drifted to one coast or the other.

Oil pollution, once seen as a major threat to life in the seas, now occupies a less dramatic position. A major tanker accident can cause catastrophic losses to fixed fishery installations, disrupt the tourist trade in the locality and cause ecological disturbance which may require a decade or more for recovery, but the effects are temporary and in most cases restored within a year or two. International regulation and national effort, as described in relevant chapters VII, X, XI of this study and in our previous studies, have done much to reduce the risk of such accidents, though inevitably it still remains. Casual oil pollution from shipping is a nuisance, though an important one, and is responsible for a disproportionate number of sea-bird deaths. For the most part such discharges of oil are illegal, but policing is difficult and successful prosecution hard to achieve under the present legal regime, though, as seen in chapter X, matters could be significantly improved if the regime instituted by the new Law of the Sea Convention were introduced either regionally or, preferably, on a global basis.

Greater attention is now directed towards conflicts of interest, principally with fisheries and conservation, resulting from the development of the offshore oil fields, than to tanker accidents. Offshore platforms and undersea pipelines exclude fishing vessels from areas which, although in aggregate small, are said to attract fish. These installations constitute a risk of pollution from blow-outs or other accidents and, on a lesser scale, from disturbance of the sea-bed and small, but continuous, inputs of petroleum hydrocarbons. The platforms, in theory, may interfere with shipping. Other mineral extraction, principally of sand and gravel from the seabed, has an impact on fisheries by altering the nature of the bottom and so the food available to bottom-feeding fish. A more important consequence for herring, which spawn in areas of fast bottom-currents on gravel beds, may be the physical removal of an appropriate environment for their eggs.

Concern about the environmental impact of fossil-fuel extraction and the problems involved in the disposal of radioactive waste has directed attention to alternative and renewable sources of energy. Tidal power and wave power are possible options in the sea, but insufficient thought has so far been given to the environmental impact of developments of this kind. Wave-energy converter arrays would lead to a prohibition of fishing and interfere with shipping in areas several hundred kilometres long and two kilometres wide. Changes in the wave-energy climate on the coast would also affect the rate of deposition of sand and of coastal erosion. Tidal barrages have attendant problems of siltation and interference with shipping and migratory fish, and, depending on where they are sited, significant consequences for conservation.

In all, it is evident that the multiplicity of uses to which waters around the British Isles may be put leads to inevitable conflicts. In these circumstances, legislation and the means to enforce it are both essential to protect the weak from the strong, and to preserve the resources and the natural environment for the common good. But such is the interaction between different activities in the sea that the resolution of conflict is rarely simple. In some instances it may be possible to regulate activities in a particular area so that all have tolerable access to the maritime resource. Often, however, the conflict is too great for compromise and particular areas of sea have to be dedicated to particular functions. This is a common enough concept on land, and land-use planning has acquired the status of a science, in theory if not always in practice. Planning the use of the sea is less advanced and, in some more extreme statements of conservationist policy, is even denied, although in fact it is practised in a rough and ready way.

These problems are not new and this volume forms the third and final part of a study undertaken by the David Davies Memorial Institute of International Studies into national and international law relating to the orderly resolution of conflicts of interest in the use of the marine and maritime resources of the seas around the British Isles.

The first, published in 1975, was concerned with the North Sea.[2] This was the report of a study group on the relevant national law of the North Sea States and international treaties regulating their activities in this body of water. The second part took the form of a conference held in Swansea in 1975, extending the discussion from the North Sea to the Celtic and Irish Seas.[3]

Events have moved rapidly since then and environmental considerations in particular have assumed a much more prominent position than they could claim when the study was first envisaged, some ten years ago. Environmental groups and parties have appeared and are already a by no means negligible political force in several countries. Several pollution-control bodies which were either not in force or were in their infancy in 1975 are now in operation and having an increasing impact on our study area, although they inevitably encounter some political difficulties in developing the regulations necessary. The European Community now plays an increasingly active role in regulating marine and maritime affairs. The long negotiation preceding the UN Conference on the Law of the Sea has stimulated, amongst other developments, a new fisheries regime, tentative moves towards the introduction of modified port state jurisdiction, an interest in protecting 'fragile' and 'special' areas, and new approaches to coastal state control over scientific research in EEZs

(Exclusive Economic Zones), even though the Convention has been signed by only five of the EC member states and will not enter into force until one year after the sixth ratification. However, its indecisive conclusion, in the light of the failure to reach the desired consensus, raises a whole new set of problems in north-west European waters.

The third part of the study, originally conceived as a brief summing up has, as a result of these developments, a more significant function. It is now possible to reappraise the situation in a different light. Uses of the marine environment have increased in complexity and the areas of conflict have increased with them. It has therefore been necessary to view comprehensively the physical and biological environment of the seas around the British Isles, and the activities that now take place there or may be envisaged in the near future, and to examine how they interact with one another. On this basis we have proceeded to examine the powers and practices of the plethora of international organizations now operating in this area, the legislative changes introduced by the third United Nations Conference on the Law of the Sea, and the organizations that exist for regional co-operation and especially to preserve the marine environment. Their adequacy to perform this task and to provide an equitable resolution of potential and actual conflicts is the final matter to which we address ourselves.

R. B. CLARK

Notes

1. Pravdic, V., *GESAMP: the First Dozen Years*, UNEP, 1981.
2. Sibthorp, M. M. (ed.), *The North Sea: Challenge and Opportunity*, Europa, 1975.
3. Sibthorp, M. M. and Unwin, M. (edd.), *Oceanic Management: Conflicting Uses of the Celtic Sea and Other Western UK Waters*, Europa, 1977.

I

The Physical Context

An Introduction to the Seas and Coasts

In order to provide an understanding of the issues and conflicts in resource management, it is necessary first to supply a brief introduction to the geographical and other physical factors which underlie the distribution and accessibility of both living and non-living resources in the north-west European continental-shelf seas. For the nature of the sea and sea-bed determines the location and exploitability, and the effects of exploitation of the resources. A knowledge of the tides and currents, for example, is essential to any discussion of pollution, just as it is also central to the dispute between the United Kingdom and the European Community on water quality standards (see chapter VII).

It is also necessary to include coastal resources in the study. The coast, as a boundary between land and sea, is a transition zone influenced by both terrestrial and marine processes; it is highly mobile, and considerable effort is devoted along some coasts to preventing erosion (caused by natural factors and human-induced ones such as sand and gravel dredging (see chapter IV) and reclamation for industrial purposes (see chapter IX)). The exploitation of the sea's resources puts great pressure on the coast as a location for the necessary support and infrastructure (see chapter IX).

The North-West European Continental Shelf

From the most ancient geological times onwards, the structural framework of western Europe has been controlled by the existence of three extensive rigid blocks or shields of rock. Relative movement of these blocks has caused the intervening area of more mobile rocks to be subjected to periods of strong compressive force which eventually produced: the Caledonian mountain belt, parts of which remain in Scotland and Norway; the Hercynian chain, the remnants of which are found in south Wales, Cornwall, Brittany and other parts of France; and the relatively recent Alpine chain. Between the eroded remnants of these mountain ranges, and in places on top of them when they subsided or became sufficiently denuded, were laid down large areas of marine sediment deposited in shallow seas that once covered most of the British Isles and Ireland. It is in these sediments, both onshore and offshore, that oil and gas reservoirs are found. Compacted now to form rock, the enormous thickness of sediment occupies a pattern of linear troughs or basins extending under the seas around the British Isles and Ireland.

The continental shelf to the west of Britain and Ireland extends into the Atlantic Ocean. Some 200 million years ago the Atlantic did not exist, and North America, Greenland and western Europe were one huge landmass. Separation of the continental blocks of southern Europe and North America was accompanied by a growing Atlantic Ocean floored by new oceanic crustal rock. The pressure from below the earth's crust at the point of separation as the continents pulled apart, followed by cooling of the new rock, set up complex tensions which gave rise to a chain of basins and troughs along the west coast of Britain and Ireland. The Rockall Plateau became separated from the European continental plate along the line of the Rockall Trough. Subsequently the Rockall Plateau and much of the continental shelf to the north and west of the British Isles became submerged, and sediments were laid down in the Rockall, Porcupine, Celtic Sea and Western Approaches Troughs. Today the Rockall Trough is a wide depression filled with over 3,000 metres of sediments and is an area of much potential interest for oil exploration.

The continental crust extends westward from Europe until it joins the oceanic crust beneath the Atlantic. The limits of this westward extension or shelf are shown in figure I.1. From a jurisdictional point of view, the delimitation of its edge is defined more precisely in the treaty which emerged from the Third United Nations Conference on the Law of the Sea (UNCLOS) in 1982 than it was in the 1958 Geneva Convention on the Continental Shelf which defined it in terms of water depth coupled with exploitability beyond that depth, as follows:

The continental shelf of a coastal state comprises the sea-bed and subsoil of the submarine areas that extend beyond its territorial sea throughout the natural prolongation of its land territory to the outer edge of the continental margin, or to a distance of 200 nautical miles from the baselines from which the breadth of the territorial sea is measured where the outer edge of the continental margin does not extend up to that distance. (Art. 1, Geneva Convention)

It was recognized at an early stage in UNCLOS III that this definition needed to be complemented by more detailed guidelines on how the limit of the natural prolongation or continental margin was to be determined. The general formula that was eventually arrived at reflected a number of differing proposals (for fuller details see chapter X). However, the confusing outcome of UNCLOS III leaves the question unsettled and contentious.

The problem with the various definitions is that the thickness of sediments in the oceans cannot always be determined accurately enough to meet the requirements of an undisputed international boundary.

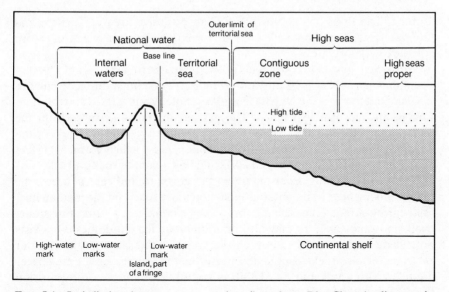

FIG. I.1. Jurisdictional zones, cross-section (based on Bin Cheng's diagram in Schwarzenberger, *A Manual of International Law*). Taken from Sibthorp, M. M. (ed.), *The North Sea: Challenge and Opportunity*, Europa Publications, 1975, p. 89.

Unfortunately, the location of the foot of the continental slope, defined as the point of maximum change in the gradient at its base, can be even more difficult to determine. Thus while it is possible to define in geomorphological terms the outer edge of the continental shelf, a legal definition has proved much more complex.

The North Sea

Lying between latitudes 51° and 61°N.,[1] the North Sea is bounded to the west by the east coasts of England and Scotland, to the south by the Netherlands, Belgium and the Federal Republic of Germany, and to the east by the FRG, Denmark and Norway. Both ends of the North Sea are subject to oceanic influences: from the south-west via the English Channel; and in the north the Atlantic Ocean directly affects the North Sea across its boundary, between Shetland and Norway. Its eastern and western shores, on the other hand, are subject to predominantly terrestrial influences. A relatively shallow sea with a mean depth of 100 metres, its surface area is estimated as 575,000 square kilometres.

The pattern of linear sediment-filled troughs referred to earlier is also a major structural feature of North Sea geology. The central North Sea trough system is approximately 1,200 kilometres long and extends from the edge of the continental shelf west of Norway, and into mainland

Europe. The floor of the North Sea is an extensive area of Tertiary and Quaternary (64 million years old to recent) sediments overlying more complex rock structures.

North Sea gas fields are mainly in its southern area, within a belt extending in a WNW-ESE direction from E. Yorkshire and Lincolnshire in England out towards the Dutch Coast. West Sole, Viking, Indefatigable, and Leman are the principal fields. The gas has migrated upwards from the underlying coal measures (now known to extend all the way across the southern North Sea) into the Rotlingende sands, which form a perfect reservoir very effectively capped and sealed by dolomite rock and salt.

North Sea oil fields occur mainly in the northern and central areas, the majority lying near to the international boundary based on the median line. Oil-bearing strata take several forms, for example dolomitic limestone, chalk and sandstone; oil may also be trapped under salt domes. Oil exists only in the minute spaces between the grains in the same way that water saturates surface rocks. In the absence of hydrocarbons these pore spaces are filled with water. Further details of the oil fields and recent production figures are given in chapter II.

Bottom sediments

The superficial or sea-bed sediments include sand, gravels and muds, the distribution of which is still only generally known. Gravel occurs in localized areas, and present tidal currents are not generally strong enough to move it around. Even where tidal currents are comparatively strong, for example off the East Anglian coast, the growth of long-lived marine animals on the pebbles indicate that the deposits remain undisturbed for a long time. Some movements can take place, however, in areas where tidal currents are aided by other water movements. Large quantities of this gravel are dredged for use as aggregates in the building and construction industries (see chapter IV).

Since almost no river-borne sand reaches the North Sea, the existing sand deposits are either reworked and/or glacial older sands, or they may be derived from coastal erosion. Massive erosion of parts of the East Anglian coast, for example around Holderness, liberates quantities of sand which are believed to move offshore. Offshore sand occurs as sand-banks and sand-waves, both of which are found only in shallow tidal seas. Sand-banks may be up to 50 kilometres long, 6 kilometres wide and 40 metres high and frequently occur in groups. They are elongated approximately parallel with the direction of peak tidal flow, but can lie at an angle of as much as 20 degrees to this direction. One side of the sand-bank is steeper than the other, the steep side facing in the direction of sand transport. Extensive sand-banks occur in the south-western North Sea (and also in the south-western Celtic Sea) where they are a significant hazard to shipping.

Sand-waves,which are also widespread in the south-western North Sea, are, on the other hand, at right angles to peak tidal flow. In appearance they are rather like the transverse sand dunes found in deserts, and may be up to twenty metres in height and several hundred metres in length. Like sand-banks, one side of the sand-wave is usually steeper than the other, and the sand waves migrate in the direction faced by the steeper slope. Migration is not continuous, but takes place only during periods when the tidal currents are strong enough. Sand-waves require frequent charting as they are a hazard to shipping and to the stability of offshore platforms. Sand from both waves and banks is exploited by dredging off the English and Dutch coasts.

The long-term movement of the sand, as deduced from the profiles of the sand-banks and sand-waves, is in general agreement with the net flow of water into the northern North Sea between the Shetland and Orkney Islands and with the north-easterly flow past Denmark towards the Baltic.

In the central and northern North Sea, large areas of the sea-bed are covered with mud and fine sand, while the deeper channels are partly filled with fine mud. The total amount of suspended matter brought into the North Sea from the Atlantic by tidal currents is believed to be large, but its concentration is very low, and it is unlikely that particles which have not settled in the ocean will do so in the North Sea where turbulence can be expected to be greater.

Suspended silts are brought into the North Sea by rivers and through the English Channel (between 5 and 10 million tonnes per year in total),[2] while other sources include the erosion of cliffs, organic production and deposition from the atmosphere. The transport of these silts follows for the most part the residual current pattern which will be described later in this chapter.

The entry of silts into the North Sea and their subsequent movement is important since heavy metals, organic materials and many radionuclides entering the rivers, estuaries and coastal waters as waste in solution, are adsorbed on mud particles and may be deposited in specific areas. Contact between seawater and suspended particles in the estuarine environment leads to a complex series of reactions in which some metals may be desorbed (i.e. re-enter into solution in the water) while others may be trapped in anoxic muds in the form of sulphides and reduced oxides. Isolated pockets of high metal content in seawater and sediments have been found offshore from estuaries as a result of these processes. The problem is particularly acute in industrial estuaries.

Organochloride compounds (DDT and derivatives, dieldrin, aldrin, endrin, polychlorinated biphenyls), carbamates, and polynuclear aromatic hydrocarbons (PAHs) are all relatively insoluble in water and may become strongly adsorbed on particles. This may result in a concentration in particulate matter many times (10^3–10^4) the concentration of these substances in water. In addition, adsorption of these substances onto particulates may enhance their stability, leading to a form of long-term storage of metals and organic pollutants.

Water movements: tides and tidal currents

Tides in the North Sea are the result not only of the gravitational forces generated by the Moon and, to a lesser extent, the Sun, but also of the response of the North Sea to the tides generated in the Atlantic Ocean. The North Sea is open to the Atlantic between Scotland and Norway, and it is through this wide gap that the Atlantic tide sweeps in.

Overall, the movement of the tidal wave is anticlockwise, with maximum tidal streams occurring close to the times of high and low water. At three points in the North Sea, called amphidromic points, the range of the tide is zero, i.e. there is no rise and fall of tide. The strongest tidal currents occur off the east coast of England, among the islands off the coasts of Holland and Denmark, and around the north of Scotland in the Pentland Firth and between the Orkney and Shetland Islands. Elsewhere, over most of the North Sea, tidal streams do not exceed 1 knot (about 50 cm/s) at average spring tides. The greatest tidal range in the North Sea—about 20 feet or 6 metres—occurs along the east coast of England, where low-lying land has been subject to periodic flooding.

In addition to the regular fluctuations in sea level caused by the influence of the sun and moon, i.e. astronomical tides, non-periodic or irregular changes are also caused by winds and changing atmospheric pressure. In extreme cases, when high winds and large pressure anomalies occur as a result of storms, the changes in sea level are known as 'storm surges'. While astronomical tides can be predicted to an accuracy of about 3 centimetres, there are much greater difficulties in the prediction of storm surges and of course their prediction can be no further ahead in time than the prediction of the storm itself.

Both positive and negative storm surges can have disastrous consequences. Early in 1953 a storm surge produced water levels up to 11 feet (3.3 m) above predicted levels at the southern end of the North Sea, causing extensive flooding and loss of life and property in Holland and south-east England.[3] Following this disaster, a flood warning system for the east coast of England came into operation in September 1953, and the Dutch have also instituted additional precautions. The serious risk of flooding in London from such surges has been eliminated by the construction of the Thames Barrage. The smaller negative surges—causing a drop in sea level—are a hazard to shipping navigating in shallow water.

Residual currents and circulation

Residual currents, often called simply currents, refer to the flow of water after the oscillatory tidal streams have been eliminated. The residual current is calculated to a first approximation by taking averages over

25-hour periods, which removes the principal semi-diurnal and diurnal constituents. The residual flow, so defined, may itself vary over periods of days, weeks or months, and is related to wind effects, the density distribution and the inflows of Atlantic and other water.

It is generally accepted that the major inflows to the North Sea consist of Atlantic water of high salinity entering from:

(a) the north, between Orkney and Shetland and Norway;
(b) the south, via the Straits of Dover; and
(c) water of lower salinity emerging from the Baltic Sea.

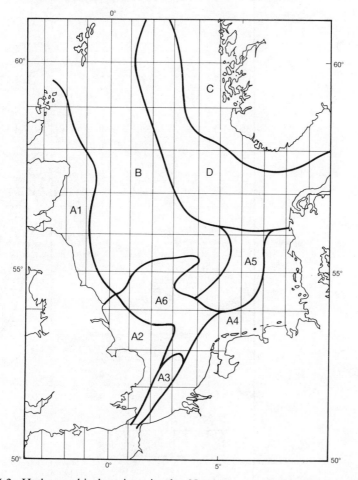

FIG. I.2. Hydrographical regions in the North Sea. Adapted from fig. 14.13, p. 488, of Banner, F. T., Collins, M. B., and Massie, K. S. (edd.), *The North-West European Shelf Seas: The Sea-bed and the Sea in Motion*, ii: *Physical and Chemical Oceanography and Physical Resources*, Elsevier Oceanography Series, 24B, 1980.

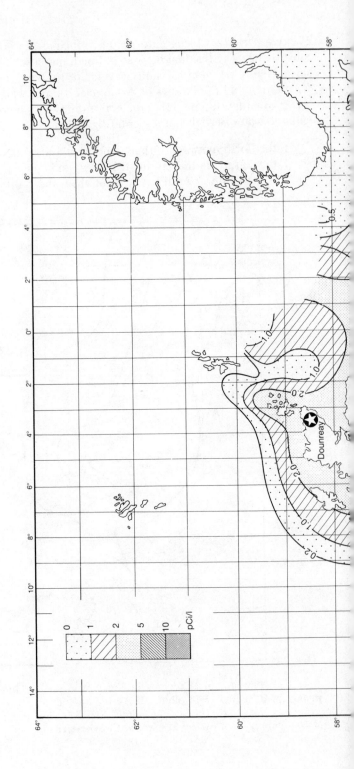

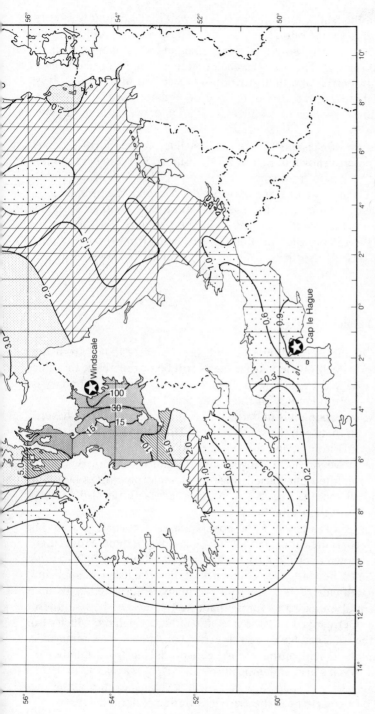
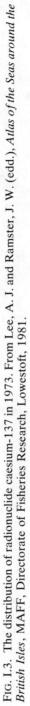

Fig. I.3. The distribution of radionuclide caesium-137 in 1973. From Lee, A. J. and Ramster, J. W. (edd.), *Atlas of the Seas around the British Isles*, MAFF, Directorate of Fisheries Research, Lowestoft, 1981.

Run-off from the land also produces coastal water masses of low salinity along the British and Continental coasts. These inflows do not mix completely, and result in the North Sea possessing a number of distinct hydrographical regions. The water in each region can be identified from a distinct set of properties and their distribution is shown in figure I.2. It is now known that most of the area of the central and northern North Sea is occupied by residual currents which are variable, weak and directly influenced by winds.

The distribution of caesium-137, a radionuclide, in the North Sea has confirmed the pattern shown in Figure I.3. Caesium-137 is discharged into the Irish Sea at Sellafield from where it can be traced in the surface water of the North Channel, along the North Sea. Despite the tremendous dilution involved, it can then be followed down the east coasts of Scotland and England to the vicinity of the Humber estuary. A significant proportion of the radionuclide also moves eastwards from the latitude of Aberdeen, crosses the North Sea, and can be traced northwards in the Norway coastal current.

The English Channel

The English Channel separating England and France extends from the Straits of Dover, which divide it from the North Sea to the east, to a line joining Lands End and Ushant, (Isle d'Ouessant). Its western boundary is therefore the eastern boundary of the Celtic Sea.

Geologically, the Channel is underlain by two main sedimentary basins: the Channel Basin (between the south coast of Dorset and Hampshire and the north coast of Brittany), and the Western Approaches Basin (between the south coast of Devon and Cornwall and the north coast of Brittany), separated by an uplifted but buried ridge of metamorphic rocks between Cherbourg and Plymouth. The Western Approaches Basin also extends further west beneath the Celtic Sea.

The Channel is of interest as a possible area for coal, gas or oil developments; coal measures could, for example, extend from their southern-most known exposures (the Somerset and Kent coalfields in the south of England) beneath the sediments of the English Channel and across to the coalfields of Belgium and Germany. Intermixed coals and shales are potential source-rocks for methane as in the North Sea, southern Holland and in Germany. Jurassic rocks in southern England, which also extend under the Channel, have been shown to contain oil. At Kimmeridge in Dorset a small oilfield onshore has been producing for a number of years, while at Wych Farm a significant oil discovery was made in 1973. Active and long-term oil seeps are known in several localities along the Dorset coast, particularly near the Purbeck Marine Wildlife Reserve.

Bottom sediments

Gravel occupies a large area in mid-Channel between Lyme Bay and a line drawn approximately from Newhaven to Dieppe; east and west of this area are extensive sand-banks. A large zone of gravelly sea-bed is also found off the north coast of Brittany. Mud is distributed in more sheltered localities, such as the Bay of Seine, Lyme Bay, and near St Malo.

Water movements: tides and tidal currents

The predominant tidal movement in the English Channel is a 'rocking' motion with high water occurring alternately at it western and eastern ends, and a region in the centre where the tidal range is smaller. Strong tidal streams occur in this central region, particularly off the major headlands. The English Channel does not act entirely as a closed basin: some tidal energy is transmitted through the Straits of Dover. The combined effects of geostrophic forces and friction on the Channel tides cause higher tides along the French coast, with particularly high tides in the Gulf of St Malo. A tidal power plant in the La Rance estuary uses this large tidal range to generate about 550 million kilowatt-hours of electricity per year. By contrast, on the English or northern shore of the Channel the range of the tides is less and tidal distortions are more noticeable with double low water near Portland Bill and double high water near the Isle of Wight.

The amount of energy contained in these tidal movements is enormous, and it has been estimated that more tidal energy is dissipated in the English Channel than in the whole of the North Sea.[4]

Water movements: residual currents

Salinity distributions of water in the English Channel were used early in this century to deduce that the general flow of water through it was eastwards into the North Sea. This was confirmed in a study which traced the distribution of caesium-137 released from the nuclear fuel reprocessing plant at Cap de la Hague near Cherbourg. It was found that the water moved at an average of one nautical mile per day, continuing along the Flemish and Dutch coasts towards the Skagerrak.

Superimposed on the mean flow are shorter-term water circulation patterns, which appear to be largely influenced by prevailing weather conditions. Measurement of currents off Land's End has led to some conflicting results, but it is likely that there is a northerly flow towards the Bristol Channel and then westwards across St George's Channel.

In the western English Channel it was thought that the circulation was clockwise in winter and anticlockwise in summer, based on salinity measurements. Data have now thrown some doubt on the conclusions; the actual circulation is likely to be more complex and to be influenced by the wind.

The Celtic Sea and Bristol Channel

The International Hydrographic Organization in Monaco has agreed that the term 'Celtic Sea' should be defined as follows (see figure I.4):

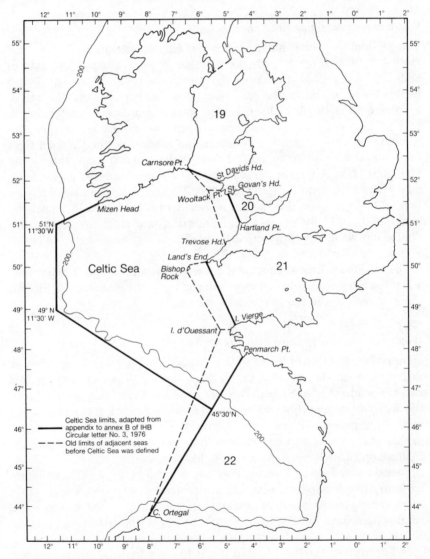

FIG. I.4. Limits of the Celtic Sea. The Celtic Sea limits are shown as heavy lines in the figure, which has been adapted from the appendix to annexe B of IHB Circular Letter No. 3, 1976. The pecked lines are the old limits of adjacent seas before the Celtic Sea was defined.

From Land's End to Isle Vierge, thence to Penmarch Point in Brittany, thence toward Cap Ortegal on the Spanish Coast as far as 46° 30′ N. and thence north-west [outside the 200-metre line] to 49° N., 11° 30′ W., northwards to 51° N., and thence to Mizen Head, along the Irish Coast to Carnsore Point; thence across to St David's Head, along the Pembrokeshire coast to St Govan's Head, across the western point of the Bristol Channel to Hartland Point and finally along the Cornish coast to Land's End.[5]

The Bristol Channel, an extension of the Celtic Sea into the Severn estuary, is generally regarded as a separate area. The length of the Celtic Sea from the continental shelf edge to its junction with the Irish Sea is about 430 kilometres, while its width decreases from about 530 kilometres near the shelf edge to 78 kilometres from Carnsore Point to St David's Head.

Geologically, the Celtic Sea is a very complex area, containing three major sediment-filled basins: the North Celtic Sea Basin, the South Celtic Sea Basin and the western extension of the Western Approaches Basin. Both the North and the South Celtic Sea Basins were sites of prolonged sedimentation, and hence are of considerable interest as potential oil and gas reserves. Geophysical exploration in the Celtic Sea has shown that these basins contain sediment well in excess of 3,000 metres (10,000 ft) in thickness, and exceed even 6,000 metres (20,000 ft) in places. Interpretation of the seismic data has been difficult because of its poor quality due to the presence of a high velocity layer (chalk) at or near the sea floor. Interpretation has been helped by a study of available seismic and drillhole data from the Grand Banks basins on the east cost of Canada since the East Canadian continental shelf was adjacent to the Celtic Sea before the opening of the Atlantic Ocean.

In the North Celtic Sea Basin, gas and some oil have been found off the coast of Ireland, and exploration is still continuing in that area.

Bottom sediments

Sea-floor sediments in the Celtic Sea include sand, gravel and marine clays. Much of the gravel is of glacial origin. The re-working of sands and gravels by tidal currents has produced areas of bare rock swept clean of all mobile sediment and in other areas large deposits of gravel, often with a high content of shell debris. Sand is dredged in the Bristol Channel for use with crushed rock as aggregate, but deposits south of Ireland are not worked. In the southern and south-western regions of the Celtic Sea occur the longest and most extensive group of sand-banks around the British Isles and these are associated with a very large field of sand-waves.

Water movements: tides and tidal currents

The range of the tide varies considerably throughout the region. At the entrance to the English Channel the mean spring range increases from 4.5 metres at Falmouth in Cornwal to 6 metres at Brest in Brittany. Along the south coast of Ireland it is about 4 metres. In the Bristol Channel the mean spring range further increases progressively from 5 metres along a line from St David's Head to Land's End, up to 12 metres at Avonmouth, which has the highest tidal range of any port in the British Isles. Serious consideration, after some thirty years of so of interest in the idea, is now being given to constructing a barrage which would convert this very large tidal range into electrical energy.

In general the tidal currents are relatively weak in the Celtic Sea, with a speed at average spring tides of less than 1 metre per second (2 knots) and in some places less than 0.5 metres per second. In the Bristol Channel the tidal currents become greater as the Channel narrows, and reach over 2.5 metres per second in the Severn estuary. Currents exceeding 1 metre per second also occur in St George's Channel, in the vicinity of the Tuskar Rock, Carnsore Point and St David's Head.

Abnormal values of sea level can be caused by storm surges, as described earlier. In the Celtic Sea such effects appear to be small, but large surges occur from time to time in the Bristol Channel and in the north-eastern part of the Irish Sea.

Residual currents and circulation

Residual circulation in the Celtic Sea has been found to be largely dependent on the wind.[6] The general circulation appears to be cyclonic. During the winter months, when the water is well mixed vertically, the wind-driven circulation extends throughout the water column. In summer however, with less wind energy available, the circulation is mainly confined to the surface mixed layer and the sea becomes stratified with a layer of warmer water overlying the colder water beneath. The interface between the two layers is known as a thermocline.

In the Celtic Sea the thermocline begins developing to the south of Ireland, usually in April, and then spreads quickly eastward to penetrate the English Channel in less than a month. Later in the year the reverse takes place more slowly. By the end of October the water of the English Channel is essentially homogeneous, but it is not until well into December that the thermocline becomes completely eroded from the region of weak tidal-mixing in the central Celtic Sea.

The transition between the well-stratified continental shelf water and the well-mixed coastal water (or the out-cropping of the thermocline at the sea surface) is revealed by large surface-temperature discontinuities, which may be followed for up to 100 nautical miles (185 km). Despite the existence of more than 50 years of hydrographic data, these discontinuities or fronts were not described in detail until recently.[7] These fronts can be identified from satellite photographs; they provide conditions for rapid growth of plankton which may develop into 'red tides'.

The Irish Sea

The Irish Sea is a semi-landlocked body of water between Britain and Ireland; it extends northwards from its boundary with the Celtic Sea to the North Channel separating south-west Scotland from the north-east coast of Ireland. It thus includes St George's Channel, between Ireland and Wales, and the broader northern area, with the Isle of Man in its centre.

The North Channel is 36 kilometres wide from Skulmartin to the Mull of Galloway, but further north it broadens out at the entrance to the Firth of Clyde. The waters of both the Irish Sea and the Firth of Clyde communicate with the Atlantic Ocean through the section, only 20 kilometres wide, between Tor Point and the Mull of Kintyre. The Irish Sea thus has the form of a channel, about 300 kilometres long and of greatly varying widths, communicating with waters of Atlantic origin at both ends. The north-east part of the sea is shallow, with depths mostly less than 50 metres and only 30 metres between the Isle of Man and the coast of northwest England, compared with a depth of 130 metres between the Isle of Man and Ireland. The deepest part of the Irish Sea is found in the North Channel, where there is a trough nearly 275 metres deep.

The Irish Sea and the Celtic Sea are joined by a series of geologically similar sedimentary basins underlying the sea-bed of each. These basins extend northwards from the Celtic Sea, through the Irish Sea, north-eastern Ireland and the Firth of Clyde, to link up with the basins off western Scotland. The southern part of the Irish Sea is separated into two distinct regions by a coastal ridge trending south-westwards from the Lleyn peninsula in north Wales towards Wexford on the south-eastern tip of Ireland. North and west of this ridge there are a number of basins which have attracted the interest of the oil exploration companies, including the Central Irish Sea Basin and the Kish Bank Basin; in the latter, two wells have been drilled, but no hydrocarbons have been found. Under the north-eastern part of the Irish Sea, the Manx-Furness Basin and the Solway Firth Basin contain large thicknesses of sediment. Many wells have been drilled in the Manx-Furness Basin and a commercial gas find has been made (see chapter II).

Bordering the eastern Irish Sea, the Cheshire Basin is a flat low-lying area extending from the Pennine uplands in the east to the Welsh Border hills in the west. It is of particular interest because of a number of seepages of oil in several places at its margin. For example, coal measures sandstones impregnated with tarry oil occur in Coalbrookdale in the English Midlands.

At Formby on the Lancashire coast, oil was produced for some years from shallow wells drilled in oil-impregnated sandstones at the surface. Unfortunately, the source of this flow of oil has never been discovered.

Bottom sediments

The sea-floor sediments in the Irish Sea include gravel, sand, and mud deposits of variable composition and thickness. Their distribution has been studied in most detail in the north-eastern sector between the Cumbrian coast and the Isle of Man. Much of this material may originate from the reworking of underlying glacial deposits.

The distribution of sediment types appears to be strongly influenced by the prevailing tidal regime rather than by sea-bed topography. The two principal areas of fine sediment accumulation are to the west of the Isle of Man and off the Cumbrian coast at Sellafield. There are extensive gravel deposits in the central sector between Anglesey and the Isle of Man. Gravel deposits also occur in the Firth of Clyde, but are not considered to be good economic prospects.[8] There is a net eastward movement of sand to the north and west of the Isle of Man, and fairly clean fine-to-medium sands are extensive in the western and eastern sectors.

The fairly extensive areas of muddy sediment act as a significant sink for several long-lived radionuclides discharged from the Windscale nuclear fuel reprocessing plant. Sedimentological processes also influence the behaviour of other industrial and domestic waste products introduced into Liverpool Bay.

Water movements: tides and tidal currents

Tides enter the Irish Sea both through St George's Channel in the south and the North Channel in the north. In St George's Channel the range is relatively small, from less than 2 metres on the coast of south-east Ireland to over 4 metres in Cardigan Bay, but larger ranges occur in the north-east part of the Irish Sea. The range increases from west to east, from about 4 metres along the Irish coast to over 8 metres at Liverpool and in Morecambe Bay, and 7.5 metres in the Solway Firth.

From the tidal point of view, the Irish Sea can be considered as two narrow and overlapping channels, each with a closed end at the Lancashire and Cumberland coast of England, one open end being in the North Channel and the other in St George's Channel. There is a large tidal range at Liverpool and in Morecambe Bay. The predominant tidal motion is a 'rocking' movement with high water occurring alternately at the open and closed ends of the sea, and a region in the centre where the tidal range is much smaller.

Tidal currents are weak west of the Isle of Man in the northern part of the Irish Sea, but are stronger in the vicinity of St George's and the North Channels, off Anglesey, Wicklow Head, Howth Head (Dublin), and north of the Isle of Man.

Residual currents and circulation in the Irish Sea

There is a long-term northward flow of water through the Celtic Sea and Irish Sea, as shown by salinity distribution. The rate of flow is very slow, and is confirmed by calculations based on the distribution of caesium-137 in seawater arising from the discharge of radioactive waste at Sellafield.

There is also a southward counter-current which enters the Irish Sea on the west side of the North Channel and there is evidence that it extends for a considerable distance to the south along the Irish coast at times. In the north-east part of the Irish Sea the surface and bottom flows differ. The surface current tends to flow parallel to the coasts, apart from a counter-clockwise circulation in the centre, eventually leaving through the North Channel. The bottom flow, on the other hand, turns towards the coast with branches approaching the Solway Firth, Morecambe Bay, and the estuaries of the Ribble, Mersey and Dee. However, in the summer months from July to October, when the prevailing south-westerly winds and the inflow of Atlantic water are less dominant, more variable conditions may exist.

While the long-term mean circulation appears to be clearly established, the residual currents over periods of several days or even weeks are very variable. Recently, data from a moored current-meter showed the occurrence of strong current surges through St George's Channel associated with the passage of weather systems across the British Isles.[9] It is likely that it takes about three years on average for a mass of water to be flushed completely through St George's Channel, the Irish Sea and the North Channel. This has considerable implications for the discharge of long-lived toxic materials which may become concentrated in water or sediments before the processes of dilution or dispersion can remove them from coastal waters.

The Continental Shelf Seas of Ireland and Scotland

The waters overlying the continental shelf west of Ireland and Scotland are part of the North-East Atlantic Ocean, with which they share biological and oceanographic similarities. This shelf extends westwards from Ireland and Scotland, and, like the other shelf zones described earlier, consists of a series of platforms or banks and deep sediment-filled troughs. This similarity in geological structure and development with the North Sea troughs has led to a great deal of interest in oil exploration, particularly west of Ireland.

The continental shelf west of Ireland extends a broad submerged peninsula into the Atlantic, where it is bounded to the north and west by the deep-water Rockall Trough (see figure I.5.). The extremity of the peninsula is almost isolated from the main continental shelf region to the east (the west Irish platform) by a northerly protrusion of deep water—the Porcupine Sea Bight. At its northernmost end this feature continues across the shoal (shallow water) region of the Porcupine Bank as a markedly shallower, narrow, sediment-filled trough—the Slyne Trough.

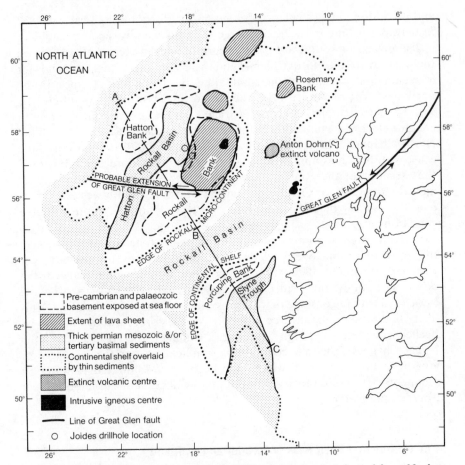

FIG. I.5. Geology of the Continental Shelf West of Ireland. Adapted from Naylor, D. and Monteney, S. N., *Geology of the North-West European Continental Shelf*, vol. 1, Graham and Trotman, 1975, fig. 18, p. 77.

Unlike the Porcupine Sea Bight, the Slyne Trough is not marked by deep water.

West of the Porcupine Sea Bight, the extremity of the submerged continental shelf peninsula forms an extensive shoal area in less than 450 metres of water—the Porcupine Ridge.

North-west of the Rockall Trough, the Rockall platform forms a well-defined shoal area some 300 miles (480 km.) from the coasts of Ireland and Scotland. It has an area of about 93,000 square miles, and is separated from the submerged continental shelf west of the British Isles by the 1,500-fathom (300 m) Rockall Trough. The Rockall Plateau is a small fragment of continental crust or micro-continent that is thought to have become separated by drifting and sea-floor spreading during the formation of the Atlantic Ocean. It is generally agreed that prior to the opening up of the Atlantic, the Rockall Plateau was attached to both the European continent and the North-American–Greenland continent. As a result, some of its geology closely resembles that of both south-east Greenland and the continental shelf west of Scotland and Ireland.

Like much of the continental shelf to the east, most of the plateau is believed to be composed of rocks unsuitable for the generation or preservation of hydrocarbons. However the Hatton-Rockall Basin, contained within the plateau and its margins, and particularly the Rockall Trough to the west, contain up to 10,000 feet (3,000 m) of sediments which are of some interest for hydrocarbon exploration.

The rocks of the plateau break the surface of the Atlantic in the precipitous uninhabited islet of Rockall. This has been annexed by Britain and an area around it designated for oil exploration. This move led immediately to a dispute between Britain and Ireland and between Britain and Denmark (on behalf of the Faroe Islands) over the right to designate areas of continental shelf around Rockall for exploration and exploitation. At the time of writing the dispute is still unresolved and bids fair to continue for some time ahead.

Closer to the west coast of Scotland, the chain of deep sedimentary basins present in the Celtic and Irish Seas is continued through the Hebridean Sea and the Minches and northwards across the shelf lying to the west of the Orkney and Shetland Islands. The basins follow a general north-eastward trend.

In the south are the Stranraer and Firth of Clyde Basins with (nearer to the Irish coast) the Portmore and Magee Basins. Between the Hebrides and the Scottish mainland, four sediment-filled basins are sunk deep into the continental shelf. Two of these, the North Minch Basin and the Little Minch (or Sea of Hebrides) Basin, form a pair of elongated troughs closely paralleling the east coast of the Outer Hebrides; the third and fourth basins (the Inner Hebrides Basin and the Colonsay Basin) form a second pair of troughs to the south-east in the vicinity of Mull.

To the north of Scotland the same north-east to south-west trend is displayed by the Sula Sgeir and West Shetland Basins lying on the Atlantic side of the Orkney and Shetland Islands. The West Shetland Basin in particular could contain significant hydrocarbon reserves and one discovery (the Clair Field) has already been made.

Bottom sediments

The composition of sea-bed sediments over such an enormous area varies very widely indeed, and they do not serve as the basis for any exploitable resources in contrast with those of shallower and more sheltered seas. The difficulty of extraction due to weather and wave climate, and the distance from markets, will also make exploitation less likely.

The only bottom sediments of any economic importance are the extensive biogenic carbonate accumulations in parts of the Minches, off north-west Scotland, and off the west coast of Ireland around Galway and Donegal.

Elsewhere there are large areas of rock, sand and gravel, extending the length of the west coast of Ireland and north to the outer Hebrides. Further offshore, sand and gravel and, in a number of areas sand alone, cover the seabed. Smaller patches of mud and muddy sand also occur offshore from the coasts of Cork, Kerry, and Donegal and in the North Minch between the Isle of Lewis and mainland Scotland and inshore of South Uist.

Water movements: tides and tidal currents

In these continental shelf waters, the tidal wave is progressive, travelling northwards along the shelf edge contours before it enters the shelf seas. South of Ireland the wave divides, one part moving into the Celtic Sea, to become further sub-divided by the peninsula of Cornwall and south Wales, and virtually causing the tidal movements in the English Channel, Bristol Channel and Irish Sea. The incoming Atlantic tide has a very powerful influence in these areas, whose tides are mainly the result of an oscillating response to it.

The tidal streams are fast moving near the coast, especially near the boundary with the Celtic Sea off the south-west of Ireland, and around the Scottish offshore islands (Inner and Outer Hebrides) and the north-west coast of Scotland.

Water movements: residual currents

The few measurements of residual currents that have been made west of Ireland and Scotland indicate a slow drift of water northwards along these coasts. The wind-induced surface currents flow towards the coast of Ireland and Scotland, and eastwards along the north coast of Ireland. These residual currents combine with those present in the Irish Sea and the Celtic Sea to produce a pattern consistent with the suggestion by Monahan[10] that there is a coastal current flowing clockwise around Ireland.

The whole of this area is affected by the North Atlantic Drift, carrying surface water from the Gulf Stream, and resulting in water temperatures being considerably higher than those at the same latitude on the other side of the Atlantic Ocean.

The Coasts

The coasts of north-west Europe have in times undergone many geological alterations and what we see today on a large-scale map is the result of a complex interaction of forces. In addition to the geological factors referred to earlier, the structure and appearance of the coast has been greatly influenced by movements of sea level, by erosion and accretion (marine, fluvial, glacial, and aerial), by volcanic action and by the detailed structure of the rocks upon which these processes have taken place. Living organisms too have contributed to the diversity and value of the coast. Salt-marsh and sand-dune plants have encouraged accretion and stabilization of suitable coasts leading in some cases to the formation of new areas of land. Maritime and cliff-top vegetation colonizing bare-rock surfaces has greatly enhanced the aesthetic and recreational value of other coasts. Inter-tidal and sub-littoral (submerged during all tides) marine algae provide food and fertilizer and serve as the basis on which a whole host of marine animals thrive. The scientific, educational and aesthetic values of these underwater habitats are now achieving recognition with the establishment of marine reserves. Despite being subject to considerable human pressure, the coastal zone also contains extensive areas and habitats in a relatively undisturbed and original state. However, the pace of land reclamation, particularly in estuaries, added to increasing industrial development, especially in areas formerly considered remote, stresses the potential for conflict with conservation and protection interests. This is dealt with in greater detail in chapter IX.

The principal types of coast found in North West Europe are described below.

Rocky shores occur most extensively where the coastal region is mountainous or rugged, and they range from steep inaccessible cliffs to wide gently-sloping rocky platforms, from smooth slopes of rock to irregular masses or beaches of great boulders. The majority of rocky shores, on open coasts, experience the relatively stable conditions of fully marine situations, while others experience the regular or intermittent low salinities and high turbidities of estuaries. The rocky shores on open coasts are exposed to oceanic swell and waves, and the violence of this wave action is a major influence on the types of living organisms found. The conspicuous and typical species of such open rock surfaces are either attached (for example, barnacles, mussels, algae) or if mobile are capable of holding tightly to the surface of the rock or of retreating to protective crevices as occasion demands (for example, limpets, periwinkles, dogwhelks). Towards low-tide level and in pools, different assemblages of fauna and flora occur. The distribution of rocky shore organisms in European waters is probably better known than for any other marine habitat, and there is an extensive literature describing the many local variations.[11]

Rocky cliffs are most frequently the landward extension of the rocky shores described above, though such shores may also be backed by earth cliffs (see below). Sandstone, limestone, slate, basalt and granite are the principal types of rock which are hard enough to lead to cliff formation. Cliff heights vary greatly from a few metres to a maximum of 274 metres in England at Countisbury, north Devon, to 426 on St. Kilda, Scotland, and 668 on Achill Island, Co. Mayo, Ireland.

Despite the hardness of the material, rocky cliffs are rarely smooth; the action of wind and wind-blown sand, spray and waves erodes the softer spots to form a complex pattern of ledges, flats, cracks and gullies. These irregularities provide surfaces on which vegetation can establish itself and seabirds can nest.

The vegetation of sea-cliffs is probably the least man-modified in western Europe, but their high scenic value and wildlife interests lead to human pressures which disturb the seabirds. This will be covered in more detail in chapter IX.

Earth cliffs, which include those made of relatively soft chalk, in an eroding coastline where the land is subsiding or the sea rising, are unstable and subject to frequent erosion, in contrast to rocky cliffs where change is infrequent. In western Europe, frequent change and instability leading to mass-movements (cliff-falls or slips) are most common in sand and clay cliffs in south and east England, north France, Denmark, and the low Baltic coast. In rapidly retreating cliffs (where erosion is more or less continuous) most of the vegetation is derived from the cliff top; whereas in cliffs where erosion is more intermittent, colonization may take place in adjacent areas of cliff face. The vegetation plays no significant part in stabilizing the cliff, nor is it of particular ecological interest. While the land near the cliff top is used for agriculture, recreation, house-building and the establishment of towns (particularly resorts), the cliff-face itself and a narrow strip of land very close to the cliff-top are rarely used for any activity. The principal value of the cliff-face is as a means of access to the beach, and the principal problems are caused by trampling of vegetation, the development of paths which may subsequently become gullies, and the further erosion of the cliff.

Shingle is the term applied to those sediments which are larger in diameter than sand (under 2 mm) and smaller than boulders (over 200 mm). Within this size-range are cobbles (60–200 mm), coarse gravel (20–60 mm), medium gravel or pebbles (6–20 mm), and fine gravel (2–6 mm). Shingle is of frequent occurrence on the coasts of Britain, Ireland, and the Atlantic coast of France. In the Netherlands, shingle is absent. Shingle beaches are the simplest and most common type of shingle structure, forming a strip in contact with the land along the top of the beach, and frequently backed by low cliffs. Shingle also occurs as spits (as at Chesil Beach and Portland Bill), bars, and offshore barrier islands. Beaches, spits, and bars are extremely mobile, and are regularly moved by storm waves.

Many of the smaller shingle structures are also associated with marsh or sand formations. The majority of shingle shores are unvegetated or have an extremely sparse cover. However, in some places on the coast larger quantities of shingle build up, resulting in stable formations that are more terrestrial in nature or in the creation of lagoons (see below).

From the conservation point of view, stable shingle formations are particularly valuable because of their importance as nesting sites for sea-birds. They remain one of the more unused types of coastline. However, shingle shores are, in general, of little economic use for the grazing of domestic animals, although this practice is quite common in the west of Scotland. Of more widespread occurrence, and of greater significance, is the taking of shingle (including gravel) from the shore for building and roadmaking. This is the main danger to the survival of some shingle beaches and to the wildlife which depends on them.

Sandy shores range in size from small pocket beaches only a few hundred metres in width and less than a hundred metres between tide marks, to vast stretches of sand extending uninterrupted for many kilometres along the coast, and with inter-tidal distances of several hundred metres. Sandy beaches are much flatter than those of shingle, but share with shingle the characterisic of never being static. At any time, a sandy beach represents a dynamic equilibrium between offshore, onshore and longshore sand transport; and such movements are often cyclic or seasonal. In extreme cases, sand may be removed completely and deposited offshore during winter, leaving bare rocks which become covered again by deposition of sand during the following summer.

Because of the lack of a stable solid surface and because of the abrasive action of its moving rock or shell particles, sandy beaches do not support either the abundant large algae found on rocky shores or the rooted vegetation which thrives on muddy shores (see below). The most abundant organisms are microscopic, firmly attached to sand grains or inhabiting the system of spaces and channels between them (the interstitial fauna). The larger animals are principally bivalve molluscs (for example, the cockle), polychaete worms (for example, ragworm), and small crustacea. All of these animals are burrowers and become active on the sand surface only when the beach is submerged by the tide. At this time also, other organisms move up the beach to feed, and important among these are juvenile flat-fish such as plaice and dabs, the adults of which are fished offshore.

Sandy beaches are of prime recreational importance and support a wide variety of activities such as sunbathing, picnicking, beach games, swimming, surfing and sand-yachting. Much of the impact which these activities might have on the beach itself is quickly obliterated by the daily rise and fall of the tides. The major pressures associated with these recreational uses are shifted to above high water mark and arise from the need to cater for large numbers of tourists: hence the proliferation of caravan sites, car parks, restaurants and other facilities in the vicinity of popular beaches.

Other uses of sandy shores include the extraction of silica sand or shell fragments for commercial uses, the exploitation of shellfish, and the discharge of domestic and industrial waste. Because of their sheltered position and gentle gradients, sandy beaches are frequently the preferred sites (for reasons of ease of construction) for sea outfalls discharging at or beyond the low-water mark. Temporary damage to sandy beaches is frequently caused by oil pollution, while accumulations of litter and refuse at the high-water mark spoil the appearance of many beaches.

Sand dunes are formed by the wind transport of marine sands, and are therefore found only where sandy beaches occur at a sufficiently high level for the surface layer to dry out between the tides, and where the shore is not backed by cliffs. Dunes occur in many places on the coasts of northern Europe and are particularly extensive on the Dutch coast where they extend almost unbroken from the Ems to the Scheldt, a distance of approximately 400 kilometres. Dunes are notoriously unstable, and complete stability may occur only after centuries of shifting. Dune landscapes investigated on the Dutch coast have been shown to be of surprising antiquity. The older dunes are considered to have been completed before Roman times; younger dunes were formed from the twelfth century onwards and completed before the end of the sixteenth century.

The colonization of dunes by vegetation leads rapidly to further accretion of sand and to eventual stabilization. Primary colonizing plants then become replaced by others more suited to the new conditions and, as a result, dunes are a complex of many different habitats influenced to a large degree by the amount of water available. On the high dunes (2 metres or more above the water table) plants are dependent on rainfall. Between the dune ridges or crests, moist or wet 'dune-slacks' occur, areas where the water table reaches the surface or comes within one metre of it. The wetter slacks become seasonally flooded or water-logged to form temporary lagoons (see below). This diversity accounts to a large extent for the considerable scientific and educational value of sand dunes. In addition, coastal sand dunes provide a habitat for many grassland species that are restricted elsewhere because of modern intensive farming and the ploughing up of old pastures. They also have high recreational and aesthetic values, and attract considerable numbers of visitors.

The economic uses of sand dunes, some of which conflict with the above uses, can in extreme cases damage and destroy them; they include afforestation, the grazing of farm animals, and their use as industrial and residential sites for golf-courses, and as military training and exercise areas.

The most serious damage has been caused by public pressure (dune grasses are particularly vulnerable to damage by trampling) and by building development. Atmospheric pollution from nearby industry and the extraction of ground-water for industrial purposes has detrimentally affected a number of such areas in Holland. These problems of industrial development in the coastal zone are taken up again in chapter IX in the context of the overall use of the coast.

Lagoons are shallow bodies of brackish or sea water partially separated from an adjacent coastal sea by barriers of sand or shingle. If the narrow opening through which the seawater can flow becomes completely constricted or closed, the now isolated lagoon becomes a coastal pond or lake, which may eventually become fresh-water if streams or a river discharge into it. Coastal lagoons are usually found only on low-lying coasts, where the relative land–sea level is changing, and where the tidal range is small. Lagoons are usually in a state of flux and generally evolve either towards total isolation behind a complete sediment barrier (and thence from a coastal pond to swamp and marsh), or into a coastal bay after erosion of the barrier. Such changes can occur in relatively short spaces of time, as a result of which the physical environment is often harsh and subject to considerable short- and long-term fluctuations, and the flora and fauna frequently show a number of peculiarities comparable to those shown by estuarine species.

In north-west Europe, coastal lagoons are found in Denmark, southern Britain, and western France. For many centuries they have been used for harbour development and for aquaculture (for example, oysters and mussels). Industrial development, including the discharge of wastes, and increasing recreational uses are damaging to lagoon ecosystems which because of their special characteristics have a high scientific and educational value. Even where the lagoon itself is not directly affected or disturbed, changes may be caused by land reclamation in the vicinity or by alterations in the river or streams which feed and maintain it. Wildfowl or waders which migrate to feed in highly productive coastal lagoons are also liable to be disturbed by these activities or by recreational uses of the open water or adjoining land.

Mud-flats are formed by the deposition of finely divided inorganic material (silt, clay) and organic debris, which has been held in suspension in the sea or in estuaries. Deposition takes place only in sheltered areas, particularly in estuaries, and, once deposited, the mud requires a strong tidal scour for its removal. In very large bays such as the Wash (east coast of England) or Morecambe Bay (west coast of England), there is a progressive decrease in particle size from the sea to the landward margin, so that sand becomes replaced by mud in the more sheltered areas of the bay on the higher level tidal flats. Similarly, in many smaller estuaries and inlets, sand-flat and sand-bars occur at the exposed mouth, with finer silts and muds settling behind them. Muddy shores behind protective dunes occur on an extensive scale on the Biscay coast of France, between the Friesian Islands and the mainland of the Netherlands, in north-west Germany, and in Denmark.

Despite their bare appearance, mud-flats are no less rich in invertebrate life than, for example, rocky shores. The immense nutrient resources of mud-flats have been utilized by mankind from the earliest times: shellfish industries were developed in many estuaries, and wildfowl and wader populations were exploited by professional wildfowlers. At high water, the flats are important feeding grounds for fish such as flounders and mullet which are taken by fish traps and nets in the drainage channels and creeks. Professional wildfowling has vanished, but commercial fishing remains and the mud-flats continue to be used for bait-digging, casual shellfish harvesting and bird watching.

The importance of mud-flats to the bird population needs to be emphasized. In north-west Europe there are large numbers of wading birds in the intertidal zone, and a large proportion of these depends heavily on mud-flats as feeding grounds. The intertidal mud and silt of north-west Europe is vital for the survival of these birds; the mud-flats sustain large proportions of the species' world population during winter months, and they serve as essential migratory staging-posts where the birds can accumulate fat reserves to complete their journeys, northward in spring and southward in autumn. Watching these birds gives pleasure to a large and increasing number of people.

Other recreational uses are few. In some sheltered creeks and bays the mud provides safe mooring or anchoring ground for small craft and may be said to contribute to the overall capacity of these areas to support sailing and other marine activities. Scientifically, mud-flats will always remain a focus of interest, but their educational value is limited since other shores offer easier access, better working conditions, and an equal variety of organisms.

The major threat to coastal mud-flats comes from reclamation. In the past, their reclamation for agricultural uses occurred widely in Britain, the Netherlands, West Germany and Denmark; but today more extensive areas are likely to be lost to industry and water storage. The discharge of industrial effluent and sewage has also in a number of locations led to elevated nutrient levels (eutrophication), with the resulting spread of green algae. Within limits, such extra growth of green algae can have beneficial effect since it is eaten by, for example, brent geese and wigeon. Beyond these limits, the physical blanketing of the mud by the algae, and the consequent depletion of oxygen levels by layers of decaying algae, have reduced the numbers and variety of worms, molluscs and other mud-dwelling organisms, reducing in turn the capacity of mud-flats to support waders and wildfowl.

Salt-marshes are a natural development of mud-flats which become colonized by seaweeds and eel-grasses (*Zostera*) in tidal areas. Mud at the higher tidal levels (mean high-water neaps and upwards) is invaded by specialized plants, the most important of which is cord-grass (*Spartina*). This plant possesses exceptional power to colonize mud and, having done so its presence slows the movement of tidal water and thus increases the rate of silt and mud deposition so that the marsh grows rapidly. *Spartina* is therefore frequently planted as an agent for mud-flat reclamation. Its attraction for wildfowl is poor (almost no herbivores feed on it), but under natural circumstances it is succeeded by other plant species.

The relationship between plants and animals in a salt-marsh is relatively simple. Only a limited number of species is involved and vegetable detritus plays an important part in the food web.

The most common use of salt-marshes is grazing, usually by sheep, but also by cows and horses, and even by domestic geese (in north-west Germany). On European salt-marshes, grazing is most common along shores from Scotland and Denmark to north-west France. Gathering plants (*Salicornia* species and *Aster tripolium*) and animals (periwinkles, *Littorina littorea*) for food is also practised locally. Cutting of turves for laying lawns and reinforcing sea-walls is also carried out in England and on the continental coast from Denmark to the Netherlands.

Coastal salt-marshes are not suited to mass recreation, but are attractive for specialist pursuits such as inshore fishing, wildfowling, birdwatching, walking and riding. The simple structure of the salt-marsh ecosystems also makes such areas valuable for education and scientific research, and they are also of interest as gene-reservoirs for further hybridization and selection of potentially valuable plants.

Some of these uses may damage salt-marshes, but by far the greatest threat to them and to the wildfowl populations which they support comes from land reclamation for agricultural purposes (by drainage, embankment or poldering) or for the establishment of industry or housing. The latter activities are usually accompanied by increased public pressure and by pollution. Near long-established industrial centres, salt-marsh sediments contain a high proportion of man-made detritus. Plastic litter accumulates at the tide-line, while urban sewage, agricultural wastes and fertilizer run-off lead to elevated nutrient levels and extensive growth of green algae. Large-scale impoundments of coastal waters for use as fresh-water storage areas, for tidal-power generation or for other purposes also threaten to eliminate extensive areas of our diminishing salt-marsh resources.

Estuaries are unique coastal environments containing many of the above types of habitat including sandy and muddy shores, rock, shingle and salt-marsh. They may be defined as the more or less enclosed regions at the mouths of rivers where fresh-water from land drainage mixes to a greater or lesser extent with saline water from a tidal sea, and their uniqueness depends on the continually changing cycle of salinity, water level and other parameters (such as temperature) within a region characterized by shelter, abundant soft sediments and a constant supply of detritus or dissolved nutrients.[12] A further outstanding feature of estuaries is their high biological productivity; they are regarded as being among the most fertile natural areas in the world, and are on average twenty times more productive than the open sea.

This productivity forms the basis for extensive and commercially valuable shellfisheries for mussels, oysters, and cockles; furthermore, many suitable estuaries are additionally valuable as sites for potential mariculture operations. The commercially caught fin-fish of estuaries include sprat and local races of herring, together with flat-fish (dabs and flounders), and the migratory salmon and sea-trout which pass through to breed in the rivers.

Human settlements, industry, the discharge of waste, port development, commercial shipping movements, dredging, reclamation, and other physical interference with estuaries have taken a heavy toll of these unique areas. Such uses are not without their particular value and may even be considered necessary in many instances, but their activities or demands are often in conflict. Examples of some of these conflicts and some possible approaches to satisfactory management of the overall resource are discussed in chapter IX.

Sources and Further Reading

Anderson, J. G. C. and Owen, T. T., *The Structure of the British Isles*, Pergamon Press, 1980.

Banner, F. T., Collins, M. B., and Massie, K. S. (edd.), *The North-West European Shelf Seas: the Sea-bed and the Sea in Motion, II: Physical and Chemical Oceanography, and Physical Resources*, Elsevier Oceanography Series, 24B 1980.

Barnes, R. S. K., *The Coastline*, Wiley-Interscience, 1977.

Goldberg, E. D. (ed.), *North Sea Science*, MIT Press, 1973.

Lee, A. J. and Ramster, J. W., *Atlas of the Seas around the British Isles*, Ministry of Agriculture, Fisheries and Food, Directorate of Fisheries Research, 1981.

Naylor, D. and Mounteney, S. N., *Geology of the North-West European Continental Shelf*, volume 1, Graham and Trotman, 1975.

Notes

1. See Sibthorp, M. M. (ed.), *The North Sea: Challenge and Opportunity*, Europa, 1975, p. 1.
2. Goldberg, E. D. (ed.), *North Sea Science*, MIT Press, 1973, p. 139.
3. Rossiter, J. R., 'The North Sea Storm Surge of 31 January and 1 February 1953', *Phil. Trans. Royal Society*, 1954, sec. A 246, pp. 371–450.
4. Miller, G. R., 'The Flux of Tidal Energy out of the Deep Oceans', *Journal of Geophysical Research*, 1966 res. 71, pp. 2485–9. Flather, R. A., 'A Tidal Model of the North-West European Continental Shelf', *Mem. Soc. Sci. Liege*, 1976, p. 9.
5. International Hydrographic Organization, Special Publication no. 22. *Limits of Oceans and Seas*.
6. Cooper, L. H. N., 'The Physical Oceanography of the Celtic Sea', *Oceanog. Mar. Biol. Rev.* 5, 1967, pp. 99–110.
7. Pingree, R. D., Pugh, P. R., Holligan, P. M. and Forster, G. R., 'Summer Phytoplanktons Blooms and Red Tides Along Tidal Fronts in the Approaches to the English Channel', *Nature*, 258, 1975, pp. 672–7.
8. Deegan, C. E., Kirby, R., Rae, I. and Floyd, R., *The Superficial Deposits of the Firth of Clyde and its Sea Lochs*, Rep. Institute of Geological Sciences, 73/9, 1973.
9. Howarth, M. J., 'Current Surges in the St. George's Channel,' *Estuarine Coastal Marine Science*, 3, 1975, pp. 57–70.
10. Monahan, E. C., *Drift Bottle Recoveries from Releases South, West and North of Ireland*, report no. 1, Surface Drifter Studies, Department of Oceanography, University College, Galway, 1979, pp. 1–75.
11. Lewis, J. R., 'Rocky Foreshores,' in Barnes, R. S. K. (ed.), *The Coastline*, Wiley Interscience, 1977, pp. 147–58.
12. Nelson-Smith, A., 'Estuaries', in Barnes, R. S. K. (ed.), *The Coastline*, pp. 123–46.

II

Oil and Gas

Introduction

Systematic exploration of the north-west European continental shelf really commenced in 1964, although there had been some exploratory activity before then. By 1964 the UNCLOS Continental Shelf Convention had come into force and the necessary domestic legislation for the exploration and exploitation of the continental shelf resources had been enacted. Norway had proclaimed sovereignty over the Norwegian continental shelf on 31 May 1963 and had passed an Act relating to Exploration for and Exploitation of Submarine Natural Resources on 21 June 1963. The first exploration licences were issued later the same year and the first production licences in 1965. Their first well was drilled in 1966.

The United Kingdom's exploration of the continental shelf began in earnest in 1964, following ratification of the 1958 Convention and the passing of the Continental Shelf Act, although some seismic exploration had already been carried out prior to this. The first licences were issued later in the same year and the first well was commenced towards the end of it.[1]

Denmark proclaimed sovereignty over its sector of the continental shelf in 1963 and granted its first licence the same year, but drilling did not commence until 1966. The Netherlands had drilled three wells offshore as early as 1962, but did not pass its law concerning the exploration and exploitation of mineral resources offshore until 1965 and did not issue its first licences until 1968, in which year seven wells were drilled, Ireland did not pass its Continental Shelf Act until 1968 and then issued its first licence in 1969. The first Irish well was commenced late in 1970 and completed in 1971.

Results of Offshore Exploration

The discovery of the giant onshore gas field at Groningen in Holland, and the knowledge that the gas originated in the underlying coal measures extending across the Channel into England led to the discovery of the West Sole gas field in 1965, only one year after the first UK licences were granted. Several other gas discoveries followed in the late 1960s, and the first major oil discoveries were made in the Norwegian Ekofisk and the

British Montrose fields in 1969. The Danish Dan field was discovered in 1971, and commercial oil production from it and the Ekofisk field began in 1972.

The first commercial oil production in British waters started in 1975 from the Argyll field, and this was followed shortly afterwards by the Forties field and the Montrose field (1976).

Irish offshore activity began in 1969 with the issue of an exclusive licence to Marathon which resulted in the discovery of the Kinsale Head gas field in the Celtic Sea with their third well in 1971. Gas production from the Kinsale Head field commenced in 1978, one year later than from Norwegian waters, and five years later than from Dutch waters.

These early successes spurred governments to issue further licences in order to encourage the oil companies to intensify their search for oil and gas and to develop fields which appeared likely to be commercially attractive.

As a result of the activity generated, Norway became a net exporter of crude oil in 1975, and by 1977 was selling natural gas to Europe by means of a pipeline laid to Emden in West Germany. As early as 1970, the UK was producing enough natural gas from the southern basin of the North Sea to meet some 90 per cent of its needs. Since then, the demand has more than trebled, with all the increase being met from the continental shelf (including supplies from the UK–Norwegian Frigg gas field in the northern basin). By 1980, the UK had achieved net self-sufficiency in crude oil production. Although the other countries of north-west Europe had not had quite the same success as Norway and the UK, significant production of oil or gas has been obtained offshore of the Netherlands, Denmark, and Ireland, making a useful contribution to those countries' needs. Oil production began in 1982 from the first offshore field in Netherlands waters.

By November 1982, there were six producing gas fields in UK waters, plus a seventh, the Frigg field, which straddles the dividing line between the UK and Norway. Work was also due to begin on developing the Morecambe Bay gas field, located in the Irish Sea between England and the Isle of Man. Producing oil fields in UK waters numbered twenty by late 1982, plus two shared with Norway (Statfjord and Murchison), while six more were being actively developed.

In Norwegian waters there are ten producing oil fields, (eight in the Ekofisk area, plus Statfjord and Murchison) as well as the Frigg gas field. One further oil field is being developed, together with two gas fields in the vicinity of Frigg. The discovery of the giant Troll gas field has probably more than doubled the total North Sea gas reserves, and may lead to the development of a Norwegian gas-gathering system. Norway's gas potential now exceeds her oil potential, and could provide a substantial amount of Europe's gas needs.

The Netherlands has seven gas fields in production with development in progress on three more, and production has just started from their first offshore oil fields. Two Danish oil fields are in production, and a third is being developed together with two gas fields. In Irish waters, the Kinsale Head gas field is the only field in commercial production so far.

With two exceptions (Morecambe Bay and Kinsale Head), all the fields in production or under development are in the North Sea. However, to the west of Shetland discoveries have been made of both gas and oil, but much work remains to be done to determine if and how these accumulations can be developed commercially. Formidable technical problems have to be solved both as regards the reservoir rocks and fluids and the environment, which is even more hostile than the North Sea.

Ireland's exploration effort resulted in the discovery of the sub-commercial Seven Heads oil field west of Kinsale Head and a number of oil and gas shows. Later, when drilling had moved to the Porcupine Basin off the west coast, Phillips and BP found oil there during 1978 and 1979. The costs of drilling in such deep exposed locations, the drop in oil prices, and the present shortage of risk capital as a consequence of the economic recession have prevented the commercial development of these discoveries. Should further reserves be proved, however, these marginal fields may well become commercial.

Further exploration work is continuing not only in the Porcupine Basin but also in the Goban Spur south-west of Ireland; while renewed interest in the Celtic Sea is being shown by exploration companies. Further drilling in the Kish Basin east of Dublin is also likely as a result of the increased probability that this area could yield gas from reservoirs similar to those at Morecambe Bay about 160 kilometres to the east.

No significant oil or gas discoveries have been made in the English Channel or in its approaches, but relatively few wells have been drilled so far. The start of exploration in these areas was delayed pending the determination of the dividing line between England and France in the Western Approaches and round the Channel Islands. However, oil discoveries onshore in both countries, in particular the Wytch Farm oil field in Dorset on the southern side of Poole harbour, give good cause for hopes of oil discovery under the waters between the two countries.

Reserves and Resources

Although over 1700 exploration and appraisal wells have been drilled already on the north-west European continental shelf to determine the magnitude of these enormously valuable resources of oil and gas, it is still not possible to quantify them with any real degree of precision. Many more wells and many more years will be needed before this is possible. At present, taking into account all the information that has been gained from the geophysical surveys and the geological results of all the wells that have been drilled, the original known reserves (i.e. those that have already been discovered and appraised, so that a reasonably accurate estimate can be made, and before deducting quantities already produced) are put at about 6.5 billion (10^9) tonnes of oil equivalent (assuming that 1 billion cubic metres of gas are equivalent to 1 million tonnes of oil). Allowing for production to the end of 1981, the remaining known reserves at that date were about 5.5 billion tonnes.

There is little doubt that this estimate is highly conservative, because many discoveries have been made which have not yet been fully appraised; and while some will prove to be non-commercial even in the long term, others will become economically attractive to develop as a result of rising oil prices, improved technology or a modified tax structure. This last but very significant factor is discussed more fully later. It is worth noting that technological advances in themselves do not guarantee commercial exploitation; the associated research, development and production costs are normally so high that further price increases will also be necessary before commercial exploitation of the more marginal fields can begin.

The total resources (i.e. adding to the known reserves a reasonable allowance for discoveries that have not yet been made; and allowing for increased recovery from known discoveries by improved techniques) are much larger, much more difficult to estimate, and much more speculative. Various estimates have been made which suggest that the original resources could be somewhere in the range of 10 to 16 billion tonnes of oil equivalent.

Investment and Costs

The investment needed to discover these resources and to develop them is also very large. Up to the end of 1980, investment on the UK continental shelf totalled some £4 billion for exploration, plus £13 billion for development. In Norway, the corresponding figures were some 8.7 billion Kroner (approximately £0.87 bn) and 54.4 billion Kroner (approximately £5.4 bn) respectively. Making allowances for expenditure on the other sectors of the continental shelf also, the total investment to the end of 1980 would appear to amount to some £25–30 billion.

In 1980 alone, the investment on the UK continental shelf totalled some £2.7 billion, and on the Norwegian continental shelf some 7.3 billion Kroner (approximately £0.73 bn.). While it is very difficult to predict with any confidence what the future investment needs will be, there is no doubt that this sort of level of investment will be needed for many years to come if the resources are to be fully explored and exploited.

Operating costs were very high—in the UK approximately £0.5 billion in 1979 and £0.7 billion in 1980. These costs are liable to increase in the years to come as more and more relatively small fields are developed to maintain the predicted production levels.

These very large investment requirements (which are at high risk, particularly in the initial phases of exploration and development) and high operating costs have caused a number of problems specific to the offshore oil industry, and these will be examined briefly later in this chapter.

Depletion Policies

In 1980, the UK produced some 80.3 million tonnes of oil and liquid products from the offshore, and 37.3 billion cubic metres of gas, while Norway produced 24.4 million tonnes of oil and 25.1 billion cubic metres of gas—a total of some 167 million tonnes of oil equivalent (t.o.e.); adding Dutch, Danish and Irish production, the total comes to some 180 million t.o.e. At £150 per tonne, this represents a value of some £27 billion, but because gas is sold more cheaply than the true thermal equivalent oil value, the actual proceeds were very much less. In 1980, the UK Government revenue accruing from fees, royalties, and taxes amounted to some £3.8 billion, and in Norway to some 18 billion Kroner or, say, £1.8 billion. According to then Government projections for 1982, the total tax revenue in the UK from the petroleum industry would amount to some £6.4 billion. Royalties would account for £1.4 billion of this; petroleum revenue taxes for £4.4 billion, and corporation tax £0.6 billion. However, oil is priced in US dollars, and the value to the Exchequer therefore fluctuates with the exchange rate.

Such vast sums of money represent a very significant proportion of the wealth of the nations concerned, and of their governments' revenues; and all governments have given considerable thought as to how these assets should be best exploited in the national interest. Although the magnitude of the resources in the UK and in Norway is similar, their needs are not. Norway, with its much smaller population consumes about 9 million tonnes of oil each year, and no gas, while the UK's oil demand is about ten times this amount, and gas consumption is approximately 40 billion cubic metres per year. Norway, therefore, can meet its needs easily, leaving a substantial surplus available for export. Consequently, from the early days Norway adopted a conservationist approach to the exploitation of its offshore oil and gas. In the 1973–4 Storting Report no. 25 it was stated that 'The petroleum finds in the North Sea mean that as a nation we shall become richer. The Government is of the opinion that these new possibilities should be used to develop a qualitatively better society. A rapid and uncontrolled growth in the use of material resources should be avoided, unless the social structure is otherwise substantially changed.' This approach prevailed, and has been continued and in the 1979–80 Storting Report no. 53 it is stated that:

The Government wishes to maintain a moderate price of petroleum production. The extent of total activities must be stipulated with a view to several factors including:

degree of safety;
situation regarding resources;
technical circumstances relating to production and transportation;
labour market and industry;
pollution problems;
preparedness;
the relation to fisheries;
objectives;
impact on the total Norwegian economy; and
energy situation in Norway and in the rest of the world.

Taking these factors into consideration, the present Norwegian policy is aimed at achieving a production level of about 70 million t.o.e. in the late 1980s, rising to about 90 million t.o.e in the early 1990s, and maintaining these levels into the next century. In order to do this it is considered necessary to discover reserves which are about twenty times the annual production. This situation obtains at present, but for it to be maintained new reserves need to be added to match the higher production levels and to replace those produced. It is estimated that some 20–30 exploration wells will be needed each year to accomplish this.

In order to control the pace of exploration and to even out the activity levels, the Norwegian Ministry of Petroleum and Energy recommends that the main principle should be the regular awarding of a small number of licence blocks at a time, at intervals to be determined by taking into consideration, *inter alia*, the extent of the reserves already proven and current development activity. To further even out activity and achieve the desired production levels, some licences have been awarded with clauses which authorize the Ministry to suspend development of a field for up to five years and to stipulate the production required.

The UK, on the other hand, with its much greater needs, initially followed a very different path. While it was never explicitly stated as such, it is apparent that at first the UK Government adopted a policy of building up production as rapidly as possible (taking into account constraints imposed by technical and safety considerations, pollution, etc.), in order to achieve a large measure of self-sufficiency as soon as possible. An indication of this policy was given as early as 1964 during the third reading of the Continental Shelf Bill when the Minister announced 'Among the general considerations by which I shall be guided in carrying out this task are the following five main factors: first, the need to encourage the most rapid and thorough exploration and economical exploitation of petroleum resources on the continental shelf.' This encouragement was provided by relatively liberal licence terms, the fiscal regime, and so forth.

There is little doubt that this policy was formulated bearing in mind the increasing uncertainty about the security of the supplies from the Middle East, and these fears were fully justified by the outbreak of the Arab–Israeli War in October 1973 which provided a further stimulus to developments in the relatively stable political climate of Western Europe.

Early production and demand forecasts suggested that the UK should reach self-sufficiency by about 1980, and this was in fact achieved, although both demand and production turned out to be lower than the original forecasts. However, even at the time of urgency it was already realized that if this policy were to continue unrestrained, an 'overshoot' situation would develop, leading to a large exportable surplus of oil in the short-term, rapid depletion of the resource and an early return to imports and dependency on Middle East crude.

In the Petroleum and Submarine Pipelines Act of 1975, therefore, powers were taken whereby the rate of development and depletion could be controlled so as to conserve the resources and prolong the period of self-sufficiency. But at the time the UK was still heavily dependent on imported crude and so there was no wish or need to slow down developments at that point.

Certain assurances were therefore given by the Secretary of State for Energy on 6 December 1974 which made it attractive for the oil industry to continue to invest in and develop North Sea oil and gas. The full test of the so-called 'Varley' assurances (he was then the Secretary of State for Energy) is appended to this chapter (appendix v); its most important features are that no delays would be imposed on discoveries made before December 1975, and that no production cuts would be imposed before 1982.

When the Conservative Government came to power in 1979, it announced that these assurances would be honoured, although by then it was apparent that the time was rapidly approaching when decisions would have to be taken to apply controls if the size of the 'overshoot' was to be limited. On 23 July 1980, the Secretary of State for Energy announced the intention that controls would be imposed (subject to the 'Varley' assurances), in order to prolong the period of net self-sufficiency. The full text of this statement is also appended to this chapter (appendix vi). In 1982, however, the Secretary of State for Energy said that there appeared to be no need to apply specific conservation measures such as development delays or production cut-backs. Controls exercised on production levels to ensure optimum economic recovery, and on gas flaring so as to prevent waste of this valuable asset, would be regarded as providing a sufficient degree of conservation.

Ireland, with as yet no commercially proven oil field and with only one gas field, can hardly be said to have a depletion policy as such. Following discovery of the Kinsale Head field in 1971, the Government commissioned a study aimed at determining the best possible use for the gas. Its conclusion was that the gas should be divided between two organizations—ESB, the state-owned electricity generating and distribution utility, and NET, the state-owned fertilizer manufacturing company—in order to reduce dependence on imported oil and to ensure security of essential supplies of electricity and nitrogenous fertilizer. Widespread protest at this decision led to a change of government policy to the extent that it sanctioned a share of the gas for domestic consumption, in the first instance by the local Gas Consumers Company, and later it allowed that a gas pipeline to Dublin, at first dismissed as uneconomic, should be constructed. Among the reasons given for the change were the fact that the operations of NET had resulted in considerable losses and that imported oil for power generation was cheaper and less wasteful of a valuable resource.

The Impact Offshore and Onshore

Offshore

The achievements to date have had an enormous impact both onshore and offshore. There are over a hundred fixed platforms either already installed in the North Sea or under construction and due to be installed shortly. These range in size from steel jackets weighing only a few hundred tons for some of the satellite gas platforms in the southern basin, to as much as 600,000 tons for the giant concrete platform in the Ninian field in the northern basin. When this was floated out in 1978 from its construction site at Loch Kishorn on the western coast of Scotland, it was the largest floating man-made fabrication to date. There are also two floating production platforms made from converted semi-submersible drilling rigs.

In addition, there are many smaller installations: flare stacks, junction platforms, and various forms of offshore loading facilities. These range from the relatively simple single point buoy moorings (SBMs) to the more elaborate articulated loading towers (SALMs) and those which incorporate floating storage such as the 'SPAR' on the Brent field. At the Fulmar field, for example, there is a specially converted, permanently moored storage tanker.

Apart from these relatively 'fixed' structures, there may be up to about fifty floating mobile drilling units and accommodation units ('flotels') in use as well as numerous other vessels such as supply boats and tugs, stand-by vessels, and about fifty diving support vessels, crane barges and pipe-laying barges. In addition there are tankers collecting oil from the various offshore loading facilities mentioned above. Thirteen fields have such facilities, but not all of these are normally in use as some of the fields are also connected to pipline systems. Their offshore loading facilities are maintained on stand-by in case of pipeline failure.

Over 4,000 kilometres of submarine pipelines of 40 centimetres diameter or larger have been laid on the sea-bed to connect offshore platforms and fields to each other and to shore terminals in order to bring the gas and oil to shore. The recently announced pipeline to take gas from the Statfjord field to shore at Karsto, a little to the north of Stavanger, and subsequently to Ekofisk for onward transmission to Germany, will bring the total to about 4,800 kilometres. These pipelines are normally wrapped with reinforced concrete to provide weight and protection against damage from ships' anchors, trawl boards, etc. Whenever practical, they are trenched into the sea-bed so as to provide extra protection. In addition there are numerous smaller-diameter lines in the oilfields themselves linking single wells completed on the sea-bed to the production platform.

Ecological effects of the drilling and other activities in the vicinity of offshore oil-production platforms have been the subject of several investigations. The general conclusion is that, given the existing controls on oily water effluents, and the degree of dispersion available in the open North Sea, effects on the water column are slight and detectable only in the immediate vicinity of the platforms. The disposal of drilling muds and cuttings can cause changes in the bottom sediments, but in the North Sea significant contamination has been found offshore only close to platforms using oil-based drilling muds.[2]

Onshore

The impact onshore is largely the result of the building of the terminals to receive the oil and gas. Some of these terminals are quite small, occupying only a few hectares of land, but others are very large, taking hundreds of hectares, particularly the Sullom Voe terminal which is among the largest in the world, and which is able to handle some 320,000 cubic metres of oil per day.

In addition, supply bases have now been created at existing harbours to handle the thousands of tons of materials used offshore. The most important of these in the UK are at Lerwick in Shetland, at Peterhead, Aberdeen, Montrose and Dundee in Scotland, and at Great Yarmouth and Lowestoft in Norfolk. Many other ports have been used, also on a lesser scale, in the countries surrounding the North Sea. In the Celtic Sea, Cork has provided the principal supply base, while exploration off the west coast of Ireland is serviced from Foynes (in the Shannon estuary) and Galway.

The establishment of platform-construction yards in Norway, Scotland, England, Holland and France has also had environmental and social impacts. This is particularly so in Scotland where the construction yards are very large in relation to the existing socio-economic environment. The principal yards are at Nigg Bay in the Cromarty Firth, Ardersier in the

Moray Firth, Methil in the Firth of Forth, Graythorpe on Teeside, and the four west-coast yards at Loch Kishorn, Ardyne Point, Portavadie, and Hunterston.

All these major facilities have in turn resulted in a need to improve the infrastructure of the areas in which they are located. There has generally been a need for more housing, schools, hospitals, and shops; roads have had to be built or improved and airports extended or improved—particularly at Aberdeen, and Sumburgh in Shetland. At Sullom Voe whole new villages have been built and at Unst at the very north of Shetland from which helicopters fly to the most northerly oil fields. The speed at which these developments have been implemented and the uncertainty about their future have caused many local planning problems (see chapter IX).

It is estimated that in the UK about 22,000 people are directly employed offshore; while the total directly employed on oil-related activities in the UK could easily be 50,000 or more. Including those indirectly employed in manufacturing, supply sub-contracting, etc., the total is likely to be well over 100,000 in the country as a whole.

Problems

Such developments taking place in a relatively short space of time have not been achieved without great effort and without giving rise to many problems: technical, financial, political and legal. There have also been many conflicts with other users of the sea and coastline—with fishing, shipping, defence, tourism, amenities, etc., and not least the conflict caused by the need for skilled labour in an industry which could afford to pay for it, while older industries could not match the higher wages and salaries offered.

Technical

The technical problems have been largely solved, or are on the way to solution, but those remaining may require further research and the accumulation of more data. These latter problems fall into two main categories—the first relating to the properties of the oil or gas reservoirs themselves and how to achieve the maximum economic recovery in general, the second to the problems caused by the nature of the environment—wind and wave forces, water depth, and sea-bed conditions, etc.

It is generally accepted that wind and wave conditions encountered on the north-west European continental shelf are amongst the most difficult anywhere in the world where oil and gas fields are being developed. When development started in the 1960s, world experience was largely confined to water depths of not much more than 30 metres and generally calm weather conditions. In the North Sea, there are rough seas for most of the year, but within 10 years platforms had been designed, constructed and installed in about 120 metres of water (Magnus field). This has represented an enormous step forward in technology and has continually pushed at the limits of human knowledge. Much research work has gone into gathering data on winds and waves, and into predicting wave climates and the force they exert on structures. The properties of materials used, notably steel and concrete, and the methods of fabrication have also had to be researched extensively; corrosion and fatigue have proved to be particularly difficult problems.

Yet more remains to be done if discoveries in still deeper and more hostile waters to the west of Shetland and Ireland are to be developed. It may well be that the limit has nearly been reached for fixed structures resting on the sea-bed and that future systems will be either totally submerged or floating, or will be a combination of both. Even in the relatively shallow waters of the North Sea, it is quite probable that similar systems will be employed as smaller fields are developed which cannot justify the enormous capital expenditure of large permanent structures. Smaller floating structures which can be moved from one field to another as required may well be employed.

One system which has been developed recently to tackle these problems is the Shell-Esso Underwater Manifold Centre (UMC) which was installed in the Cormorant field, some 90 miles north-east of Shetland in the summer of 1982. Although the water depth here is 150 metres, the system is also designed to work in several thousand feet of water, to handle a number of wells, and to be operated entirely by remote control without the need for diver intervention. It weighs some 2,300 tonnes, is the height of a four-story building, and covers an area half the size of a football pitch. At Cormorant, control is exercised electronically from the main Cormorant A platform over 6 kilometres away to which the oil produced is also piped. In deeper waters, the UMC could be controlled from a floating vessel.

Another system being developed is BP's Single Well Oil Production System (SWOPS). All the equipment is mounted on a converted tanker which is anchored or dynamically positioned over the well and the oil is produced into the tanker through a special production riser linked to the well-head on the sea-floor. Because the tanker would be susceptible to storms, special arrangements have to be made to close in the well and disconnect the riser without causing pollution.

Deep water also poses problems for pipe-laying. Although many large-diameter pipelines have been successfully laid in water depth of up to about 180 metres, it is only recently that one has been laid in over 300 metres of water—not in north-west European water, but across the Straits of Messina. The Norwegian Trench, a 600-metre depression in the sea-bed close to the Norwegian coast, has so far prevented the laying of pipelines from the Ekofisk complex of fields to Norway. Consequently the oil comes by pipeline to Teeside in the UK, while the gas goes to Emden in West Germany. This problem has now been overcome and the Norwegian Government has decided that in accordance with the principle that petroleum produced on the Norwegian continental shelf should be landed in Norway, gas from the Statfjord field will in future be piped to a terminal at Korsto where the gas liquids will be removed and the dry gas then piped to Ekofisk for onward transmission to Emden.

For even deeper water, further improvements in technology are needed. Over 160 kilometres west of Ireland, on the Porcupine Bank, exploration has resulted in two oil finds in almost 460 metres of water. This part of the continental shelf is completely exposed to the full force of the Atlantic weather, and tentative production plans being drawn up for Aran-BP allow for interruption of the oil flow in severe stormy weather. Because the water depth is too great for a conventional platform, it may be necessary to use subsea completions on the well-heads and to load the oil into a moored tanker through a flexible pipeline—a system similar to the SWOPS described above. Alternatively, if a large discovery was made, it could be developed by multiple sub-sea completions linked to a manifold and riser to a guyed tower or tension-leg platform.

The problems are likely to be even greater if oil is found in the Goban Spur area, some 275 kilometres south-west of County Kerry, where seismic studies began in 1979. In this location, water depths range from 600 to 1,500 metres, far beyond the depths in the Porcupine Bight, in the Celtic Sea or in the North Sea.

Financial

The development of the oil fields in the European continental shelf waters around the British Isles has presented all the problems normally encountered in providing finance for industrial development but has presented them in extreme form for the following reasons:

(a) the sums involved in individual projects are very large;
(b) hugh investments are necessary before any return can be expected;
(c) profits cannot be expected to build up quickly;
(d) the risk of loss is high in the initial phases;
(e) new untried technology is often involved.

The banking system has been called upon to meet much of the financing needs of oil development on the continental shelf and has done so despite a number of risks. The exploration phase of searching for oil involves the highest degree of risk, and finance for the exploration and for the appraisal phases is essentially equity finance, risk capital which must be raised directly or be provided out of a company's own equity resources.

While exploration entails the highest risk development, even after adequate appraisal, still entails major problems and substantial risks. It is indeed mainly because of the large sums involved and the substantial risks to be run that most developments on the continental shelf have been undertaken not by single companies, but by consortia of companies, and financed by consortia of banks.

Among the risks may be mentioned:

The reservoir risk—even the skills of the present technical experts cannot guarantee that early estimates of reserves will be realized, and indeed the risk remains high that oil may not be there at all or may not in the event be producible in the volumes anticipated, or be producible only after additional expense.

The construction period risk—the costs of accident and of delay during the construction period can be severe and any delay in completion has an immediate effect on cash flow. With the sums of money involved such delays can be extremely costly.

The consortium risk—the successful prosecution of any project depends to a very great extent on the technical, managerial and financial competence of the field operator, the company appointed by the members of the consortium to undertake the exploration and development of the field.

If a member of a consortium cannot meet its financial obligations, the remaining members will either have to meet them or find another partner; but even if they do find a willing partner with the financial strength required, transfers of licences from one company to another must be approved by Government and are subject to restrictions, controls and consequent delays.

The product-pricing risk—North Sea crude has to be priced internationally (i.e. depending upon world prices and levels of production), but it attracts a premium for its lower sulphur content and its crude quality; it is, however, comparatively expensive to produce.

Although of vital interest to the UK and indeed to Europe, the North Sea reserves of oil and gas are believed to represent only 3 and 2 per cent respectively of *world* reserves. The North Sea, as has been seen over recent years cannot establish a price for oil—it can only reflect the world price. Ever-increasing costs, a heavy tax burden, and falling oil prices have already led to the postponement of certain developments.

Legal risks—the lending institutions found themselves in unfamiliar legal territory in financing North Sea projects. The legislative basis was new, the physical location of fields outside territorial waters was an unusual feature, and the legal framework had been built up to deal with a quite different situation. It also happens that oil fields and oil pipelines can come under the jurisdiction of more than one sovereign government, and companies can thus find themselves unwillingly involved in disputes between governments with consequent delays.

Unforeseeable risks—these include *force-majeure* risks, war risks, hazard risks such as blow outs, fires or collisions. Such risks are in principle insurable, but the large sums involved in an essentially restricted market have caused difficulties for underwriters.

Political and fiscal risks—governments have revenue ambitions, and rates of tax and royalty, as well as other elements of total government take, can change, as can governments' attitudes to other rights and obligations.

Within the UK the frequent changes which have occurred in the oil taxation regime have caused difficulties for the oil industry in their forward planning; to some extent this has hindered developments. The industry's attitude to the 1980 changes were well documented in submissions made to the Chancellor of the Exchequer in September and October 1981—by BRINDEX (The Association of British Independent Oil Exploration Companies) and by UKOOA (United Kingdom Offshore Operators Association Ltd.) respectively. The rate of taxation and the pace of development are intimately connected, with taxation acting as a regulator. Should the desire be to maximize production, a lowering of the taxation rate will enable marginal fields to be developed, while a high taxation rate will ensure conservation of more marginal resources.

Further major changes to the UK offshore tax system have been proposed by the Chancellor, partly in response to the industry's representations, but they have been received with disappointment by the industry which continues to maintain that future developments are threatened by the overall tax regime.

Despite the risks involved, however, the financial institutions have responded with considerable success to the heavy demands made on them by the oil industry. Moreover, whereas in the early days of development much of the finance was provided against company balance sheets, with full recourse or at least limited recourse to the corporate credit of the companies involved, banks are now accepting responsibility for aspects of projects which would have been unthinkable a few years ago. This increasing responsibility has come from the confidence gained in offshore operations. It was stated by the Committee to Review the Functions of Financial Institutions (the Wilson Committee) that 'The inherent risks and novelty of North Sea oil financing gave rise to many additional problems. But the financial system has proved equal to the challenge, solutions have been found and there is no sign that any shortage of finance has held up North Sea oil development'.[3]

Financial problems can also work in the opposite direction. Massive oil discoveries and their rapid exploitation can, of course, seriously influence a country's economy and, in particular, its existing industries. Many of the current economic difficulties in Holland, Norway, and the UK (some of which stem from onshore conflicts detailed later in this chapter and in chapter IX) can be attributed to an increase in the real costs of their exportable commodities. Other contributing factors have been the use by governments of the very large petroleum-derived revenue for social services, military uses and other non-wealth-creating outlays; and the failure to add sufficient value (through processing) to the petroleum before it is exported or used locally. It is important, if further economic conflict is to be avoided, that appropriate steps should be taken to offset the inevitable damage to existing industries. These could include:

(a) a depletion policy which prevents the economy from 'over-heating';
(b) using the government revenues to pay off overseas debts and to provide an infrastructure which would make existing industries more competitive and encourage new industry;
(c) using a substantial proportion of the gas or oil as petrochemical feedstocks and power or heat sources, or both, in a wide range of basic and secondary processing and manufacturing industries to produce higher value products.

Gas flaring and the gas-gathering pipeline system

The problem of conserving the maximum amount of the associated gas produced at the offshore oil fields has not yet been solved. By the mid-1970s it was already becoming evident that there were several oil fields in the northern part of the North Sea which individually had insufficient gas to justify separate collection by pipeline to shore, but that taken together they might justify a common gas-gathering system. If this were not done, large quantities of gas would have to be flared and a valuable resource wasted. A study of the problem was commissioned in 1975 by the Department of Energy in the UK. The subsequent report, entitled 'A Study of Gas-Gathering Pipeline Systems in the North Sea' was published in May 1976 and suggested that such a system was feasible and probably economically justifiable.

To take matters further, a joint public-sector/private-sector company—Gas Gathering Pipelines (N. Sea) Ltd. (GGP)—was set up in December 1976 to plan and commission detailed studies of gas reserves, markets, methods of financing etc. Its report, submitted in April 1978, concluded that there appeared to be insufficient gas at that time which could not be collected through other lines already planned (from the Frigg field to St Fergus, and the Flags line from the Brent field to St Fergus). But there was room for uncertainty. Another study was initiated in July 1979. This was commissioned by the Department of Energy and carried out by the British Gas Corporation and Mobil North Sea. It recommended that such a scheme should be undertaken.[4] But this again has foundered, largely on the financing of the project which has been estimated at about £1 billion. Because of the uncertainties referred to earlier, the banks and other financial institutions were not prepared to undertake the financing without guarantees from the government. These the government was unwilling to give as they could have represented future commitment against the public-sector borrowing requirement.

It is likely that the private sector may yet produce a simplified scheme of its own, but in the meantime large quantities of natural gas are being flared. It should be borne in mind that the longer a decision is delayed, the longer it will be before a system is built; more gas will be flared in the meantime and consequently less will remain to be brought ashore, to be consumed usefully. In this field it would seem that there is considerable conflict between a policy of immediate economic gain, governed by market forces, and a longer-term view which would conserve the resources but at some considerable financial risk.

By contrast the Norwegian Government has taken the long-term view over the disposal of Statfjord gas and has made a positive decision which, even though it may not be the optimum financial solution, does at least ensure that the gas will not be wasted.

Marginal fields

One major issue which brings in the whole range of technical, financial and political problems is the development of the so-called 'marginal fields'. A marginal field may be defined as one which, in the light of present knowledge and technology, and under the present fiscal regime, appears unprofitable to develop, but where a change in one or more of these factors may make it profitable.

Marginal fields present technical problems; how to get more oil out at the same cost, or as much oil out at less cost, or preferably more oil out at less cost. To achieve these objectives, new technology must play a large part, and much research and development work is thus being carried out. Particularly where small fields are concerned, it is probable that custom-designed floating systems will come into being. It will be possible to move these relatively cheaply from one location to another as the need arises. But although such systems will be cheaper to build, this may have to be achieved at the expense of sacrificing some equipment such as water-injection or gas-compression facilities. Yet without such equipment, it will not be possible to recover the maximum amount of oil.

On the other hand much research work is also being done on how extra oil can be extracted from known oil reservoirs by sophisticated oil-recovery techniques. Improving conventional oil recovery by only a few per cent could make a great deal of difference to the profitability of a marginal field and it is to be hoped that some adequate technique will be developed for use offshore.

If it proves impossible to increase the profitability of a marginal field by technical improvements, it may be possible to alter the fiscal regime to achieve the same effect; for example by reducing royalty payments and/or taxation. Again it raises the question of whether the emphasis should be placed on immediate revenue or future yields.

Conflicts

Conflicts offshore

Some of the areas of conflict which can arise between the development of oil and gas offshore and other activities have been mentioned already. A further conflict of interest may also be identified between the exploitation of offshore resources and the military uses of the continental shelf and coastal waters. The protection of oil and gas installations is an important and necessary task of a country's defence forces; in addition, both existing and past uses of the sea for military purposes has caused difficulties. For example, some areas of the Dutch Waddenzee were out of bounds in the 1970s because of uncleared explosives; and some other areas of the Dutch sector of the North Sea remain dangerous as a result of unexploded mines buried in the sea-floor.

Practice and exercise areas also lead to conflict of interest. Around the shores of the United Kingdom, for example, are many areas which the Ministry of Defence uses for naval exercises, the testing of weapons, submarine operations, etc. Fortunately, many of these lie where there is little or no oil or gas potential and no conflict arises, but sometimes it is necessary to accommodate both interests. For example, when BP proposed to drill offshore in Weymouth Bay, problems arose as a result of the proximity of the Portland torpedo-testing range. Although the drilling rig was not in the line of fire, there was a slight risk of it being hit by a stray (but unarmed) torpedo. Eventually a procedure was negotiated, but at the same time oil exploration was restricted and areas closer to Portland were not explored.

At the 1976 International Arbitration in Geneva, which was concerned with the international boundary of the continental shelf in the Western Approaches and the Channel Islands, it became understood that the single deep longitudinal channel (the Hurd Deep) was of great interest to the French for submarine operations; hence the UK proposal to use the Hurd Deep as marking the midline was strongly opposed. Furthermore, the Hurd Deep coincides with a belt of faulted Mesozoic rocks of potential interest for hydrocarbon exploration.

The installation of extensive detection arrays on the sea-floor on both sides of the Atlantic can also affect exploration for hydrocarbons. For security reasons, their exact nature and location remain secret, and yet they could be damaged by seismic survey operations.

So far no serious conflict with military uses has occurred. But as oil and gas exploration activities increase and move further offshore into deeper water, the time will come when political decisions will have to be taken on whether a particular area is more important to the country concerned for reasons of defence or for commercial exploitation.

Conflicts also occur between the shipping industry and hydrocarbon developments offshore. Such conflicts arise primarily as a result of the need to avoid collision between ships and fixed or mobile drilling-installations, particularly in the vicinity of coastal shipping clearways; these are examined in chapter VI.

Conflicts between oil developments and fishing are more serious. Many drilling activities are in areas which are regularly fished, while pipelines traverse other fishing grounds, as do the routes taken by supply vessels when navigating from shore bases to offshore fields. The principal concerns of the fishermen are:

(a) possible loss of fishing grounds and disturbance of fishing by the proliferation of offshore structures;

(b) damage to or loss of fishing-gear caused by pipelines, suspended well-heads or debris from oil operations left on the sea-bed, and the question of liability and compensation for such loss or damage;

(c) pollution;

(d) interference as a result of lack of consultation and notification of seismic, drilling, construction and pipelaying activities.

In order to provide a forum at which such problems could be discussed and resolved, a Fisheries and Offshore Oil Consultative Group (FOOCG) was set up in 1974, chaired by an official of the Scottish Office. The Scottish Fishermen's Federation, the British Fishing Federation, and the United Kingdom Offshore Operators' Association (UKOOA) are all represented on it. Government departments represented include Trade, Energy, Agriculture and Fisheries (Scotland), and Agriculure, Fisheries and Food (England and Wales). Apart from the matters of concern listed above, the fishing organizations were also consulted on future licensing for oil and gas, and as a result of representations made by them, a new code of practice was drawn up for the seventh round of licensing to cover the Inner Moray Firth area which is particularly important to fishermen.

At the same time (December 1980) the Department of Energy announced contingency plans to deal with the possibility of oil spillages occurring within 40 kilometres of the British coast. These contingency measures were designed to cover possible spillages resulting from activities on those coastal blocks included in the seventh round of licensing from which oil could rapidly reach the shore (within one day under the worst possible conditions). The measures include the following essential items which all licences (including those in the Moray Firth) are required to provide for:

(a) a capability to be present near the installation at all times for spraying dispersant at 30 minutes notice, with stock sufficient to deal with a 10-tonne spill; or an effective oil recovery system;

(b) additional clean-up or recovery resources to be available within half the minimum time it would take the oil to get ashore;

(c) provision for aerial surveying to take place within 4 hours of any incident;

(d) trained personnel to be available to chart and predict the likely path of any oil spilled;

(e) prior consultations and arrangements to be agreed with the relevant MAFF and DAFS and the Nature Conservancy Council on the identification of vulnerable natural resources, and the adoption following an incident of all reasonable measures to ensure their protection.

A significant change was also made at the same time in the arrangements for compensating fishermen for loss or damage to gear or loss of fishing time caused by oil-industry debris. The voluntary compensation fund, financed by the UKOOA and managed by the fishermens' organizations, was extended to cover damage from unidentified oil-related debris. The fund paid out over £100,000 between 1975 and 1980 in 220 compensation cases. Scottish fishermen are also continuing to press for an experimental clean-up of oil-related debris in specific areas of the UK sector of the North Sea. It is interesting to note that although there has been some loss of access to fishing grounds because of the offshore oil installations, there is no conclusive evidence to support allegations that there has been any consequent loss of catch. It appears probable that any loss may be compensated for by increased quantities of fish around the installations which provide suitable surfaces for the attachment of algae and other food organisms.

As mentioned above, pollution is one item of great concern to the fishermen. It is of equal concern to others because of its effects on sea-birds as well as fish and on the amenity use of the shores when contaminated with oil.

The other side of the picture needs to be presented as well. Just as the shipping and fishing industries may suffer from the activities of the oil companies, so also do the oil companies have cause for concern at the activities of some fishermen and some ships' captains. Proper regard has not always been paid to the 500-metre safety zones established around oil installations in accordance with the 1958 Convention, and occasionally vessels have passed perilously close to installations, no doubt attracted by the fish which tend to concentrate around them. This is made even more dangerous by the presence of other vessels with legitimate reasons for being there—supply boats, work boats, etc., from which divers may be operating—and by the fact that many pipelines on the sea-bed lie in the proximity of installations. Modern trawlers with their heavy 'trawl doors' or 'otter boards' can damage smaller-diameter pipelines as can anchors. The damage that can be done is well illustrated by the incident which occurred in April 1980 when the pipeline connecting the BNOC *Thistle* field with the Royal Dutch Shell Dunlin A platform was damaged by a supply boat's anchor: some 1,154 tonnes of crude oil were lost, and oil production was suspended for a time. Repairs to the pipeline cost nearly £5 million.

The enforcement of safety zones is a very difficult problem. The oil companies have no legal powers to take action themselves, but by the time a vessel on offshore protection duties could be summoned to the scene, many hours would elapse and the offending trawler could be many miles away. While the operator can collect evidence of the infringement, and refer it to the appropriate authorities for action, it is by then almost impossible to prove beyond doubt that an infringement of the safety zone has taken place. Enforcement can be particularly difficult when foreign-flag vessels are involved. The problems of defending and policing these installations are examined in chapter VII.

Drifting barges or vessels out of control are other causes for concern; oil companies have, on several occasions, had to evacuate all personnel from a platform because of the danger of collision. There have been many instances of barges, some of which weigh hundreds of tons, breaking their tow-lines during storms. They may travel at a rate of several knots, driven by currents and winds, and could cause severe damage if they should strike an oil platform. Vessels out of control are potentially even more dangerous but fortunately not so common. Sometimes ships can suffer engine or steering-gear failure, and in one instance the crew abandoned a 490-ton coaster, the *Manor Park*, when its cargo shifted in a storm. The crew left the main engine running, as a result of which an oil booster platform on the Ekofisk-Teeside line had to be evacuated (December 1979). There was no immediate risk of collision, but the unmanned vessel under power passed within a few miles of the platform. An even more dangerous situation can be envisaged: that of a fully laden vessel proceeding at full speed under automatic control with no look-out or anybody on the bridge (or alternatively in fog with radar out of action) and colliding with an oil-producing platform. It may be perfectly safe for ships to proceed in such a manner well out to sea, but there have been reports of this happening in the English Channel. So far no significant oil discoveries have been made there, but if one were made, the possibility of such a catastrophe which might endanger many lives and cause severe pollution becomes very real. Fortunately, most of the North Sea fields lie away from the heavily used shipping routes.

Conflicts onshore

On land other conflicts have arisen, mostly over the requirements for land for associated storage facilities. Generally speaking, these have been resolved without great difficulty by following the normal procedure for obtaining planning permission for any industrial development. Particular objections may be raised if the proposed development is situated in an area of outstanding natural beauty, or if the proposed development might be harmful to particularly rare fauna or flora found in the area. Other objections may be raised on safety grounds.

In some cases the objections can be met by good planning, careful landscaping, and the use of suitable paints—the Flotta terminal in Orkney is a good example of how the visual impact of such a large-scale industrial development can be minimized. In other cases it may be necessary to relocate the proposed facility—for example the first site selected for bringing the gas shore from the Frigg field was one where the fauna and flora had to be protected. A new site was therefore selected at St Fergus, a few miles away.

Where objections are raised on safety grounds, these objections have to be carefully examined to establish their validity and, if justified, extra safety precautions have to be incorporated in the design of the facility.

It should not be thought, however, that there is always opposition to on-shore developments. On the contrary; proposed developments have frequently been able to take advantage of derelict sites no longer needed for their original purposes. These sites have then been rejuvenated and fresh employment provided in areas which were rapidly becoming run down. In the longer term, although the numbers employed will be less, a greater degree of skill will be required and this helps to keep in the area young people who would otherwise move to places of greater opportunity.

However in areas where there was little unemployment, the advent of the oil industry, and its demand for skilled labour for which it pays high wages, brought different problems, not least for other employers of labour in the area who could not afford to pay such wages. This is particularly true in the short term, when large amounts of labour are often needed during the construction phase of a project. In a number of cases, for example the Gulf Oil Terminal at Bantry Bay, the proposed crude oil refinery at Nigg Bay in the Cromarty Firth, the Sullom Voe oil terminal in Shetland, the impending development has had the effect of polarizing the community into pro- and anti-industry groups. It may bring prosperity, but it also brings strain. On the whole, however, there is little doubt that the oil industry will continue to provide substantial employment opportunities in north-east Scotland, Orkney and Shetland for some fifty years or perhaps longer.

Safety of Offshore Installations

No account dealing with the extraction of petroleum from under the sea would be complete without reference to the safety of the people working in this hazardous environment. The seas are always potentially dangerous and when at the same time one is dealing with the problems of handling dangerous substances, the risks are compounded. Many of the operations carried out offshore are similar to those performed onshore and have attached to them the normal type of industrial risks associated with working with machinery, cranes, welding apparatus, pressure vessels, etc. Added to these are the risks imposed by the environment itself and those associated with producing oil and gas. The whole is made worse by the limitations of space on an offshore installation. In designing a platform, therefore, particular care must be taken to ensure than an event in one location does not have disastrous consequences in another. Fire is a particular hazard and can have very serious consequences. Elaborate fire- and smoke-detection systems are fitted which can automatically activate quenching systems as well as sounding alarms.

However, despite the precautions that are taken, there still remains the possibility of a disaster caused by human error or equipment failure, or more likely by an unforeseen combination of several causes, so that it may be necessary for an installation to be evacuated. During 1981 there were 6 fatal accidents on UK offshore installations and vessels, 59 serious injuries and 135 dangerous occurrences. Whenever time and conditions permit, evacuation would normally be by means of helicopters; when this is not possible, evacuation has to be by sea. Consequently, installations in the North Sea are equipped with survival capsules or totally enclosed lifeboats equipped with water-spray capacity. These give a reasonable chance of escape from an installation in the worst possible case of burning oil on the surface of the surrounding sea. The lowering of these survival craft is controlled from within the craft themselves so that no one has to be left behind.

In some cases, these survival craft are supplemented by the provision of inflatable life-rafts which can be thrown overboard, and in addition there is generally a standby vessel in the vicinity which can shepherd the survival craft and provide extra accommodation and first-aid support. Unfortunately, as the *Alexander Kielland* disaster showed, these arrangements are still not entirely foolproof and more thought needs to be given to the problem.

Governments and oil companies have paid particular attention to these problems from the early days. The UK enacted the Mineral Workings (Offshore Installation) Act in 1971 which specifically dealt with the safe design, construction and operation of oil and gas installations on the UK continental shelf, and provided for detailed orders to be promulgated under it over a period of time as knowledge developed. Later, relevant sections of the Health and Safety at Work Act 1974, which is of more general application, were applied offshore by Order in Council in 1977.[5]

The earlier UK legislation was principally directed at minimizing the likelihood of a major disaster such as the structural failure of an installation, or a 'blow-out' or an uncontrolled escape of oil and gas from below the sea-bed which could put at risk the lives of everybody on board, perhaps numbering hundreds of people. Such structural failures have happened.[6]

Blow-outs have also occurred. These are potentially extremely hazardous and could cause severe pollution. Fortunately, although there have been several blow-outs in the North Sea, there has been no loss of life or serious injury caused by them.

Safety is one area of activity in which governments and the oil industry have common objectives and is an ideal subject for co-operation and collaboration between the countries of north-west Europe, and in particular those surrounding the North Sea where there is a mutual interest in protecting the lives of nationals working on offshore installations, and safeguarding coasts against pollution. Consequently in 1973 the UK convened a conference of these states in order to establish how national requirements and safety standards could be harmonized and improved so as to promote safe working practices in the North Sea and to facilitate the movement of mobile installations from one sector to another. Following this conference, a series of working groups was set up to examine particular aspects of the subject and to make proposals for harmonized requirements. This work was followed by another conference held in the Hague in 1978 which identified what still remained to be done, a final conference being held in Norway in 1982.

To a certain extent this work has been paralleled by that more recently undertaken by the International Maritime Organization (IMO) which has produced a code of practice for mobile offshore drilling units. But the north-west European states believe that this does not go far enough and they may wish to enforce more stringent requirements in their own waters.

It is necessary to keep safety standards continually under review and to this end the UK Secretary of State for Energy set up a committee in 1978 'To consider so far as they are concerned with safety, the nature, coverage and effectiveness of the Department of Energy's regulations governing the exploration, development and production of oil and gas offshore and their administration and enforcement. To consider and assess the role of the Certifying Authorities. To present its report, conclusions and any recommendations as soon as possible.' This commitee, which became known as the Burgoyne Committee after its chairman Dr J. H. Burgoyne, commenced work in January 1979 and issued a report 'Offshore Safety' which was presented to Parliament in March 1980.[7] This report contained over sixty recommendations, mostly of a detailed technical nature, and the majority of these have been accepted and acted upon. In fact, action was already taking place on many of these while the committee was meeting.

However, not all the recommendations could be implemented, even though they appeared desirable. For example, one was that the size of the 500-metre-radius safety zone around an installation should be increased. But the authority for these safety zones is provided in the 1958 Convention and the size cannot be increased without further international agreement, which is unlikely.[8] In addition, there would be opposition to any increase from shipping and fisheries interests.

Probably the most important, but also the most controversial, recommendations contained in the report concerned the responsibility for the formulation of offshore safety policy and its enforcement. At the time the committee was meeting, there was divided responsibility, with the Health and Safety Executive having responsibility for occupational safety matters and the Department of Energy being responsible for other safety matters such as structural safety, pipeline integrity, etc. The Petroleum Engineering Division of the Department of Energy was responsible for the enforcement of all the regulations.

All members of the committee agreed that this situation of divided responsibility was unsatisfactory and that one agency alone should be responsible, but they were unable to agree as to which agency that should be. The majority favoured the Department of Energy. The government eventually accepted the majority report, including its recommendation that the Petroleum Engineering Division of the Department of Energy should be strengthened by transferring to it a few selected members of the Health and Safety Executive staff.[9]

Emergencies

Finally, reference must be made to the arrangements for dealing with major emergencies. Essentially, these are in the hands of the oil companies themselves, since they have the knowledge and the resources, subject to the overriding supervision and approval by governments of the action taken by the companies. Major emergencies are those which may cause an installation to be evacuated, such as structural failure, or a blow-out, fire or explosion, or any combination of them. Operators are required to have procedures to deal with such emergencies, and to practise exercises and drills.

In order to deal with the wider consequences and to regain control of a situation if it should get out of hand, a 'Sector Club' system has been set up which covers all North Sea operations and provides for mutual aid in case of emergency. In each of the six sectors, which may cross national boundaries, one company has been nominated to take the lead in co-ordinating emergency action, while other companies operating in that sector provide aid as necessary. In each sector there are vessels equipped with fire-spraying equipment and it is the intention to have emergency support vessels also available, suitably equipped with heavier gear, including cranes. When not needed for emergency work, these vessels are used for maintenance purposes and are therefore kept in a state of operational readiness at all times. Stocks of dispersant chemicals and spraying equipment are also available to combat pollution should it occur.

The British Government has also set up an organization known as the 'Blow-out Emergency Team' (BET) to co-ordinate government action in the event of an emergency involving a blow-out and to liaise with the oil company, sector club co-ordinator and others concerned, such as the coastguard and police. Government departments represented on this team include Energy (which provides the chairman), Trade, Fisheries, Defence and, if in Scottish waters, the Scottish Office. If pollution should result from the blow-out, the BET would coordinate its activities with those of the Marine Pollution Control Unit (MPCU) of the Department of Trade. The BET would concentrate on the measures being taken to control the blow-out and prevent loss of life, while the MPCU would concentrate on containing the spillage and its dispersion or clean-up, taking into account the possible effects on fish and bird life.

The role of the Government and of the BET is essentially supervisory, relying on the oil-field operator and the sector club to provide the first line of defence while offering any assistance that may be required. In the exceptional case of an operator's organization and resources proving inadequate, and of valuable resources being threatened, the Government could take over command of the clean-up operation.

This arrangement for dealing with emergencies was reviewed by the Royal Commission on Environmental Pollution.[10] The Commission concluded that the division of responsibility offshore appeared to be suitable, but that for nearshore installations, for example in the Moray Firth, a different response system was required. Instead of the existing arrangement under which the Department of Energy is responsible for ensuring that proper measures are taken by the operator to halt the flow of oil, as far as possible, and the Department of Trade is responsible for clean-up or dispersal of the oil at sea if required, the Royal Commission suggested that, when central government involvement becomes necessary, the MPCU should take control of all the counter-pollution operations, including any onshore. For this purpose, the MPCU should be strengthened, and should become more involved with the local authorities. Action has subsequently been taken in both these areas.

Notes

1. For background discussion to these developments see Mason, C. (ed.) *The Effective Management of Resources: The International Politics of the North Sea*, Frances Pinter, 1979.
2. Davies, J. M., Hardy, R. and McIntyre, A. D., 'Environmental effects of North Sea Oil Operations', *Marine Pollution Bulletin*, vol. 12, no. 12, 1981, pp. 412–16.
3. *Report of the Committee to Review the Functions of Financial Institutions*, HMSO, 1980, Cmnd. 7937.
4. Energy Paper no. 44, Dept. of Energy, HMSO.
5. Criticism of the UK position can be found in Carson, W., *The Other Price of Britain's Oil: Safety and Control in the North Sea*, Martin Robertson, 1982.
6. *1965 — Sea Gem*: 13 lives lost

    Ocean Prince
    Constellation } mobile drilling rigs; no lives lost
    Trans Ocean 3

    1980 — Alexander Keilland —floating accommodation, 123 lives lost. This last incident caused more deaths than the combined total of all causes in the UK sector since the start of operations in 1964 up to the present time.
7. Offshore Safety: Report of the Committee Chaired by Dr. J. H. Burgoyne, HMSO 1980, Cmnd. 7866.
8. In certain circumstances the new Law of the Sea Convention does make provision for extensions. But this is not yet in force and not all the W. European states have signed the convention.
9. See Carson, op. cit. n. 8.
10. *Oil Pollution of the Sea*, eighth report of the Royal Commission on Environment Pollution, HMSO 1981, Cmnd. 8358.

Appendix i

Oil fields in production (November 1982)

United Kingdom	*Norway*	*Denmark*	*Netherlands*
Argyll	Albuskjell	Dan	Helder ⎫ Block Q1
Auk	Cod	Gorm	Helm ⎭
Beatrice	Edda		
Beryl	Ekofisk		
Brent	W. Ekofisk		
Buchan	Eldfisk		
Claymore	Murchison (Nor.)		
N. Cormorant	Statfjord (Nor.)		
S. Cormorant	Tor		
Dunlin	Valhall		
Forties			
Fulmar			
Heather			
Montrose			
Murchison (UK)			
Ninian			
Piper			
Statfjord (UK)			
Tartan			
Thistle			

Oil fields under development (or due to be developed shortly)

United Kingdom	*Norway*	*Denmark*	*Netherlands*
Beryl B	Gullfaks	Skjold	Horn (Block Q1)
Brae	(N34/10)	(formerly Ruth)	
Hutton	Valhall		
NW Hutton			
Magnus			
Maureen			

Gas fields in production (November 1982)

United Kindom	*Norway*	*Netherlands*	*Ireland*
Frigg (UK)	Frigg (Nor.)	K8	Kinsale Head
Hewett		K11	
Indefatigable		K13	
Leman Bank		K14	
Rough		K15	
W. Sole		L7	
Viking		L10	

Gas fields under development (or due to be developed shortly)

United Kingdom	*Norway*	*Netherlands*	*Denmark*
Morecambe Bay	NE Frigg	K7	Roar
	Odin	K10	Tyra
		L4	
		P6	

Appendix ii

Exploration and appraisal wells drilled on the north-west European continental shelf (south of 62° N.)

Year	United Kingdom	Norway	Netherlands	Denmark	Ireland	France	W. Germany
1962	—	—	3	—	—	—	—
1963	—	—	—	—	—	—	—
1964	1	—	—	—	—	—	—
1965	10	—	—	—	—	—	—
1966	28	1	—	1	—	—	1
1967	58	5	—	1	—	—	—
1968	38	11	7	7	—	—	—
1969	52	14	16	2	—	—	—
1970	24	15	14	3	1	—	—
1971	28	13	19	3	2	—	—
1972	41	17	17	1	3	—	—
1973	61	18	19	3	5	—	2
1974	100	23	17	2	4	—	5
1975	116	21	18	4	7	1	6
1976	86	31	19	4	6	2	11
1977	105	20	28	5	6	—	1
1978	62	19	23	3	15	1	—
1979	48	28	21	2	8	2	—
1980	54	33	31	1	3	4	1
1981	73	34	28	4	8	2	3
TOTAL	985	303	280	46	68	12	30

Note: Inter-country comparisons should be made with caution. Some countries report well-commencements, others well-completions. Similarly there are differences in the counting of suspended, aborted, and re-drilled wells.

Appendix iii

Oil and gas reserves of the north-west European continental shelf

	Original reserves	Cumulative production to end 1981	Remaining reserves as at 1/1/82
(a) *Oil* (including Natural Gas Liquids) (million tonnes)			
UK	1977	352	1625
Norway	1100	129	971
Netherlands	8	—	8
Denmark	150	3	147
TOTAL	3235	484	2751
(b) *Gas* (million tonnes oil equivalent)			
UK	1425	418	1007
Norway	1589	90	1499
Netherlands	176	50	124
Denmark	80	—	80
Ireland	38	3	35
TOTAL	3308	561	2745
TOTAL OIL AND GAS	6541	1045	5496

Oil and gas resources of the north-west European continental shelf

		Rounded totals (m.t.o.e.)
United Kingdom		
Oil (inc. N.G. Liquids)	2100–4300	
Gas	1230–2045	
TOTAL	3330–6345	3330–6350
Norway		
TOTAL		6500–8500
Netherlands		
Oil	20	
Gas	300	
TOTAL	320	320
Denmark		
Oil	200	
Gas	200	
TOTAL	400	400
Ireland		
TOTAL		40
GRAND TOTAL		10,600–15,600

Note: No estimates are available for offshore of Germany, France and Belgium, but in any case these are believed likely to be small in comparison to the UK and Norwegian resources and would not significantly affect the overall total.

For the distinction between reserves and resources, see p. 40.

Sources for appendices i, ii, iii:

UK: Report To Parliament: 'Development of the Oil and Gas Resources of the United Kingdom 1982'.
Norway: Storting Report no. 53 (1979) 'Concerning the Activity on the Norwegian Continental Shelf', and Fact Sheet, The Norwegian Continental Shelf 1981:1. Published by The Royal Ministry of Petroleum and Energy.
Netherlands: *Natural Gas and Oil of the Netherlands: Annual Review 1980*, issued by Ministry of Economic Affairs.
Press Reports.
Twentieth Century Petroleum Statistics 1980, O. C. Golyer and MacNaughton.

Appendix iv

Oil and gas production from the north-west European continental shelf

(a) Oil (million tonnes)

Year	United Kingdom	Norway	Denmark
1971	—	0.3	—
1972	—	1.6	0.1
1973	—	1.6	0.2
1974	—	1.7	0.1
1975	1.1	9.3	0.2
1976	11.6	13.6	0.2
1977	37.3	13.4	0.4
1978	52.8	16.9	0.5
1979	76.5	19.0	0.4
1980	78.7	24.4	0.3
1981	87.6	25.9	0.7
Cumulative Total	345.5	127.5	3.1
+ *N.G. Liquids*	7.0	1.1	—
TOTAL	352.5	128.6	3.1

TOTAL OIL (rounded): 484 m tonnes

(b) Gas (million tonnes oil equivalent)

Year	United Kingdom	Norway	Netherlands	Ireland
1967	0.5	—	—	—
1968	2.1	—	—	—
1969	5.1	—	—	—
1970	10.9	—	—	—
1971	18.3	—	—	—
1972	26.5	—	—	—
1973	28.9	—	0.01	—
1974	34.8	—	0.01	—
1975	36.3	—	1.0	—
1976	38.4	—	3.1	—
1977	40.3	2.6	4.8	—
1978	38.5	14.2	6.3	0.1
1979	39.2	20.8	10.9	0.6
1980	37.3	25.1	12.1	1.1
1981	37.4	27.0	11.3	1.4
Cumulative Total	394.4	89.7	49.5	3.2
+ Flared	23.6			
TOTAL	418.0			

GRAND TOTAL GAS (rounded): 561 m.t.o.e.

Total Oil and Gas: **1045 m.t.o.e.**

Appendix v
Statement by the Secretary of State for Energy on depletion policy, 6 December 1974

In my statement to Parliament on 11th July on United Kingdom offshore policy I said that the Government proposed to take powers to control the rate of depletion of oil. I already have power to decide on the timing, nature and extent of future licensing rounds, and in the forthcoming petroleum legislation I shall be proposing powers to control the rate of production.

How or when such powers may be used in the 1980s and 1990s will depend on the extent of the total finds, on the world oil market and on the demand for energy. On all these points great uncertainty prevails. Policy will also be influenced by our general economic situation and in particular the outlook for our balance of payments. The Government cannot, therefore, be expected to define, before any oil has come ashore, and when large parts of the sea remain unexplored, a long-term production pattern. On the other hand, these powers may be needed in the future to safeguard national interests. However much oil we find, it is limited and can only be used once. This and future Governments must, therefore, ensure that this vital national resource will be used at a rate which secures the greatest long-term benefit to the nation's economy, and in particular to Scotland, Wales and other parts of the United Kingdom in need of development.

We propose, therefore, to take powers of control for use in the future, but it remains the Government's aim to ensure that oil production from the United Kingdom Continental Shelf builds up as quickly as possible over the next few years to the level set out in paragraph 4 of the White Paper (Cmnd, 5696). This will help our balance of payments, contribute to Government revenues, stimulate our industries and make our energy supplies more secure. It will also be an important British contribution to the development of the indigenous energy resources of the industrial world. I wish therefore, to assure the oil companies, and the banks to which they will look for finance, that our depletion policy and its implementation will not undermine the basis on which they have made plans and entered into commitments. Our future policy will be based on the following guidelines:

(*a*) No delays will be imposed on the development of finds already made or on any new finds made up to the end of 1975 under existing licences. If it should prove necessary to delay the development of finds made in 1976 or later, there will be full consultation with the companies so that premature investment is avoided.

(*b*) No cuts will be made in production for finds already made or from new finds made before the end of 1975 under existing licences, until 1982 at the earliest or until four years after the start of production whichever is the later.

(*c*) No cuts will be made in production from any field found after 1975 under an existing licence until 150 per cent of the capital investment in the field has been recovered.

(*d*) If we later need to use these powers we will have full regard to the technical and commercial aspects of the fields in question and this would generally limit cuts to 20 per cent at most. We shall be consulting the industry on the period of notice to be given before any reduction in production comes into effect.

(*e*) In deciding on action to postpone development or limit production, the

Government will also take into account the needs of the offshore supply industry in Scotland, Wales and other parts of the United Kingdom, for a continuing and stable market.

Longer-term conservation strategy is being and will be formulated as progressively more information becomes available. At this stage the regime for depletion of any finds made in the Celtic Sea should be regarded as settled. The British National Oil Corporation, to be established by the Petroleum Bill next year, could have an important role to play in exploring areas yet to be licensed, and in establishing potential fields whose reserves could be husbanded or developed quickly in accordance with the widest national interest. This is for the future, and does not affect present licences but I think it right to state our more immediate intentions now.

Appendix vi
Statement by the Secretary of State for Energy on depletion policy, 23 July 1980

We expect that from later this year UK oil production will regularly reach a level equal to UK consumption. Thereafter on present forecasts production would rise to a peak in the mid-1980s giving significant surplus over UK consumption in the 1980s as a whole. We are likely to become net importers of oil again about 1990.

Recent events underline the fragilities of the world energy scene. The Government believes that on strategic and security of supply grounds it is in the national interest to prolong high levels of UKCS production to the end of the century. This requires action to increase exploration, which we have already taken, and to defer some oil production from the 1980s. Such action accords fully with the recommendations to maximise indigenous hydrocarbon production on a long term basis and with our other international commitments including net exports of 5 million tonnes in 1985 as agreed in the Community and the International Energy Agency.

There are of course, major uncertainties about future levels of North Sea production and UK consumption. There can therefore be no rigid plan. We shall continue close supervision over reservoir performance at existing fields and scrutinise new applications for field developments to ensure good oil field practice consistent with optimum oil and gas recovery in the national interest. We shall also continue to take decisions on a case-by-case basis, but giving greater emphasis to the need to limit the sharpness of the peak in production. We shall, of course, honour the assurances given by the Rt Hon Member for Chesterfield [Eric Varley] on 6 December 1974 on the basis of which heavy investment has been underaken by the oil companies.

In particular the Government will consider delaying the development of fields discovered after the end of 1975, which are not covered by the assurances given by the Rt Hon. Member for Chesterfield. The Government will also continue to tighten control on gas flaring.

The Government has taken no decisions on whether to have production cutbacks which, under the assurances given by the previous Administration, cannot be made before 1982.

I believe that this flexible approach is the right one and takes account of both the needs of those involved in the difficult business of oil production and, more important, the long term national interest.

III

Renewable Energy from the Sea

The reserves of oil and gas are dwindling; fossil fuels are becoming more expensive, and the environmental effects of their consumption in large quantities are being studied with growing concern; the future of nuclear power is in doubt. As a consequence, increasing attention is being given to renewable energy sources. The principal sources that concern us here are waves and tides, by which we can capture energy directly from the sea; and winds, the exploitation of whose power will most likely be located either on the coast or offshore. Both wave and wind power are derived ultimately from the energy of the sun modified by the earth's weather systems, while tidal energy depends upon the gravitational effect of the moon (and to a lesser extent the sun) on the world's oceans.

Tidal Power

Harnessing the energy of the tides is a goal which has been achieved in only a few locations even though the potential energy available is very large and is environmentally 'clean'. What, then, are the problems, and is it likely that economic or physical constraints on the exploitation of tidal power will severely limit the contribution which it can make to our energy requirements? In order to answer these questions, we must examine how the potential energy of tides may be harnessed, the limitations imposed by coastal topography and by society's energy needs, and most importantly the impact of tidal power schemes on other coastal resources. Although the exploitation of tidal power is non-polluting, its ecological effects can be very disruptive.

From the eleventh century, tidal power was used to grind grain, and as late as 1940 a dozen tidal mills were in operation in Britain. Tidal energy may also be used for pumping water, but in our century such direct uses have very little potential. By far its most effective use is for the generation of electricity. The simplest means of doing this is to build a single barrier across a bay or estuary, equip the barrier with sluices and turbines, allow the basin to fill through the sluices with the rising tide, close the sluices at high water, and release the impounded water through the turbines when the tide has fallen. A tidal range—or difference between high water and low water—of at least 4 or 5 metres, depending on local energy and construction costs, is needed before such a system can generate electricity economically. Such higher tidal ranges are the result of particular hydraulic or topographical circumstances, and are confined to relatively shallow coastal inlets. Constructing a tidal barrage across such an inlet will, of course, alter its characteristics including the velocity, quantity, and timing of the water-flow passing the barrage line. Predicting the energy and power available becomes a complex task, and it is important that the hydrodynamic situation is modelled mathematically.

One of the major limitations affecting the use of tidal power is that the tides (and hence the generation of power) vary according to a lunar rather than a solar cycle. Thus peaks in generation do not generally coincide with peaks in demand, and the power output also varies over the spring—neap tidal cycle. However, the two-pool system allows for continuous generation of power. The turbines are installed between two basins, one of which is regularly filled from flood tides, the other being drained on the ebb. Such double-basin schemes usually incorporate some degree of storage, and their power output can be 'retimed' or concentrated so as to coincide with peaks in electricity demand. Tidal power is predictable and can be used to displace the operation of other, generally fossil-fuelled plants. But in a system with a very high proportion of nuclear stations, this may not be possible since nuclear plants operate most efficiently on continuous load.

Further control over the timing of the output may be obtained by using the turbines as pumps. There is little or no energy-gain, but the availability of power to coincide with peak demand is improved.

Existing tidal power schemes

The only tidal power station on the European coast is that at La Rance near St Malo on the north coast of Brittany. This is a single-basin scheme, commissioned in 1966 and connected to the national network in 1967. The turbine-generators are reversible and are capable of operating as turbines or as pumps in either direction. Pumping can be used either to augment the natural filling of the basin to achieve storage and increased output at peak load, or to lower the water level in the basin below sea-level at low tide, again increasing peak load output. It is possible to generate either one-way on the ebb only, or two-way on both ebb and flood.

Twenty-four turbine-generators produce a total net electricity output of about 0.5 terawatt (10^{12}) hours per year. The scheme has developed only minor faults since commissioning, and energy availability has been about 96 per cent.

Other tidal power schemes under consideration

In Europe some of the sites with the greatest potential are on the coast of the British Isles. The Solway Firth, the estuaries of the Dee, Mersey, Humber and Severn, and Loughs Strangford and Carlingford on the east coast of Ireland have all been considered at one time as possible sites. Of these, the most outstanding site is the Severn estuary, for which a number of schemes have been proposed. In 1981, a pre-feasibility study, costing about £2.4 million, concluded that a barrage could generate up to 10 per cent of Britian's electricity needs at a cost only marginally greater than nuclear power.

There are considerable, but no insurmountable, technical difficulties involved in building the barrage or constructing the power station. Other problems, however, including conflicts with other resources, are not so easily dealt with. The Severn estuary carries a considerable load of industrial and domestic pollutants together with silt, and silting up behind the barrage could pose a problem. Improved effluent treatment facilities would be required upstream, while the more difficult liquid wastes may have to be piped to an outfall located well to seaward of the barrier. The silt may also cause abrasion and wear in the turbines and sluices, and additional work would need to be done in order to quantify this effect. By contrast, the La Rance estuary is very clean and virtually silt-free.

The barrage would also have to be equipped with navigation locks capable of taking the largest ships currently using the ports. However, this would have the benefit of making some harbours usable over a longer period of time.

It is in relation to the environmental effects that the greatest uncertainty lies. The extensive system of sand and silt flats which border both sides of the estuary are colonized by invertebrates which provide food for large numbers of wading birds and wildfowl, particularly shelduck. The salt marshes along the estuary are also an integral part of the whole ecosystem and provide a roosting and breeding area for birds. The whole of the Severn estuary is of international importace as a wintering ground for five species of wading birds and shelduck. Near the head of the estuary, the New Grounds at Slimbridge are important as a winter haunt of wildfowl, especially the European white-fronted goose and the Bewick swan. Downstream of the proposed barrage line, on the English (south) side of the estuary, Bridgwater Bay is important not only on account of the numbers of wintering waders and wildfowl, but also as providing apparently the only moulting grounds for shelduck (*Tadorna tadorna*) in Britain. Furthermore, the marsh and shingle areas around Bridgwater Bay are also of considerable interest, and they are designated as a wetland site of international importance.

Potential environmental impact and conflict with other marine resources

The operation of the La Rance power station and the Severn Barrage feasibility study provide some data on the environmental impact of tidal power schemes, but a great deal still remains to be investigated.

At La Rance, the closure of the estuary was followed by a progressive freshening of the water in the basin and by the restriction of the tidal range within the basin. No adverse biological effects have been reported. Pleasure craft use the lock in large numbers, while the road along the top of the barrage carries a great deal of traffic.

The Severn estuary barrage proposal is a much larger project, and its potential effects could not be compared directly with La Rance. The Severn Barrage Committee, in their report to the Secretary of State for Energy, concluded that the technical feasibility of the scheme was not in doubt and that a further phase of more detailed investigations should be undertaken to establish the acceptability of the barrage. Environmental, social and industrial factors were seen as key issues on which a great deal of further work was needed, along with preliminary design studies and economic evaluation.

In May 1983 the Government agreed to provide half the cost of a feasibility study for the Severn Barrage, in partnership with private enterprise.

The necessity for, and effectiveness of, multi-disciplinary studies in dealing with the development of this particular resource, is clearly shown by the way in which it was found necessary to organize the components of the pre-feasibility study. The overall programme of studies was made up of over eighty individual but closely interrelated items. These were carried out by a variety of organizations including civil, mechanical and electrical engineering contractors and consultants in industry, government laboratories, research institutes and university departments. Co-ordination is therefore a vital feature of this type of feasibility study and we shall be returning to the need for co-ordination and planning in a more general sense in chapter IX and in our recommendations.

Wave Power

In contrast to tidal power, where the technology of exploitation is known and the principal constraints are economic and environmental, the technology of extracting energy from waves is still largely theoretical and experimental. Nevertheless, there are very good grounds for believing that the various systems now being developed may eventually enable us to capture energy from ocean waves, convert it into electricity or some other form, and transmit it ashore at a cost similar to that of generating electricity from fossil or nuclear fuel.

Wave power has the possibility of becoming a significant energy source in the next couple of decades, and its environmental effects and interactions with other continental shelf resources must be considered with care. Before proceeding to discuss these issues, a very brief introduction to, and assessment of, the technology is necessary.

Geographical distribution of wave energy

Wave energy is ultimately derived from the sun's energy falling on the earth's surface and atmophere, and creating winds which cause the formation of waves on open water surfaces. The windiest areas of the world lie between 40 and 60 degrees of latitude both north and south of the equator.

In the northern hemisphere, the west coast of Europe is situated at the downwind end of one of the windiest sea areas of the world, with the result that wave conditions are severe and the average concentration of wave energy present is high. Locally, the west coast of Ireland, the Outer Hebrides and the Orkney and Shetland Islands are appreciably more windy than the remainder of Europe's coasts. Since the winds have blown without obstruction over the Atlantic before reaching these islands, the energy of the ocean waves is correspondingly higher, and ocean swell is also present. By contrast, the southern North Sea, the English Channel and the Irish Sea are more sheltered—wind speeds are generally lower and the fetches (namely, the open water distances over which the wind can blow) are more restricted. Even more importantly, the shallower water in these seas has reduced wave energy levels due to the influence of the sea-bed. The most likely locations for wave energy collectors will therefore be the west of Orkney and Shetland, west of the Hebrides, and off the north-west and west coasts of Ireland. Locations in the Celtic Sea (off the coast of Cornwall) and off the east coast of Scotland have, however, also been considered.

Wave energy conversion systems

In order to capture the energy of waves, a device is required to convert the wave energy into mechanical movement and eventually into usable energy. The problems in achieving this are formidable. The device must be able to withstand the worst possible storms, and yet retain some degree of efficiency in extracting energy under near-calm conditions. Regular maintenance would be extremely expensive and frequently impossible and therefore the device must be able to work unattended for long periods. The wave spectrum at any one location includes waves of very different heights and periods, arriving from different directions; therefore the device must be reasonably efficient in extracting energy under a wide variety of conditions at sea.

In engineering terms, the energy conversion system used must be able to handle large short-term variations in the instantaneous power level, and must be capable of dealing with a peak power level many times greater than the average.

Some proportion of the available power in, for example, storm conditions has, therefore, to be shed in a controlled manner. The large short-term variations in power output can be smoothed by connecting together several wave energy conversion devices. Such interconnection also assists with bulk transmission of the energy to shore, the energy being carried as electricity, pressurized fluid, chemical or secondary fuel energy, and heat.

The generation of electricity from wave energy poses a number of severe mechanical problems. Converting the random oscillation of waves to mechanical power can be carried out by means of gear or belt-drive arrangements, hydraulic pumps or, uniquely in the case of the Salter Duck by means of gyros. Air or water turbines have been proposed for other designs. In all cases it is essential to ensure that the electrical and mechanical components are separated from the salt-water environment and that they have a long maintenance-free life. Transmission of the electrical energy ashore, including the use of flexible submarine cables, will require some advances in technology. As with tidal power, there will be a mismatch between the output of the wave energy devices and the needs of a national network. Wave energy, being a function of sea-state and weather, does have the advantage, however, that maximum output is available during winter months, thereby following broadly the pattern of electricity demand. Over shorter time scales, calm periods of a couple of days or a week would require either an associated pumped storage scheme or the use of fossil-fuel plants to provide the energy needed when the output from the wave energy scheme falls.

A further factor affecting the location and economics of wave energy schemes is the configuration of the existing national electricity transmission networks in Britain and Ireland, the two countries off whose coasts the optimum sites are located. If the electricity generated is to be used primarily to supply remote or island communities (a viable and practical end-use with marked social and economic benefits), then this factor is not of great importance. However, if large-scale wave energy systems were designed to feed energy into either of the national networks, then major transmission costs could become significant. In the case of a wave power system located off the Outer Hebrides, lengthy transmission-line reinforcements would be required in order to connect it, at full potential, to the remainder of the network. Equally, prime locations off the north-west coast of Ireland would require similar additional transmission lines, but the distances involved would be less. Off the west coast of Ireland, lines to existing turf-burning power stations could carry some of the load, but would need to be augmented if a very large-scale wave power scheme was installed.

On the north-east coast of England, the east coast of Scotland, and in the Celtic Sea off Cornwall, wave power schemes would be sufficiently close to the present grid network to avoid significant transmission line reinforcements. The proposed electricity interconnector between Ireland

and Wales would, as a result of the greater system-stability obtained, permit relatively larger inputs of energy to the combined grids.

Instead of generating electricity on the wave energy converter at sea, oil or water under pressure may be pumped ashore, particularly if the device would in any event use a hydraulic system for energy conversion. Such a method would have the advantage of putting all the electrical equipment on shore, and the necessary technology for this is well developed. Nevertheless, the cost of long-distance hydraulic transmission is so great as to make it uneconomic except as a means of transferring energy from an array of devices to a nearby large-scale generator unit.

The third option, that of utilizing wave energy to produce chemical products which can be taken ashore by pipeline or tanker, offers the advantages of freedom in the siting of the wave energy converters and the onshore reception points. Most chemicals can also be stored cheaply and easily for long periods, thereby eliminating the problem of mismatch between the wave energy supply and the demand for electricity. The conversion of wave energy to chemical products is based on the initial production of hydrogen by the electrolysis of sea-water. Electricity still has to be generated on or near the wave energy device, but storage and transmission problems are now avoided. On the other hand, desalination of the seawater becomes necessary before electrolysis can be carried out, and the cost and complexity of the whole operation is greatly increased.

Further processing to yield ammonia has also been suggested since ammonia is a vital raw material and basic feedstock for the manufacture of fertilizers and other widely-used chemicals. The production of methanol, methane and gasoline using electrolytically-generated hydrogen is also a possibility, but a further difficulty here is that the necessary carbon would have to be delivered by tanker or pipeline to the production site.

Uranium could also be produced by a floating factory using cheap wave power. The major barriers to the extraction of uranium from seawater are the energy costs required to pump large volumes of water through a small ion-exchange resin bed, and to keep the depleted seawater discharge away from the intake. A wave-powered factory could overcome both of these problems.

However, 1982 cost estimates for the production of hydrogen, ammonia or synthetic hydrocarbons from wave energy indicate that the products will be two to four times as expensive as those made from fossil fuels. Therefore there is little prospect in the immediate future for considering hydrogen or its derivatives as providing suitable carriers for the energy produced from waves. Direct supply of electrical energy to offshore islands or the national networks remains the most likely form of power output: the technology is established, cable costs are comparatively low, the efficiency of transmission is comparatively high, and there is a market for the product.

The principal types of wave energy converter

Contrary to popular belief, the concept of wave power is not a recent entrant to the energy scene, but has been in existence for at least 200 years. It is estimated that between 1856 and 1973 over 340 British patents for wave energy devices were granted.

Design and testing of wave energy converters have yielded a number of possible devices, which may be categorized as rectifiers, tuned oscillators and untuned dampers. Generally, rectifiers and tuned oscillators fall into the class of devices known as 'terminators'; while untuned dampers are classified as 'attenuators'. The meaning of these terms is explained in the appendix to this chapter; the appendix also includes a brief description of the principal features, mode of operation, and probable cost-effectiveness of the various devices. Current research in the UK, where government support amounted to £13 million between 1976 and 1981, has already reduced the unit cost of available energy from different devices and may change the order of the candidates most likely for further support, but the essential principles have by now been well studied and the problems remaining are primarily in the field of engineering reliability and cost reduction.

Research, economics and efficiency

The ultimate measure of wave power viability must be in pence per kilowatt-hour (kWh). Base-load electricity generation (i.e. power produced by large stations operating continuously at high efficiency), costs about 3–4p per kWh to produce and it is unlikely that wave power can compete with this figure. On the other hand, 'marginal' or 'peak lopping' stations, which are run only when electricity demand requires them to do so, generate at costs much higher than this. It is in this area that wave power will be competitive, provided that its availability, when required, can be assured.

The research programme funded by the UK Department of Energy since 1976 has resulted in significant improvements being made in the efficiency and economics of a number of devices. In December 1978 an initial costing exercise produced estimates of between 30p and 50p per kWh for five reference designs. A year later, a similar exercise produced estimates of between 5p and 15p per kWh.

Further testing of selected devices is continuing, and in the UK the Government planned to spend £3 million on wave power projects in 1982/3. This is about the same amount as in the 1978/9–1980/1 period, but £900,000 less than in 1981/2. A decision will also have to be taken on whether to pursue the goal of a large 2-gigawatt (10^9) station for mainland supply, or to concentrate on smaller schemes for isolated or island communities.

Interaction with other marine resources

Environmental and social aspects of large-scale wave energy conversion arrays were also studied as part of the Department of Energy's research programme. These studies concentrated on the effects that would result from using the optimum wave power locations west of the Outer Hebrides and in the Moray Firth.

In considering the environmental impact of wave energy systems, the impact of the wave-energy converters, the transmission of power to the shore, the shore-based installations, and the availability of electricity for community or industrial development must all be considered. Resources affected include the shoreline (through changes in the wave regime), fisheries, shipping, and amenity uses of the coast and nearshore waters.

Wave climate and the shoreline

Since the purpose of wave energy converters is to extract some of the energy from the waves over a part of the total wave spectrum, it follows that there will be some reduction in the wave climate to leeward of them.

This could be important on the west coasts of South Uist, North Uist, and Benbecula which consist of beaches of shingle or shell sand in a state of dynamic equilibrium. Over the yearly cycle, this equilibrium involves movement of sand in summer up the beach towards high-water mark, where it then dries and is blown inland to form the 'machair' so essential in maintaining the grazing economy of these islands. The effect of wave energy converters offshore might be to reduce the erosion caused by winter storms and encourage further accretion of sand. Such an effect is likely to be beneficial because it could increase the supply of wind-blown shell sand to the machair.

On the other hand, it has also been pointed out that wave energy converters may increase the degree of erosion. Existing understanding of wave dynamics shows that long low waves build up beaches, while short steep waves erode them. With a line of wave energy converters offshore, the longer waves will be partially absorbed, and the major component of the wave spectrum arriving onshore will be the short steep waves generated locally between the converters and the shore.

Interactions with the fishing industry

One of the major considerations in the deployment of wave energy converters must be the possible effect on fisheries. Areas of considerable potential for wave power, such as the shelf seas off the west coast of Ireland and west of the Outer Hebrides, are also important fishing areas, particularly for pelagic fish such as herring. Salmon are netted at sea off these coasts and the effect of the wave energy converters on the migration of smolts and adult fish must be considered. Wave energy devices may deflect homing salmon swimming near the surface and there is the additional possibility that their above-water surfaces might create an environment favourable to large colonies of predatory sea-birds which feed on smolts attracted to the area. Large floating or semi-submerged objects will in time accumulate dense growths of algae and sessile marine animals which will attract shoals of fish. If sufficiently stable, the wave energy converters could also attract seals which would feed on the adult fish, and further exacerbate the conflict between seal conservationists and salmon fishermen.

Of great significance also would be the loss of those fishing grounds occupied by the wave energy converters, their moorings and the sub-sea cables to shore. Wave energy converter arrays would lead to a prohibition on fishing in zones up to several hundred kilometres in length and perhaps two kilometres wide. Gaps in the line of converters, perhaps two kilometres wide, would allow passage of vessels, but not while engaged in fishing. Even inshore of the converters, where the reduced wave climate may permit an increased number of fishing days per year, trawling would have to be curtailed in certain areas in order to avoid sub-sea cables. Sub-sea electric cables would have to be heavily armoured as well as buried in order to avoid the spectacular consequences of the insulation being penetrated by a 10-ton steel trawl door.

Interactions with navigation and shipping in general

The deployment of wave energy converters will present a hazard to shipping, particularly since the devices have a very low freeboard (height of the device above sea-level) which will render them relatively invisible to ships, either by sight or by radar, under most sea states. For small boats especially, which only infrequently carry radar and from whose decks the range of visibility is much less, wave energy devices could present significant hazards. Lights and radar reflectors will therefore be necessary on wave energy devices.

In the case of very large vessels, the risk of collision must be avoided at all costs. The consequences of a tanker travelling southwards from Sullom Voe, taking the westward route around the Hebrides and west coast of Ireland, and colliding with a wave energy device en route would be environmentally disastrous. Tankers have collided with charted rocks marked by the presence of nearby lighthouses or light-vessels, and there is little to suggest that the record will be improved. The siting of wave energy converters should therefore be as far away from regular shipping routes as possible. Clearways currently being considered for the passage of deep-draught oil tankers west of the Hebrides should be located well away from wave energy converters and vice versa.

There is a much greater density of shipping in the Celtic Sea and the western end of the English Channel where possible sites for wave energy converters have been under discussion. Sites off the Scilly Islands may conflict with internationally agreed schemes for traffic separation. Even if new agreements are made and revised schemes adopted, there is the danger that ships' captains may not take the trouble to learn about them, or may even ignore the new regulations. A survey carried out by the Anglo-French Safety of Navigation Group provided disturbing evidence that even in recognized shipping lanes, a significant proportion of vessels ignore the rules and sail in the 'wrong' direction. The probability of collision is high enough to cast serious doubt on the practicability of sitting wave energy devices off the coast of Cornwall.

Given the expected difficulties of mooring these devices, the occurrence of occasional 'break-away' wave energy converters must be anticipated. These could cause considerable danger to shipping.

Interactions with the development of offshore oil and gas resources

The discovery of oil west of Shetland and west of Ireland in areas otherwise well suited for the exploitation of wave energy has added a further dimension to the conflict. While these hydrocarbon finds have not yet been declared economic, provision must be made to resolve conflicts that will undoubtedly occur over the designation of the sea-bed for hydrocarbon exploitation, the movement of supply vessels, and the drilling rigs themselves. Much will depend on the relative location of the oil fields and the wave energy converters. Oil fields on the shore side of a line of converters will benefit from the easier wave climate expected, but the prospect of one or more wave energy converters breaking their moorings and drifting down on an oil production platform during a westerly gale would require special precautions and additional vigilance.

Interactions with amenity and conservation

Being sited so far out to sea, wave energy converters would cause little visual intrusion and would probably be visible only from high points on the nearest land. Their effect on the recreational use of the sea for offshore sailing has already been commented upon.

The transmission of wave power to the shore will require sub-sea cables, onshore reception facilities (including perhaps transformers and switching stations) and the provision of transmission lines to connect with the national electricity network or grid. Since the most suitable wavepower sites lie off high-scenic-value coasts, it will be almost essential to avoid overhead transmission lines, towers and other visually intrusive objects. The careful siting of buildings and burial of cables may be required by the planning authorities.

Shore-based wave energy converters, sited in narrow creeks on west-facing coasts, where the natural configuration of the rocks magnifies the amount of energy available, are also under active consideration. Experiments are in progress and larger devices are proposed for Islands off the west coast of Scotland and for Bull Rock off the south-west coast of

Ireland. Both schemes are based on use of the Wells Turbine (see appendix). Construction will also cause some impact. Present designs for converters are very large and would require massive quantities of construction materials. While construction could take place in specialist yards elsewhere, assembly of the units must take place nearby or on site. Sea-bed-mounted converters, as opposed to floating devices, may also require additionally large quantities of material for the preparation of the sea-bed. This material would have to be obtained by quarrying, and its emplacement on the sea-bed could significantly change the local ecology.

In the event of a converter, or a string of them, breaking loose in a westerly gale, the task of retrieving them from down-wind beaches would be most difficult, and there might be a temptation on the part of the owners to leave large chunks of concrete shell in situ. A similar problem arises with sea-bed mounted converters at the end of their useful life; some acceptable method for their removal must be agreed before permission is given to install them.

Economic and social aspects

Some preliminary attention has already been given to this problem in relation to the proposed site off the Outer Hebrides. These islands have no large-scale industries and are characterized by emigration, a declining population, and relatively high unemployment. Installation of wave energy converters on a large scale could provide employment through the labour force needed to operate and maintain the system, and through the possibility of using some of the power to establish new industries on the islands.

The provision of maintenance bases, tugs, workboats, and diving and other specialized services will bring other community benefits. Land is available for industrial use, and there are many examples of the successful establishment of major technologically based industries in remote areas, such as at Sullom Voe, Flotta, Fort William, and Loch Kishorn. Furthermore, in contrast with oil- or gas-related developments, wave-energy-based developments will not exhaust their resources. Nevertheless, it will be important to recognize, as is being done by the Highlands and Islands Development Board and by Comhairle nan Eilean (the Western Islands Council), that communities and lifestyles, language and culture are unique and closely interrelated on these islands, and that their weakening or destruction could cause many undesirable social consequences.

Wind Energy

Even though the energy of the wind cannot truly be regarded as a marine resource, many locations with the greatest wind energy potential are on the coast or in shallow coastal waters. Exploitation of wind power on a large scale is therefore most likely to add to the growing pressure on coastal lands and nearshore waters, and thus falls within the scope of this study. While being environmentally very 'clean', the overall impact of large aerogenerators or extensive 'wind farms' will require careful assessment, particularly as wind energy is now economically competitive with energy from fossil fuels in the generation of electricity.

North-west European coasts, and those of the British Isles in particular, are fortunate in being situated in one of the windier parts of the world. The west coast of Ireland, the Outer Hebrides, the Orkney and Shetland Islands, and the north of Scotland generally, are considered to be the best areas in which to exploit the available wind power. The British Isles are also surrounded by large areas of shallow windy sea in which numerous wind turbine towers could be situated. Areas considered for such developments include Morecambe Bay in the Irish Sea, Carmarthen Bay in the Bristol Channel, and east of the Wash off the east coast of England.

In Western Europe the seasonal availability of wind energy correlates closely with the seasonal demand for energy, most wind energy being available in the winter months. In the UK, the Central Electricity Generating Board believes that, in principle, aerogenerators could provide about 10 gigawatts, or about 25 per cent of current peak demand in England and Wales, if the right machines were available. There is a theoretical limit of about 59 per cent to the amount of energy which can be extracted from wind, and modern wind turbines can convert more than two-thirds of this limit into electricity.

The energy recovery period of a modern wind turbine is short, typically about six to twelve months; in other words, the energy invested in the construction of the wind turbine will be returned within the first six to twelve months of its operating life.

Modern wind turbine design

There are two distinct categories of aerogenerators. One, which has evolved from the more traditional design, has a horizontal axis of rotation, while the other has blades which rotate about a vertical axis.

Horizontal axis machines must have an orientation system to point the rotor into the wind. They have accumulated many thousands of hours of operating experience and have demonstrated the practicality of completely automatic, unattended operation.

The vertical axis wind turbine possesses two distinct advantages: firstly, this type of machine does not need to be pointed into the wind. Secondly, heavy items of equipment, such as the speed increasing gearbox and the electrical generator, can be mounted at or close to ground level, thereby reducing the cost of the support structure and improving access for maintenance.

The three principal types of vertical axis turbine are the Savonius rotor, the Darrieus, and the Musgrove. While the Savonius rotor is not considered a candidate for large wind energy machines, the Darrieus rotor is the subject of extensive studies in the USA and Canada, where measurements have shown that its overall efficiency is as high as the best horizontal axis wind turbines.

Current European wind energy research development and demonstration programmes

In Britain, the Secretary of State for Energy announced in January 1981 the decision to erect a 60-metre-diameter 3-megawatt aerogenerator on Orkney mainland at a cost of £5.2 million. Together with a smaller 250-kilowatt model (expected to be in operation by 1984), the 3-megawatt machine will begin supplying about one seventh of the island's electricity requirements by 1986. The overall research programme of the Department of Energy also includes:

(a) supporting the development of a 100-kilowatt Musgrove design;
(b) studying the problems and benefits of the offshore siting of wind turbines;
(c) acquiring additional data on wind, particularly in relation to the interactions between closely spaced aerogenerators;
(d) generic studies of materials, aerodynamics, generation and transmission, engineering structures and interactions with the environment.

Funding of wind power research by the Department of Energy rose from an estimated £900,000 in 1981/2 to an expected £3.2 million in 1982/3. Much of the increase will, however, be taken up by the building of the two machines in Orkney.

A further significant development in Britain has been the announcement by the Central Electricity Generating Board that it plans to buy and install a medium-sized wind turbine of proven design on its Carmarthen Bay power-station site by 1982. It then intends to install an array of up to 10 multi-megawatt machines on an east coast site during the period 1985/90.

Among other European countries, Sweden, Denmark, Germany, Ireland, and France all have continuing research, development and demonstration programmes. In the Swedish programme, two machines are now under construction.

The European Community's wind energy research programme, in which all member states participate, has five project areas covering the techno-economic evaluation of wind power, the preparation of a wind atlas, a grid interface study, and the collection and rationalization of existing and new data on wind energy machines.

Offshore wind energy systems

As mentioned above, the UK Department of Energy is undertaking a detailed study of offshore wind energy systems. Similar investigations are under way in Sweden, the Netherlands and the USA. Preliminary results indicate that the construction of large wind turbine arrays pose no major technical problems. Large areas of shallow sea, no more than 20 or 30 metres deep, lie off the east and west coasts of England and these would provide suitable locations for offshore wind farms. The foundations of the wind-turbine towers would rest on the sea bed, and in such shallow water only a small fraction of the tower need be submerged. Costs of such a system will be dominated by the civil engineering requirements (construction of tower and foundations), with a much smaller cost associated with the generation and transmission of power. Preliminary estimates by Dr Musgrove suggest that electricity delivered to the shore from such a scheme would cost about 4p per kilowatt-hour, with substantial cost reductions being expected as a result of further development and mass-production of the aerogenerators. Department of Energy estimates would, however, undoubtedly be higher.

Interactions with other marine resources

As in the case of wave energy systems, offshore wind energy arrays will interact with other marine resources, but the scale of the interaction will be less. In the first place, the energy being captured by the system is being taken from the wind, and any effects on the wave climate and hence on the stability of nearby sandy shores will be minor and incidental, resulting from the presence of the wind turbine towers. The space occupied by wind farms will also cause less interference with navigation than the extensive linear configuration necessary for wave energy systems, and it is also likely that the wind farms will be situated in shallower water, away from the principal navigation channels. Wind turbine towers are also good radar targets, they can be well lit, and their position will be fixed (in contrast to the more mobile wave energy devices).

Nevertheless, the arrays of towers and the sea-bed cables connecting them to the shore will, even if the cables are buried, have the effect of severely curtailing any trawling in their vicinity, and large areas of the sea-bed may be lost to fishing. Careful siting of the towers and connecting cables may reduce the impact, but prior consultation with the fishermen is essential. Some amelioration of the impact may be possible, first by siting the towers—where it is feasible—in areas that are not fished, and secondly by burying the undersea cable to such a depth that it will not be exposed by erosion or by changes in sea-bed topography.

Locating the towers away from the principal shipping routes and navigation channels, and marking them prominently with distinguishing lights will minimize the risk of collision with shipping, though such a risk can never be eliminated entirely.

Interference with oil or gas operations offshore is unlikely, although care will have to be taken to avoid sub-sea electric cables being laid across gas or oil pipelines. This may give rise to some routing problems. Onshore reception facilities and transmission lines will require careful design on coasts of high amenity or scenic value; and in some locations burial of the transmission lines will be essential. The towers will be more than 5 kilometres offshore, so their visual impact from the shoreline will be minimal. Construction of the towers could take place at existing shipyard or oil platform construction sites, but large quantities of material may have to be barged to the proposed tower locations in order to prepare the sea-bed for emplacement of the towers.

Wind energy on the coast

The siting of wind energy machines on the coast would have a much more dramatic effect on the visual quality of the coastal scenery. Since uninterrupted air movement is essential for efficient operation of the aerogenerators, the most probable locations will be on flat, low-elevation coasts or a short distance inland on hill summits. In either case, the effect of the tall towers on the predominantly horizontal landscape elements will be considerable. There is no way in which the structures could be disguised or hidden, so the best approach may be to rely on good design. Initial public reaction to wind turbines in the USA has been very encouraging, and modern wind turbine designs can be aesthetically elegant. Wind turbine towers will occupy very little land space, and will not compete with certain other land uses, such as short-rotation forestry or sheep-rearing, in exposed coastal areas.

On the whole, however, wind energy is one of the least disruptive renewable energy sources. No further technological advances are required other than the application of existing knowledge and the further improvement of first- and second-generation machines now operating. As far as the impact on our coasts and coastal waters is concerned, the principal factors will be, firstly, the location and extent of offshore wind turbine tower arrays, and, secondly, the balance of cost-effectiveness between large-scale megawatt-size aerogenerators in a few locations and many smaller machines serving local communities. Both large and small machines would be connected to the national electricity supply network, but in the latter case the network would serve principally as a back-up system to ensure peak-demand needs and reliability of supply. In either case, there is no doubt that the visual character of some of the windier stretches of Europe's coast will be changed dramatically during the next two or three decades.

Sources and Further Reading

Tidal Power

British Ecological Society, Industrial Ecology Group, abstracts of papers presented at an open meeting on the Ecological Implications of the Severn Barrage, held at University College, Cardiff, 21–2 September 1982.

Mitchell, R., 'Nature conservation implications of hydraulic engineering schemes affecting British estuaries', *Hydrobiological Bulletin,, vol. 12*, 3/4, 1978, pp. 333–50.

Severn Barrage Committee, *Tidal Power from the Severn Estuary, a Report to the Secretary of State for Energy*, Department of Energy, Energy Paper no. 46, HMSO, 1981.

Wilson, E. M., 'Tidal power', in Banner F. T., Collins, M. E. and Massie, K. F. (edd.), *The North-West European Shelf Seas: the Bed and the Sea in Motion*, 1980, Elsevier Oceanography Series 24B, pp. 573–81.

Wave Energy

Cottrill, A., 'Wave energy: main UK contenders line up for 1982 decision', *Offshore Engineer*, January 1981, pp. 25–36.

Dawson. J. K., 'Wave energy: a review paper prepared for the Department of Energy', Energy Paper no. 42, HMSO, 1979.

Hurley, L., 'Wave Power—turning the tide with new technology', *Technology Ireland*, January 1982, pp. 17–20.

Mollison, D., *Productvity Analysis of Salter Ducks*, 25 Nov. 1981.

Mollison, D., 'The Irish Wave Power Resource', a report to the NBST and ESB, 1981.

Proceedings of the Wave Energy Conference held at the Heathrow Hotel, London 22–3 November 1978, Energy Technology Support Unit, Harwell.

Salter, S. H., 'Wave Energy, Problems and Solutions', *Journal of the Royal Society of Arts*, August 1981, pp. 568–83.

Salter, S. H., 'Recent progress on ducks', *IEE Proceedings*, vol. 127, pt. A., no. 55, June 1980, pp. 308–19.

Wave Energy Steering Committee, *Maidenhead Workshop Proceedings 16–18 December 1979*, Energy Technology Support Unit, Harwell.

Wind Energy

Department of Energy, *Renewable Energy News*, issue no. 5, June 1981.

Musgrove, P. J., 'Offshore wind energy systems', *Meteorological Magazine*, vol. 109, 1980, pp. 113–19.

Musgrove, P. J., 'Wind energy', *Journal of the Royal Society of Arts*, August 1981, pp. 553–67.

Pooley, D., *The Wind Energy Research and Development Programme of the UK Department of Energy*, Harwell, Energy Technology Support Unit, 1981.

Appendix
The Principal Types of Wave Energy Converter

Rectifiers

A rectifier is essentially a device for converting energy flowing in alternate directions into a uni-directional energy flow. The wave energy rectifier proposed by the Hydraulic Research Station uses a principle similar to that in a tidal power station. Wave peaks (corresponding to high water) drive seawater through non-return flaps into a high-level reservoir. Outlet flap-valves in a lower reservoir discharge water to the sea during wave troughs (corresponding to low water) and power is generated by means of water flowing between the reservoirs driving turbines. High-level and low-level reservoirs are placed alternately side by side, the flap-valves are on the vertical seaward face, and the converter sits on the sea-bed facing the oncoming waves. Its efficiency is low, and structural costs are high; hence work on it was discontinued in 1979.

Tuned Oscillators

Tuned oscillators operate by providing a 'tuned' working component which is excited by a chosen part of the wave spectrum and damped by a power take-off system. The principal devices classified under this heading are: the Oscillating Water Column (OWC), the Cockerell Raft, the Salter Duck, the Belfast Buoy, and the Bristol Cylinder.

The concept of a column of water oscillating vertically in tune with the oncoming waves has for many years been thought of as a promising wave energy converter. Pioneering work by Masuda in Japan has led to the installation in Japanese waters of more than 300 generators delivering 70–120 watts for powering light-buoys and light-houses. Around the coast of Ireland, some 15 navigation buoys are powered by battery systems which are kept charged by wave energy.

The trapped oscillating column of water can be made to work in a variety of ways; the favoured method is to allow it to operate as a piston to pump air through a turbine. In Britain, the National Engineering Laboratory (NEL) and the engineering firm of Vickers have developed two designs, one of which lies afloat across the wave path, whereas the other is submerged on the sea-bed. The NEL device is based on the rise and fall of water in an inverted box forcing air back and forth through an orifice at the top of the box. This two-directional air movement is rectified by power-operated louvre valves into a uni-directional pulsating flow which operates an air turbine.

The Vickers oscillating water column uses the pressure changes caused by the varying head of water as a wave passes over the submerged device in order to induce a resonant and amplified oscillation in a water column. The water column is made so that its natural frequency oscillation is approximately equal to that of the waves with the result that the water column will resonate, capturing energy from an area larger than that occupied by the device. Initially designed as a submerged duct with a closed-air reservoir, the device was improved by linking the main water column to a second column alongside it. The open end of the main water column faces upwards on top of the structure, where it senses the full effect of wave pressure variations and can be placed as near to the sea surface as is desirable. The open end of the secondary column is directed horizontally near the base of the device, at a depth where pressure fluctuations are much less. In addition, this second opening is displaced laterally, so that the two openings are beneath different parts of the wave cycle at any given time. The oscillating airflow between the two columns operates self-rectifying turbines.

The oscillating water column principle has been used extensively in the Japanese research programme on wave energy. A vessel named the *Kaimei* was equipped with twenty-two separate chambers containing oscillating water columns open to the sea at the bottom. In a preliminary assessment of sea trials, the vessel produced much less electrical output than expected, this being attributed to the relative shortness of the barge-like structure compared with the dominant wavelength in the test area. Rather than remain as a steady reference point, the vessel tended to move wherever the waves were over a certain size. Nevertheless the *Kaimei* has provided a focus for the major international collaborative effort in wave energy research.

The Cockerell Raft, developed by Sir Christopher Cockerell, is a shallow pontoon hinged so that it can follow the contours of the waves passing under it. A wave energy converter based on this principle would consist of a string of rafts moored so as to face the prevailing wave directions, power being extracted by hydraulic pumps placed at the hinge and operated by the relative angular movements of adjoining pontoons. Hydraulic fluid under pressure from the pumps drives a generator situated on the raft or alternatively on a central platform to which the high-pressure fluid is fed from a number of rafts. Even though it has the advantage of simplicity and ruggedness, after detailed study it was found to be among the more expensive devices.

The Salter Duck is perhaps the most widely known wave energy converter that can be described as a tuned oscillator. In this device it is not a column of water which oscillates, but a steel or concrete cam or vane, nodding up and down under wave action as it rotates on a spine at its rear. It is a very efficient absorber of wave energy, possessing at the same time the ability to survive under very rough conditions. The mooring forces required under such conditions are also small because in shedding some of the excess wave energy, the ducks generate secondary waves astern of them which counteract the principal force pushing them shoreward.

Power is extracted through pairs of contra-rotating gyroscopes situated inside the duck's 'beak'. Under wave action the gyro assembly 'processes', which causes it to rotate in a horizontal plane, swinging through 180 degrees and back typically once every ten seconds. The resulting force is harnessed through ring cases attached to the gyro gimbals. A circle of hydraulic pumps which bear on the ring are activated by cams as the gyro assembly turns, the hydraulic fluid being fed to separate motors driving the gyroscope flywheel and an electrical generator.

From the viewpoint of electrical generation, the gyroscope-based system possesses a number of advantages. The reserves of energy instantly available from the flywheels consitute a 'spinning reserve', stabilizing the national transmission network to which it is connected rather than causing it problems. With each flywheel weighing 17 tons, up to 45 minutes of energy storage is available. Sophisticated micro-processor control can be used to increase the life of the overall system by reducing the wear on components which may show signs of failure. Thus, while catastrophic failure of a duck becomes more unlikely, the power output can be expected to decline over the proposed 25-year lifespan. A small excess number of primary pump units, held in reserve initially, would allow for this decline; and normal power output could therefore be maintained.

In any event, existing design philosophy for large-scale wave energy conversion is based on pairs of ducks on a long jointed backbone or spine, parallel with the wave fronts. The motion of the joints, and hence the flexibility of the spine, can be controlled by double-acting hydraulic rams arranged around the circumference of the backbone section. The joints will not only allow the spine to deflect in waves of amplitudes greater than the ducks wish to absorb, but they will be able to act as a power-generating mechanism in their own right. The amount of spine flexibility can therefore be controlled to an optimum level (stiff spine for low wave heights; compliant spine in heavy seas) and unwanted oscillations damped out. Lastly, there is the possibility that some of the energy could be used for dynamic positioning, thus giving some degree of mobility to the string (limited only by the flexible cable conveying electrical energy ashore) and ensuring that it always remained at the correct angle to the waves.

In a full-scale system, each duck would be 26 metres wide, built probably of concrete at a cost of £2.1 million, and displacing 3,000 tons. Each duck would generate 2 megawatts (2×10^6 watts), and for a 2-gigawatt station (2×10^9 watts), 1,000 ducks would be required, moored in 100 metres of water and stretching for 30 kilometres.

Problems of the reliability and long life under arduous conditions of the machinery in the ducks still require further investigation, and there is as yet no adequate design for a flexible submarine cable to act as a link between the moving duck string and a rigid cable on the sea-bed.

The Belfast Buoy is, by contrast, a much simpler device. Based on the oscillating water column principle, it is circular and can absorb energy from waves arriving from any direction. A pressure chamber, floating high in the water, is rigidly connected to a ballast chamber below the surface and designed to stabilize the buoy against heaving vertically. As waves pass the open bottom of the pressure chamber, an oscillation is induced, sending air back and forth through a narrow upper neck. The unique feature of the buoy is the Wells turbine whose blades have a symmetrical aerofoil section, allowing it to rotate in the same direction regardless of which way air flows through it. The device has considerable potential, and the self-rectifying turbine in particular has wider application in other devices, including shore-based wave energy converters.

The Bristol Oscillating Cylinder is a relatively new concept, experimental work having began only in 1978. Totally submerged, it floats below the water surface, parallel to the approaching wave crests. It is also buoyant, and is held down by chains connected to mooring points on the sea-bed via hydraulic pumps. The orbital motion of water particles in the pressure field of a wave as it passes overhead causes the cylinder to orbit around its static position, thus varying the tension in its moorings. The varying tension operates the hydraulic pumps, from which a high-pressure fluid (which could be seawater) is sent to a turbo-generator on the sea-bed, or to an offshore platform or onshore. The advantages of the Bristol cylinder are that it is not exposed to storms at sea, it is smaller than most devices, and it is mechanically simple. Ensuring long-term reliability of the mooring and pumps, and increasing its overall efficiency in capturing wave energy are the principal problems awaiting solution.

Untuned dampers

Wave energy dampers, or attenuators as they are frequently called, extract energy from the waves working on a flexible hull. In contrast to the previously described devices, all of which, with the exception of the Belfast buoy and the Bristol cylinder, possess a long horizontal absorbing side facing the waves, attenuators are ship-like structures which lie ahead to sea and extract energy from the waves running along their hulls. The best-known of these, the Lancaster flexible bag, consists of a number of flexible air bags attached along the top of a sumberged hull lying head-on to the sea. In appearance, it resembles a submarine, complete with conning tower in which an air turbine is situated. As waves run along the device, the crests compress the bags, forcing air through non-return valves into the higher-pressure manifold in the hull. Meanwhile, the troughs allow the air bags to be reinflated by air drawn through another system of valves from the low-pressure manifold. An air turbine is then driven by the pressure differences, the bags, ducts and turbine comprising a closed-air system. A number of problems remain, however, and these are concerned primarily with the need to increase the life of the flexible bag material.

Vickers have also produced a design for a device based on the same principle, but in this case the 'hull' sits on the sea-bed. Waves passing overhead excite a secondary wave travelling along the free surface of a chamber running full length inside the structure, end-on to the wave crests. Air trapped in the chamber is used to drive turbines. Being submerged, it is less likely to be damaged by storms, but maintenance and the effect of the salt-laden air on turbines requires further development work. Two designs are under development, an attenuator and a terminator. Both are concrete structures mounted on piers piled to the sea-bed in about 25 metres of water.

The Lanchester Sea Clam is also an untuned damper, consisting of flexible rubber air bags attached to a hollow concrete spine at a slight angle to the incoming waves. Power generation by self-restricting turbines occurs on both inhalation and exhalation. An early design had an outer metal plate or 'shell' to absorb the wave power and operate the bellows, hence the name 'clam', but direct wave contact was found to be as useful and much cheaper.

IV

Mineral Resources of the Sea

In addition to the sub-seabed minerals dealt with in chapter II, the sea also provides a source of minerals and chemicals which serve as raw materials for construction and process industries. Like the energy-producing minerals (oil, natural gas, coal), these raw materials are not renewable; the quantities available, though very large in some cases, are finite, and their extraction may give rise to significant environmental impact and conflict with other activities.

This chapter will examine first the coast and offshore sea-bed as a source of sand and gravel, then other mineral deposits on the sea-bed, and, finally, dissolved chemicals in the seawater.

Sea-dredged sand and gravel form the raw material for the largest and most advanced marine mining activity in the world today, and their extraction is a subject of increasing concern. Yet for many centuries sand and shingle were removed directly from beaches for use as animal bedding (sand), as a soil conditioner, and for building. It may therefore be appropriate to begin with a brief note on this ancient practice.

Removal of Beach-sand and Shingle

The formation of deep man-made and very fertile soils around coastal districts in certain parts of Scotland and Ireland is due to the continued application of large quantities of calcareous sea-sand mixed with seaweed, stable-manure or peat. On the western shores of the Outer Hebrides, the naturally wind-blown sand is colonized by a rich vegetation and is fertilized by animals and sea-birds to give a unique environment known as 'machair'. The taking of sand from beaches to build up such soils became so wide-spread that in 1641, for example, the Irish House of Commons contemplated introducing legislation to regulate its removal. Yet, in Ireland at any rate, the removal of sea-sand continued to increase; and reached a peak in the nineteenth century. In the early part of the present century there were still many coastal dwellers whose sole occupation was the collection of sea-sand, and the removal of sea-sand and shingle still continues in a small number of locations in Kerry and Donegal.

The primary effect of beach-sand or gravel removal is to cause a reduction in the level of the beach, and this is usually followed by erosion of the coast. Material which would otherwise take part in the natural cycles of build-up and erosion is removed from circulation and may not be replaced by material from further offshore. Dunes in particular become prone to undercutting by wave attack, and may be permanently lost. The effects are similar to those caused by offshore dredging which removes the supply of sand from the sea-bed below the low-water mark.

The best known and most frequently cited example of damage through sand or gravel is the destruction of the village of Hallsands on the south coast of England. This village was built upon a raised beach platform at the foot of the cliffs in Start Bay. But in 1887 the shingle beach was used as a source of supply for the construction of dockyards at Plymouth, some 660,000 tonnes of shingle being removed from the intertidal zone. Since there was no sublittoral shingle reservoir, the material removed was not naturally replaced, the shore level was reduced by about four metres, erosion of the cliffs followed, and the village was attacked and destroyed by wave action.

Offshore Sand and Gravel Dredging

Removal of sand from beaches was extended seaward during the latter part of the nineteenth century by using barges which were floated out on the ebb tide, beached on a tidal flat at low water, filled by hand shovelling, and returned to shore on the incoming tide. The first offshore dredging proper began in the United Kingdom in about 1936 in the Bristol Channel, and after the Second World War was extended to the south coast of England, Liverpool Bay and the Outer Thames estuary. By about 1960, open-sea dredging began with the development of the suction pump (which replaced the barge-mounted grab).

After some initial doubts about the suitability of marine aggregates for concrete manufacture had been dispelled, production rose rapidly. Total offshore production from the UK sector of the continental shelf reached 13.5 million tonnes annually from 1969 to 1971, and by 1980 had risen to 17 million tonnes. A survey carried out by the Sand and Gravel Association of Great Britain in 1968 recorded 76 sites where sea-dredged aggregates were delivered alongside a wharf.[1] In 1979 there were nine major dredging companies of which six were operating in the North Sea, four on the south coast of England, and six in the Bristol Channel. These companies operated about 52 dredgers ranging in capacity from 500 tonnes to 8,000 tonnes, and supplied around 14 per cent of all UK gravel production.

The principal markets for marine sand and gravel are the large conurbations bordering the southern North Sea, such as the London and Rotterdam areas. To supply the London market there are some twenty installations for unloading and processing marine aggregates between Battersea and the mouth of the Thames estuary. In 1970 some 2.3 million tonnes were brought into this area, and by 1979 production in the Thames estuary had risen to 4.1 million tonnes.

During the period 1969 to 1973 at least 6 million tonnes of marine gravel were transported from the British continental shelf to the Netherlands to be used in the construction of breakwaters for the new harbour entrance of Rotterdam Europort. If additional quantities (not recorded in the UK Department of the Environment statistics) supplied from other parts of the British continental shelf directly to Europort are taken into account, the total could well be in the region of 20–25 million tonnes[2]

Large quantities of gravel were also exported from the UK for construction work at Zeebrugge harbour in the late 1960s. More recently, exports from the UK to mainland Europe have averaged between 3.5 and 4 million tonnes annally. However, it is estimated that in order to satisfy the demand for gravel in the London area alone, marine gravel will no longer be available for export within 45 years from now.

Similar shortages are expected on the continental side of the North Sea. The inland gravel resources of the Netherlands along the banks of the Meuse, heavily exploited during the last twenty-five years, will be exhausted within a period of twenty years from now. Unfortunately there is no other gravel-bearing formation known in the Netherlands, and further supplies will have to be imported. Demand for gravel in Denmark, Germany and France is also expected to put increasing pressure on their available offshore deposits.

The International Council for the Exploration of the Sea, in the first report of the Working Group on Effects on Fisheries of Marine Sand and Gravel Extraction, noted the following trends:[3]

(a) demand for marine aggregate will increase, and at an increasing rate;
(b) the continued decrease in availability of farming and building land, together with increasing road congestion, will lead to a disproportionate increase in production from marine sources;
(c) despite the increase in the size of dredgers, and in their depth of operation, the costs of transporting this low-value commodity will ensure that marine aggregate production will continue to be concentrated in the (relatively) nearshore zone, close to the main metropolitan centres of demand, and will move to more distant deposits only as the nearshore beds become depleted and the market price of aggregate increases.

Furthermore, A. A. Archer noted the increasing public resistance to the land exploitation of minerals and, despite the environmental effects of dredging, he envisaged an increase in marine sand and gravel extraction. Yet, despite the existence of extensive sea areas surveyed under prospecting licences, only relatively small areas have been approved by the

Crown Estate Commissioners for commercial dredging, and less than 50 per cent of commercial licence applications submitted are granted. Aggregate production from Liverpool Bay is also declining in importance due to deteriorating quality inshore, and while a great deal of survey work has been carried out around the Scottish coasts, widespread deposits have not been discovered. Interest in hitherto unexploited areas, such as the sand- and gravel-banks off the east coast of Ireland between Dublin and Wexford, began in the late 1970s, but to date no commercial dredging has been licensed. A summary of the existing and planned exploitation of marine sands and gravels is given in the report of the third meeting of the ICES Working Group on Effects on Fisheries of Marine Sand and Gravel Extraction.[5]

Conflict with other uses

The extraction of marine sand and gravel may cause damage to the sea-bed, affect marine life on the bottom, make the dredged area less attractive for spawning fish, and reduce commercial fish catches. The degree of conflict or impact will depend to a considerable extent upon the extraction method, the amount of fine material present in the sand, the mobility of the bottom, and the extent to which the area being dredged supports commercially fished species.

Most of the sea-going aggregate dredgers are of the suction type, and recover a mixture of sand and gravel; some keep only the gravel, rejecting the sand at sea. If any finer material, such as silt or mud, is present, this too is washed back into the sea, creating a plume of turbid water. Decreased primary production (due to less light being available) and reduced zooplankton abundance have been associated with dredge-induced turbidity. The secondary effects of turbidity, namely the smothering of immoble benthic fauna with a layer of fine silt, is also likely to occur under certain conditions. In locations where the dredged material contains appreciable amounts of adsorbed toxic substances, for example in the vicinity of harbours or ocean outfalls, the toxins may be resuspended in the water and cause harm to benthic fauna or fish. On the other hand, dredging has also been found to have beneficial effects on primary productivity in the water, as a result of the resuspension of nutrients derived from the sea-bed sediment.

The dredge will also take a very high proportion of benthic animals living in the sand or gravel. These will be returned to the sea with the finer material, but most are damaged leading to a temporary impoverishment of the fauna. If the area remains subsequently undisturbed, a more diverse fauna can gradually establish itself within two or three years. If the area is dredged regularly, a stable, diverse, benthic community may never be attained.[6]

Dredging activities have a number of consequences for fisheries. If the sea-bed has been made uneven by pits or tracks, this will make it less suitable for trawling. Alteration of the benthic fauna or of the type of bottom material may also affect fish stocks directly. The most important consequence of dredging is the effect it has on the spawning grounds of herring. Herring usually spawn on a gravel bottom where currents in excess of 1 metre per second prevent smothering and ensure a continuous supply of clean water. Dredging, by altering the nature of the bottom, is likely to create difficulties for spawning herring. It has also been suggested that the adult herring may use sound characteristics of the sea-bed under the action of bottom currents as a clue to recognizing their spawning site, and that dredging would alter these characteristics,[7] but conclusive evidence has yet to be found. Similar concern has been expressed about the vulnerability of the sand-eel to dredging.

Effects of Dredging on the coast

There are a number of possible ways in which dredging can affect an adjoining coastline:

(*a*) if the dredging is too close to the shore, beach material may be drawn down during storms into the deepened area;

(*b*) the dredging may affect the onshore movement of shingle and interrupt the natural supply which maintains the shingle beaches;

(*c*) if bars or banks are dredged, the coast may become more exposed to wave attack;

(*d*) the refraction of waves over the dredge site could cause changes in the pattern of longshore shingle or sand transport.

Because of the importance of the coast, and of the need to maintain coastal stability and prevent erosion, care is now taken by the governments concerned to restrict dredging to areas in which these effects are unlikely. The criteria applied are discussed below.

Control of dredging

Control of the exploration for and exploitation of minerals on the British sector of the continental shelf lies with the Crown Estate Commissioners (CEC) who are responsible for the proprietary rights of the Crown in tidal waters. Formerly, the Commissioners' control was restricted to territorial waters, but this was extended under the 1964 Continental Shelf Act. A prospecting licence is initially required, and this is issued by the CEC after consultation with fisheries interests. After proving the presence of suitable material, the dredging company then applies for an extraction licence, and at this stage the CEC request the opinion of the Hydraulics Research Station (HRS), on whether dredging at the proposed rate is likely to affect adversely the adjacent coastline.

If the opinion of the HRS is favourable to the application, then the CEC carry out further consultation with the following agencies:

(a) the Department of the Environment, who are responsible for coastal protection;

(b) the Ministry of Agriculture, Fisheries and Food, who are responsible for fisheries laboratories and for whom the district inspectors of fisheries consult with fishery interests including the local sea fisheries committees;

(c) the Department of Trade, who are responsible for navigation;

(d) the Department of Energy, who are responsible for offshore oil and gas installations;

(e) the Ministry of Defence, who are responsible for practice and exercise areas;

(f) the Post Office, who are responsible for undersea telephone cables;

(g) the coastal local authorities, who are responsible for coastal protection;

(h) the regional water authorities, who are responsible for water quality in estuaries.

In Scottish waters the Department of Agriculture and Fisheries for Scotland and the river purification boards, as well as the relevant agencies of the Scottish Office, are consulted. The departments in turn take advice from their own consultative bodies, such as Trinity House.

These opinions are received by the Minerals Planning Division of the Department of the Environment, which is responsible for co-ordinating the consultative procedure and for considering the objections. There is no right of appeal against a decision. Finally a licence is issued by the CEC, who have the right to levy a charge on each tonne of material loaded. There are no formal provisions for carrying out an environmental impact assessment of the proposals nor for subsequent environmental monitoring.

Pospecting licences are normally issued for a period of two years and may cover an area of up to 1,000 square miles. No more than 1,000 tonnes of exploratory samples may usually be removed. Production licences stipulate the annual rate of gravel removal, which is usually chosen so as to allow the deposit to be worked for fifteen to twenty years.

In other European countries, similar controls and licensing systems are in operation. These have been summarized by the ICES Working Group on Effects on Fisheries of Marine Sand and Gravel Extraction (1975, 1977, 1979), but the following points are of particular relevance:

(a) **Norway:** Accurate data including results of all surveys, samples, etc. must be supplied to the Ministry of Industry; and the exploration must as far as possible not interfere with fishing or with marine fauna and flora.

(*b*) **France:** Regulations approved by a government commission in 1978 require dredging companies to answer a comprehensive check-list dealing with the possible effects of the extraction on the marine environment; to finance impact studies if required by the licensing authorities; to supply detailed returns of quantities extracted and bathymetric data; to allow observers on board the dredgers; and to finance a post-dredging benthic survey.

(*c*) **Netherlands:** The Law on North Sea Soil Materials governs the licensing of dredging, and it is framed in general terms to allow the appropriate authorities to add their own regulations. Extraction is not allowed within about 20 kilometres of the coast, but consideration is being given to replacing this with a depth limit of a minimum of 15 metres.

(*d*) Both **Sweden** and the **USA** require a survey before a licence can be issued. In Sweden a government survey and regular monitoring are carried out, the costs of which are borne by the dredging company. In the USA an environmental impact statement must be produced before a licence is issued, and the operator must then comply with the strict guidelines laid down.

On the whole, controls in the various countries appear to work reasonably well in preventing conflict. Their aim, to quote the UK Code of Practice for the Extraction of Marine Aggregates (1981), is based on the view that 'the fishing and extraction industries are legitimately exploiting the sea's resources; no one industry or activity can have an absolute priority'.

Other Mineral Deposits

In addition to deposits of sand or gravel, other areas of the sea-bed contain minerals which can form the basis of an extraction industry. Perhaps the best-known deposits of this type are the manganese nodules, but since these occur in economically exploitable quantities only on the deep ocean floor and not on the continental shelf, they are outside the scope of this study. Of more immediate interest are the minerals which can be dredged from shallow water around the shores of north-west Europe, and these include cassiterite, magnetite, ilmenite, zircon, and rutile.

The distribution of these placer deposits is determined by the nature of the underlying geological formations from which the minerals have been ultimately derived and, to a lesser extent, by the current and tidal movements. Thus, for example, the North Sea can be considered a highly unpromising area in the search for such minerals, but certain inshore areas close to the ancient metamorphic and granite terrains flanking the western coastlines of the British Isles may be considered to offer rather more exploration potential.

There has been active interest in commercial retrieval of tin from off the coast of Cornwall for over a century, but methodical exploration of the sea-bed has been carried out only in the last few decades. Cassiterite, an oxide of tin, is found in shallow water adjacent to the onshore tin-mining areas. Cassiterite-bearing sands are known from a number of locations, but at present dredging is restricted to a 20 kilometes square area between Perranporth and St Ives Bay.

Pockets of sand rich in zircon (which is the source of zirconium, a metal used for alloys, photo-flash bulbs and in nuclear engineering) have been found in the Thames estuary, particularly in an area a short distance east of the Maplin sands. Other high concentrations of zircon occur sporadically on westward-facing beaches on the coast of south Wales, but are not capable of economic exploitation at present. Zircon is also known to occur with rutile (titanium oxide), ilmenite (oxide of iron and titanium) and monazite (a source of thorium, yttrium and europium) as black sand in Budle Bay, Northumberland, but no workable deposits have been found. The presence of magnetite and ilmenite in sands off the coast of western Scotland has been confirmed, and may be worth further examination. Studies have also been made of the concentration of copper, lead, zinc, and cadmium in shallow marine sediments in Cardigan Bay (west coast of Wales), but no potentially economic resources have yet been located.

Potentially exploitable carbonate accumulations of biogenic origin also occur off Ireland, Brittany, and the west coast of Scotland. Some of these accumulations consist of either living or dead masses of the coraline alga *Lithothamnium*, which concentrates calcium carbonate from seawater. The alga is very slow-growing and, as suggested in chapter V, this resource should be regarded not as a renewable living material, but as a finite irreplaceable resource to be exploited with care. Small quantities of *Lithothamnium* or maërl have been dredged off the coast of France since the nineteenth century, and by 1974 the amount had increased to around 648,000 tonnes annually. No large-scale extraction has taken place off any of the other coasts, although proposals to dredge have been considered. One extraction licence has been issued in Ireland, but commercial operations have not yet commenced. Under the terms of the licence the Shellfish Laboratory of University College, Galway, will monitor the operation and, if any adverse effects are found, processing or extraction will be stopped until a solution to the problem is obtained.

An alternative soure of carbonate is, however, available in the enormous calcareous sand deposits which occur in many areas around Europe. Not only are these sediments a renewable resource, but in many cases they are associate with an impoverished faunal community of sea-bed organisms, in contrast to the richness of animal life found inhabiting the maërl beds. Mollusc debris comprises the bulk of many littoral deposits (up to 80 per cent by volume) off the west coast of Ireland. The coasts of the

Netherlands and north-west Germany are particularly short of limestone, and the shell deposits at the mouth of the river Jade have been exploited for centuries, both for limekiln supplies and for road-metal. The tidal flats to seaward of the Jade estuary support dense populations of bivalves, and their shells accumulate continuously. The deposits are up to 4 metres thick and one company alone is reported to have dredged 70,000 cubic metres annually. Local demand has stimulated the exploitation of these reserves, whereas similar accumulations of shell on the British coast have not been exploited because of the proximity of adequate supplies of quarried limestone. Extensive accumulations of shells, resulting from local cockle fisheries in south Wales and calcium-rich shell sands in the English Channel, are unable to be worked economically and remain unexploited. Nevertheless, mollusc and other shell debris contributes largely to the amenity value of a number of shorelines, especially the unique Shell Strand beach of north-east Herm in the Channel Islands, and the 'coral' strands of Connemara, west of Galway. Offshore exploitation of the calcareous deposits could endanger the continuity of supply to such beaches unless particular care is taken.

It may also be worth mentioning that a large part of the southern North Sea overlies an extension of the north German salt basin, continuing nearly to the English coast. The salt domes contain large quantities of halite and potash; these are at present in abundant supply from other sources, but the domes could provide a future resource. The tops of some of the domes are close to the sea-floor and the minerals could be mined from artificial islands. If such mining operations were undertaken, it is unlikely that they would conflict with hydrocarbon production.

Potash also occurs under a large part of Yorkshire, and the deposit extends for a considerable distance under the North Sea. It is mined by ICI near Saltburn-by-the-Sea, and the workings extend beneath the coast. Extraction of the mineral leaves large quantities of a liquid effluent which is pumped out to sea and discharged three miles offshore.

Dissolved Materials in Sea-water

If dissolved substances in seawater could be extracted economically (and this would depend to a great extent on very cheap energy), they would provide an almost inexhaustible resource for most of mankind's needs. However, only four substances—salt, magnesium, bromine, and fresh water—are at present being recovered commercially from seawater. On a world scale, very large quantities of these substances are extracted at over one hundred centres of production, but of these only a few are situated in north-west Europe.

Sea salt is produced on a small scale at Maldon in Essex (south-east England) by solar evaporation. Production amounts to about 200–250 kilograms per day and the product is sold mostly as a high-quality table salt.

Magnesium is the third most abundant element in seawater, and the metal is an important constituent of light, strong alloys used mainly in aircraft construction. Its oxide, magnesia, is also widely used as a refractory material in steel furnaces, cement kilns and other high-temperature applications, and as a chemical in paper pulp, rubber, animal foodstuffs, effluent treatment and uranium-extraction industries. It is extracted from seawater using burnt dolomite (a limestone rock) as a precipitant. Steetley Refractories have operated a magnesia extraction plant at Hartlepool on the east coast of England since 1937, with a present capacity of 250,000 tonnes per year. A second plant was built by the Quigley Magnesite Division of the Pfizer Chemical Corporation at Dungarvan on the south coast of Ireland, with a capacity of 75,000 tonnes per year, and operated until 1982.

Magnesium metal was once produced in the UK to meet wartime demand, at a plant at Harrington, Cumbria, but the cost of electric power made the process uneconomic in peacetime. In Norway, however, relatively cheap hydroelectric power has made the country second only to the USA in magnesium production. The plant at Heroya, near Oslo, currently extracts 60,000 tonnes of magnesium per annum from seawater.

Seawater is the principal commercial source of bromine, most of which is subsequently made into di-bromo-ethane, used for the manufacture of lead alkyl anti-knock compounds for addition to petrol. A plant at Amlwch, Anglesey, built in 1954 and operated by the Associated Octel Company, has a production capacity of about 30,000 tonnes per annum. Approximately 16 million litres of seawater are pumped through the plant for every tonne of bromine produced. The final effluent is a slightly diluted seawater containing sulphuric and hydrochloric acids and small amounts of free chlorine and bromine. In the early 1970s, concern was expressed about the environmental effects of the effluent, but some years later a slight improvement in conditions was reported.

The desalination of seawater in order to produce fresh water is widespread in arid coastal regions, for example in the Middle East, but at present the only desalination plants operating in north-west Europe are at Terneuzen in the Netherlands and on Guernsey in the Channel Islands. The former produces around 10.5 million tonnes per annum; the latter is a very small plant, operated seasonally, and produces about 1 million tonnes per annum which are used to supplement normal water supplies in the summer.

The only other materials which have been seriously considered as being economically recoverable from seawater are potassium salts and uranium. The UK Atomic Energy Authority investigated the technical problems of uranium extraction and went as far as to commission a study of the operating parameters of a hypothetical plant located in the Menai straits. As the concentration of uranium in seawater is only of the order of 3 parts per trillion (3 pg/l), any method would involve the processing of very large volumes of seawater. Although an initial outline energy-and cost-estimate might indicate the viability of such a plant, a serious constraint would be in finding a suitable site. With the present risks and uncertainties about the future of nuclear power, it is unlikely that uranium extraction will be undertaken except for military or strategic purposes.

Conflict with other uses

Extracting dissolved materials from seawater may be compared with any other chemical processing industry located on the coast, the principal difference being that the volume of effluent (namely 'spent' seawater) discharged is much greater. Desalination and extraction of salt by solar evaporation produce a more salty brine which, provided it is diluted quickly by normal seawater, should cause no adverse effects. The extraction of magnesium and bromine results in the discharge of large quantities of treated water which may prove damaging.

For example, the discharge of effluent from the bromine extraction plants at Amlwch was found to cause various lethal and sub-lethal ecological effects throughout the whole of Amlwch Bay.[8] Furthermore, M. Guiry, in a survey of the biology of Dungarvan Bay, found extensive deposits of a magnesite/dolomite silt derived from the overflow of effluent lagoons onto the foreshore in the immediate vicinity of the Quigley magnesite plant.[9] In both cases the damage could be attributed to either poor design or faulty operation, and did not extend so as to produce demonstrable effects on commercial fisheries. In both cases also, amenity use of the adjacent foreshore was not an important factor.

Sources and Further Reading

Advisory Committee on Aggregates, *Aggregates: The Way ahead*, report of the committee chaired by Sir Ralph Verney to the Department of the Environment, Scottish Development Department and Welsh Office, HMSO, 1976.

Bonner, F. T., 'Sea-Bed Resources, Potential and Actual (excluding Hydrocarbons)' in Banner, F. T., Collins, M. B., and Massie, K. S. (edd.), *The North-West European Shelf Seas: The Sea-Bed and the Sea in Motion*, II: *Physical and Chemical Oceanography and Physical Resources*, Elsevier Oceanography Series 24B, 1980, pp. 54–67.

Dickson, R., and Lee, A., 'Gravel extraction: effects on sea-bed topography', *Offshore Services*, August 1973, pp. 32–9, and September 1973, pp. 56–61.

Hess, Harold D., *Marine Sand and Gravel Mining Industry of the UK*, NOAA Technical Report, ERL 213-MMTC, NTIS, 1971.

Jolliffe, I. P., 'Beach-Offshore Dredging: some environmental consequences', paper presented at the sixth Offshore Technology Conference, Houston, May 6–8, 1974, OTC 2056.

Oele E., 'Sand and gravel from shallow seas,' *Geologie en Mijnbouw*, vol. 57 (1) 1978, pp. 45–54.

Price, W. A., Motyka, J. M., and Jaffrey, L. J., 'The effect of offshore dredging on coastlines' *Proceedings of the 16th Coastal Engineering Conf., ASCE, Hamburg, West Germany, August 28–Sept. 1, 1978*, pp. 1347–58.

Quinn, Ann C. M., *Sand Dunes: Formation, Erosion and Management*, 1977, An Foras Forbortha.

Shelton, R. G. J., and Rolfe, M. S., *The biological implications of aggregate extraction: recent studies in the English Channel*, ICES, C. M. 1972/E:26.

Notes

1. Chapman, G. P. and Roeder, A. R., 'Sea-dredged Sands and Gravels', paper presented at the Fourteenth Course in Quarry Management.
2. Chillingworth, P. C. H., 'Marine Sand and Gravel: Prospects for the Future, *Quarry Management and Products*, April 1980, pp. 92–5.
3. ICES Co-operative Research Report, 1975, no. 46.
4. Archer, A. A., 'Progress and Prospects of Marine Mining', paper no. OTC1757, presented at the 5th Offshore Technology Conference, Houston, Texas, 29 April–2 May 1973.
5. ICES, Marine Environment Quality Committee, C. M. 1979/E:3.
6. de Groot, S. J., 'The potential environmental impact of marine gravel extraction in the North Sea', *Ocean Management* 5, 1979, pp. 233–49.
7. de Groot, S. J. *The Consequences of Marine Gravel Extraction for the spawning of Herring*, ICES, C. M. 1979/E:5, pp. 1–30.
8. Hoare R., and Hiscock K., *Estuarine and Coastal Marine Science*, 2, 1974, pp. 329–48.
9. Guiry, M., Dungarvan Bay Biological Survey, manuscript 1970.

V

Living Resources of the Sea

The living resources of the sea satisfy a significant proportion of the protein needs of mankind. In this chapter we examine briefly the contribution they make in north-west Europe, focusing in particular on the wild stock fisheries of the area; a brief examination of the contribution that mariculture may make to supplementing these resources will also be made, and the chapter will conclude with a summary of the value of marine algae and sea-birds for human consumption.

An Introduction to the Sea Fisheries

The annual world catch of commercial fish is now about 70 million tonnes. The maximum catch available from all the world's seas using conventional gear has been estimated at 80 million tonnes per annum, which might be reached within the next decade or so.

Fisheries remain an important resource in north-west Europe. In 1977, for example, the total value of demersal (bottom-dwelling) food fish landed in Britain reached a total of £190 million; pelagic (surface or mid.-water) landings in the same year were worth £32 million and were still increasing. Demersal tonnage landed reached a peak of 750,000 tonnes in 1969–70, but thereafter declined due to the reduction in available distant-water fisheries. During this period there was also a very large increase in the quantity of smaller fish caught for industrial use, primarily for reduction to fish-meal. This development exploited a different segment of the fish population and it has caused serious conflicts with the interests of traditional fisheries.

Primary fishing is only a small contributor to gross domestic product in the countries of the European Community, as in the rest of the world. In no country does the value of all marine fish and shellfish landings exceed one per cent of GDP. Denmark's fish landings, the highest in the EC, were worth 0.7 per cent of GDP in 1976 and this was twice the percentage contributed by the next highest landings, which were those of Ireland (0.29 per cent) and Italy (0.21 per cent) respectively. The figure for the UK was 0.18 per cent in 1973–6, and during this period Ireland was the only country in the EC in which the value of landings as a percentage of GDP increased (from 0.282 per cent in 1973 to 0.294 per cent in 1976): The proportion for France, West Germany and Italy remained virtually

TABLE V.1. *Total international landings in the North Sea of the main commercial fish (thousands of tonnes), 1966–1980*

Year	Demersal				Pelagic		Industrial		
	Cod	Haddock	Whiting	Plaice	Herring	Mackerel	Norway		Sand-eel
							Sprat	Pout	
1966	220	269	158	100	895	530	113		
1967	253	167	92	109	696	930	71		
1968	286	139	145	112	718	822	72		
1969	199	639	216	122	547	739	70		
1970	224	672	182	130	563	322	63	290	195
1971	315	258	112	114	520	243	86	385	404
1972	341	213	109	123	497	188	108	510	366
1973	228	191	140	130	484	326	262	461	307
1974	204	188	184	113	275	298	313	833	532
1975	186	174	140	109	313	263	641	664	445
1978	213	205	191	112	175	306	621	575	517
1977	185	151	120	118	46	259	304	455	803
1978	261	90	103	97	11	149	378	347	810
1979	231	87	141	143*	19	153	379	1	
1980	239*	101*	101*	98*	11*	95*	323*		

Note: These figures come from ACFM data tabulations, 1971–80. Those for Norway pout and sand-eel include landings from the Skaggerak and Kattegat. An asterisk indicates provisional data.

constant, while the Netherlands and the UK experienced significant decreases. These percentages appear very small when viewed in national terms, but they do not include the value added in processing and distribution. The share-added value can often be a multiple of 3, 4, or 5.

However, despite its small contribution to the GDP of many countries, fishing remains a politically sensitive and emotive issue for two main reasons. In the first place, it is an ancient industry, with strong traditions of independence and pride. In the second place, although its overall contribution to GDP is small, fishing can be an important local source of income and employment. In the British Isles and Ireland, for example, it is important in regions such as parts of the west, south, and east coasts of Ireland and the west coast of Scotland, the Moray Firth, Orkney and Shetland, parts of the Scottish east coast, the coasts of Lincolnshire and Norfolk in eastern England, and southern Cornwall. Many of these areas are physically and economically isolated from the mainstream of national economic activity. In many similar coastal regions on the periphery of north-west Europe, fishing ports contribute substantially to the income of their hinterland areas and provide employment, directly or indirectly, for a relatively large number of people.

In terms of habitats and methods used to catch them, fish may be divided into several categories, of which the most important representatives are listed in table V.2.

There are basically five methods of catching fish currently in use in the north-east Atlantic: hook and line; gill or drift net; trawl (bottom and

TABLE V.2.

Category	Species	Method
demersal food fish	cod, haddock, whiting, saithe, plaice, sole, megrim, hake	bottom trawl and seine
pelagic food fish	mackerel, herring, sprat (some)	mid-water single trawl and pair trawl; purse seine
industrial fish (demersal and pelagic)	Norway pout, sand-eel, sprat (other), blue whiting	light trawl and mid-water trawl
anadromous fish	salmon, sea-trout	drift netting, fixed nets
crustaceans	*Nephrops*, crab, lobster, prawn, shrimp	light trawl, and creels
molluscs	scallops (demersal), squid (pelagic), oyster, mussel (benthic)	dredge mid-water trawl dredge

mid.-water); seine (Danish and purse); and traps (pots and creels). Long lines and gill nets are not used on a major scale nowadays in this region; the former are still used to catch demersal fish in certain coastal regions (for example cod off Scotland), while drift netting is employed for catching migratory species of salmon in coastal regions and estuaries. Long lining is becoming more widespread and may even stage a come-back following the success of experiments with automatic baiting machines. The effectiveness of both trawling and seining is greatly increased by accoustic methods of fish-finding sonar, which are now almost universally used. Pots and creels, baited with fish, are used to trap lobsters, crayfish and crabs in shallow waters close to the shore, and are usually worked by small boats.

Present State of the Main European Sea Fisheries

Certain adverse factors have influenced fisheries generally in recent decades. One is that the operating costs of fishing vessels, especially the cost of fuel, have increased markedly since the oil crisis of the mid-seventies. This has put a premium on the use of smaller, very highly mechanized vessels and intensive fishing methods.

Economic problems have been greatly exacerbated for some countries by the progressive unilateral extension of exclusive fishing limits by Iceland, Norway and the Faroe Islands. West Germany and the UK, despite extending their own limits, have been particularly badly hit, and many of the larger distant-water trawlers, which were too big and uneconomic to use on near-water grounds, have been sold or laid up. In Britain, for example, some important fishing ports are facing serious difficulties, having been abandoned by the large trawling companies: for instance, in 1972 there were more than 120 trawlers at Lowestoft, but in 1979 the figure was down to 70 and in 1982 there were only 30 middle-water vessels; in 1975 about 120 freezer trawlers operated out of Hull, but by 1982 this fleet had fallen to 12.

The third general factor, which has added to these problems, was the length of time taken by the EC to agree on a Common Fisheries Policy (CFP). The fundamental difficulty was in reaching agreement on the broad allocation of catches (both in relation to quantities and species taken) between member countries, which needed to take into account historic patterns of fishing, loss of fishing grounds elsewhere, and the needs of regions heavily dependent on fisheries. The final achievement of a CFP in January 1983 should enable improved conservation measures to be taken, and has also enabled funds to be provided for the further modernization of fishing fleets and for further fisheries research. Nevertheless, the new policy does not provide a complete solution; major problems still exist, and the impact of the CFP has yet to be fully realized.

To analyse adequately the present situation, it is necessary to consider separately the main groups of fisheries shown in table V.2. Although herring has been fished for centuries, the exploitation of other pelagic fish such as mackerel and sprat on the present very large scale are relatively new developments. Before 1950, the fisheries of the north-east Atlantic were almost exclusively for human consumption. Subsequent years saw a large growth of 'industrial' fisheries (i.e. those producing fish meal and similar processed products for feeding to farm animals, notably pigs.) These industrial fisheries began with herring (though this ceased in 1976). Small-meshed nets are used to catch small species such as Norway pout (*Trisopterus esmarkii*) and sand-eels (*Ammodytidae*), thus utilizing a hitherto untapped source of fish production. Also caught, either deliberately or as an incidental by-catch, are young specimens of certain of the main species usually caught for human consumption. Herring, for example, are caught in the fishery for sprats. The overall result is not necessarily the best use of the natural productivity of the stocks. The market value of catches of industrial fish tends to fluctuate more than that of catches for human consumption, partly in response to the volume of imports of fish meal and other fish products from overseas and also to the availability of supplies of non-fish protein.

The best assessments that can be made about the present state of the individual fisheries of the North Sea and adjacent waters are contained in the 1980 report of the ICES Advisory Committee on Fishery Management. For four of the demersal species shown in table V.2 (cod, haddock, whiting and plaice) the conclusion is that although none appears to be in danger of collapse, the fishing intensity is still substantially higher, by a factor of two or three, than that corresponding to the Maximum Sustainable Yield. The high catches of certain years were caused by the occasional exceptionally good year-class and have not been sustained. The productivity of all four species, taken individually, would be improved if considerably larger mesh sizes were used in the trawl fisheries.

Cod

The cod fishery off Greenland has been an issue of particular importance in relation to Greenland's membership of the European Community, and is the cause of a legal dispute between Denmark and the Commission. Following a vote by the Greenlanders in February 1982 to withdraw from the Community, the Commission agreed to review the problem of access to the cod stocks. For 1982, a total allowable catch (TAC) of 75,000 tonnes was recommended, of which 62,000 tonnes would go to Denmark (to be fished by Greenland's fishermen), 10,000 tonnes would go to West Germany and 3,000 tonnes to Britain. Denmark insisted that the TAC should be reduced to 62,000 tonnes, all of which should be reserved for the

Greenlanders. This was not acceptable to Germany, which is heavily dependent on the catch of Greenland cod for its deep-sea fleet.

Herring

The collapse of the North Sea herring fisheries, referred to above, is self-evident from the data of table V.1. Until the mid-sixties the catch was in the region of three-quarters of a million tonnes annually. The herring stock in the southern North Sea had begun to collapse by 1954, while at the same time a predominantly Danish industrial fishery for immature herring was developing in the eastern North Sea. In 1964 the Norwegian purse-seining fleet switched their efforts to herring in the northern North Sea when the fishery for the Atlanto-Scandinavian herring further north failed. In addition, the development of technical developments which permitted single-boat purse-seining on the high seas allowed the Norwegian purse-seining fleet to extend greatly its catching power. Finally, the distant-water trawlers of several countries, with their access to traditional grounds off Iceland and the Arctic becoming restricted, found that they could profitably use large mid.-water trawls for catching herring congregating on their spawning grounds, particularly at the eastern end of the English Channel.

This enormous increase in fishing effort, superimposed on the traditional drift and trawl fisheries, caused rapid depletion of the stocks. From an estimated level of nearly 2 million tonnes in the early 1960s, the stock of spawning herring in the North Sea had fallen by 1975 to a mere 130,000 tonnes. The evidence that the reproductive capacity of stock had been seriously impaired by excessive fishing was incontestable and in 1977 a ban on all fishing for adult herring was imposed. This was lifted in the southern North Sea in October 1981 to allow a catch of 20,000 tonnes of herring during the winter season. By March 1982, however, the European Commission told member states to halt herring fishing as the TAC had already been reached. Unofficial estimates put the Danish catch alone at around 11,000 tonnes,[1] in contrast to their recommended quota of 1,000 tonnes. British fishermen, whose quota was 2,000 tonnes, are reported to have caught only 1,500 tonnes. Unfortunately the inividual quotas for each country were not legally enforceable, since the Council of Ministers had failed to agree upon the legislative proposals made by the Commission. Throughout the period, however, a by-catch of immature herring, taken unavoidably in the industrial fisheries for other species, has been permitted. Following ICES publication of scientific evidence showing a healthy increase in stocks, the ban on the North Sea herring fishery was lifted in May 1983. There is, however, no provision made in the EC's Common Fisheries Policy for the allocation of herring in northern and central belts of the North Sea.

To the west of Scotland, the Minch herring fishery followed a similar sequence of events, but the decrease in stock size which occurred in the mid.-seventies was diagnosed much more quickly. As a result of experience in the North Sea, the need for decisive action to close ICES Division VIa (the Minch and offshore areas west of Scotland and north of Ireland) to herring fishing was accepted without hesitation in 1978. By 1981 a major recovery of the stock had occurred and in that year a TAC of 55,000 tonnes was advised which was not much lower than the long-term average yield from this stock. The Isle of Man herring stock is the most recent to show signs of depletion and severely reduced TACs are now being enforced in this area.

In the intervening area—the Firth of Clyde—the herring population, which was once dependent on a now depleted stock which spawned in the Firth of Clyde, is now drawn from all the surrounding spawning stocks. Owing to the difficulty of quantifying the proportions of each stock, however, the Clyde herring fishery is managed as a separate unit, the size of the TAC each year (2,000 tonnes during 1979–81) depending on the state of the stocks in the adjacent areas.

Similar difficulties with the herring fisheries have been faced by the authorities in Ireland during recent years. Herring was until very recently the most important species taken by Irish fishermen, mainly because it is readily caught, easily marketed, and was relatively high-priced.

There are two main winter fisheries off the Irish coast: one in the Celtic Sea and the other off the north and north-west coasts (including ICES Division VIa referred to above).

Because of its relatively high value, herring was heavily exploited in the Celtic Sea, despite warnings by both Irish and international scientists that such excessive fishings could not be continued without depleting stocks. The declining catches then indicated that the depletion had become serious. As a result, quotas were imposed in the main herring fisheries, but at a level which scientists generally concluded were too liberal. The fishery was subsequently closed in 1977 and remains so. However, in October 1982 there was some controversy as to whether it might be reopened. The Fisheries Research Centre at Abbotstown, County Dublin, who had supplied the information to ICES in 1976 on which it based its recommendation for the closure of the fishery, recommended that the Celtic Sea should be reopened. ICES, however, maintained that further evidence of the recovery of the stock was needed and this view prevailed in Brussels. Table v.3. provides a clear example of the way in which a species reacts to increasing fishing effort.

The closure of the Celtic Sea herring fishery caused serious problems for the local fishing communities at Dunmore East and Kilmore Quay, who were almost entirely dependent on the fishery and who sought government aid to ease their financial difficulties. The anger of the local fishing

TABLE V. 3. *Fishing for Herring in the Celtic Sea, 1963/4 to 1975/6.*

Fishing season	Total catch (tonnes)	Fishing effort exerted*	Catch per unit effort (tonnes)
1963/4	3,786	502	7.5
1964/5	2,999	318	9.4
1965/6	3,553	389	9.1
1966/7	8,180	515	15.9
1967/8	10,947	643	17.0
1968/9	12,174	646	18.8
1969/70	16,673	867	19.2
1970/1	19,060	970	19.6
1971/2	13,724	1,179	11.6
1972/3	18,800	1,159	16.2
1973/4	10,697	960	11.1
1974/5	11,819	1,062	11.1
1975/6	6,582	1,063	6.2

* Number of fishing nights by pelagic trawlers.

Source: Sea and Inland Fisheries Report, 1975 (Dublin, Stationery Office, Prl. 614).

communities, and the strength of their case for compensation was increased by reports that vessels of other nationalities, ostensibly fishing for mackerel in the area, were taking as a by-catch (allowable under the existing regulations) a quantity of herring equal to that formerly caught by the local inshore boats now lying idle. Similar problems were caused by the closure of the herring fishery in ICES Division VIa. More recently (1982), and adding further to the herring fishermen's problems, large quantities of herring have had to be dumped at sea because of the lack of a market.

Mackerel

The mackerel fisheries have also been faced with problems. As herring stocks decreased, in the North Sea, and subsequently in other areas, purse-seine fishing was diverted to mackerel, at first in the northern North Sea and particularly in the area around the Shetlands in summer. Two stocks of mackerel mix to feed there, one spawning in the North Sea, the other to the west and south-west of the British Isles. Whereas the latter has, until recently, maintained its stock size, the North Sea mackerel stock has decreased every year since 1972, falling to a critically low level, in part due to exploitation and in part because recruitment of young mackerel has been at a very low level.

The principal mackerel fisheries are now in the Minch, off the south-west coast of Britain and off the Irish coast. Fishing pressure on the stock increased when herring fishing was banned, 606,000 tonnes being taken in 1979, 39 per cent in excess of the TAC. In addition, large numbers of small young fish were taken during the winter fishery off south-west England, which is potentially damaging to the stock. However, new control measures have now been instituted to protect this fishery.

On the west coast of Scotland, landings of mackerel in 1976, 1977, 1978 and 1979 totalled 14,748 tonnes, 39,558 tonnes, 91,740 tonnes, and 94,407 tonnes respectively. Mackerel is also landed at different ports to herring, and the fishery is now based mainly on a trans-shipment operation, referred to as 'klondyking', at Ullapool. Up to 30 factory/processing ships, mainly from eastern European countries, and 180 fishing vessels are involved.

The total catch of mackerel by Irish vessels also rose from 1,000 tonnes in 1970–71 to 50,000 tonnes in 1980–81, and fears were expressed by ICES and the UK Department of Fisheries that the species may go the way of the herring stocks. The total spawning stock of western mackerel in the waters from the Faroe Islands to France is estimated to have fallen from 3.5 million tonnes in 1973 to 1.8 million tonnes in 1981.

Industrial Fisheries

The last three columns of table V.1 show the catches of the three most important industrial species: sprat, Norway pout (a small fish of the cod family) and sand-eel. The figures for Norway pout and sand-eel include catches from the Skaggerak and Kattegat, but most of the Norway pout is caught in the northern North Sea and most of the sand-eel catch comes from the central North Sea.

Sprats are caught in the North Sea for canning, pet food, and for reduction to fish meal and oil. Small quantities are also used for immediate human consumption. Until the recent increase in landings took place, the former outlets predominated and the fish were caught mainly in coastal fisheries during the winter when sprats concentrate in estuaries. With the ban on industrial fishing for herring which came into force in 1976, the Danish and Norwegian industrial fishing fleets diverted to fishing for sprats in more offshore areas of the North Sea, most of the landings being used for reduction to fish meal. Despite the increase in landings, there had not, until 1980, been any evidence that this short-lived species with limited growth was being over-fished. As a precautionary measure, however, an upper catch limit of 400,000 tonnes was regularly set. That limit was never reached; yet there was a dramatic decline in the stock in 1980 and 1981, with a change in its distribution, the remaining sprats now being confined to the southern North Sea. It is not yet clear to what extent this decline has been caused by over-fishing or by environmental or biological changes. Until 1982 no regular stock assessments were made for either Norway pout or sand-eel, and no limits to their catch set, but so far they have shown no obvious signs of being over-fished. However, there is some concern about the effect on the salmon fishery of the industrial fisheries for capelin and sand-eel, which form a large part of the diet of salmon.

The total catch from the North Sea of fish for industrial purposes, which includes quantities of small herring, mackerel and some other species in addition to the three mentioned above, rose to over 2 million tonnes in 1974. Although catches have since declined to around $1\frac{1}{2}$ million tonnes, and although the market value of industrial fish is a good deal lower than that for human consumption, it is clear that economically, and probably biologically also, the growth of the industrial fisheries is important. This is especially so because they have to use small-meshed nets and are therefore liable to take, unavoidably as a by-catch, young undersized specimens of the species more valuable for human consumption. The worst offenders in this respect are the sprat fisheries, which frequently take quantities of immature herring, and the Norway pout fisheries which in some areas take large quantities of immature haddock and whiting. The problem of Norway pout intermingling with juvenile haddock and whiting generally occurs only at the immature stage; as the individual fish grow older, they tend to be found separately rather than intermixed. The problem of the by-catch has been the subject of contentious regulations by the UK during the CFP negotiations.

Salmon

Salmon is another species under extensive pressure, particularly by drift-net fishermen, and a brief consideration of the attempts and the failure to manage it provides a good example of the problems involved.

On the Irish coast, for example, drift-netted salmon accounted for 23 per cent of the value of all landings by sea fishermen in 1976; but by 1978, this figure had fallen to 11 per cent. As a result of this decline, very stringent controls were introduced in 1979 in an attempt to preserve stocks. In 1963 drift-net fishermen took only 25 per cent of the total catch, whereas in 1978 the figure was 71 per cent. This changing pattern of salmon landings over the years has given rise to serious controversy, since it represents a redistribution of a lucrative species between categories of fishermen. It was asserted that the drift-net fishermen were endangering stocks and that failure to control them would do irreparable damage to the industry. An equally important problem caused by drift-net fishing at sea is that it prevents the management of salmon stocks on a regional basis.

From a political and social point of view, however, it is difficult to reduce the number of drift-net licences and hence the number of fishermen. Many of these fishermen are otherwise economically disadvantaged, most of them live in the more remote or peripheral regions of the country, and the returns from salmon catches are an important part of their income. In many places, entire communities traditionally depend on commercial salmon fishing for the major part of their livelihood. Excessively stringent restrictions would therefore hit these communities hard, but equally so would a continuing decline in salmon stocks. The volume of drift-netted salmon in Ireland dropped from 1,482 tonnes in 1975 (valued at £Ir.2,048,000) to 836 tonnes in 1978 (valued at £Ir.2,831,000) and when these figures became available it was obvious that very severe controls were essential. An additional factor which complicates the situation further is the very high value to the tourist industry of the salmon caught by rod-and-line by visiting anglers in inland waters. In addition, a significant proportion of salmon caught in drift-nets are captured by unlicensed, and therefore illegal, nets.

In 1979 regulations were introduced in Ireland in an effort to protect the species. These include:

(a) A shortening of the salmon fishing season at both ends.
(b) An extension of the week-end close time to three days.
(c) Boats over 15 metres are not allowed to fish for salmon.
(d) The maximum length of net is set at 730 metres, except in Donegal where the maximum is 1,370 metres. This regulation is the same as in previous years.
(e) Depth of net cannot exceed 30 meshes.

In Scotland, salmon fishermen are equally concerned about declining stocks, and it is suggested that in some rivers, stock depreciation may have reached danger point. The situation here is different to that in Ireland, however, in that fixed nets are allowed but not drift nets.

In England and Wales the position is again different, there being (with one major exception) no licensed drift netting for salmon, and fixed nets are generally prohibited. The major exception is the salmon drift-net fishery off Northumbria and Yorkshire which has been in existence for over a hundred years and makes an important contribution to the livelihoods of a large number of local licensed fishermen. In recent years the use of highly efficient monofilament nets has caused problems about the catch levels. More recently, following complaints by Scottish salmon fishermen, the Ministry of Agriculture, Fisheries and Food (MAFF) examined the effect of fishery on Scottish salmon catches, the results showing that probably more than 94 per cent of the salmon caught in the fishery were returning to Scottish waters.

MAFF has now proposed that the fishery be restricted to within 3 miles rather than 6 miles from baselines; that the responsible management authorities should be required to maintain and enforce tight limits for drift netting and, to the fullest extent possible, create opportunities for coastal fixed engines (i.e. nets attached to the shore) to replace existing drift net licences; and that the Minister should have powers, to be used when considered necessary, to override local regulations by introducing at short notice emergency provisions for increasing the weekly closed times in order to protect stocks.[2]

In addition to the conflicts between salmon netsmen and river anglers, and the possible detrimental effect upon salmon stocks of the industrial fisheries for capelin and sand-eel referred to earlier, two further issues complicate the management of wild-stock salmon, and make sea ranching unlikely.

In the first place, salmon have been caught at sea for a number of years off Greenland and the Faroe Islands. These fisheries intercept salmon in their winter feeding grounds. The Greenland catch has remained steady for some time, and the present quota of 1,190 tonnes annually is likely to be reduced.[3] Until very recently, the Faroe Islands presented a more difficult problem. In the five years from 1976 to 1981 the Faroe Islanders increased their catch from 20 to 1,000 tonnes, using long-lines which hook large numbers of small fish, which, though returned to the sea, may not survive. Under threat from the Commission of the EC, which stipulated that Faroese fishing rights in EC waters were conditional on discussion of a salmon quota, the Islanders agreed to limit their catch. In return the Commission agreed to maintain the Faroese catch of other species in EC waters.

The second dispute is between salmon fishermen and seal conservationists, the former insisting that seals not only damage nets, but also consume large numbers of salmon. On the Scottish coast the numbers of the grey seal are reported to have greatly increased and concern has been expressed about the resulting mortality of salmon. On the west coast of Ireland salmon fishermen took matters into their own hands when in October 1981 they killed an estimated 150 seal pups and 20 mature seals on the Inishkea islands off the Mullet peninsula. There has been increasingly widespread public protest about the slaughter of seals, which undoubtedly contribute to the aesthetic qualities and scientific and recreational interest of rocky coasts, so the conflict of interests is likely to be very difficult to resolve satisfactorily.

Shellfish

Shellfish (crustacean and molluscan) fisheries differ from other fisheries in several respects. Shellfish are relatively sedentary, and most species are exploited locally by small-boat fishermen close to shore. There is evidence that lobsters, for example, exist in a large number of small stocks around the coast. International regulation is accordingly less important here than it is for mobile fish such as mackerel and herring. Most gear used in shellfish capture is highly specific and the problem of by-catch seldom arises. The major exceptions to this are the fishery for Norway lobster (*Nephrops*), which is trawled in the Irish Sea, the Celtic Sea, the Minch and the North Sea, and is frequently accompanied by a by-catch of small whiting; and the shrimp fisheries of the European continental coast which take as a by-catch large numbers of juvenile sole and plaice.

High demand for shellfish has increased their economic importance in recent years. Total shellfish landings in England and Wales, for example, fluctuated between 37,000 and 48,000 tonnes in the years 1973–8, but the market value of the catch increased markedly from £4 million in 1973 to £11million in 1978.

Year-to-year variations in spatfall (number of larvae finding suitable settlement sites) are thought to be the main cause of fluctuation in catch rate of escallops, queen scallops and cockles. Exploitation of such species as winkles and mussels is at present limited by difficulties in marketing rather than by biological constraints. For the more important crustaceans (lobster and *Nephrops*), however, the available data suggests that they are at present maximally exploited.

Heavy fishing pressure has reduced north-west European lobster stocks considerably, and catch rates and the average size caught have decreased. The ICES Lobster Working Group has concluded that the main priority was to increase the minimum landing size while holding fishing mortality at its current level, and they have suggested a minimum mesh size of 70 millimetres for *Nephrops* trawls.

Naturally occurring stocks of oysters have been greatly reduced during this century by disease, pollution and land reclamation. However, the rearing of oyster larvae under artificial conditions can now assure their continued availability. Other shellfish are also being cultivated, both on experimental and commercial scales.

Incentives in an Unregulated Fishery

The picture emerging from the foregoing assessment of the state of the fisheries in north-west European waters is both clear yet paradoxical. On the one hand, the economic conditions under which industries operate could hardly be described as favourable. Some countries and some kinds of fishing vessels have been hit more than others, but overall the various sections of the fleets have faced difficulty as first one and then another stock declined, or running costs escalated faster than could be matched by consumer demand. Climatically induced variations and other oceano-graphic and biological factors have caused major, and usually unpre-dictable, changes in fish stocks, to which the fishing fleets have then had to adapt.

Yet, apart from this, the biological evidence is also unmistakable: in nearly all the long-established fisheries, both demersal and pelagic, the present amount of fishing effort is two or three times greater than that which would ensure the highest average yield over a long period. To put it another way, half or more of the money, time and resources at present expended by fishing fleets is not just wasted, but is actually depressing the yield which could have been achieved with much less fishing effort.

This is not a new phenomenon: it is probable that the maximum sustainable yield (MSY) in some North Sea fisheries, notably for plaice haddock, and cod, was attained if not exceeded, before the turn of the last century, when sailing smacks still formed the bulk of the beam-trawl fleets. Certainly, by the 1930s the increased catching power of the Vigneron-Dahl trawl gear, with otter boards and bridles instead of a heavy beam, resulted in the steam trawler fleets of that period generating fishing intensities on the main demersal stocks comparable to those of the present day.

This picture is not unique to the north-west European seas. It is typical of the world's long-established fisheries that in the absence of external restraint, the amount of fishing tends to increase until the profit margin under which each vessel operates has fallen (because of stock depletion) to the point at which the economic incentive for further expansion has disappeared. Whether or not the stock is then biologically overfished depends primarily on the economic cost of fishing that stock; on how far the fishing grounds are from their ports of landing; on the vulnerability to capture of the species in question; and the market demand for it.

The driving force behind the intrinsic expansionist tendency of unregulated fishing is competition for a common property resource, the legal status of which permits free and open access for all states, in the absence of the establishment of any overall international authority. The subsequent assertion of national jurisdiction over 200-mile fisheries zones has reduced greatly the area of high seas and thus free access for all states, though fish remain a common property resource; the conclusion of the CFP establishes a regulatory regime for fisheries in the EC 'common pool'. However, outside the EC 'common pool' the situation remains that if a more efficient gear modification or fish-finding device is introduced by one vessel, it will give that vessel an immediate advantage over its competitors. As that modification is taken up by the rest of the fleet, the advantageous position of the first vessel declines, but the fishing intensity of the fleeet as a whole increases. Inevitably, natural variations aside, the average catch per unit effort of each vessel (including the pioneering vessel) will become lower than before the modification was introduced because the stock will be less abundant. If the resulting fishing intensity is already higher than that generating the MSY, the total catch will also be lower, although that is not a statistic that influences the short-term tactics adopted by individual fishing units in a free fishery.

The profitability of a fishing vessel (i.e. unit profitability), together with the availability of capital for further investment, are the major factors which determine the size of fishing fleets. If it appears that further investment in more fishing units would give a better return than alternative forms of investment, then there will be a tendency for additional units to be added to the fleet. This tendency may be encouraged by government policy in giving loans or grants to fishermen to enable them to purchase larger or better-equipped vessels. The same considerations apply to gear selectivity, where this can be varied. If, in the interests of making the best use of the growth potential of the species, a minimum permissible mesh size is laid down, it will release an appreciable number of fish of a size large enough to be worth marketing. An individual fishing unit that uses a mesh smaller than the legal minimum therefore increases its catch rate compared with its competitors; if the smaller mesh becomes widely used, it will intensify 'growth over-fishing' and possibly deplete the spawning stock to a point at which recruitment over-fishing becomes noticeable.

From this admittedly highly simplified analysis, it is possible to visualize something of the complexity of attempting to achieve rational exploitation of multi-national, multi-species regions such as the North Sea, Celtic Sea, Irish Sea and the shelf areas bordering them. The fishing industries of each country operate under different economic conditions and serve different markets and consumer preferences. Their fleets exploit a different 'mix' of species and use a variety of gear for the purpose. The distribution of the main fish species overlap to a large extent, so that the operations of the various national fleets are strongly interactive, even though they have their own characteristic preferences.

It is hardly surprising, therefore, that practical fisheries management and conservation in such circumstances is highly complex and strongly influenced by political considerations. Before examining these management problems it is first necessary to establish the factors governing the natural productivity of fisheries and how this may be influenced, beneficially or detrimentally, by fishing operations themselves.

Biological Productivity of Fisheries

The fishing industry, like agriculture, has to contend with a range of factors that affect its output and efficiency. Some of these are man-made, such as the economic, social and political conditions under which the industry, both catching and marketing, has to operate. Others are natural, such as the biological productivity of the resource which is being cropped and the influence on it of disease, the weather and so forth. The fisherman is very much at the mercy of factors beyond his control. This is partly because he does not own the resource he is cropping, and partly because the natural productivity of fish stocks is typically far more capricious than that of agriculture, except perhaps in marginal land farming or in harsh tropical environments. More important still is the fact that he cannot directly replenish the stocks, and the way in which he harvests them affects not only the present yield from it, but also its future productivity.

Most marine fish, particularly in temperate regions, spawn at a certain time of year, when conditions for survival of the larvae are optimum. The resulting progeny constitute the 'year-class' of the year and are recognizable as a 'cohort' through their subsequent life. When the fish become large enough to be fished commercially, the year-class is said to be 'recruited' to the fishery. Recruitment may coincide with the onset of maturity and some commercial fisheries, particularly of pelagic species, are based exclusively on annual spawning aggregations.

So what happens after a year-class is recruited to a commercial fishery? If the selectivity of the gear is low (for example a small mesh in the case of trawls) or fishing is intense, or both, a high proportion of the year-class will be caught while they are still relatively young and small. Conversely, if fishing is light or the gear retains only the larger fish, many fish will survive and attain their individual growth potential, but only a small proportion will be caught before they die from natural causes. Almost always the highest yield from the year-class throughout its life will be obtained at some intermediate level of fishing, the precise amount depending on whether the species is slow-growing and long-lived (favouring large meshes and light fishing) or fast-growing and short-lived (favouring small meshes and heavier fishing). If the intensity of fishing is greater than that resulting in the maximum catch from the year-class throughout its life, this results in 'growth over-fishing'.

In practice, a fish stock consists at any moment of a number of year-classes of different ages that have been recruited in the preceding years. Nevertheless, the same intensity of fishing which would have resulted in the maximum yield from any one year-class throughout its life will also result in the MSY from the whole stock each year, with one very important proviso: that the size of future year-classes is not affected by the previous intensity of fishing applied to the stock.

It is necessary to examine this last point further, since it seems at first sight paradoxical. The very high fecundity which typifies most commercially important species (for example, a large female cod will spawn several million eggs each year) and the correspondingly high mortality rate of the resulting young, mean that the relationship between the size of the parent stock and the number of recruits which eventually survive, perhaps several years later, to enter the commercial fishery, is very uncertain. Indeed, natural factors—predators, food supply, weather and general environmental conditions—have a dominant and often dramatic influence determining the size of the recruiting year class. The 1962 and 1967 year-classes of North Sea haddock, for example, the largest since age-censuses began in 1916, were between 20 and 50 times larger than the year-classes preceding or following them, and were the progeny of spawning stocks which were either below average (1962), or about average (1967). This is an extreme case; year-class strength in most fish species does not fluctuate to this extent, although large fluctuations are not uncommon. These fluctuations, together with other biological and environmental factors, are reflected in wide variations in the annual catch of different species. Such marked changes in catches usually occur only in the case of fisheries which rely on a relatively small number of year-classes. Among European-caught species, this occurs chiefly with pelagic species such as sprats, mackerel and herring, and Norway pout and sand-eels which are used for fishmeal production. The catches of these species can vary fairly markedly from year to year through natural causes. Stocks of herring and cod, for example, have exhibited erratic, indeed dramatic, natural fluctuations ever since the fifteenth century.

It is hardly surprising, therefore, that until a few years ago it was not possible to establish any consistent relationship between size of parent stock and numbers of subsequent recruits, nor hence to determine whether fishing was affecting future recruitment. Within the last decade or so, comprehensive age-censuses of fish stocks maintained over long periods have established beyond reasonable doubt that in at least two major fisheries, the north-east Arctic cod and the North Sea herring, sustained heavy fishing has been accompanied by a dramatic decline in recruitment. When this effect is superimposed on a stock which is already over-fished in the 'growth over-fishing' sense, the result is a rapid decrease in stock size and possibly a 'collapse' of the fishery as a viable commercial undertaking.

To summarize, biological over-fishing can be the result of:

(a) growth over-fishing, in which too large a proportion of each year-class is caught while still young and small; and/or
(b) recruitment over-fishing, in which the spawning capacity of the parent stock is insufficient to maintain future year-class strengths and leads to stock collapse.

From our present understanding of the dynamics of exploited fish populations, it can be said that in the long-lived, slow-growing species the onset of growth over-fishing is likely to occur well before the adult stock is reduced to the point at which its spawning capacity is insufficient to maintain future recruitment. In contrast, in short-lived species with a limited growth span, this may not occur until much higher levels of fishing intensity are reached, the balance between growth and natural mortality being such that nearly the same 'yield per recruit' is obtained over a wide range of fishing intensity. In such situations, spawning stock may have been reduced to a level well below that necessary to sustain future recruitment before it can be diagnosed, owing to a combination of the masking effect of year-class fluctuations and the time lag necessary for the cumulative effect to become apparent.

The biological fishery assessments prepared for the North Sea and adjacent waters by the Advisory Committee on Fisheries Management

(ACFM) of ICES, and transmitted on an advisory basis to the apropriate regulatory body of the European Commission or NEAFC, are of necessity based largely on growth and mortality (i.e. per recruit) calculations. On these are superimposed whatever limiting or qualifying assumptions can be made to take into account the possibility of a relationship between stock and recruitment. The most recent assessments of North Sea herring, which have led to a limited reopening of the fishery, are one of the few instances in which a formal stock-recruitment relationship has been incorporated.

In deciding whether, on biological grounds, the intensity of fishing should be increased, decreased or held steady, the point of reference is usually the level which it is estimated would generate the MSY or, if the stock and recruitment curve is not known, the MSY per recruit. Yield per recruit is used when the data which are required to estimate total catches in absolute terms are not available; for example, to determine the effects of a change in mesh size when only growth and mortality rates and selection factors are known. When absolute recruitment to the fishery is known or can be estimated with some degree of confidence, advice can be given in terms of absolute yields, i.e. as MSY, but economic, social, political and ecological factors, applied rationally or irrationally, may well have to be taken into account and may cause the fishery to operate at some other level of intensity. Article 61, part v, of the Law of the Sea treaty, for example, requires the coastal state to take into account, *inter alia*, the economic needs of coastal fishing communities and developing states, when determining the allowable catch of the living resources in the Exclusive Economic Zone. What can certainly be said biologically is that a fishing intensity significantly higher than that required to generate the MSY will result in lower catch per unit of fishing effort (and hence profitability) and, depending on the characteristics of the fish stock in question, may cause it to become unstable. Today the inadequacy of the species-by-species approach is being stressed. Consideration of the ecosystem as a whole, including prey-predator relations, is increasingly seen as indispensable to the formulation of a sound management policy and this is also taken into consideration in the Law of the Sea Convention (Article 61(2), (3), (4)).

Fisheries management options

Although a very desirable step forward, the existence of a Common Fisheries Policy does not mean that, at long last, all our fisheries problems will now be solved. There are many complex issues involved, and the management tools we have available are, even when applied in the appropriate circumstances, crude and unreliable. A brief discussion of some of these fisheries management problems and the options available may therefore be desirable here.

The impact of fishing on any kind on any fish stock is characterized by two principal factors, namely:

(a) its intensity, as reflected in the fishing mortality rate generated in the fish population; and

(b) its selectivity, i.e. the incidence of fishing mortality on different-sized fish of the same species, or fish of different species.

In principle, both factors need to be controlled to enable the MSY to be obtained from the stock, or to meet whatever overriding economic or social criteria may be required while still ensuring that the stock is exploited as efficiently, biologically speaking, as possible.

The fishing intensity is determined *directly* by the amount of fishing and the efficiency of the gear. For a given size of stock, the annual catch is an indirect measure of the fishing intensity exerted during that period. Control of catch, by setting national catch quotas, seems at first sight the most straightforward way of regulating the fishing mortality rate and this is the method recently adopted in the NEAFC/EC region and in some fisheries for a longer period.

The apparent simplicity of management by catch quotas is, however, deceptive. The catch that corresponds to a given desired fishery mortality rate cannot be predicted unless the stock size is known. To set a catch quota that will have known biological significance, it is therefore necessary to predict stock size at least a year in advance, and preferably for a longer period. In EC waters this has necessitated research-vessel surveys of pre-recruit year-class strengths organized internationally under the auspices of ICES. Even with the pooled efforts of several countries, these surveys are demanding and the resulting data are, inevitably, subject to some error.

Catch quotes also involve problems of other kinds. If intended to reduce the amount of fishing of an over-fished stock, they must be set initially at less than the catch that would otherwise have been obtained by the contemporary fishing effort. This leads to a contraction of the fishing season on that stock or to a reduction of quotas over the same period, although this may not matter initially if alternative stocks are available. However, if these alternative stocks are being fished to the maximum, the additional attack on them may cause a domino effect, with stocks declining in turn. Another difficulty is to decide how a national quota is to be divided between vessels in the fleet. A procedure in the UK is to limit the catch by individual vessels, usually weekly, and there is renewed interest in the literature in extending this approach to the concept of *quantitative rights*, or freely transferable fish quotas to each fishing unit.

An important disadvantage of any quota system, whether bought or allocated free, arises through the practice of discarding fish at sea. This occurs in most fisheries for unavoidable reasons such as complying with the minimum legal size for fish landed. However, under a boat-quota system it is not uncommon for a crew to select only the largest or otherwise preferred best quality specimens well above the minimum legal size and to return the rest of the catch (almost always dead) to the sea. In the Clyde herring fishery referred to earlier, it was suggested that twice the TAC was actually caught, though not landed.

The other approach to control of the fishing mortality rate is that of limiting the amount of fishing effort by some form of licensing system. Experience in the UK of this method has so far been confined to an attempt to restrict the fleet fishing the Manx herring fishery. This involved the Isle of Man authorities placing an eligibility criterion of participation in the fishery during the two previous fishing seasons before granting a licence for the 1977 season. The result was to allow only 100 British vessels, 24 Irish vessels and the Manx fleet to take the 8,0000-tonne TAC. Partly as a result of rising herring prices, the authorities gave way to pressure from producer groups to relax the entry conditions. There was also a proposal to limit entry to the mackerel fishery during 1980. Since the general exclusion of Comecon fishing fleets fleets, this fishery has developed spectacularly in about three seasons to provide around a third of the total British catch.

Limitation of entry is less effective in a multi-species fishery with vessels capable of switching from one stock to another. For example, the fleet now deployed on mackerel includes freezer trawlers displaced from traditional distant-water grounds, and purse-seine and pair trawlers no longer able to fish for herring, and is greatly in excess of the capacity required to harvest the mackerel. This is symptomatic of the over-capitalization that exists, for example, throughout the British fleet. However, this is rather an extreme case, and there are advantages, in terms of stability for the industry, to be gained from limited entry, even if the precise way in which the effort then distributed over the various stocks is not fully predictable or controllable. The question of allocation of licences might be dealt with by auction or by free transfer, but neither method is at the moment acceptable to the British industry.

It has been suggested in the UK that steps should be taken through vessel licensing to restrict entry to all commercial fishing. These licences would be endorsed to indicate the fisheries in which the vessel had participated in certain previous fishing seasons. This could be used initially to limit the number of vessels allowed to participate in particular fisheries in the future. They could also be used to hasten the process of attrition, by removing the endorsement whenever a vessel was not used for a particular fishery for which it was eligible. However, if this system was developed to the point where endorsements also specified a quantity entitlement, and these were made freely transferable, a system of quantitative rights would have evolved. Such a system would allow regional preferences of real and lasting benefit to be given, and is the most likely long-term basis for optimum fisheries management.

Some form of control of the size of fish caught is also essential in most fisheries. For those with a large growth span caught with a trawl or seine, such as cod and plaice, a much larger mesh than the minimum specified by present regulations would certainly improve the sustainable level of catch by a substantial margin, provided net material of adequate strength is used. The difficulty is that few vessels fish exclusively for these large species all the time, and the mesh size suitable for them would retain few if any of the smaller species such as haddock, whiting and sole.

The present minimum mesh size of 80 millimetres is very much a compromise weighted in favour of the smaller species, but even this is much too large for the even smaller fish caught for industrial purposes, namely sand-eels, Norway pout and sprat, and for herring and probably mackerel also. To the extent that these fisheries can be conducted in areas and at times when the young of the large species are not present, there is no conflict, provided of course that the small-meshed nets are not deliberately used illegally in other fisheries. The sand-eel fishery can be segregated fairly well in this way, but the distribution of Norway pout overlaps that of young haddock and other human consumption species to a considerable degree. The quantity of young haddock caught as a by-catch in the pout fishery became so large in the seventies that the UK defined, and the EC subsequently agreed to, what became known as the 'pout box'—an area in the northern North Sea to the east of Scotland, where juvenile haddock are plentiful and in which fishing for Norway pout has been banned. The tonnage of 'banned' Celtic Sea herring taken as a by-catch in the mackerel fishing has, as we have noted, been a cause of aggravation in the fishing communities affected by the herring ban.

The enforcement of properly selective fishing has always been a problem. Because of the ease with which the cod end of nets can be masked or doubled, thus much reducing selectivity, minimum legal sizes for fish landed have for long been imposed as a deterrent. The selectivity of nets is not, however, sharp or well-defined, and often large quantities of undersized fish are unavoidably retained, even when the net size is legal. Since, as already noted, virtually all die before they are returned to the sea, a considerable degree of wastage is inevitable. For this reason it is sometimes advocated that it would be better to allow small fish to be landed for fishmeal than discarded dead; but if that were to be done, the deterrent effect of the minimum-size limit would be removed.

No matter what strategies are adopted for better management of the fisheries, there is no avoiding the need for effective supervision, with powers of arrest or endorsement of licences at sea. With the largest sea area to cover, Britain's MAFF stepped up its surveillance of inshore fishing grounds in September 1982. In recent years Ireland has also increased its fishery patrol fleet. Nevertheless, the areas to be patrolled in total are so large that it has frequently been suggested that the task should be co-ordinated (or even operated) by the European Commission itself, and that it should not be left to the competency of individual member states. It is, however, unlikely that any policing policy will be successful unless the fishermen accept the necessity for the regulations to be implemented.

The management of salmon—a special case

Salmon, as we have seen earlier in this chapter, present special problems for future management of sea fisheries in several European countries, particularly Norway, Ireland, and Scotland. The MAFF Consultation Paper on the Review of Inland and Coastal Fisheries in England and Wales (July 1981) described the problem of managing the mixed fishery stocks of migratory (salmon, sea-trout, and eels) and non-migratory, or sea, fish as the main management problem in estuaries and on the coast.

The present state of knowledge about migrations of salmon simply does not permit accurate evaluation of the rivers of origin of salmon taken offshore or in coastal drift-net fisheries. Since this drift netting now accounts for nearly two-thirds of the total salmon catch, the likelihood of serious over-fishing of runs from some rivers approaches certainty.

All the evidence suggests that to increase salmon catches it will be necessary to curtail severely or even to ban the interceptory fisheries off Greenland, the Faroe Islands, Norway, Shetland, and Ireland, and possibly to reduce the industrial fisheries for capelin and sand-eels in the north Atlantic. A long-term research programme is also vital, backed up by a management system that would permit monitoring and control of catches on a stock basis. It is also clear that expansion of drift-net fishing has simply diverted catches from anglers and estuarine commercial fishermen, and prevented traditional management on a catchment basis. The rather ineffective enforcement of regulations governing drift-net fishing and widespread poaching in rivers suggests that total catches may be well above the reported figures.

The most urgent need is clearly to establish firm control over fishing effort. In the longer term, acquisition of the data required to identify catches by rivers of origin, and development of a rational basis for the sharing of catches by river system among anglers, drift netters and fixed nets, is also essential.

Even while the difficulty of regulating intercept fisheries in international waters remains largely unsolved, and capelin and sand-eels continue to be exploited, there is still a choice of some more limited control measures available to national fishery authorities.

A number of alternative policies, ranging from modest to severe, might be considered. If the number of licences can be held at present levels and the restrictions on size and composition of nets, and days of fishing, strictly enforced, the situation might to some extent be stabilized.

A second, tougher option would require reduction in the total salmon harvesting capacity. Harvesting of Atlantic salmon at sea by drift-netting is inefficient in both biological and economic terms. Moreover, virtually all of the growth in harvesting capacity in recent years has come from new entrants to drift-net fishing. It would seem logical, therefore, to reduce effort by cutting back on drift-net capacity. This could be done in either of two way (or both in combination). One is to implement vigorously those regulations relating to the phasing out of larger boats, most of which have entered the fishery fairly recently, and which have alternatives to which they can be diverted. In addition, it might be possible slowly to reduce the number of remaining licences by failing to re-issue them when licence-holders leave the fishery for any reason, for example on the death of the holder. Such a policy would be strenuously resisted. Nevertheless, it would be in the long-term interest of the fishermen themselves if the number of licences could be slowly reduced to a level which approximates to the fishing effort applied during the period when drift-netting was a traditional small-boat fishery. Finally, the most effective measure would be a complete closure of some salmon fisheries for periods long enough to permit recovery of the severely stressed stocks.

In addition to these measures, European salmon stocks require protection from illegal fishing and from pollution or habitat destruction. Protection from illegal fishing requires much more effective enforcement of existing regulations, affecting both the fisherman and the buyer. As long as there are both willing sellers and buyers of illegally caught fish, compliance will be low. Any effective programme to reduce illegal fishing must apply with equal force to buyer and seller alike, but probably the most effective means of protecting salmon from illegal drift-netting is to impose very heavy penalties which include not only fines and confiscation of gear, but also confiscation of the boat.

Control of pollution in rivers and estuaries is also essential. During the last century many salmon rivers in England became so polluted that salmon runs virtually ceased. In Norway, Scotland, and Ireland, most salmon rivers escaped significant damage, and current legislation and pollution-control technology are such that, if properly applied, no further pollution damage need occur. Indeed, in some English rivers, particularly the Thames, enforcement of water quality standards has resulted in a marked improvement, such as to allow fish to penetrate the tidal zone, and salmon runs have taken place since 1980.

Arterial drainage schemes and canalization of rivers pose a more serious threat to salmon stocks. Their effects are more difficult to determine than those of pollution, but are more dangerous to the fish in the long term. A paper prepared in 1982 drew attention to the very disturbing results which have emerged from the pre- and post-drainage studies on the major tributaries of the Boyne.[4] Only very small numbers of young salmon have become established in these rivers, and most of these are stocked fish. An undoubted conflict of interests therefore exists between the need to improve the agricultural value of poorly-drained land and the need to conserve salmon and sea-trout.

A useful step forward in this regard was made with the signing on 2 March 1982 of the Convention for the Conservation of Salmon in the North Atlantic Ocean by Canada, Denmark (for the Faroes), the European Community, Iceland, Norway, Sweden, and the USA. Two other states especially concerned with these salmon are Spain and Porugal which, it is assumed, will be included when they join the EC. The withdrawal of Greenland from the EC will no doubt be the subject of future negotiation.

The convention aims at providing the basis for international co-operation in acquisition, analysis and dissemination of scientific information relating to salmon stocks and for the conservation, restoration, enhancement and rational management of these stocks. To this end it established the North Atlantic Salmon Conservation Organization (NASCO), the headquarters of which are to be in Edinburgh.

The convention, which enters into force one month after the fourth ratification, applies to salmon stocks which migrate beyond the areas of fisheries jurisdiction of the north Atlantic coastal states lying north of latitude 36° N., though the precise outer limits are unclear. Salmon fishing beyond the national zone is banned, and further restricted to within 12 nautical miles of the territorial sea baselines (except for west Greenland, where 40 miles is provided, and the NEAFC area round the Faroes). Article 18 provides that the convention 'shall apply, insofar as the European Economic Community is concerned, to the territories in which the Treaty establishing the European Economic Community is applied and under the conditions laid down in that Treaty', in other words to the same areas as are subject to the Common Fisheries Policy. Canada has already agreed, in 1982, to limit salmon catches in the west Greenland area and the Faroese authorities had similarly agreed to abide by a quota for 1982 and 1983 in their zone.

It is intended that NASCO will *inter alia* establish working arrangements with, and recommend scientific research programmes to ICES as well as other fisheries, and scientific organizations. Although the council can initiate studies and measures, it is not given powers to manage salmon harvesting in parties' EEZs. Objection procedures are also provided concerning the regulatory measures for the international area, and enforcement is left to national means. However, despite these limitations, which are common to most fisheries treaties, the setting up of NASCO represents a significant co-operative advance in north-west Europe.

Existing Management of the Fisheries of the North-West European Coastal and Continental Shelf Waters

Government intervention in fisheries dates back to the sixteenth century. However, it is only in the twentieth century that international co-operation has grown as the combined fishing power of interested nations increased. The first convention which covered the north-east Atlantic was the 1937 International Convention for the Regulation of the Meshes of Fishing Nets and the Size Limits of Fish, but this was never implemented, except in the North Sea, because of the 1939–1945 war. In 1946 another convention, of the same name but commonly termed the Over-Fishing Convention, was agreed, although a further seven years passed before all the states concerned had ratified it.

The 1946 Convention was, however, of limited scope. Its remit covered only mesh sizes and the associated size limits of fish. Any regulation required the voluntary agreement of the member countries, and there were no powers for international enforcement. By the 1960s the persistent warnings of the fisheries scientists that control of the size of fish caught and gear selectivity were insufficient to prevent over-fishing was heeded, and in 1963 the NEAFC finally achieved sufficient ratifications for it to enter into force. Under this convention, measures to control fishing effort were included for the first time, directly by limitations on the amount, place and duration of fishing effort, and indirectly by catch limits.

These measures could be effectively applied only by unanimous agreement within the Commission and unfortunately this was never achieved. The NEAFC failed because its convention contained an objection procedure which allowed its member states effectively to object to the agreements reached by the majority at its annual meetings; objecting states were not bound by the agreed regulations.[5]

Under article II of the NEAFC convention, the ICES was recognized as the body providing impartial scientific advice to the commission, which administered the new convention; this advice covered assessment of the stocks and of the probable consequences of proposed policies for management, including lack of action. As a result the commission has each year received from ICES the best assessments that can be made of the fisheries coming under its jurisdiction.

During the first decade of the NEAFC, the commission attempted to formulate policies which used its wider powers of control of fishing activity, as compared with the restriction on mesh regulation and size limits of earlier convention. In so doing, it encountered the fundamental problem which had been anticipated by fisheries biologists and economists, namely that the criteria for achieving the MSY from a stock give no indication as to how that yield is to be allocated among the participating nations and fleets. The failure to act in time to prevent the collapse of the North Sea herring fisheries, described earlier, was largely attributable to the difficulty of arbitrating between claims for national quotas based on historic catches. The difficulty of reconciling the differing economic interests of member countries with an overall exploitation regime which is biologically sound was not confined to herring. The Netherlands did not accept the strong evidence for gross over-fishing of sole, nor hence the requirement for reducing the TAC for this species. It is perhaps as well that so far this stock has shown a remarkable capacity to maintain recruitment despite heavy fishing.

The mid.-seventies saw two major developments which had a direct influence on the attempts that were being made under the NEAFC to develop the regulatory framework for the fisheries under its jurisdiction and, indeed, on the status of the commission itself. One was the accession of the UK, Ireland and Denmark to the EC in 1973; the other was the declaration by the countries whose coastlines border the north-west Atlantic of a 200-mile exclusive fisheries zone during 1976 and 1977. As a consequence, the relative importance of the NEAFC and the EC in fisheries management and in the determination of policy changed dramatically. Until then, freedom of fishing on the high seas was the dominant legal principle, and it could be limited (for purposes of preventing over-exploitation) only by the common consent of the participating states.

The failure of the NEAFC referred to above, coupled with the growth at UNCLOS III of a general consensus in favour of recognition of coastal states' sovereign rights for purposes of exploring, exploiting, conserving and managing the living resources in zones up to 200 nautical miles from their shores, led to a further change of position by most European states. Following agreement within the EC, on 3 November 1976, UK asserted jurisdiction over fisheries in areas 200 miles from its baselines (including the use of Rockall Islet as a basepoint) in the Fishery Limits Act 1976.[6] Most other coastal EC members gradually followed suit.[7] Belgium intends formally to extend its limits, but deferred enactment of its Bill until the conclusion of the CFP, since it has the smallest national area and the greatest interest in access to the Community 'pool'. Some member states have fishing limits in other geographical areas, including in some cases overseas dependencies, but the CFP is likely to apply only to French overseas territories.[8] Iceland had extended its limits in 1972; Norway did so with effect from 1 January 1977. It should be noted that the actual extension was within the power of member states, not the Community institutions, and was linked, in accordance with the Council resolution recommending it, to the North Sea and north Atlantic; for the first time this introduced uniform fishery limits in those areas. The problem of establishing boundaries, however, where zones overlap between states opposite or adjacent to each other, was not considered within the EC; the boundaries remains formally undelimited. It will be seen in chapter X that the Law of the Sea Convention provides only a vague formula for the delimitation of such boundaries.

These declarations of national jurisdiction over fisheries, whatever the ultimate boundaries, severely curtailed the activities of the NEAFC, which has had to be renegotiated and reconstituted to accommodate the resultant reduction of much of its area of operation. Article 116 of the Treaty of Rome requires that in an international organization of an economic character its member states should proceed only by common action. The EC thus demanded that in future it should proceed in the NEAFC as a community. This required renegotiation of the NEAFC to permit the EC as such to adhere, since the existing convention provided only for states and organizations to become parties to it. The seven EC state members of the NEAFC (Belgium, Denmark, France, FRG, Ireland, Netherlands, UK) gave notice of withdrawal in 1976/7.[9] Pending conclusion of a new convention, the NEAFC was unable to set quotas in the interim.

As mentioned above, until 1976 the NEAFC, in spite of its general failure to cut quotas to levels recommended on biological grounds, had progressively extended the scope of its regulatory measures. From merely restricting mesh sizes, it progressively moved to use of closed seasons, closed areas, use or prohibition of use of specified gear and then to specification of a TAC allocated by an increasingly sophisticated quota system, eventually limiting both national and species quotas. However, the decline of some species, especially herring, continued, and it was widely suspected that many fishermen were disregarding the regulations and that their flag-states were either unable or unwilling to enforce effectively the nationally enacted NEAFC regulations. The system of joint enforcement described in our North Sea study was negotiated in 1967, but was put into effect only in 1972. Even then it was limited to mutual inspection; offending vessels could not be arrested when detected by a participating state, only reported to their flag state which retained the discretion to prosecute. The USSR did not concede until 1976 the right of other states to inspect suspected vessels below deck.

The failure to enforce NEAFC regulations stringently was coupled with the failure of the co-operative commission system to reduce fishing effort on over-exploited species to levels appropriate to effective conservation based on the MSY. The TACs of the NEAFC consistently exceeded those recommended by ICES.

The NEAFC established a working group to consider a new convention and submitted a new draft convention to a special meeting in 1977. However, it omitted several difficult issues which it left to the commission itself to decide, including the status of the EC within the new body, financial contributions and methods for implementing the new treaty. By the fifteenth NEAFC meeting, several member states had effectively withdrawn;[10] others soon followed,[11] leaving only ten members.[12] None the less, at its fifteenth meeting the NEAFC considered as ICES report covering a full range of scientific advice on stocks and asked ICES to produce the same in 1978 so far as part i of the report was concerned, i.e. covering stock assessment and management recommendations on stocks in the NEAFC area. However, it merely noted the 1977 advice without recommending conservation measures since the area now fell mainly under national jurisdiction. Part ii of the ICES report concerned biology, distribution and exploitation of major shared stocks in the North Sea; the NEAFC asked ICES to extend this for 1978 to cover other shared stocks. The NEAFC did agree that existing recommendations could be carried over into the new convention. It was decided to replace the ICES–NEAFC Liasion Committee with an Advisory Committee on Fishery Management to which reference has already been made; its structure is described later in relation to ICES.

During 1978–80, the NEAFC continued to wrestle with the knotty problem of its own future within the dramatically changed regulatory environment. In 1978 the UK convened a diplomatic conference on Future Multilateral Co-operation in the North-East Atlantic Fisheries; this did not succeed in drafting a new convention, but did agree a number of points: the convention area should remain the same; the new convention should exclude marine mammals, sedentary species and such highly migratory and anadromous species as are covered by other conventions: that voting and other procedures should remain the same;[13] that the new commission should be enabled to make recommendations concerning fisheries and control measures for areas beyond states parties' national jurisdiction (subject to objection procedures); and that for areas within states parties' national jurisdiction, the new commission should give advice only if formally requested to do so by the state concerned. This left only one major contentious issue—the EC's status in relation to the convention, since the USSR adhered to its habitual position that intergovernmental organizations cannot be full parties. This problem was finally resolved in 1980 when the USSR withdrew its objections to this proposal and a new North-East Atlantic Fisheries Convention was opened for signature.[14] The impending changes stimulated an interesting development, for the purposes of our study, in existing NEAFC practice; in 1980, for the first time, the NEAFC appointed an observer to attend 'future dialogue meetings to be arranged by ICES';[15] until then it had a practice of not appointing observers to other bodies.[16]

The new convention finally came into force on 17 March 1982 and the new commission, effectively replacing the old one, had its first meeting in November 1982. The new convention has now[17] been ratified by Denmark (for the Faroe Islands); the EC, the GDR, Iceland, Norway, Sweden, and the USSR, but four signatories (Cuba, Poland, Portugal and Spain) have not yet ratified.

Unfortunately, however, the net result of the changes in the NEAFC is that the wrangles on quotas which led to the old NEAFC's failure have been largely transferred to the EC forum, while the new NEAFC has no substantive powers in most of the area.

The International Council for the Exploration of the Sea (ICES)

Founded in 1902, ICES originated from proposals made in 1895 for international co-operation in marine scientific research,[19] based on a programme in which 'scientific investigation would be accompanied by a practical exposé of the steps to be taken in order to bring exploitation of the sea fishery more in accord with the natural conditions regulating the growth and increase of fish'[19] and thus increase supplies to European markets. The economic and scientific objectives were coupled from the start.

It now has eighteen members, including Community and non-Community states bordering north-west European waters. Its activities are limited to the Atlantic Ocean and its adjacent seas, interest being concentrated on the North Atlantic. It is a purely co-ordinating body with an exhortatory rather than a regulatory role. Its structure and general aims are discussed at greater length in chapter XI, including the many significant changes which took place at its 1977 meeting in response to new demands. One of these changes was the transformation of the old NEAFC–ICES Liaison Committee into the Advisory Committee on Fishery Management (ACFM) since the terms of reference of the former had altered following developments in the EC, NEAFC and national fisheries management; its composition was also changed to meet the needs of extended national jurisdiction over fisheries.

The ACFM's advisory function is being made increasingly difficult by the deteriorating standards of reporting statistics of catches and fishing effort by some member countries. This is a matter for concern, because without reliable information of this kind, effective management is not possible, however competent the science. Nevertheless, up to now the reports of the ACFM, and those of the various specialized working groups on which the ACFM's conclusions are based, have been of great value, with standards of scientific judgement and objectivity which are admired the world over.

For purposes of collecting and collating information, ICES divides its area on a grid system, each square of approximately 30 square miles being allotted a number in relation to which the scientific information is supplied. The system is, as a result, also used by the commissions who rely on ICES for their scientific advice (including NEAFC, the Oslo and Paris Commissions and the EC) and enables a detailed picture of the fisheries and environmental factors in the area to be built up, continually added to, and re-evaluated.

In 1979 the EC established its own Scientific and Technical Committee on Fisheries, which prepares an annual report on the state of fish stocks and on conservation needs, and which liaises closely with ICES. ICES thus presents the sole means of integrating the comprehensive advice on all fish stocks, their interrelationships and independences in, and bordering, north-west European continental shelf waters, a role vital to effective conservation and ultimate maintenance of the optimum utilization required by both the NEAFC and present EC policies.

ICES can also evaluate the effect on fisheries of other activities in the area, such as those causing pollution, and sand and gravel extraction, by making use of its other committees or working groups. ICES has also drawn attention to the need for continued dialogue between fisheries scientists and fisheries administrators, especially in regard to the new ocean regime. This has presented some problems, but ICES is taking the initiative to promote such discussions in co-operation with member governments and intergovernmental commissions which receive scientific advice on fisheries management from ICES.[20] Clearly such a dialogue is essential for the adoption of effective measures to conserve fisheries.

The European Community (EC): The Development of a Common Fisheries Policy

The unilateral declarations of jurisdiction over fisheries in 200-mile zones by north-west European states,[21] and their effects on the NEAFC's scope and membership, have enabled the EC to begin to develop and apply the Common Fisheries Policy (CFP) to this vast new area. The CFP is based on two regulations[22] extending the Treaty of Rome provisions, which were fully described in our North Sea study.[23] The resultant problems are considered below in some detail since they reflect on the suitability of the EC as a co-ordinating or management body in north-west European waters.

The first regulation established the principles of equal access and exploitation for flag-vessels of all member states in so-called 'maritime waters' under their sovereignty or jurisdiction and on non-discrimination between member states in the systems applied by them for fishing in these waters. The second regulation aimed at establishing common organization of the market for products of the fishing industry. Our North Sea study pointed out that the mutual concessions required by these regulations were not particularly great for the original six members, but that the CFP did not commend itself to the UK, Denmark, Norway, and Ireland, which had applied for membership before the regulations were adopted. On their accession to the Community, therefore, they sought concessions; some were accorded, though not enough to persuade the majority of the Norwegian people to endorse accession to the Community. The other three states, however, entered on the basis laid down in the 1972 Treaty of Accession, namely that limited derogations from the full effect of the policy would be permitted for a time.[24] This meant that firstly, in an inner belt of 6 miles of coastal waters only, they would be able to restrict fishing to vessels which fished traditionally in those waters and which operated from ports in that geographical coastal area as long as existing restrictions on fishing were observed. Only the three new member states and France and Germany have taken full advantage of this however; Belgium and the Netherlands retain equality of access, and Italy has used the 6-mile exclusive limit only around Sicily. In addition, in certain specified areas (where regional communities were specially dependent on fishing), an outer belt of a further 6 miles could also be reserved to local vessels. These areas included various UK offshore areas such as the Shetlands and the Orkneys, and areas off Denmark (including all offshore Faroes and Greenland), France and Ireland.

The EC coastal states, subject to these derogations, prima facie retained their national jurisdiction over the waters within their 200-mile fisheries zones and could subject them to national conservation measures, *inter alia*, as long as this was done without discrimination between other member states' and their own fishing vessels. The Community as such has no maritime jurisdiction and it is thus somewhat misleading to refer to 'Community waters'. However, as this is such a convenient term by which to refer to waters subject to the fisheries jurisdiction of member states, this phrase will be used hereafter to describe these areas. It should also be noted that the term 'maritime jurisdiction' has proved disputatious. The Commission and the European Court of Justice have taken a broad view of the Community's external powers to conclude international agreements as a community;[25] it has also held that the Council's obligation to determine conditions for fishing and conservation applies not only to fishing in the waters under member states' jurisdiction, but also to fishing by their vessels on the high seas or in the waters of third parties.[26]

In addition, the Accession Treaty (article 102) provided that from the sixth year after accession at the latest, namely by at least 1 January 1978,[27] the EC Council, acting on a proposal from the Commission, must determine 'conditions for fishing' with a view to ensuring protection of all fishing grounds and conservation of the biological resources of the sea. While this obligation was in ambiguous terms, there was some evidence for saying that the EC must adopt both a conservation and an allocation regime.[28]

It was not until five years after this date that a CFP was finally agreed, even though the time limit had expired and article 102 had thus been rendered academic as a legal basis of a CFP. Under article 103 the

Accession Treaty also required that the Commission should submit a report to the Council before 31 December 1982 on the economic and social development of the coastal areas of member states and on the state of stocks. In the light of that report and the objectives of the CFP, the Council was required to examine the provisions which might supersede existing derogations from the CFP.

The task of producing an acceptable regime governing the conditions of fishing in EC waters proved one of the most difficult and contentious issues yet faced by the Community: attempts to allocate equitably the TAC found in these waters so exacerbated divisions between fishing member states as to threaten one of the basic objects of the Community, namely 'to promote throughout the Community a harmonious development of economic activities . . . and closer relations between the states belonging to it'.[29] The delay in reaching agreement on an internal fisheries regime, however, did not prevent negotiations—and by the Community as such—with third countries. Until 1977 increasing numbers of new states had entered the area and since not all of them were members of the NEAFC, they were not subject even to that body's weak and inadequate controls. The serious threat of over-fishing which resulted was overcome by subjecting the area to national jurisdiction. It was recognized both in the so-called 'Gentleman's Agreement' reached at the Hague in October 1976, and in the Council resolution which endorsed it, that a concerted Community approach would make it easier to restrict and even eliminate third parties fishing in Community waters. This the Community swiftly proceeded to do;[30] foreign vessels accepted the reductions and even total bans without protest. USSR vessels left the EC zone, never to return, when it proved impossible for either the EC or the USSR to accept the drastic cuts proposed by each for their respective zones.

The Community experienced very much greater difficulty in negotiating internally than externally. It had to modify both its original and subsequent proposals for a CFP to meet the objections of the new member states, particularly the UK, Ireland and Denmark. The situation was enormously complicated by the unilateral extension of fishery zones by states, most notably Iceland and Norway. Access to these distant water grounds was then obtainable only by negotiation and the negotiations had to be conducted by the EC Commission. The UK found that failure to conclude a CFP prevented any agreements with Norway and with others since the quid pro quo for the fishing opportunities in their zones was uncertain in the Community zone. The UK had been the greatest loser from the closure of distant fishing grounds both in terms of quantity (378,000 tonnes) and value (158 million units of account), though Germany suffered the greater percentage loss (67.8 per cent). The greater part of the Community catch was also taken in the UK zone (about 60 per cent). Yet it could not make available to any non-EC states what was surplus to its own requirements or harvesting capacity in its own zone or even enter into negotiations with them on a bilateral basis except in rare circumstances.

The Commission's initial proposal was that the Council should fix an annual catch rate (ACR) for all stocks beyond a 12-mile territorial sea (in which fishing would be exclusive to the coastal state). The Council's total ACR, plus total catches allocated to the Community in waters of third parties, minus third-party catches in the Community zone fixed by bilateral agreements (with possibly a reserve being retained for allocation to cover exceptional circumstances), would be allocated in the form of quotas. The remaining TAC would be allocated by the Council among member states on the basis of their catch of species during an unspecified reference period, expressed as a proportion of the Community catch for period.

The proposals were immediately criticized as being totally unacceptable by the new member states. The UK for example, questioned the reliability of the catch figures used and their limitations to one year's catches (1973) when catches in other years had fallen. It was also highly critical of the absence of any recognition of the fact that 60 per cent of Community catches would be taken from the UK zone and that the UK had been a net loser from the closure of distant water grounds (a view later acknowledged by the Commission as a factor that needed to be taken into account).[31] The UK later contended that a further factor which ought to be considered was that it fished mainly for human consumption and not for industrial purposes. This was a point of particular concern to the Danes. They took the view that industrial fishing should not be a scape-goat, as if it alone hampered rational exploitation for human consumption. They pointed out that the Dutch and British had discarded some 34,000 tonnes of whiting in 1976 and 40,000 tonnes of haddock in 1977, ostensibly in the interests of effective enforcement of existing rules, though the discarded fish had little chance of survival.

In its final stages, the dispute over the CFP tended to take on the character of an Anglo-Danish conflict. But other member states too were critical either of the Commission's proposals or the British counter-proposals or both. The British proposal for exclusive rights in 'variable belts' or zones, varying in extent from 12 to 50 miles depending on the importance of the area to local regional fishermen, aroused particular concern among the French and Dutch. Both tended to see the proposal as a way of excluding their fishermen from traditional fishing grounds within 12 miles of the British coast. The threat was regarded as all the more serious because of the difficulties already being experienced by their fishing fleets. It should be added that the French fishing industry had been largely responsible for the 'Common Market means a common sea' approach adopted by the Community when it faced the problem of remaining competitive when stocks were beginning to decline, but French domestic demand was rising. Initially, indeed, only the Irish supported the

UK but even this support began to wane after 1977 in the face of the quotas demanded by the UK and the provision by the EC of financial aid to Ireland to enable the purchase of fishery protection vessels and aircraft.

West Germany, the greatest loser in percentage terms from reduction of access to distant water grounds, inevitably sought compensation in free access to Community waters and high quota allocations therein. It was also particularly interested in the conclusion of external agreements, for instance with Canada. Its distant-water fleet in 1980 and early 1981 was tied up in German harbours and it was said that to keep it profitable it would need to catch at least 80,000 tonnes of fish outside Community waters, including 10,000 tonnes in Canadian waters. It was particularly resentful, therefore, of the fact that Britain's stand on quota allocations and limits prevented conclusion of a six-year access agreement between the EC and Canada in 1980/1.[32]

Thus it appeared that, all too soon, the old economic and political wrangles over the allocation of fisheries which had so undermined the effective maintenance and conservation of stocks by NEAFC (since it so often had to compromise and set quotas higher than those advised by ICES, or face the use of objections-procedure by its members, thereby rendering the objectors subject to no quotas at all) were transferred to the EC forum, with similar dangers to the maintenance of an optimum yield of stocks.

During the second half of 1982, the Community member states considered a set of new proposals on access, quotas, the organization of a common market in fisheries and fish products and on structural policy. The proposals were acceptable to nine of the Ten, including the British; they were opposed by the Danes. Some progress was made: Community regulations for the control of catches were adopted in July 1982 and the Commission was able once again to negotiate with Norway for increases in the quotas for common stocks in the Skaggerak. But the Danish government, under strong pressure from its Parliamentary European Committee, rejected the Commission's main proposals and, indeed, held out for access to 20,000 tonnes of mackerel off the west of Scotland and for the issue of seven licences off the Shetland Islands, both new claims. It also insisted that its vital national interests were at stake and that, in accordance with the Luxembourg Compromise of 1966, it would not accept that the issue could be put to a vote.

In the absence of any Council regulation, the position was that on 31 December 1982, the derogation from the free access regulations permitted under the Act of Accession expired. This would have allowed free access to all waters under the maritime jurisdiction of the member states from 1 January 1983. In order to prevent free access to the Danes, other member states began enacting the Commission's proposals into their national legislation, allegedly in conformity with the European Court's judgment in the UK fisheries case of 1981.[33] France, Germany, Italy, the Netherlands and the UK all notified the Commission of adopted national measures. Those taken by the British were in fact put to the test by Mr Kent Kirk, a Danish MEP and owner of several fishing boats, who entered British waters and was arrested by British enforcement official. His request to have his case transferred to the European Court of Justice was refused and he was convicted and fined £30,000.

Faced with an increasingly complex legal situation, the Commission on 5 January 1983 provisionally authorized the measures adopted by member governments without prejudice to its formal valuation of their substantive merit. Denmark, in addition, announced the initiation of legal actions in the Court of Justice against the Commission and Britain. Trilateral meetings between the President of the Council of Ministers, the Commission and the Danish Minister of Foreign Affairs ensued. Faced with the pressures emanating from the actions of the nine and the Commission, and with the offer of minor amendments in the CFP package, Denmark finally agreed. On the 25 January 1983 the CFP was officially signed by all ten Community Fisheries Ministers.

It has been well stated that this was a major economic, political and legal event and that

Its long-term economic and political importance becomes apparent when one realizes that the CFP is the first common policy through which the Commission allocated a rare natural resource—fish. Its short-term legal significance results from the fact that the consensus eliminates the element for a major institutional crisis which might have opposed one Member State, Denmark, against all—or at least most—other Member States and the Commission.[34]

In essence the Danes had accepted a political deal, but it was one which also saved the Commission from the embarrassment of having to defend the legality of the national measures. The result was a further small step forwards by the Community.

Concluding Remarks on Fisheries

It is clear from the foregoing that many of the problems encountered by the NEAFC in attempting to formulate and put into practice the effective management of the fisheries of the north-east Atlantic are still present after jurisdiction over the fisheries of the North Sea and adjacent waters has been largely transferred to the European Community, and a Common Fisheries Policy has been established.

The main requirement is to bring about the restructuring of the industries while at the same time beginning the process of reducing the present excessive fishing-capacity which is being deployed in the EC area. It has been suggested that the obstacles facing the rational exploitation of a multi-national common property resource are such that it would be better to divide the EC area into exclusive fishery zones assigned one to each member state, and then to leave each country to manage its own fisheries and to arrange by negotiation to fish in one another's zone, if desired. Attractive though this solution may appear, there are several objections to it. One is that the task of reaching agreement on what would be a permanent and legally binding allocation of territorial fishing rights would presumably be at least as difficult as, if not a great deal more than, that of agreeing on shares of catches or fishing effort, which could easily be adjusted subsequently. Another is that any zoning that would have any chance of being agreed would bear little relation to the natural distribution of the fish stocks, most of which would range over several national zones during their lifespan. In these circumstances, the resultant fishing intensity that was effective on each stock would be difficult to predict and the incentive for a country to control the exploitation of young fish that moved into its area would be less than at present. Finally, such an option may be illegal under the Treaty of Rome!

There seems to be no alternative, therefore, but to continue to attempt to reach agreement with the current methods of regulation, treating the fish in EC waters as a common property resource. It is likely that a combination of methods will eventually be used, with the better features of catch quotas and limitation of entry being combined to achieve a more sensible and flexible management regime than would be possible by either method alone.

The theoretical ideal of the achievement of the MSY from each of the major fish stocks in the area is unattainable in practice, even if desirable. The prime requirement is to have sufficient knowledge and capacity to act promptly, so that a disaster such as the collapse of the herring fisheries never recurs in that or any other stock. Beyond that, it is a matter of a steady move towards smaller and more efficient fleets so as to realize some at least of the potential productivity of which the stocks are capable, and at an economic efficiency twice or three times the present.

In working towards these objectives, the situation under the EC regime is more favourable in at least some respects than under the NEAFC. One is that the EC has agreed to negotiate as an entity with outside countries which are important in the fisheries context, such as Norway and Canada, thus avoiding the disturbing consequences of the former unilateral agreements with individual EC countries. Another is that the EC has, in theory, powers of enforcement of fishery regulations; even if there is reluctance to use these powers, their very existence may be instrumental in bringing about a better compliance with regulations. Lastly, the CFP is not an isolated concept, but is part of the overall package of political and economic measures which apply in various forms to each member state. Whether these circumstances will facilitate the development of a better management regime for the EC fisheries remains to be seen, but it offers the potential of so doing, and enables social grants to be given to disadvantaged areas and to fishermen.

Whatever form of management develops in the future, it is certain that much will depend on sound and impartial scientific assessments of the state of the stocks and the likely effect of any proposed regulatory measures. Because most member states of the EC have their own fishery research organizations investigating the same stock, it is vital that these various sets of data are pooled and that the scientists come together in a neutral forum to agree on what can be said with reasonable assurance, and what has to be regarded as uncertain. ICES, through its Advisory Committee on Fishery Management, has provided just that forum since the late 1950s, advising first the Commission under the 1946 conventon and then the NEAFC. It is to be hoped that the European Commission in Brussels will continue to look to ICES to provide the scientific basis for its policy decisions.

Additional Marine Resources

In addition to the wild-stock fisheries, the sea's living resources also include marine algae or seaweeds which form the basis of a specialized and regionally important industry in north-west Europe. Seaweeds, traditionally, have been used for centuries in Ireland, Scotland, and Brittany as a soil conditioner and fertilizer. Cut, dried and added to the sandy well-drained coastal soils, the weed provides organic matter and essential minerals. On the Aran Islands, the soil itself was made by mixing sand with seaweed, and the small enclosed fields provided rich all-year grazing and renowned crops of potatoes and other vegetables, In the Shetlands, sheep graze on intertidal seaweeds in winter when snow has covered the land above the high-water mark.

There is a well-established industry in Norway, Scotland, and Ireland for the extraction from seaweed of algin, which is a polysaccharide used for a variety of pharmaceutical and food products. It is also possible that other substances of value to medicine will be found in seaweeds as a result of a renewed interest in their exploitation.

The basis of the resource is the quantity of brown seaweeds which grow on rocky shores throughout western Europe. These include the intertidal species which become uncovered at low water and the sub-tidal species which are washed up on shore after gales. A good growth of these plants is found mainly in sheltered areas since as a result of the scouring action of the waves on exposed coasts, little or no weed is able to grow. The sub-tidal species (principally *Laminaria*) form forests below low-water mark; these forests are deciduous and cast their fronds during May, when the wind is favourable. They are deposited on nearby beaches. Also, during winter gales from the west, whole plants including the stem of 'sea-rod' may be cast up on the beach.

Seaweed is exploited mainly by coastal farmers and crofters who cut the intertidal species on a falling tide and tow the raft of cut weed to a pier or jetty where it can be stored and collected for processing. The collection of *Laminaria* can be done only after a gale has brought in a fresh cast of weed, and is generally carried out using a tractor and trailer on the beaches at low tide. Only the stipe (stem) of the *Laminaria* is used for algin extraction, and the fresh weight of material processed amounts to 3,000–6,000 tonnes per annum in Ireland and 2,000–4,000 tonnes per annum in Scotland, the wide variation being due to its availability depending upon weather conditions. The actual growth probably amounts to several million tonnes, but so far no efforts have been made, or are contemplated, to exploit the weed directly on the sea-bed, independently of the action of storms. By contrast, on the coast of Norway the weed is trawled from the sub-littoral beds. During 1981, one Norwegian firm showed interest in trawling for *Laminaria* around Orkney, but there was opposition to the proposal on the ground of the possible long-term detrimental effect of such an operation upon the traditional hand-gathering methods.

The principal intertidal weed cut for processing is *Ascophyllum nodosum*, and this is exploited throughout the Outer Hebrides, on the west coast of Ireland from Donegal to Galway, and on the coast of Norway. Potential yield is approximately 35,000 fresh wet tonnes per annum in Ireland, and about 15,000 tonnes per annum in Scotland. At current levels of cropping, approximately 60 per cent of MSY is taken from Irish shores, and about 80 per cent from Scottish shores. In Norway, about 40,000 fresh wet tonnes of both *Laminaria* and *Ascophyllum* in total are taken annually. Overall, the algin-processing industry suffers from competition from South America, where the harvested weed can be left to dry in the sun, and from Iceland where free heat from thermal springs is used for drying.

The other marine alga which has been commercially exploited only on a small scale, but which constitutes an important potential resource, is *Lithothamnium* or maërl. Interest is centred on deposits off the coast of Brittany, England (Falmouth area), and Ireland (Galway Bay), where the alga is found in sufficient quantities to make commercial utilization worthwhile. Small quantities have been dredged off the coast of France since at least the nineteenth century, and in 1974 the amount had increased to 648,000 tonnes. Maërl is very rich in calcium, and possesses valuable properties as a fertilizer and soil conditioner.

The extensive deposits of dead alga are either formed beside the actively growing maërl, as off the coasts of Brittany and Ireland, or appear to be quite separate from the present-day growing areas, as in Falmouth Bay. In all cases, the banks require strong currents for their formation and are the result of the collection of dead material over very considerable periods of time. Replenishment of the banks is apparently very slow, since maërl species have been observed to grow only about 1–2 millimetres per year, and the formation of new plants occurs only as a result of the infrequent release of reproductive spores. In the long term, the effect of dredging will be to exhaust all supplies of maërl within the extraction zone, and to destroy the rich and productive animal community associated with living maërl (dead maërl is poor in living organisms) if this too is exploited. The slow growth rate of this alga means that replacement of the resource will not take place in the foreseeable future and indicates that it should be regarded not as a living renewable resource, but as a finite irreplaceable material to be exploited with care and forethought.

Sea-birds

On remote islands off the coast of north-west Europe some species of sea-birds have traditionally been harvested for food, but the resource is not a significant one in modern terms. Men from Ness in Lewis take an annual harvest of young gannets each year from the islet of Sula Sgeir, while puffins are regularly taken in the Faroe Islands. The exploitation of these birds, which was naturally regulated by the difficulty of access to the islets and sea-bird cliffs and by the small local populations which consumed them, has had no effect on their overall numbers in recent times. In contrast , oil pollution has killed far larger numbers of them.

Mariculture

Farming of the sea can be regarded as a 'natural' progression from the hunting of wild-stock fish and the gathering of naturally occurring shellfish populations. In the period from 1975 to 1980, world-wide aquaculture production grew by 54 per cent to 9.4 million tonnes, with farmed shellfish accounting for some 37 per cent of world shellfish production by 1980. For high-value species such as oysters, salmon and trout, it is already becoming more economically viable to farm them rather than to rely on harvesting the natural populations. Artificial rearing of trout in fresh water is already a well-established practice, and indeed is essential if regular supplies of such fish are to be available. A hotel or restaurant could hardly offer trout on the menu if it had always to be caught by rod and line! In the case of marine fish and shellfish, the advantages of mariculture[35] are that it not only has the potential to provide a more reliable supply, but it may be able to do so more economically. For some countries, mariculture has the additional advantage of being located within territorial waters or on the national territory, thus avoiding international disputes over the sharing of the harvest of wild stocks.

The significance of the contribution that mariculture can make to the economies and employment prospects of north-east Europe is an open question; for it is almost certain that however highly developed, it will never achieve a level of production equal to that obtainable by wild-stock species in the open sea. Indeed it is generally considered that Europe will be doing well if 10 per cent of all seafood is eventually obtained from culture operations, although some authorities would regard this as a pessimistic outlook, and argue that mariculture has a much greater potential.

The degree to which fish, shellfish and marine algae (for seaweeds also can be cultured) are manipulated by mariculturists varies enormously. Oysters and mussels, for example, are frequently moved from one area to another to improve growth and condition, but have originated in most cases as naturally-occurring wild seed, and may remain in a natural environment throughout their life cycles. The aim of the shellfish farmer in this type of operation is to obtain the greatest productivity from the natural environment at his disposal. On the other hand, most fin-fish under cultivation are spawned in artificial hatcheries from brood stock in captivity and spend their entire lives confined, being fed specially formulated food, being innoculated against disease, and so forth. The aim in this case is to 'improve upon' the natural environment by exercising greater control over the ever-present variables. The first type of approach is termed *extensive cultivation*, the second is *intensive cultivation*.

Intensive cultivation generally uses enclosed production units, intensive management, high-density stocking, specially prepared food and selective breeding, and it operates on the basis of a high capital cost, high operating costs, and high yield per unit area. Examples include salmonid culture in floating cages, eel culture in tanks using thermal effluent, and hatchery culture of seed molluscs. *Extensive cultivation* normally involves large areas, less management, low capital costs, low operating costs and low yield per unit area. A good example is the transplanting of seed mussels from the Irish Sea to Wexford Harbour on the Irish coast, from Morecambe Bay to the Menai Straits in North Wales, and the collection of naturally-occurring mussel and oyster spat (seed) in large areas on the coasts of France and Holland.

Extensive cultivation may be either *artificial* or *natural*, depending on whether the source of the seed or spat is a hatchery or a naturally occurring spawning population. When the source of the seed is a hatchery, we have what are termed *culture-based fisheries*, in which an animal is reared intensively during the early part of its life cycle before being released into the wild. A further extension of culture-based fisheries, and one which is practised with increasingly sophisticated methods, is *salmon ranching*. In this case the success of the operation is dependent on the ability of the salmon to find its way back to the river where it was spawned. Juvenile salmon are produced in hatcheries, they are then released to sea to feed and grow (free range), and finally, they are harvested when they return to the place of release.

The requirements of a successful mariculture development will vary enormously depending on which of the above types of cultivation is envisaged. It is very important, therefore, to assess objectively the advantages and disadvantages of each potential site or stretch of coast in order to determine its suitability for the proposed development, to assist in choosing a method of cultivation which will make the best use of the local or site characteristics, and to minimize conflicts with existing uses.

Factors influencing the development of mariculture

The success of mariculture in Japan, Spain, the Netherlands, and Norway is well known; while in other European countries, and particularly in Ireland, Scotland and England, progress is generally considered to have been disappointingly slow. It is fair to say that in these latter countries mariculture has failed in very many cases to justify the optimism, or realize the potential, so often ascribed to it over the past ten or fifteen years. Old established techniques have not always transferred with success to new or extended areas. New techniques have been developed, but many have failed to yield the commercial rewards suggested by pilot-scale research projects. In other cases, the introduction of new species and new techniques have increased production only to find the market unwilling to pay an economic price for the new product. With the exception of the very significant developments which have taken place in marine culture of salmonids, the returns from other forms of commercial mariculture have generally fallen below expectations.

Analysis of such failure is vital for further progress, and it is convenient to begin the analysis by considering the particular features of those countries where mariculture has become well developed. Five factors in common emerge from such an examination:

(a) They have a *good natural position* for mariculture in terms of climate, sites, stocks and water quality (environmental factors).
(b) They have a *strong seafood-eating tradition* and therefore a good home demand for seafood products (internal market).
(c) There is *strong government support* for the industry over the wide range of services and back-up facilities required.
(d) There is *good co-operation* among the fish farming units.
(e) There is a local *population with a tradition of fishing*, knowledge of the sea and skills in boat handling, and who are also willing to accept and participate in appropriate mariculture developments, including the possible restrictions of long-established 'rights' and habits.

The presence of all these factors is necessary to some extent. While the absence of any one or even two of them can be overcome by strengthening other areas, the industry will nevertheless remain weak and vulnerable.

Environmental factors

Climate and water temperature are the most important environmental factors. The west coasts of Ireland and Britain and the Brittany coast of France possess a moist maritime climate, and their coastal waters are warmed by the North Atlantic Drift which prevents icing and creates higher than average temperatures for such latitudes. In summer, the oceanic influence provides a cooling effect and prevents the water rising much above 17°C on the Irish coast where the annual range is between 5°C and 16–17°C. This range is ideal for cooler-water species such as salmonids, scallops and mussels, but falls just below the optimum for many other species which thrive on the French coast. The cooler North Sea water, especially in Norway, provides very suitable conditions for salmonid culture.

Wind and exposure to wave action are important factors when considering the location of floating structures, since a great deal of mariculture activity is based on rafts, floating net pens and hanging ropes. Ireland and Scotland have exceptionally windy climates. In addition, both of these west-facing coasts have a high and persistent rainfall. This causes problems when there is a run-off of fresh water in enclosed inshore areas and salinity can fall sharply. Species such as the flat oyster (*Ostrea edulis*) and the scallop (*Pecten maximus*) are particularly vulnerable to very low salinities. A further drawback in these areas is that high winds and driving rain make outdoor working conditions difficult for most of the year.

Site availability is, of course, a major factor in determining the location of mariculture. The present state of mariculture technology necessitates production in sheltered coastal waters, and within north-west Europe the coasts of Scotland, Norway and Ireland possess desirable characteristics with many sheltered deep-water inlets and island archipelagos. However, many of the best potential sites lie open to the prevailing westerly winds. If *floating structures* are to be used—as in intensive mariculture—the two main site-related factors to be considered are shelter and depth of water. Suitable locations are rare and in some cases either have been or are being developed by competing interests (Holy Loch—naval installation; Killybegs harbour—fishing; Cork harbour—shipping, industrial development; Waterford harbour—navigation). Many other factors also have to be considered including growth potential, currents, oxygen content of water, turbidity, biological factors (fouling, red-tides), bottom type and accessibility.

Cultivation on the sea-bed is much less vulnerable to lack of shelter, the main requirement being for adequate areas of firm, intertidal or shallow-water ground. Suitable areas of this type are available in Britain and Ireland, usually in estuaries. There are also many sites in Europe where *land-based mariculture* could be carried out using hatcheries, onshore tanks and artificial ponds. Future development of this type of mariculture will be dependent on the energy costs of the systems being used (i.e. how much pumping and heating is required). There are good but limited possibilities for using thermal effluent from large power stations; experimental work at Hunterston in south-east Scotland has already shown the potential to achieve elevated growth rates in artificially warmed water.

Finally, the availability of land-based services and facilities such as piers, slipways, phone services, fresh water, boatbuilding and marine engineering, fish and shellfish storage, haulage and distribution facilities, and processing plants both for mariculture and traditional fishing must be considered. In this area of general marine infrastructure, the position of the most suitable areas in Ireland and Scotland must be regarded as distinctly weak. Less suitable sites from the purely physical point of view in the south-west of England or on mainland Europe possess a considerable advantage in their infrastructure and proximity to markets.

Water quality

Water free from toxic substances is very important for mariculture, and this requires not only the control of landbased discharges but also the minimizing of maritime accidents, particularly those causing spillages of oil or other toxic cargoes. Industrial pollution has ruined many estuaries in the Netherlands and England; but extensive stretches of unpolluted coast can be found in Norway, Scotland, Ireland, and Brittany.

Nevertheless, the continuing development of industry on estuarine locations, together with expanding populations on the coast, and the effects of agricultural drainage and run-off are causing further deterioration of water quality in certain coastal and estuarine locations. While some organic enrichment is acceptable and even desirable for the growth of mussels and oysters, most shellfish will accumulate bacteria, viruses, heavy metals and pesticides on long-term exposure to small concentrations of such substances. It will be essential to maintain the quality of any coastal waters suitable for mariculture by means of monitoring, control, and appropriate planning.

Internal market for mariculture products

Norway, Denmark, the Netherlands, Belgium, Luxembourg, France, Spain and the UK all possess a strong seafood-eating tradition, although in the UK, particularly, the range of the seafoods consumed is narrow. Ireland, despite increasing its fish consumption per capita by 60 per cent over the years 1963–77, remains one of the lowest fish-consuming nations in the

EC (table V.4), along with Italy and West Germany. If the consumption of shellfish is considered separately, France, Denmark, Belgium and Luxembourg emerge as the major shellfish eaters, with Italy, the UK and Ireland following, and Germany consuming the least. The low consumption of shellfish in Ireland and the UK can be seen as a major factor in the slow development of shellfish culture in those countries. Both of them export a very high proportion of their fish production (Ireland exports 70 per cent of total production and a higher percentage still of cultivated species such as salmon, trout, oysters and mussels).

Constraints in the development of mariculture

In the north-west of Europe as a whole, the market for any mariculture operation is likely to be concentrated on luxury items with a high financial return. However, in order to maintain the high prices necessary to meet the production costs and to sustain the luxury image of the fish, the market must remain small; hence the scope for expansion is limited.

Some reasons for the success or failure of different types of marine farming in recent years have been briefly mentioned already. In many cases, mariculture failed to live up to expectations because those earlier hopes and targets were unrealistic.

Mariculture operations also compete with other activities for the limited resources of the coastal zone, and these are coming under increasing pressure from urbanization, industrial development and a growing range of leisure pursuits. The reclamation of estuarine and coastal wetlands, the discharge of sewage and industrial waste, and the spread of port-related industries and shipping movements have destroyed the mariculture potential of otherwise suitable areas.

Many legal problems have also been encountered. They differ in each country according to the particular legal code and tradition, but in general they revolve around the concept of ownership and exclusive rights to operate in the traditionally free and open environment of the sea. Various forms of licensing have been devised or proposed in order to solve the problems, but the legal principles are so basic that totally new legislation is required. The present constraints are very severe in the case of sea ranching of, for example, salmon.

A single mariculture operation may be affected by any one or by a combination of problems; overall the reasons for the slow development and partial failure of mariculture are complex. Nevertheless, four types of constraints can be identified:

(a) lack of scientific knowledge concerning the life-cycle, nutrition, and reproduction of species of interest;
(b) lack of an integrated policy for mariculture development; which in turn reflects the lack of policy for the coastal zone and its resources;

TABLE V.4. *Per caput consumption of fish and shellfish in EEC countries, 1962–1976 (live weight; kg per person)*

Year	West Germany	France	Netherlands	Italy	Luxembourg/ Belgium	UK	Ireland	Denmark
1962/3	10.9	18.5	10.1	11.4	13.2	19.1	5.3	28.0
1966/7	9.9	20.4	11.7	13.1	15.8	19.5	5.8	45.2
1970/1	11.2	20.4	11.3	12.4	14.8	17.8	5.3	28.7
1974	11.1	20.5	14.3	11.6	13.7	16.8	8.4	26.8
1976	10.2	21.1	12.7	11.7	18.0	18.1	12.4	26.0
Average 1972–6	9.9	20.5	12.6	12.1	13.9	17.7	9.9	28.3
Consisting of:								
Wet fish	9.3	14.6	9.2	10.1	9.5	15.8	8.0	23.7
Shellfish	0.6	5.9	3.4	2.0	4.4	1.9	1.9	4.6

Sources: (i) *Eurostat: Fisheries, Fishery Products and Fishing Fleet 1976–1977*, Statistical Office of the European Communities, 1979; (ii) O'Connor, R., Crutchfield, J. A., Whelan, B. J., and Mellon, K. E., *Development of the Irish Sea Fishing Industry and its Regional Implications*, Economic and Social Research Institute, paper no. 100, Dublin, 1980.

(c) administrative, organizational, and social difficulties which hinder the formulation of a policy on the broad front, and which in some cases have prevented a mariculture venture from becoming successful;

(d) the legal difficulties concerning ownership of the stock being cultured, whether on the sea-bed, suspended from rafts, in floating cages or free-swimming.

Mariculture policy

Experience in Japan and the USA has shown that harmonious development of mariculture with other uses of the coastal zone can be achieved only through a national plan which seeks to tackle the many areas of constraint and conflict simultaneously. Some countries are now preparing, or have prepared, national aquaculture programmes to guide mariculture development in a co-ordinated manner and to consider how mariculture should operate in the coastal zone and in the national economy of the country.

Problems in mariculture research and development are similar in several Western countries, and some degree of co-ordination between the present overlapping research programmes would enable effort to be concentrated more efficiently on the outstanding problems. Some collaboration already exists through the European Mariculture Society and the Conference on European Peripheral Maritime Regions, but this is only a beginning.

The two countries with the greatest unexploited potential in north-west Europe, Ireland and Scotland, need national programmes to consider the overall position of the industry and its conflicts with other coastal resources.

Research, development and demonstration

The lack of scientific knowledge referred to above can be remedied only by a programme of research, development and demonstration. Such a programme necessarily will be long-term and costly and will require a high proportion of public funding. The mariculture industry is still embryonic and largely unable to sustain research to the necessary degree except in those countries where mariculture has traditionally been a significant industry. Even in such countries, however, and Japan in particular, the industry continues to receive strong government support for research and development.

It should also be emphasized that, as in many other areas of resource development, basic and applied research must be integrated. The biological and technical problems that have hindered the growth of aquaculture are numerous and complex, and they cannot be solved on a piecemeal basis. Interaction between university research, government-sponsored or departmental laboratories, and the efforts of individual mariculturists is therefore a key requirement.

Government support

The full potential of the mariculture industry is therefore dependent to a considerable extent on government support over a wide range of activities, including research facilities, pilot-scale and demonstration facilities, advisory services, analytical services, pathological testing services, marketing advice, access to information, and education and training. Progress in mariculture development since the 1960s has brought fish farming to a point where it might be possible to go forward successfully and relatively quickly with some government support of research and development until the industry could afford to pay its own way. The appropriate legal, fiscal, and economic climate in which the industry can develop must also be provided by government. While a number of European governments have been consistent in their efforts to provide the required support and climate, the approach of others has been patchy and uncoordinated.

Some Conclusions

While human populations remained small and did not possess an advanced technology, the living resources of the sea could be harvested without endangering or diminishing the stock of living organisms on which the resource depended. Technology, from the steam trawler to the present-day fishing vessel equipped with a wide range of electronic fish-finding and navigation aids, has allowed the exploitation of new stocks to the extent that markets have to be found rather than existing needs met. This commercialization of the sea's resources, along with the urbanization of coastal lands discussed in chapter IX, has placed under severe pressure the vital living resources of north-west Europe's coastal and continental shelf waters. Instead of an adequate yield being available for every fishing community, there is, as we have seen a bitter and strenuous argument over the sharing of scarce resources. Scientific knowledge of the quantitative dynamics of marine ecosystems has failed to keep pace with our ability to exploit, and economic pressures have led to the disregarding of scientific advice based on what we do know. Such scientific advice may be adequate in a situation where long-term decisions can be taken with care and forethought, but it is apt to crumble under the onslaught of the race to harvest more. The principal hope therefore lies in greater sharing of scientific knowledge coupled with the will (and the necessary power) to control the exploitation of living resources at all levels. We also need more awareness, from fishermen particularly, that overexploitation can eliminate stocks, not merely of whales, but of many fish species as well, and can have a disastrous effect on the viability and livelihoods of fishing communities. The development of mariculture techniques may begin to take some of the pressure off wild-stock fisheries, but it is likely to be several decades before mariculture production makes a significant contribution to overall fish and shellfish supplies, and it will probably be concentrated on a few high-value species. Clearly, it will be a major challenge to manage rationally the biological resources of coast and sea—a theme which will be elaborated as we continue to examine the consequences of our other uses of these environments, and the limitations of the numerous *ad hoc* organizations which exist.

Further Reading

Comhairle nan Eilean, *The Fisheries in the Western Isles: A Study in Conservation and Development*, Western Islands Council.

Ireland, J. de Courcy, *Ireland's Sea Fisheries: A History*, Glendale Press, Dublin, 1981.

Scott, I. R. (ed.), *The Fisheries in the Highland Region: A Study In Conservation and Development*, White Fish Authority, Fishery Economics Research Unit, M & D Report no. 450.

Notes

1. *Financial Times*, 4 February 1982.
2. MAFF Consultation Paper on the Review of Inland and Coastal Fisheries in England and Wales, July 1981.
3, When Greenland withdraws from the European Community, a new quota agreement will almost certainly be necessary.
4. Bruton, R., and Connelly, F. J., *Land Drainage Policy in Ireland*, Policy Research Series 54, no. 4, Economic and Social Research Institute, Dublin 1982.
5. See Sibthorp, M. M. (ed.), *The North Sea: Challenge & Opportunity*, Europa, 1975, p. 106.
6. Fishery Limits Act 1976, Elizabeth II 1976, ch. 86; in force 1 January 1977. The Act extended British fishery limits to 200 miles from the baselines from which the territorial sea adjacent to the UK, Channel Islands, and the Isle of Man is measured. It referred only to fishery limits and did not establish the Exclusive Economic Zone proposed in UNCLOS texts.
7. For full details see Churchill, R., '200 mile limits: recent claims' *Marine Policy* 1 (3), 1977, pp. 255–8; 'Revision of the EEC Common Fisheries Policy', *European Law Review* 5, 1980, pp. 3–37, at pp. 9–12; Denmark, the Federal Republic of Germany, France, Ireland, Netherlands and Belgium have all now asserted 200-mile fisheries jurisdiction though only four did so by the recommended date of 1 January 1977. Denmark included the Faroes and Greenland.
8. Churchill, R., 'Revision of the EEC Common Fisheries Policy', p. 11.

9. The notices were not effective until 1977/8; FAO Activities of Regional Fishery Bodies during the International Period COFI./78/inf. 6, May 1978, p. 9.

10. Belgium, Denmark, France, Netherlands, the UK (December 1977), FAO, COFI/78/Inf. 6, May 1978, p. 9.

11. Norway (January 1978), Ireland, the FRG (1978); ibid.

12. Bulgaria, Cuba, Finland, the GDR, Iceland, Poland, Portugal, Spain, Sweden, the USSR; ibid.

13. An EC proposal that voting should be weighted in ratio to budgetary contributions was withdrawn.

14. On 18 November 1980; the UK is the depository state. The new convention is concluded between contracting *parties*, not contracting states, thus providing for EC inclusion. For the USSR's previous position, see NEAFC seventeenth report (1978) p. 2.

15. NEAFC nineteenth report (1980) p. 4.

16. See NEAFC's sixteenth (1978), seventeenth (1978), eighteenth (1979) reports, pp. 5, 5 and 4 respectively.

17. As at 5 May 1983.

18. For historical details see Went A., 'Seventy Years Agrowing: A History of ICES 1902–1972, *Rapp. Conf. Int. Explor. Mer.*, 165, 1972.

19. Ibid. p. 5.

20. IMS *Newsletter*, no. 24, Winter 1979–80, p. 12.

21. For a description of the events leading up to this and the relevant UNCLOS III texts, see Birnie, P. 'The History of the EEC Common Fisheries Policy', *Marine Policy*, 2(2), 1978. It should be noted that the UK Fishery Limits Act 1976 applies only to fishery limits, not to the continental shelf resources. So-called 'sedentary species' remain subject to the legal regime governing the latter, which includes molluscs and most crustacea within the definition. Strictly it could be argued that they are not subject to the CFP, being shelf not 'water' resources. However, they are not exempt from the Community rules governing the common market in fisheries products, even if they can be withdrawn from the equal access provisions. The EC has made no attempt to allot TACs or quotas for these species.

22. The original regulations 2141/70 (the so-called structural regulation) and 2142/70 (the so-called market regulation) were replaced in 1976 by regulations no. 101/76 and 102/76 respectively, though they remain substantially unchanged.

23. *North Sea*, pp. 109–13. For a good account of the history of these regulations, see Brown, E. D. 'British Fisheries and the Common Market', 25 *Current Legal Problems*, 1972; see also references cited in n. 1.

24. Articles 100–3 of the Treaty of Accession, Brussels 22 January 1972 (entered into force 1 January 1973), UK Misc. no. 3, 1972—part I (Cmnd. 4862–1). But there is some doubt concerning the EC's *obligation* to develop a CFP on these principles. See Churchill, 'Revision' op. cit. n. 7, pp. 4–5.

25. For a full description of the interpretation of these powers and the relevant decisions of the European Court of Justice, see Koers A. W. 'The External Authority of the EEC in Regard to Marine Fisheries', 14 *Common Market*

Law (1977), n. 269; also Churchill, op. cit. n. 7. 'Revision' pp. 95–111, for their exercise.

26. European Court of Justice in Dramer *et al*. Joined Cases nos. 3/76 and 6/76, 14 July 1976, p. 54 para. 14, and p. 37.
27. The precise date was clarified in the Van Dan Case, Cases 185–204/78.
28. Ibid.; see also Churchill, 'Revision', op. cit. n. 7, p. 14.
29. Treaty of Rome, article 2.
30. Birnie, op. cit. n. 21, pp. 108 and 112.
31. Birnie, op. cit. n. 21, pp. 114–15.
32. *Financial Times*, 28 January 1981, 'EEC Ministers Reject German fish deal plan'.
33. Case 804/79 Commission of the European Communities v. United Kingdom; Judgement of 5 May 1981, ECR 1045.
34. Editorial Comments 20 *Common Market Law Review*, 1983 p. 8.
35. The artificial rearing of organisms in water is known as *aquaculture*, and when this is carried out in the sea it is called *marine aquaculture*, or *mariculture*.

VI

The Use of the Seas for Transportation

Introduction

Western Europe has always been ideally suited to the development of shipping as a medium providing the cheapest and often the only mode of transport, with short sea-crossings separating Britain from the mainland of Europe, and Britain and Ireland from each other.

Since the mid-nineteenth century the volume of goods transported by sea has grown enormously. The use of iron, and subsequently steel, made the construction of much larger vessels possible. The growth of the petroleum industry had a very significant effect on shipping. The oil tanker became the largest carrier of cargo (both overall and in terms of individual ship size), and the turbine-powered ship drawn by steam generated in boilers rendered the coal-burning steamship obsolete. In short-sea trades the diesel-powered motor-ship predominated. Within the past four decades, the advent of very large vessels has made possible some considerable economies of scale as a result of their ability to carry large amounts of cargo over long oceanic distances, at relatively high speeds, at very low costs per ton-mile.

Vessels also began to become more specialized, and at present almost every ship is designed for a specific trade, commodity or function. The steep rise in petroleum prices which began in 1973 and 1974 had considerable repercussions on sea-borne trade, both directly and through its effect on the economies of the trading countries. Fuel efficiency is now at a premium, there is a surplus of vessels, and significant numbers of older ships have been scrapped, laid up, or converted to floating storage. Faced with declining freight rates, increased costs and much reduced profits, the shipping industry is undergoing a series of changes which make its future direction difficult to predict. Allied to these changes, the new Law of the Sea Convention has introduced many new elements of legislation which affect the shipping industry. Details of these can be found in chapter X.

This chapter is primarily concerned with the impact of shipping and port-related developments on the exploitation of other resources, the identification of actual and potential conflicts, and trends and developments which might cause additional problems and intensify the need for control or surveillance. The focus is the British shipping industry, but the overall picture that emerges is applicable to north-west Europe as a whole.

Current Developments in Shipping

The character of shipping, both world-wide and in Europe, has changed greatly over the past twenty years. Ships have become larger, and the increase in the number of container ships and roll-on/roll-off (ro-ro) ships has had a major impact on coastal and short-sea shipping trades.

Containerization has now penetrated general cargo markets throughout the world, and nowhere is this more evident than in the case of trade between the countries of Europe. Its most dramatic impact has been the concentration of port terminal activities on considerably fewer sites, and the need for much greater areas of land at each port. The increasing size of berths has demanded greater depth of water with the result that dock and terminal construction has tended to move from shallow estuaries to the open coast. The rapid turn-around needed for the economical operation of modern ships has also reduced the number of berths required, and this trend has been facilitated by the increased cargo-handling capacity of each berth. Ship scheduling is often much stricter so that the berths can be more intensively used than under conditions of random arrivals and first-come, first-served rules. Nevertheless, between one and two days, and occasionally longer, are required for container ships to discharge and reload cargo; much less than would be required for a general-cargo, non-container vessel, but much more than that required to turn round a ro-ro ship.

Ro-ro ships encompass a wide range of alternative cargo-handling and ship-design approaches; five major types can be distinguished:

(a) the multi-purpose ferry, carrying passengers, cars, trucks and other rolling cargo;
(b) the truck ferry, carrying mainly driver-accompanied trucks, but no other passengers;
(c) the trailer ferry, accommodating no more than twelve non-crew members and carrying predominantly road trailers;
(d) the ro-ro container ship, carrying a variety of rolling and non-rolling cargo, including trailers, but also containers, packaged timber and palletized goods;
(e) the specialist trade car carrier.

Ro-ro ships are generally significantly faster than load-on/load-off (lo-lo) ships and are also more expensive to build. Traffic accompanied by drivers can be handled at remarkably fast rates, and many ro-ro ferries can clear a berth within 60 minutes. The essential components of the terminal are a large area of paved parking-space and a ramp between the ships and the shore.

In the deep-sea trades, plying between European countries and those of other trans-ocean continents, a number of significant changes have also taken place. Containerization (lo-lo) has made a great impact, as has also the increasing proportion of bulk carriers. The carriage of crude oil and its products employs 44 per cent of the world's shipping fleet (measured in Gross Registered Tonnes—GRT), dry-bulk and combination carriers account for 26 per cent and a further 22 per cent is general-cargo and container vessels. The remaining 8 per cent comprises a mixture of passenger vessels, car ferries, liquid-gas containers, fishing and fish-carrying vessels, and a large number of miscellaneous ships.

With the tanker and dry-cargo markets in a slump and the world trade recession affecting the container trade, shipping companies have concentrated on cutting costs to a minimum. Since energy costs occupy such a high proportion of overall running costs, much effort has been expended in using fuel more efficiently. In the case of older ships, slow steaming brings substantial cost-saving and is widely practised for ballast passages or when a vessel is not under charter. For even older ships there may be no alternative but to scrap them. Forty large oil tankers with an average age of about 11 years were sold for scrap in 1981, equivalent to a reduction of 5 per cent in the very large crude carrier (VLCC) fleet. Yet several of these tankers were equipped with the latest safety and anti-pollution equipment. Some 75 tankers are also being used around the world for floating oil storage.

Other economies practised by ship-owners have included using smaller crews and registering their ships in countries where costs are lower. The latter practice, of using so-called 'flags of convenience', is an old one, but has taken on a new dimension. Strike-prone or inefficient ports, and ports which charge higher harbour dues, are also being avoided by ship-owners. These developments, and the others noted earlier, have caused enormous problems for traditional ports which have invested heavily in outdated facilities and surplus manpower. In Britain, for example, the two largest ports of London and Liverpool have suffered very badly, and Bristol, the Clyde Ports and Manchester are also in difficulties.

Moreover, the pattern of trade has changed in favour of continental Europe and, save for London, the ports listed are now on the wrong side of the country. The most profitable ports in 1978 were those handling short-sea ro-ro and lo-lo ships—the British Transport Docks Board ports (a surplus of 12.4 per cent), Dover (8.6 per cent) and Felixstowe (7.3 per cent). Manchester, Liverpool, and London are subject to tidal constraints, Dover, Felixstowe, and the BTDP ports are not. Furthermore the port of Dover is operated by a non-profit-making harbour board, and Felixstowe is owned by European Ferries, which provides them with a degree of commercial security. In order for ports to operate economically, it has been necessary to reduce the dock labour-force. During this period several continental ports have grown rapidly, in particular Rotterdam.

Other recent developments in shipping have included the appearance of hovercraft and hydrofoils for carrying cars and passengers on the short sea-routes between Britain and the European mainland. Specialist chemical carriers and liquefied natural-gas carriers have increased greatly in numbers. In 1966 the world fleet of LNG carriers was 150 with a total of 500,000 cubic metres, while in 1979 it had increased to over 600 ships with a total capacity of 14 million cubic metres. These too, however, were badly hit by the oil price rise and subsequent recession. Many new ships in Europe, ordered before the recession, have come into operation; and some of the older ships have been sold to Mediterranean, Middle and Far East, and Latin American buyers.

Some particular problems of the UK shipping industry

The UK registered fleet has decreased substantially in the past ten years—from a peak of 50 million d.w.t. in the 1970s to 37 million d.w.t. in 1980, though the world merchant fleet has doubled in size since 1970. The average age of the 1,200 UK ships is no more than 7 years old and the fleet includes a large number of specialized vessels. It is not being rebuilt at a rate which will maintain its present size. The decline of the UK fleet has been significant as a percentage of the total EC fleet (from 46.6 per cent in 1965 to 37.9 per cent in 1980), but most striking has been its decline as a percentage of the world fleet (19.2 per cent in 1965 to 6.5 per cent in 1980; see table VI.1). Tables VI.2 and VI.3 illustrate the change in numbers of ships and gross registered tonnage in European states between 1970 and 1980. The UK, Germany and the Netherlands, it should be noted, show a similar picture of declining ship numbers and a small increase in overall tonnage registered.

The total amount of cargo carried by the UK fleet has remained steady (377 million gross tonnes in 1973 to 384 million gross tonnes in 1979), but while imports dropped from 220 million tonnes to 157 million tonnes, exports doubled from 54 million to 108 million tonnes in the same period. These changes are due almost entirely to the shipping of North Sea crude oil (see table VI.4) and are reflected in the volume of traffic handled by the principle ports (table VI.5). The latter table shows clearly the fall in trade in the Bristol channel. Ports on the west coast and in the Thames estuary suffered considerably, while Tees and Hartlepool, Forth, Felixstowe and Dover gained trade. Changes in the type of trade have reflected the overall European developments referred to earlier. Ro-ro and container traffic increased from 29 million tonnes in 1975 to 42 million in 1979, the main increase being to the European mainland (12.9 to 19.4 million tonnes) and mostly in goods carried in road vehicles (10.8 million to 19.2 million

TABLE VI. 1. *Gross registered tonnage of ships registered in the European community states (excluding Greece) as a percentage of the European Community fleet and as a percentage of the world shipping fleet, 1965–1980*

Year	Belgium	Denmark	France	Germany	Ireland	Italy	Netherlands	UK
(a) as a percentage of the EC fleet								
1965	1.8	5.6	11.3	11.4	0.4	12.3	10.6	46.6
1970	1.9	5.8	11.2	13.7	0.3	13.0	9.1	45.0
1975	1.8	6.0	14.5	11.5	0.3	13.7	7.6	44.6
1978	2.2	7.2	15.9	12.7	0.3	14.9	6.2	40.2
1979	2.4	7.6	16.3	11.7	0.3	16.0	7.4	38.3
1980	2.5	7.5	16.6	11.7	0.3	15.5	8.0	37.9
(b) as a percentage of the world fleet:								
1965	0.5	1.6	3.9	2.6	0.1	3.9	3.7	19.2
1970	0.4	1.4	2.8	3.5	0.1	3.3	2.3	11.4
1975	0.4	1.3	3.1	2.5	0.1	3.0	1.7	9.7
1978	0.4	1.4	3.0	2.4	0.1	2.8	1.3	7.6
1979	0.4	1.3	2.9	2.1	0.1	2.8	1.3	6.8
1980	0.4	1.3	2.8	2.0	0.1	2.6	1.4	6.5

Source: Eurostat 1980, table 1-5 (1982).

TABLE VI. 2. *Numbers of merchant ships registered in European states (including EC Member States) 1970–1980*

Flag state	1970	1973	1976	1978	1980
Belgium	95	96	102	96	104
Denmark	874	1040	957	869	746
France	514	560	561	527	469
Germany	2409	1858	1553	1563	1491
Greece	1604	2382	2737	3386	3634
Ireland	47	54	47	54	63
Italy	1127	1255	1209	1150	1158
Netherlands	1173	917	766	670	655
UK	2355	2297	2133	1967	1780
Spain	755	803	819	773	804
Portugal	152	185	159	123	118
Norway	1860	2007	1863	1701	1537
Sweden	680	661	577	506	495

Source: Eurostat 1980, table 5-2 (1982)

TABLE VI. 3. *Gross registered tonnage of merchant ships registered in European States (including EC Member States) 1970–1980 (1000 tonnes)*

Flag state	1970	1973	1976	1978	1980
Belgium	974	1099	1427	1593	1698
Denmark	3013	4020	5009	5385	5233
France	5906	7990	10919	11846	11557
Germany	7519	7622	8971	9406	8053
Greece	10675	19218	24962	33868	39381
Ireland	152	216	187	194	188
Italy	7023	8698	10869	11279	10861
Netherlands	4989	4831	5650	4865	5345
UK	24689	29237	31927	29870	26103
Spain	2864	4327	5393	7415	7496
Portugal	721	1122	1018	1094	1208
Norway	18826	23355	27593	25674	21530
Sweden	4677	5618	7894	6423	4134

Source: Eurostat 1980, table 5-2 (1982).

tonnes). Over the same period, traffic between Britain and the other European countries increased, while the number of passengers travelling by sea to the rest of the world has been falling.

Port-related Developments

In order to cater for the increasing size and variety of vessels, and to provide additional land close to deep-water berths, many traditional ports

TABLE VI. 4. *Great Britain —Foreign traffic in crude petroleum (million gross tonnes)*

Year	Imports	Exports
1973	115	4.0
1974	112	1.5
1975	88	2.5
1976	84	13.0
1977	66	27.0
1978	63	35.0
1979	57	54.0

Source: *Annual Digest of Port Statistics* 1979, vol. 1.

TABLE VI. 5. *Volume of traffic, in million gross tonnes, handled by selected British ports, 1973 and 1974*

	1973	1979	% change
London	51.3	40.2	−22
Medway	27.1	18.6	−33
Tees, Hartlepool	26.0	37.1	+43
Clyde	18.1	10.1	−44
Bristol	6.0	4.5	−25
Newport	4.6	1.7	−63
Felixstowe	3.4	5.3	+56
Southampton	29.1	22.6	−22
Liverpool	27.3	13.1	−52
Manchester	15.9	11.9	−25
Forth	10.3	28.8	+180
Hull	5.6	3.6	−36
Cardiff	3.4	2.2	−35
Dover	2.8	6.0	+114

have extended downstream from their historic locations at the heads of estuaries. The most successful ports have been almost completely rebuilt, and around them in many cases are clustered industries which are facilitated by the bulk transport of liquid or solid raw materials or finished products.

The petro-chemical industry, including refining, has always favoured deep-water locations with extensive areas of suitable land for the construction of tank farms and process units. Milford Haven is one example of a port successfully developed in a deep-water harbour by the petroleum-refining industry. It was developed by Esso and BP to receive very large 200,000 tonne tankers (VLCCs). It opened in 1959. However, tankers had soon reached a size that even Milford Haven could not handle and the oil companies began looking for deeper water to accommodate the ultra-large tankers (ULCCs). Gulf Oil established a transhipment terminal at Bantry Bay, on the south-west coast of Ireland. Smaller tankers then transported the oil from the terminal to ports including Milford Haven, Le Havre, Cherbourg, Huelva, and Rotterdam where water depths were more limited. The terminal experienced an increasing through-put of oil until 1973/4, but declined from then onwards as a consequence of decreasing oil consumption and competition from other ports. In January 1979 the French-owned tanker *Betelgeuse* buckled and broke in two while taking on ballast alongside the terminal; the structural collapse of the ship was immediately followed by a fire and explosion which damaged the terminal to such an extent that its repair was considered to be uneconomical.

The exploitation of Britain's North Sea oil has, in addition to its effects on the import and export of petroleum referred to above, resulted in new oil terminals being constructed at Sullom Voe in Shetland and Flotta in Orkney. The former is by any standards an exceptionally large terminal, receiving 1 million barrels per day of crude oil via two 36-inch-diameter pipelines from the Brent, Cormorant, Dunlin, Murchison, Ninian, and Heath Fields. At Sullom Voe the oil is processed, stored and loaded on board tankers bound for other British and continental ports.

Other oil-related port developments have included the use of traditional ports such as Aberdeen and Lowestoft as service bases for exploration and production drilling. Expansion of this type of activity has been particularly notable at Aberdeen, where oil-rig supply ships have been in frequent competition with fishing vessels for berth space.

Another location in the UK which is likely to be developed for additional marine terminals and port-associated industries is the Cromarty Firth on the east coast of Scotland. Already the site of an oil-production-platform construction yard and a crude-oil stabilization plant and shipment terminal, the Firth possesses the required characteristics of deep water and an adequate area of industrially zoned land.

On the west coast of Ireland the Shannon estuary also possesses the necessary characteristics of deep water and suitable land. Recent industrial development in the estuary has included the expansion of an existing 600-megawatt oil-fired power station, the construction of a new coal-fired power station (900 megawatts increasing to 1,200 megawatts by 1987), and the construction of a plant for the processing of bauxite to alumina. Possible future developments include an oil refinery.

The primary consequences for other resources of these and similar port-related developments include:

(a) the loss of estuarine wetlands, intertidal rocky and sandy shores, and
.   shellfish beds, as a result of the 'reclamation' of land for industrial purposes;

(b) the loss of adjacent agricultural land, often of high quality, for industrial and transport purposes;

(c) the loss of fishing and recreational waters as a consequence of harbour development;

(d) discharges from port-associated industries and pollution from ships using the ports have contributed to a decline in estuarine and coastal water quality;

(e) shipping accidents and loss of cargo near ports have led to the fouling of beaches by oil and the destruction of sea-birds;

(f) the overboard discharge of garbage and debris by ships using the ports has led to the fouling of nearby beaches by plastic containers and other non-destructible waste, and to the fouling of the sea-bed by heavier items;

(g) the necessity to maintain deep water channels in the ports or their approaches requires dredging and the subsequent disposal of dredged spoil.

The loss of intertidal and agricultural land has long been a consequence of the development of ports and their associated industries. In this context too must be seen the impact and loss of additional land caused by the building of roads to serve the port and its industry. The consequences of additional vehicular traffic generated by the need to move goods to and from the port, particularly if ro-ro facilities are provided in the port, may also include air pollution and urban dereliction caused by traffic and the widening of streets. The effects of providing a supporting infrastructure can be more significant in environmental terms than the impact of the port itself or its industry. Particularly in scenic locations (which frequently possess the sought-after deep water for berthing), a sudden proliferation of housing and other developments can damage amenity and aesthetic value.

Proper land use and coastal-resource planning are essential if detrimental consequences are to be controlled; they may never be totally eliminated, but they can be reduced to an acceptable level depending on the particular location.

Harbour and port developments will by their very existence reduce the amount of water-space available for commercial or sport fishing, or for water-based recreational activities. Yet in most instances such losses have either been negligible in terms of the overall sea area available for these activities, or the developments have brought about compensating benefits. In Milford Haven, for example, marine terminals have been established and large tankers manoeuvre, discharge and load in a sea inlet containing semi-commercial cockle-beds, a herring spawning and fishing ground, and through which salmon and sea-trout ascend. Yet the fisheries have not been detrimentally affected. Bantry Bay also contains locally important herring and scallop fisheries; these were affected not by the terminal operations, but by the oil spillages from the *Universe Leader*, *Afran Zodiac* and *Betelgeuse* incidents.

In order to deal with such a wide range of issues connected with the development and operation of ports, some reorganization of port authorities has been considered necessary. In 1962, the Rochdale Committee examined the organization of ports in Great Britain and recommended a number of changes. The National Ports Council (NPC, now disbanded) was established under the 1964 Harbours Act, and its principal duties were to formulate and keep under review a national plan for the development of harbours in Great Britain, advise harbour authorities and the Secretary of State for Transport, promote training and research, keep statistics, etc. In its 1978 report to the minister, the NPC argued, though in vain, that the industry needed to maintain a central independent body such as itself to continue its very necessary tasks.

One interesting recommendation in the 1978 NPC report was that the case for a national Maritime Agency should be re-examined. It was suggested also that marine and port responsibilities should be under one minister and not two. It is significant that while there have been enormous changes at sea—in the size, draught and type of vessels, in the cargoes they carry, the navigational aids they have at their disposal, and their communications with the shore—there have been few changes in the shore-based organizations which deal with the safety of their movement as they come from deep sea through coastal waters to their berths. Most of the other leading maritime countries have a much simpler organization than that of Great Britain. The Japanese Maritime Safety Agency is a good example, while Britain's own Civil Aviation Authority, set up under the Act of 1971, with responsibility for safety, but leaving the ownership and operation of airports separate, could provide a lesson for marine affairs.

Appendix 12 to the report also distinguishes between the 'conservancy' function of a port authority (the regulation of ship movement including channel-marking and lighting, usually with the maintenance of dredged channels), which is fundamentally non-commercial, and cargo operations, the ownership of wharves, etc. The Rochdale Report, 1962, had suggested that these two functions should be combined, but the increasing number and size of ships carrying hazardous cargoes, and other changes since 1962, indicate the need for a new approach to shore control of, and assistance to, ship movement. A maritime agency, on the Japanese lines, could take on responsibility for the conservancy functions of ports and for most if not all of the functions of the marine division of the Department of Trade, the lighthouse authorities, and the coastguard. It would be essential to retain local autonomy as far as possible, but in fact most local matters at present need clearance with one or more of the various central authorities concerned with marine safety.

In 1978 there were 63 separate harbour authorities in England, Wales,

Scotland, and the Isle of Man, responsible for the safety of shipping in 96 harbours, 44 separate pilotage authorities, and 2 lighthouse authorities. Marine research was done by 6 different government departments and their subsidiary bodies, various research councils and associations, and a number of other bodies, with insufficient co-ordination. This plethora of bodies with a marine safety function leads to problems of training and management, career prospects and, on an operational level, to different standards of marine traffic services, and conflicting boundaries (e.g. different port and pilotage limits), which leads to such anomalies as some ports displaying entry signals with a meaning directly opposite to the signals of neighbouring ports.

Towards Cleaner Shipping Operations

Shipping is not intrinsically a 'dirty' industry, yet it has become associated with pollution of the sea and coast, particularly by oil. Apart from accidents, such operational pollution constitutes the most noticeable impact of shipping on the marine environment. IMO has consequently enacted a number of conventions in this field, details of which can be found in chapter X.

Following the change from coal-burning to oil-burning and diesel-motor ships, small discharges of oil regularly accompanied movements of shipping. Oil tankers added to the amount of oil discharged at sea because of the need to wash tanks used for ballast. Since washing, or the discharge of oily ballast, cannot take place in port unless special reception facilities are available, tank-cleaning usually takes place at sea. Some dry-cargo vessels will occasionally use empty but dirty fuel-tanks to hold ballast, while all ships have to discharge oily bilge-water periodically. In addition, spillages of oil occur during the course of on-board fuel-transfer operations, during bunkering in ports or during the handling of oil cargo at terminals. Most spillages which occur in ports or at anchorage under the control of a harbour authority can be assigned to a particular vessel; operational spillages at sea are rarely so attributable, and their control therefore requires a different approach.

Concern about pollution caused by tankers discharging tank washings and oily ballast led to the introduction in the early 1960s of a technique for separating the oil residues from the water in the cargo tanks and retaining the residues in a holding tank or 'slop' tank (usually one of the cargo tanks designated for this purpose). In general, it is possible for the next cargo of crude oil to be loaded on top of these residues, thus giving the procedure its name of 'Load on Top' (LOT). Its use enables nearly all the oil that would otherwise be discharged into the sea to be retained on board, with both economic and environmental benefit, but this procedure is not suitable for short journeys, such as across the Mediterranean or North Sea, and this fact is responsible for much of the illegal discharges which occur.

Crude Oil Washing (COW) is a relatively recent innovation developed in part as a response to the practical problems of operating the LOT system. The technique is based on the use of the crude oil itself as a tank-cleaning agent during discharge. COW has considerable incidental advantages as an efficient first stage in tank cleaning, but to be fully effective it must be followed by tank washing with seawater and the LOT procedure applied. The main difficulty with the COW technique is the need to ensure the correct operation of an inert gas generator. Recent in-port inspections of tankers by the Health and Safety Executive in the UK have revealed a significant proportion of ships with incorrectly operated and dangerous inert-gas systems.

Many new crude-oil tankers are now fitted with segregated ballast tanks (SBT) designed for the sole purpose of holding clean ballast water. Separate pumps and piping systems are also fitted to ensure that contamination of the ballast is prevented. But under adverse weather conditions, additional ballast has to be carried in cargo tanks; thus SBT can never eliminate the need to handle dirty ballast water except possibly in the summer months. Clean ballast tanks (CBT) are cargo tanks used only for ballast and maintained in an oil-free condition. In practice, CBT are an interim measure to facilitate the introduction of SBT and to achieve the aims of SBT on existing tankers without incurring the heavy costs of installing a truly segregated system.

Oil–water separators are used on board many vessels (including dry-cargo ships) to remove oil from bilge water before it is discharged, or to clean dirty ballast which has been held in empty fuel or bunker tanks. However, they are costly to install and, with the exception of vessels over 80 GRT using fuel tanks for ballast water, ships are not required to have them. The International Chamber of Shipping has recently produced a voluntary code of practice recommending that ships fit separators in order to comply with the standards of the 1973 International Convention for the Prevention of Pollution from Ships (MARPOL 1973).

Reception facilities in ports[1] are also essential for the reduction of operational discharges of oil or oily water. In major oil ports and at oil-storage sites, facilities are generally provided by the oil industry to receive and process dirty ballast-water. In other ports, facilities may be provided by port authorities or the municipality. Nevertheless, many ports and harbours are not equipped with any facilities at all, and the waste oil from ships, fishing vessels, and pleasure craft is simply dumped overboard. Even where facilities for receiving waste oil are provided, they do not entirely eradicate discharges; there are many reasons why a vessel may pump waste oil or dirty ballast overboard at sea. As the transport of chemical cargoes in bulk also increases, specialized reception facilities for residues and wastes are needed, but in most cases these are provided by the relevant industry.

In addition to tank washings and oily bilge-water, the operation of ships also leads to the discharge of sewage and garbage. The problem of sewage from ships is not a serious one; at sea, the sewage is rapidly dispersed and degraded, while in port it may be held temporarily in tanks or, if discharged, is small in volume compared to the sewage discharges which are common in most ports. Litter and garbage is a more widespread problem. Litter on beaches is seemingly ubiquitous throughout Europe and most of it comes from ships. Local coastal authorities have therefore a continuous job in cleansing them. Floating refuse in estuaries and coastal waters is not only unsightly, but it also poses possible dangers to fishing and pleasure craft.

The procedures and equipment designed to prevent operational pollution from ships would be useless without adequate training and commitment by the officers and crew. Causes of incorrect operation of equipment include failure to understand the equipment or the instructions for using it, inadequate command of the appropriate language, lack of proper allocation of responsibility for its use, or simply human error. Efforts made by the shipping industry to cut costs have included a reduction in the number of crew on board and an increasing degree of automation of engine-room and other equipment. The use of more complex equipment, particularly in areas of high shipping density, has added to the need for a higher level of vigilance and increased training requirements. Excessive reliance on the equipment, and failure to detect possible malfunctions at an early stage may lead not only to pollution but also to accidents. There is evidence that standards of crew manning and competence have declined, despite the efforts being made by the ILO and IMO to establish international standards through international conventions and codes of practice. The most important of the conventions is the IMO International Convention on Standards of Training, Certification and Watchkeeping for Seafarers 1978 (STCW) which came into force in April 1984. It lays down basic principles to be observed in keeping navigational and engine-room watches, and it contains mandatory minimum requirements for the certification of masters and officers. Separate certificates are required for flammable/combustible substances, dangerous liquids and liquefied gas; and ships carrying these substances in bulk are required to have as Master, Second-in-Command and Chief and Second Engineers, officers whose certificates carry endorsements appropriate to the type of cargo being carried. The convention has a particularly important role to play in the prevention of accidents at sea. A second major convention in this field is the Minimum Standards in Merchant Ships 1976, drawn up by the ILO. A further useful development is the establishment by IMO of a World Maritime University, opened on 4 July 1983 (see chapter X).

Finally, in order to ensure compliance with regulations, and to check the general condition of ships carrying dangerous or polluting cargoes, it is essential that countries in whose ports the ships are loading or discharging should be given stronger powers to inspect and, if necessary, to detain any ships which do not meet certain standards. Under the conventions already in force, port states have powers to inspect vessels voluntarily in their ports to ensure compliance with international requirements; such inspection is restricted largely to safety certificates and to oil record books. The 1978 STCW Convention, among other things, increased the powers of port states to inspect and, if necessary, to detain foreign vessels in port. These strengthened powers of inspection and detention are a welcome step in the prevention of pollution and accidents, but it remains to be seen how effective they will be in practice. Delay to a vessel is very costly for the owner, and harbour authorities may be reluctant to enforce the new regulations. Moreover, while effective inspection is obviously crucial, the world-wide economic recession has led to a reduction in the number of inspectors.

The Prevention of Shipping Accidents

In earlier decades a shipwreck on the coast frequently brought material benefits to the local population; now it is more likely to bring pollution by oil or chemicals, damage to fisheries or amenities, or injury to persons opening containers washed up on nearby beaches. The prevention of shipping accidents therefore becomes not merely a question of saving lives, ships and cargoes, but of avoiding destruction of port facilities or pollution of the sea.

Despite advances in shipping technology, the number and tonnage of ships lost continues to increase even though the percentage of ships lost has decreased (table VI.6). An analysis of world merchant-shipping losses for the years 1967 to 1975 shows that during this period some countries had five times as many ship losses per number of ships at risk as had other countries. Loss rates and serious casualties involving tankers of more than 10,000 dead-weight tonnes also show that ships registered in certain countries were more at risk (table VI.7). A study of loss rates in merchant

TABLE VI.6. *Shipping losses worldwide, 1950 and 1979*

	1950	1979
Number of ships in service	30,852	71,129
Number of ships lost	222	400
% of ships lost	0.71	0.56
Tonnage in service (GRT)	260,026	2,034,000
% of tonnage lost	0.31	0.49

TABLE VI. 7. *Loss rates and serious casualties involving tankers of more than 10,000 tonnes d.w.t., 1968–1975*

Flag state	Serious casualties		Total losses	
	Number	Rate %	Number	Rate %
France	10	1.3	nil	nil
Greece	72	3.9	19	1.0
Italy	11	1.3	4	0.5
Japan	16	1.1	2	0.1
Liberia	178	2.9	42	0.6
Norway	45	2.0	6	0.3
Panama	36	2.9	12	1.0
UK	57	1.8	4	0.1
USA	39	1.5	5	0.2
Other flags	111	1.7	26	0.4
All flags	575	2.2	120	0.4

Source: IMO tanker casualty sub-group.

fleets (table VI.8) showed and even wider gap between states with good and bad safety records. While some of the states with a high average loss rate are the traditional 'flag of convenience' states, such as Liberia, Greece, Singapore, Panama and Cyprus, others with a similar loss rate, such as Japan and Canada, are not regarded as flags of convenience.

Unfortunately the term 'flags of convenience' makes little distinction between the owners operating under the various flags; the term is too much of a generalization to be useful. From a financial and operational viewpoint, registration under a flag of convenience can be beneficial; of very much greater importance is whether or not the owner maintains and operates the vessels in such a way that the risk of accident is kept to a minimum. The role of the flag state is therefore one of supervision or control over owners, some of whom may fail to comply with internationally accepted operational standards. The vessels which do not measure up to the regulations are generally old, were purchased second-hand (often from nations such as the UK), may be inadequately manned, are poorly maintained, badly navigated, and suffer many equipment failures. Even when the ships themselves are well maintained, the equipment is often old and works poorly. Yet many of these vessels comply with current international regulations—a situation which reveals an urgent requirement for an accident-prevention approach more closely related to the realities of ship-board life and attitudes and to current management practices.

The cost of shipping accidents, particularly those involving oil tankers, has also risen enormously.[2] The *Amoco Cadiz* spillage in 1978, for

TABLE VI.8. *Loss rates in merchant fleets, as a percentage of ships at risk, 1976 and 1967–1976*

Flag state	Number of ships at mid-1976	Number of ships lost in 1976	% of existing fleet at mid-1976	Average loss rate 1967–76
USSR	7,945	3	0.04	0.03
Poland	733	—	—	0.14
Yugoslavia	423	—	—	0.19
UK	3,549	9	0.25	0.32
Finland	350	—	—	0.39
West Germany	1,957	8	0.41	0.40
India	526	2	0.38	0.40
France	1,388	4	0.29	0.42
Sweden	764	1	0.13	0.44
Netherlands	1,325	7	0.53	0.46
USA	4,366	11	0.25	0.48
Denmark	1,413	6	0.42	0.51
Brazil	520	1	0.19	0.52
Norway	2,759	13	0.47	0.53
Italy	1,719	5	0.29	0.54
Spain	2,792	19	0.68	0.64
Japan	9,748	52	0.53	0.69
Liberia	2,600	17	0.65	0.83
Canada	1,269	9	0.71	0.91
Singapore	722	4	0.55	1.05
Greece	2,921	23	0.79	1.22
Panama	2,680	50	1.87	1.90
Cyprus	765	19	2.48	2.63
TOTAL WORLD FLEET	65,637	345	0.53	0.62

Source: *Lloyds Register of Shipping.*

example, is believed to have cost several hundred million dollars to clean up. The explosion on board the *Betelgeuse* in 1979 completely destroyed the ship and marine terminal; costs of salvaging the damaged tanker were about £Ir.5 million, and the repairing of the terminal was estimated at £Ir.50 million. Clean-up costs amounted to more than £Ir.700,000; the tribunal of inquiry cost several million pounds; further costs included those of the ship, the cargo of oil, payments made to relatives of the crew who died in the disaster, and to fishermen whose livelihood was temporarily affected. Total costs are thus liable to be over £Ir.100 million. The tribunal of inquiry pointed out in its report that the repairs to the ship which were not carried out, and which led to her being in a seriously weakened condition, would have cost about £Ir.155,000.

Insurance coverage of shipping casualties is a highly significant factor not only in shipping operations but in international schemes for the compensation of victims. The most noteworthy developments in compensatory systems were directed to oil pollution emanating from tankers, following upon the *Torrey Canyon* disaster. Protection and Indemnity (P and I) Clubs provide mutual insurance for shipowners' third party liabilities and the major burden of compensation was borne by the carriers until the late 1970s when the contribution of oil companies markedly increased. This contribution was made not only through the International Oil Pollution Compensation Fund, a mechanism created by treaty in 1971 to round out the liability and compensation system devised internationally in 1969 for shipowners, but also through the Tanker Owners Voluntary Agreement Concerning Liability for Oil Pollution (TOVALOP) and the Contract Regarding an Interim Supplement to Tanker Liability for Oil Pollution (CRISTAL). Thus the tanker and cargo owners have funded compensation schemes which, in the case of CRISTAL, provided some $80 million in the 1978–81 period. In 1979 the OECD Member States contributed 95 per cent of the compensation available in the 1971 IOPC Fund, and in June 1981 the liabilities falling on that Fund were in excess of $74 million.

Such sums point to the high importance which insurance assumes in the victim-oriented systems of compensation, but it is generally accepted that the existing limits of compensation are inadequate owing to the erosion of inflation, the effects of massive oil pollution and the high costs of clean-up. The oil and tanker industries have emphasized to IMO's Legal Committee that it is necessary to revise existing compensation machinery, as a matter of urgency, in particular the compensation limits. The Member States of IMO have agreed that this revision should be done at a diplomatic conference which will be convened in 1984. A very complex draft of a revising instrument is already in being and it will, in general terms, be aimed at providing as extensive insurance cover as possible having regard to the current level of claims and the capacity of the insurance market. In 1981 the Eighth Report of the Royal Commission on Environmental Pollution reflected the view that the 1969 and 1971 limits had become unsatisfactory owing to large oil spills, escalation of costs associated with them and inflation. It stated: 'There is some urgency to bringing the compensation conventions into line with the realities of a major spill.'

Whilst the level of insurance premiums is in itself a strong incentive to shipowners to ensure that their ships are in conformity with international standards, the occurrence of costly oil spills continues and victims will greatly benefit from international efforts at IMO to enhance the financial protection available to them.

The question of insurance for the possible loss of cargoes of nuclear waste or noxious materials is a most contentious subject which is still under discussion. In view of the time which it has taken to establish an acceptable solution in the case of insurance for oil spillage, it looks as though the present unsatisfactory situation will continue to prevail for some time ahead.

The number of lives lost in tanker accidents (both oil and chemicals) is also significant. According to IMO, 1,593 seamen lost their lives in tanker accidents in the 12 years from 1968 to 1980. Moreover, the number of lives lost in 1979 (255) was the highest recorded and was more than twice the previous annual average of 115.

The frequency of collisions and the density of shipping are closely connected. The most significant focal points of shipping are in the English Channel, Irish Sea, and Celtic Sea. Through these areas pass nearly all of the shipping bound to or from north-west Europe. The most densely populated seaway is the English Channel; it also has the record for the highest number of maritime accidents. The Celtic Sea is another high-risk area. It is noted for its rough sea conditions, bad weather and poor visibility; and ships making landfalls in Britain or Ireland have met with many accidents, even when carrying sophisticated position-finding equipment.

With the development of oil and increased offshore activity in the North Sea, including increased tanker traffic around the coast of Scotland, have come greater risks of accident and spillage. A number of incidents during 1980 in the Pentland Firth highlighted the hazards. A US-registered tanker, the *Ultrasea*, came close to going aground, and a laden Japanese tanker was forced to stop in a narrow channel with strong tidal currents in order to avoid a collision with a bulk-cargo carrier.

Actions taken to prevent maritime accidents can be divided into those aimed at making the ships themselves safer and those aimed at making the seas safer for the growing variety of ships. In the first category are included improved standards for training and watchkeeping, collision avoidance systems, and improved control over the management and registration of ships. In the second category are included hydrographic surveying, special charts, lighthouses and buoys, traffic-routeing schemes, and shore-based radar and reporting-in systems for vessels carrying dangerous cargoes.

Making ships safer

International conventions require that every sea-going vessel complies with the standards prescribed by the marine administration of the country of registry. In their own right, classification societies also make extensive rules concerning the quality of materials used, design and construction of ships, their machinery and equipment. These are not mandatory, but an owner would find it difficult to obtain Load Line and Safety Construction certificates, insurance and cargo contracts without them. Classification is upheld by a series of regular inspections throughout the ship's life, and classification societies are being asked to undertake these more frequently. The *Betelgeuse* tribunal of inquiry also recommended that more of a ship's equipment should come within the scope of the surveys of the classification societies, and that there should be minimum standards for the type, quantity and quality of equipment fitted to vessels. It should not be left to the shipowner to decide what he shall, or shall not, fit. The tribunal also recommended that the classification societies should review their methods of supervising repairs in large vessels, since it was not possible for one surveyor to supervise repairs adequately during a major overhaul.

Classification societies have traditionally not concerned themselves with navigational equipment or the ergonomics of ship-control systems. However, the increasing levels of automation and reduced manning levels are now such that the proper design, installation and maintenance of equipment are becoming of vital importance. A series of accidents in recent years, including the *Betelgeuse* and the *Energy Concentration*, drew attention to the stresses imposed on very large tankers during loading or discharging, particularly if the hull has already been weakened, or if incorrect procedures are employed. As already stated, the *Betelgeuse* broke in two while taking on ballast at the Gulf Oil terminal in Bantry Bay, her hull structure being seriously weakened by the failure of her owners to ensure essential maintenance. The *Energy Concentration* broke in two during cargo discharge in Rotterdam Harbour on 22 July 1980. The hull fracture was a result of uneven offloading, some of her cargo having been discharged at a previous port of call. The ship was in excellent condition and met international standards, but was not provided with the necessary equipment to enable loading stresses to be calculated and cargo distribution to be worked out.

A study carried out by the Salvage Association in 1980[3] blamed badly trained crews and shipping company management for a dramatic increase in shipboard fires and explosions on tankers. The study found that of 71 major casualties between 1974 and April 1980, 30 involved vessels under the Liberian flag, 10 Greek, and 7 British. 37 incidents leading to substantial damage or total loss occurred between January 1979 and April 1980, compared with 34 in the previous five years. Inadequacy of crew training and pressures to meet commercial deadlines were considered to be the principal factors causing accidents, together with the return to service of a number of older tankers which had been laid up. Owners of these older vessels are now being encouraged to scrap them and to build new ships; many have, however, been sold to developing countries anxious to build up their national merchant fleets.

A further study in 1981 yielded a similar conclusion. An industry working-group established by the Oil Companies International Marine Forum (OCIMF), the International Chamber of Shipping (ICS), and the

International Association of Independent Tanker Owners (INTERTANKO), identified human failure as the cause of all recent major shipboard fires and explosions. Most of the vessels involved complied, in full, with IMO requirements in vital areas. The critical problems were seen as inadequate training, poor management, and lack of awareness of the basic hazards of operating crude-oil carriers; tougher technical standards were seen to be of little use in the prevention of accidents. The study was critical of management, both ashore and afloat. Safety was stressed as a management responsibility; yet management's dangerous practice of appointing people to responsible positions for which they are quite inexperienced has remained all too common. At the same time, some managements also fail to take responsibility for key safety decisions and neglect to provide the ships' masters with the guidance they need. The study uncovered much evidence of mounting work pressures on crews with senior ships' personnel so overburdened with obligations as to impair safe operations. Ships' officers reported being faced with a deluge of new rules, recommendations and advice which they considered excessive and only adding to the confusion. There is no doubt that these findings are important, not least in emphasizing the need for the human element to be taken into account when framing new regulations.

These studies have also focused attention on the problems faced by the masters of vessels carrying hazardous cargoes. In law the master is responsible for the safety of the vessel, yet in many instances he cannot make vital decisions without referring to the owners. Such decisions might involve the purchase of charts or other navigational equipment, the repair of such equipment, or the hire of salvage tugs in a situation of near emergency. The investigation into the *Zoe Colocotroni* spill revealed that the master could not purchase or repair necessary navigational equipment without prior authorization by the owners, the Colocotroni brothers, one of whom had his office in London, the other in Greece.

In the case of the *Christos Bitas*, a Greek-owned tanker which ran onto rocks near the Smalls Light off the Welsh coast in October 1978, a Greek Government inquiry revealed the following inadequacies:

(a) the ship's main radar set, a 19-year-old model, was not working;
(b) the second radar set broke down about five hours before the ship went aground;
(c) the radio direction-finder had not been adjusted for four years, and its margin of error had grown so wide that it was not used;
(d) the ship's gyro-compass was working, but the repeaters on the bridge were not, and the helmsman had to rely on the magnetic compass;
(e) the distance-run indicator dial (log) on the bridge was not working;
(f) the ship did not carry a Decca Navigator system.

Despite these deficiencies, the ship was maintained at full speed in poor visibility, the appropriate signals were not sounded, and adequate look-outs were not kept. While the master was clearly found by the inquiry to be grossly negligent, the degree to which the poor maintenance of the equipment was the responsibility of the owners was never clarified.

From this it can readily be seen that the division of responsibility between master and owner for compliance with statutory safety obligations is in urgent need of clarification.

The role of the country of registry, or 'flag state', is also coming under scrutiny by the European Community. In the view of the European Commission, the problem of 'flags of convenience' or open registers has been clouded by an artificial distinction between open registers and conventional registers. In reality, many registers are 'open' to some degree, and substandard conditions can arise on shipping under any flag. The European Commission believes that a more rational and less divisive approach would be to seek international agreement on conditions or circumstances which should not be allowed to arise on any ship, whatever its flag. These conditions would include failure to meet international safety and pollution-prevention standards, or to observe decent working and living conditions on board. But they might also cover the present impossibility of finding out who is making the decisions about a particular ship and of how to reach that person if needed.[4] If such a list of undesirable conditions or circumstances could be agreed, it might also be possible to reach further agreement that port states and flag states together should ensure that such conditions do not arise, or are quickly dealt with if they do. Both IMO and the ILO have enacted legislation in this field.

Increasing the powers of port states would form an important part of such a process, and this is already being done to some extent. In 1980 the European Commission proposed to the Council of Ministers a draft directive for the enforcement, in respect of shipping using Community ports, of international standards for shipping safety and pollution prevention.[5] The purpose of the proposed directive is to ensure the identification and inspection of substandard ships visiting Community ports, and it would establish a type of port state jurisdiction similar to that envisaged by the European Ministers responsible for shipping safety at a meeting in Paris in December 1980. Under the draft directive, member states would undertake to:

(a) ensure that on each visit to port, a ship will lodge with the appropriate authorities a declaration of the nature and date of expiry of the ship's and crew's certificates;

(b) extend to all ships the requirements of the 1979 Council Directive which applied only to tankers, i.e. that all ships should now inform the competent authorities of any deficiencies or incidents which may

decrease the normal safe manoeuvrability or seaworthiness of the vessel;
(c) inspect the ship if its certificates are missing, invalid, or if there are clear grounds for believing that the ship or her crew does not correspond with the particulars of a certificate;
(d) follow the provisions of any relevant international conventions if deficiencies are revealed during the inspection or examination.

The directive will have the effect of harmonizing procedures among member states for in-port inspection of ships, for the reporting of defects, and for their remedy. Deficient or substandard vessels will effectively be prevented from sailing in EC waters, and a good measure of control will be given to port states. It is also recognized that the implementation of the directive will require additional inspection staff, and it is proposed to spread the burden of the work by asking each member state to inspect only 25 per cent of foreign merchant ships visiting its ports. Vessels which have been inspected by any of the other member states' authorities within the previous six months need not be inspected again unless there are clear grounds for repeating the inspection. The establishment of a data bank on shipping accidents and infringements, which is available to port authorities, is also proposed as a means of providing the necessary information required by the inspecting authorities. Thus a port authority in any member state will have immediate access to data about a vessel seeking to enter the port, and this data will include the results of previous inspections (if any), details of accidents in which the ship has been involved, any reported deficiencies or infringements of relevant international conventions or codes, and information about the ship's builders, owners and operators. A decision can then be made by the port about whether to turn the ship away, inspect before admitting, admit the ship and inspect later, or treat her as being safe in all respects.

On a broader front, the powers of port states have been augmented with the coming into force of MARPOL and through the provisions of the Memorandum of Understanding on Port State Control which was signed by fourteen West European states on 26 January 1982 and has replaced the Hague Memorandum of 1978.[6] It appears also to have superseded the EC Draft Directive on port state inspection.[7] The fourteen states are Belgium, Denmark, Finland, France, West Germany, Greece, Ireland, Italy, Netherlands, Norway, Portugal, Spain, Sweden, and the UK. The new memorandum has followed the recommendations of a 1980 Regional European Conference on Maritime Safety.

Making the seas safer

The greatest hazards of collision or grounding exist in the crowded inshore shipping lanes, especially in the English Channel and Celtic Sea, where precise seamanship is needed in order to avoid accidents. The growing size and number of ships using these areas has increased the risk; while the consequences of any accident are made worse by the hazardous nature of many of the cargoes carried.

A number of serious collisions in the English Channel in the 1950s, where 90 per cent of the ships to pass through the Dover Strait each day were using a narrow passage under 5 miles wide between the Varne Bank and the English coast, led to suggestions for the separation of traffic. A separation scheme in the straits was introduced in June 1967, the first of over 100 traffic separation schemes now in operation throughout the world. The decreasing incidence of collisions indicated the undoubted benefit of the scheme, but some modifications proved necessary, and more changes were introduced in 1982.

In 1972, the new Convention on the International Rules for the Prevention of Collisions at Sea for the first time included a rule for the 'conduct of vessels in traffic-separation schemes' and when the convention came into force in July 1977 it regulated the movement of vessels in or near the schemes, although it has not been made obligatory for vessels to use the schemes if they do not wish to (for schemes through straits such as the Dover Strait or the Straits of Gibraltar there is, of course, no practical alternative for very large ships).

Meanwhile, despite the significant reduction in the number of collisions, serious accidents to large vessels continued to occur. In 1967 the stranding of the 120,000 tonne tanker *Torrey Canyon* on the Seven Stones reef off Cornwall caused the largest oil spill in the world up to that time, and focused attention on such incidents. The collision in 1970 between the *Pacific Glory* and the *Allegro* south of the Isle of Wight was followed in 1971 by a series of accidents near the Varne bank. The tanker *Texaco Caribbean* sank following a collision with the Peruvian ship *Paracas* which was steaming against the flow of traffic; its wreckage was struck, before it had been marked, by the German ship *Brandenburg* with much loss of life; and, even after marking, it was struck again, by the Greek ship *Nikki*. These accidents led, *inter alia*, to a new internationally agreed system of buoyage, and to the introduction of traffic-surveillance centres, with radar coverage of the Dover Straits, on both sides of the Channel. Work commenced at the same time on operational research into marine traffic problems, using the information obtained from, among other sources, the Channel surveillance radar systems.

After a period with fewer serious accidents, the *Olympic Bravery*, a 278,000 d.w.t. tanker in ballast ran aground at Ushant on its maiden voyage in January 1976. There was no oil pollution, but Brittany was not so lucky when the *Amoco Cadiz*, 238,000 tons, ran aground in the same area in March 1978 causing the largest oil spill to date. There could have been an even greater disaster if the *Al Faiha* had run aground on the South

Falls Bank shortly afterwards, but, following a unique example of intervention from the shore, the ship altered course in time; the Dover Strait Information Service, which on this occasion was able to correlate the radar echo with the ship's name, although this is usually impossible, saw that it was heading for disaster, made radio contact and prevented a disaster.

Major accidents spur on safety measures. Just as *Torrey Canyon* and the 1971 accidents stimulated international action against oil pollution and on buoyage, traffic surveillance and routeing, and as the *Argo Merchant* disaster off the east coast of the USA led to the US government imposing requirements on vessels entering their waters to carry position-fixing equipment over and above that required internationally, and also for more sophisticated radar equipment (a requirement that will be international in due course, but which the US is already imposing much against the wish of the shipowners), so the *Amoco Cadiz* disaster led to a flurry of activity at the request of France, supported by the UK and other maritime states.

At its spring meeting in 1978, barely a month after the accident, IMO agreed a new traffic separation lane off Ushant that pushed inward-bound tankers and other ships carrying hazardous cargoes further offshore (27 miles from the French coast at its nearest point), and restricted use of the lane to ships equipped with an electronic position-fixing appliance, the first occasion on which traffic lanes have been earmarked for specially equipped ships; and also altered the traffic separation scheme off the Casquets, moving it further away from the Channel Islands. These changes came into effect on 1 January 1979.

The European Commission has also been considering offshore vessel traffic management on a regional basis. As well as the moves aimed at increasing vessel safety, it has also undertaken a co-ordinated programme on research on maritime safety, with particular emphasis on shore-based maritime aids to navigation. The draft EC directives on port state control and on the establishment of an information system for preventing and combatting hydrocarbon pollution of the sea will include compulsory ship-reporting procedures. The compulsory identification of each ship, as well as notification of its position and estimated time of arrival at the port, must be made as soon as it enters the traffic management zone. This is essential in order to secure systematic interaction between the ship and the shore-based traffic observers, so that action can be taken if the ship does not co-operate or supply the required information. Compulsory pilotage services, which at present are confined to harbours and their approaches, could also be extended to heavily trafficked areas such as the English Channel.

Pilotage

After concern had been expressed in many quarters that the Pilotage Act of 1913 was in many respects out of date, inflexible and cumbersome, and that the arrangements for pilotage in the UK were in need of revision, the Government appointed a committee, the Steering Committee on Pilotage (SCOP), in 1973. It was the first inquiry into pilotage since 1911. Its unanimous report in 1974 recommended an extension of compulsory pilotage certificates for masters and chief officers familiar with the pilotage district; a Central Pilotage Board with authority to initiate major organizational changes, including some reduction in the role of Trinity House, which was the largest pilotage authority licensing some 720 pilots; and the ending of the restriction of pilotage certificates to British subjects.

All these recommendations proved highly controversial and the government decided to appoint another committee to prepare legislation in the light of the various representations made. The Merchant Shipping Act of 1979 which set up a Pilotage Commission and retained the powers of Trinity House followed.

The new policy on pilotage certificates has also run into acute controversy. In July 1980 certificates became available to EC nationals on EC flag ships and a surge of applications followed. Certificates have been issued at Plymouth and to ferrymasters using the IOW pilotage district, but there has been little or no progress elsewhere. The DFDS Shipping Company took Trinity House to court unsuccessfully, and then issued a writ against the Pilotage Commission over refusals to examine their officers for certificates.

It may seem surprising that pilotage problems, involving only about 1,600 pilots, should be so intractable. UK pilots, like those of many other countries, are self-employed with their earnings directly related to the traffic at their own pilotage district. By the nature of their profession (going aboard ships as strangers and having to take charge of the navigation, with possibly difficult relationships with the master, the shipowner and at times the port authority), pilots are inclined to take an independent stand, while remaining concerned, at the same time, to safeguard their position in the face of all the changes taking place. Shipowners view extensions of compulsory pilotage as unnecessary and expensive, arguing that their own masters know their ships better and know the waters sufficiently to navigate safely. The development of marine traffic systems in port approaches, operated by the port authorities, can lead to conflict with the pilots if the schemes are not introduced and operated in full co-operation with all the interested parties including the pilotage authorities and the pilots.

Between 1973 and 1979 the number of pilots in England and Wales fell from 1,466 to 1,358, though there was an increase of 50 in Scotland, mainly for the new oil ports. Changes at individual ports have been much more marked and the new Pilotage Commission is faced by a number of difficulties which require solution. It could be argued that a national maritime agency, employing pilots and those involved in shipping movements in port approaches, could offer a better career structure for all concerned and overcome many of the problems arising.

Hydrography, nautical charting, and buoyage

The nautical chart is an essential part of the equipment for any maritime activity whether it be safe navigation, fishing, offshore exploration or exploitation of hydrocarbons or minerals, delineation of offshore boundaries or recreational usage. A nautical chart has to be kept constantly up to date, but can only be as accurate as the hydrographic survey data available to its compilers; the task of searching the world's continental shelves to locate and height the many hidden rocks, wrecks and sand-banks has always been too vast for the means available to carry it out. Hydrographic surveyors have therefore concentrated on those areas where depths were thought most likely to be critical to the deepest-draught vessels expected to use the area.

Until the mid-1930s, the only available method of obtaining depths at sea was to obtain spot depths with a lead weight on a marked line, held as near vertical as possible, in positions fixed by horizontal sextant angles, in clear daylight conditions only, either of fixed marks on land or of beacons moored in shallow water; as the deepest draught of any vessel was then less than 16 metres, detailed examination of the sea-bed was stopped once general depths of 20 metres were obtained. The possibility of isolated pinnacles and wrecks between each cast of the lead was accepted and the experienced, dedicated surveyors acquired an uncanny knack of finding dangers. Many, however, were missed.

With the introduction of the echo-sounder in the mid-1930s, it was possible for the hydrographic surveyor to obtain a narrow profile of the depth along his track, although the probability of obstructions between his tracks remained until the advent of the sidescan sonar in the late 1970s. This instrument, when towed at slow speeds astern of the vessel, close to the sea-bed, reveals all irregularities up to 200 metres either side of the track; these can subsequently be examined in more detail. Since the mid-1950s, electronic position-fixing equipment has enabled surveyors to position themselves anywhere on the continental shelf, with great accuracy and regardless of visibility.

Despite the improved techniques now available, the growth in the draught of merchant vessels and the need to tow concrete production platforms at draughts of over 80 metres—more than three times that of even the largest tanker—represent developments which have outstripped the world's total hydrographic surveying resources. There are, for example, now known to be some 17,000 wrecks lying within the area of the UK continental shelf, but the exact position is known of less than 4,000 of these and the exact least depth is known of even fewer. The southern North

Sea—that is from the latitude of about Flamborough Head to Folkestone—as well as parts of the Irish Sea, Celtic Sea, Bristol Channel, the Solent, and many port approaches, are known to be so unstable as to require regular monitoring of the depths and adjustment of the navigational aids in consequence.

The responsibility for providing very high-precision surveys of the UK continental shelf lies with the Hydrographer of the Royal Navy. While various port and harbour authorities accept responsibility for maintaining surveys within their port limits, the Surveying Flotilla of the Ministry of Defence is largely engaged in surveys of the UK continental shelf. The agreed British national surveying programme is co-ordinated with those of the other six members of the North Sea Hydrographic Commission (NSHC)—Denmark, Federal Republic of Germany, France, Netherlands, Norway, and Sweden—to ensure common standards, avoidance of duplication and the use of standardized vertical and horizontal data and equipment. Ships operated by Service Hydrographique de la Marine (SHOM) used stations in south-west England when surveying the western English Channel; in the eastern English Channel, British and French ships on survey have shared position-fixing chains with stations in France and southern England; the Hifix-6 survey chain, owned and operated jointly with stations in England and on the Continent, was used by the Netherlands and the United Kingdom in their 1981 survey of the deep-water channels leading to western European ports and the Baltic.

Ireland has as yet no hydrographic service, but a number of surveys have been carried out in recent years by commercial organizations in the vicinity of expanding ports. Apart from these special surveys, commissioned either by government agencies or by port authorities, the majority of the 80 or so charts covering Irish waters are based on surveys carried out by the British Admiralty using the old-fashioned lead and line method of the nineteenth century. Because of the increasing number of deep-draught vessels using Irish waters, numerous reports have been made in recent years of uncharted outcrops and depth inaccuracies. These have been detected around the whole coast, but particularly in the south-east, east and south.

In 1979 the National Board for Science and Technology (NBST) was given the responsibility of co-ordinating hydrographic activities. In 1981 it commissioned the Senior Regional Hydrographer of the Pacific Region (an officer of the Canadian government) to examine the state of hydrographic surveying in Irish waters and to recommend appropriate action.[8] This study recommended a civilian organization for the hydrographic service—a model adopted by Canada and a number of other countries. Such an arrangement offers a solution to those countries afflicted with the perennial problem of who pays for the navy's hydrographic work; its removal from the defence sphere makes for a more direct and accountable customer–contractor relationship.

Overall co-ordination of hydrographic surveying and charting world-wide is carried out by the International Hydrographic Organization (IHO), based in Monaco since its foundation in 1921. All 48 member states freely exchange data of concern to mariners since failure to do so—or, even worse, to tamper with the accuracy of supplied data—would inevitably result in the stranding of a vessel with probable pollution of one's own coastline and coastal waters and possible loss of life. Under the auspices of the IHO, considerable progress has been made in the standardization of the nautical charts published by the member states concerned. Unfortunately, despite the unique extent of international co-operation, it will take very many years to complete the basic surveys needed and to amend all the nautical charts.

In the meantime, to enable individual users to assess the adequacy for their purposes of the material used to compile any areas of any chart, source data diagrams are now being inserted on all British Admiralty charts as well as on those of many other countries. Mariners at sea are kept informed of significant changes to their charts and nautical publications by means of the international series of Radio Navigational Warnings; area co-ordinators receive such information from a wide range of sources within their area, as well as from adjacent areas, and arrange for these to be broadcast by radio stations powerful enough to cover the whole area at least. The Hydrographer of the Royal Navy has the responsibility for Area 1, covering north-west Europe. Less immediate changes are promulgated by means of daily Notices to Mariners; bound copies of these are distributed weekly to all who need them and all copies of BA charts held in stock by the Hydrographic Department, Taunton, are corrected by hand as are the copies supplied to customers by the major 'A' class agents.

But, however excellent a hydrographic and chart publication service might be, there is no guarantee that a particular ship will have the correct charts on board or will use them. The 1979 Annual Report of the Hydrographer of the Royal Navy (UK) commented upon the large number of vessels which fail to carry appropriate or up-to-date charts. During the summer of 1979, British and French maritime authorities visited merchant ships arriving in their ports and inspected the charts in use for the area of the Ushant and Casquets traffic separation schemes. In British ports, of the 229 vessels inspected, 39 carried charts which did not show the Ushant scheme, and 46 had charts which did not show the Casquets scheme. Both of these schemes had been so altered on 1 January 1979 that in some areas the recommended direction of passage had been reversed; yet seven months later a large number of owners were allowing their ships to use charts which led them the wrong way down the English Channel.

However, as from May 1980, the Safety of Life at Sea (SOLAS) Convention (1974) became effective and this requires, among other things, that all sizeable vessels should carry an adequate set of up-to-date charts and navigational publications. National legislation has been passed in several countries—including the UK—but enforcement of this essential requirement has proved difficult.

Buoyage

An agreed system of standardized buoyage is just as essential as internationally standardized charts. The accidents in the Straits of Dover in the early 1970s, referred to above, brought renewed pressure on buoyage authorities to adopt an internationally agreed system. As long ago as 1889, certain countries had agreed to mark the port hand side of channels with black can buoys and the starboard hand with red conical buoys; unfortunately, when lights for buoys were introduced, some countries placed red lights on the black, port-hand buoys to conform with the red lights marking the port-hand side of harbour entrances, while others (including the American continent, Japan, and others in Asia) placed red lights on the red, starboard-hand buoys. Of subsequent attempts at standardization, the 1936 convention drawn up under the League of Nations at Geneva was the most nearly successful in that many countries agreed with the idea of a Lateral system and a Cardinal system; however, the Second World War intervened and subsequently wide interpretations of the 1936 convention resulted in *9 distinct systems being used in north-west Europe alone*.

In 1975, the International Association of Lighthouse Authorities (IALA) agreed that, whilst a single world-wide system was not practicable at that time, a standardized 'System A' should be introduced, combining the Cardinal and Lateral (Red to Port) systems, for all of Europe, Africa, Australasia, and the western part of Asia. While speed in adoption was important, it was accepted that to change the thousands of buoys and fixed marks would be an enormous task—not only for the national and port buoyage authorities, but also for the national hydrographic offices—particularly those providing world coverage.

An implementation programme was agreed and the first stage in 1977 saw the introduction of 'IALA System A' buoyage in the southern North Sea and Straits of Dover. By the end of 1981, the whole of north-west Europe, as well as the western Mediterranean and other smaller areas, had adopted 'System A'.

At the five-yearly IALA Conference in November 1980, it was agreed to harmonize 'System A' (Red to Port) with 'System B' (Red to Starboard) into a single IALA buoyage system. It is hoped that a complete global plan will be accepted whereby all the world's buoyage will be standardized in time to celebrate the centenary of the first attempt at standardization in 1889.

The Response to Accidents at Sea

One of the most vital components of any response system is of course the 'search and rescue' operation. Marine SAR, as civil search and rescue facilities are called, is the responsibility of appropriate government departments or specialized agencies. An outline of the SAR network in the UK is given in chapter VII.

The coastguards' total regular strength of about 550, assisted by 8,500 auxiliary coastguards, has not changed much over the last ten years, but there has been considerable reorganization within the service, mainly by concentrating staff at fewer rescue centres, with much more emphasis on their function of co-ordinating marine SAR via their VHF, telephone and telex networks, and much less emphasis on the traditional visual watchkeeping, though the closure of some of the smaller look-out stations has not been without local protest, especially in the south-west of England.

The marine SAR organization works well in spite of its heterogeneous nature (ranging from MOD units deployed for military purposes to RNLI lifeboat stations dependent entirely on charity) and the various units have an excellent public image. But it is many years since it has had to deal with a really major disaster at sea, the 1979 Fastnet race being perhaps the most difficult. Most ports have their plans to handle emergencies in their estuaries and there are of course plans for coping with high-seas incidents. Exercises have been held including some jointly with France. On paper, the arrangements are all ready and it must be hoped that they will be fully effective when called upon in spite of there not being a clear chain of command running right through the SAR system.

In a wider context, IMO's SAR Convention, adopted in 1979, needs only three further ratifications for it to enter into force. This convention regulates the arrangements for provision and co-ordination of search and rescue services on an international basis. As at 31 December 1982, France, West Germany, the Netherlands, Norway, Sweden, and the United Kingdom were contracting states.

The 1969 International Convention Relating to Intervention on the High Seas in Cases of Oil Pollution Casualties[9] gives governments the power 'to take such measures on the high seas as may be necessary to prevent, mitigate or eliminate grave and imminent danger to their coastline or related interests from pollution or threat of pollution by oil, following upon a maritime casualty or acts related to such a casualty, which may reasonably be expected to result in major harmful consequences'; it was a power which some claimed to already exist under customary international law. However, the convention is in force; in the UK its powers are exercised by a minister at the Department of Trade. The intervention powers of the UK Secretary of State are more sweeping than provided for by international convention—for example, the Secretary of State does not have to consult the state against whose ship it is proposed to take action.

Once the Secretary of State has invoked powers of intervention over a ship casualty, the D.o.T. is responsible for taking steps 'to prevent, mitigate or eliminate grave and imminent danger . . . from pollution . . .'. This often requires firm direction of salvage operations to try and suit the best advantage of all interests—a nearly impossible situation. Sharp differences of opinion have arisen over the cases of *Eleni V*, *Christos Bitas* and *Tarpenbek* as to the best strategies to employ. Since *Eleni V* (May 1978), a pollution clearance advisory panel has been consulted by the Department of Transport, *inter alia* with regard to disposal of a damaged ship and its burden of oil. The Maritime Consultative Council represents nature conservation interests on this panel, which is useful in ensuring that interested parties are aware of the latest position and of each other's views, and can influence subsequent events. Nevertheless, an advance study of options for action is not available, and this does not improve matters in divisive situations. Furthermore, the Department of Trade is ill equipped to take immediate decisions, which are obviously dictated by the circumstances. In particular, a review of ports and places of refuge capable of receiving a casualty, their advantages and disadvantages, should be undertaken and incorporated into a national contingency plan. Fundamental to these powers of intervention are the problems of salvage and of ports of refuge.

The difficulties of salvaging large crude-oil carriers were highlighted by the *Amoco Cadiz* stranding, and by the collision between the *Atlantic Empress* and the *Aegean Captain* north of Trinidad and Tobago in July 1979. The latter incident highlights the problems faced by salvors in dealing with large tankers, especially those of protecting other marine resources, and of getting paid for their services. Following the collision, three major salvage contractors began to tow the seriously damaged *Atlantic Empress* away from the beaches of Trinidad and Tobago. While under way, they fought a serious fire on board the 288,000 tonne d.w.t. tanker. The towing and damage-control efforts continued for two weeks, and the fire was almost under control when an explosion occurred and the vessel sank shortly afterwards.

It was widely reported that one salvage contractor had five tugs on the scene for the whole two weeks, at a cost of $15,000 per tug per day. Largely as a result of the salvage contractors' efforts to tow the damaged vessel away from Trinidad and Tobago, there was no significant oil pollution damage to any Caribbean island coast, despite the fact that the 275,976 tonnes of crude oil lost was the largest cargo volume ever lost from one ship. Yet under the 'no cure, no pay' agreement of Lloyd's Standard Form of Salvage Agreement, the salvage contractors were not compensated in any way for their efforts to save the ship and her cargo and to prevent pollution.

Since that incident the problem of 'no cure, no pay' has been partially solved by the development of a new Standard Agreement, known as Lloyd's Open Form 1980 (LOF 80). Under LOF 80, the salvor's efforts to prevent the escape of oil can now be compensated and, most important, an exception has been made to the no cure, no pay principle. The exception applies only when the casualty is a laden or partly laden tanker carrying crude, heavy diesel, fuel, or lubricating oil; the salvor must be free of negligence, and the salvage operation must have been wholly or partially unsuccessful. Within these narrowly-drawn terms, the salvor is entitled to his reasonably incurred expenses plus 15 per cent. Thus, in theory at least, the salvor can do no worse than to break even on tanker salvage contracts; though it is still uncertain whether measures to prevent the escape of oil can be included in the expenses claimed.

However, the new agreement does little or nothing to solve an even more intractable problem, that of where to bring a disabled and possibly leaking tanker. Under the former Lloyd's Open Form, the salvor was required to take the salvaged vessel to a place of safety, normally a port or safe anchorage. Under LOF 80, the salvor can now take the ship and cargo to a safe haven of his own choice. But this does not take into account the action frequently taken by coastal states of barring the salvor and the disabled vessel from their waters or ports. An early example of this problem arose with the Greek tanker *Andros Patria* (218,665 d.w.t.).[10] In December 1978 the *Andros Patria* developed a crack in her hull and began leaking oil 38 kilometres west of the Spanish coast. Abandoned by her crew, the tanker was taken under tow in deteriorating weather conditions. Despite the imminent danger of the ship sinking and spilling her cargo, the Spanish government ordered the *Andros Patria* away from its coast, and The French, English, and Portuguese authorities closed their ports to the ship. Eventually, the *Andros Patria* was towed towards the Azores and most of her cargo off-loaded outside the Azores' 200-mile limit. When off-loading was completed, the tanker was able to steam under her own power to Portugal, even though Portuguese officials still required a thorough inspection of the ship before allowing her to enter one of their ports.

Three more recent cases were followed by the sinking of the vessels concerned. In October 1980 the passenger liner *Prisendam* caught fire in the Gulf of Alaska; she was taken under tow to sheltered water, but was then denied entry to Alaskan territorial seas by the Alaskan government, which feared an oil spillage from the vessel's bunkers if she sank. Ten days after the fire began, the vessel sank at sea and no oil spill was observed. In February 1981 the bulk carrier *Eastern Mariner I*, damaged in heavy seas and carrying a cargo of ammonium phosphate, was granted refuge in Bermudan waters. Then, citing the danger of oil pollution from the ship's bunkers, the Bermuda government ordered the ship to depart. Ignoring the master's argument that the vessel was unseaworthy, tugs chartered by the government towed the ship to the open sea. The ship then began taking water too quickly for her pumps to handle, was abandoned, and sank. Finally, in April 1981, the Polish gas-carrier *Stanislaw Dubois* collided with a Sudanese ship and needed to put into a port for survey and repair. After finding that no port would admit their ship, and after exhausting all other possibilities, the owners were left with no alternative but to scuttle the vessel.

These cases raise the question of whether it is appropriate or correct for a government to export (by refusing entry to a stricken vessel) the environmental problems caused by a shipping accident. In most cases, the government or the port authority are aware that the vessel has nowhere else to go, and that the owner or salvor may have to scuttle the ship in deep water. Such an action may be a rational and safe last resort if the cargo has been made safe, for example, if most of it has been pumped out or off-loaded, or if, in the case of crude oil, the temperature of the deep water is low enough to retain the crude as a stable non-polluting material. The *Christos Bitas*, damaged off the coast of Wales and sunk in the Atlantic south of Ireland in October 1978 was such a case though it did raise the question of whether the scuttling of such a vessel might violate the provisions of the Oslo or London Ocean Dumping Convention (see chapters X and XI). But what if the disabled vessel is carrying a toxic cargo miscible with water, for instance chlorine, chlordane, hydrogen fluoride or radio-active materials? In the last case, there may be no alternative but to make every attempt to recover the vessel and her cargo; ocean dumping would not be an acceptable solution.

These problems *must* be dealt with before they arise; and the only way to do this is to formulate a policy on the issue. Such a policy will of necessity have to dedicate specific harbours or sheltered inlets of the sea as 'ports of refuge' for these vessels. Salvage and anti-pollution equipment could be located at the port of refuge, which would be chosen for its shelter and other physical advantages including proximity to densely trafficked shipping-lanes or other areas where casualties are likely to occur.

Because of the understandable reluctance of governments to act unilaterally in Europe, the European Commission and the member states of the Community should undertake the task of designating ports of refuge, and of negotiating their establishment on the coasts of other European countries. A fundamental requirement of such a move would be the prior implementation of coastal resource management programmes and policies.

Conflicts with Other Uses

Many shipping operations come into conflict with the natural environment, as a consequence of pollution or port development. These problems have been addressed earlier in the chapter and they are not new. However, as the size of ships increase and cargoes become more hazardous, the possibility of damage also becomes greater.

In order to avoid collision or damage further away from the coast, shipping activities have to be separated geographically from areas where exploration for, or production of, oil or gas is being undertaken. In UK waters, for example, the consent of the Department of Trade is required for any activity that could affect the safety of navigation. Initially, any drilling for oil or gas requires a licence from the Department of Energy and the consent of the Department of Trade. Depending on the navigational risks in particular areas, special conditions may be imposed such as 'summer drilling only', only one rig to be drilling at any one time, jack-up rigs to be used rather then semi-submersibles, requirements concerning support and patrol vessels, in addition to the standard conditions relating to the marking and lighting of rigs and mooring, etc. These special conditions are nowadays usually imposed in the licences.

Many of the areas recently licensed, or likely to be licensed, are quite sensitive from the navigation point of view, such as areas in the Channel, Firth of Forth, off the Humber, and in Liverpool Bay. There is consultation between the departments concerned: Energy, Trade, Defence, MAFF, DAFS, and ministers are now consulted about any new licensing proposals. A grading 'star' system has been introduced to assess roughly the navigation risk, ranging from a 4-star block in which the risk is considered too great to allow licensing at all to a nil-star block where the risk is negligible. Coastal shipping clearways, for example, where there are no off-lying dangers or restricted channels, such as category 'A' clearways off the coast of Scotland and north-east England, would probably be no-star. There are two categories of clearways in the UK continental shelf, agreed with the General Council of British Shipping. These include the routes most commonly used by merchant ships. Six months notice of any drilling or other oil or gas operations is required in the category 'A' clearways which cover all the English Channel, the east coast and some other areas, but only six weeks notice is necessary in the remaining areas of the shelf, including the category 'B' clearways.

In the Channel some licences have been issued for blocks west of the Greenwich Meridian, for example, south of the Isle of Wight, but none so far east of the Meridian. Over the last few years, the number of rigs drilling has varied between 15 and 30.

As the search for oil and gas extends to the higher risk areas, the conflict of interest with shipping will increase. The IMO has had to produce a list of approved methods of making temporary changes to routeing systems to allow drilling in or very near traffic lanes. An instance of these procedures having to be invoked was in August 1981 when the south-west-bound lane of the Texel traffic separation system was temporarily altered to allow drilling, as reported to shipping by Notice to Mariners 1360(T) of 1981. In 1980 there had to be a similar alteration to a United States scheme.

There can also, of course, be problems with production platforms. For example, there is now an approved deep-water route running east of the Indefatigable Bank off the Humber, and six suspended gas wellheads lie in or very close to this route. If the gas industry wishes to reopen them and erect platforms when extraction becomes profitable, there could be problems, since deep-water routes (which consist of routes that have been surveyed to a minimum depth, sometimes involving wreck clearance) are less easy to alter temporarily than traffic schemes. It might be necessary to insist on extraction through pipelines with sub-sea completions rather than allow either platforms or offshore loading of tankers in all areas near IMO traffic separation schemes or deep-water routes.

There are 500-metre safety zones round all rigs and platforms, prohibited to shipping. From time to time, fishing vessels infringe these zones as does an occasional merchant vessel. Trouble has also been caused by vessels, mainly fishing boats, passing between individual rigs or platforms within an oil or gas field (though keeping outside the 500-metre zones round each rig). So with the agreement of the Royal Navy, the fisheries departments and the General Council of British Shipping, much larger areas, called somewhat oddly Development Areas, have been marked on Admiralty charts round fields such as Ninian and Brent, which all vessels are recommended to avoid.

One other problem is that of the eventual removal of rigs, wellheads, platforms, and so forth. Under the Coast Protection Act, the Secretary of State requires removal to be to a safe depth to avoid danger to surface navigation, but the 1958 Geneva Continental Shelf Convention requires *total* removal (though this has been modified by the proposed new Law of the Sea Treaty to refer only to removal to meet requirements set by IMO). The fishing industry would like to see total removal to sea-bed level of all abandoned constructions, but the oil industry wishes to keep expenditure on clearance to a minimum, even though under the offshore tax arrangements it would be an allowable expense.

International Control of Shipping

Freedom of navigation was one of the earliest and most important activities protected by international law. But, as we have seen, developments recently have made it necessary to bring about certain changes giving greater powers to port states and coastal states. Most of these changes have been negotiated within the forum provided by IMO. In recent years, IMO has made great efforts to overcome the criticism that its conventions take too long to come into force. Because of these delays a number of states took unilateral action, leading to the introduction of different standards in various parts of the world, thus endangering both the safety of ships worldwide and the natural environment of seas and coasts.

Yet it must be recognized that IMO has no powers other than those granted to it by its member states and delays in enforcing conventions continue to be caused primarily by the slowness of its members' states to enforce them (see chapters X and XI). IMO has none the less taken rather seriously the need to encourage its individual member states to ratify conventions speedily, to adopt and implement the necessary legislation, *and* to enforce it in order to promote safer ships and cleaner oceans. This task may become easier in global terms within the framework provided by the Law of the Sea Treaty if the treaty is ratified, or the relevant parts are adopted into customary law.

In north-west Europe however, with which this study is concerned, regional efforts to promote the relevant conventions can make a significant contribution and the importance of the regional approach has been stressed by IMO officials and by individual governments.[11] Regional consultation and co-operation agreements on marine pollution prevention and abatement in specific areas where the risks are high, such as the Baltic, Mediterranean and North Seas, have been steadily encouraged by IMO. Regional initiatives to improve maritime safety according to IMO standards, such as certain actions undertaken by the United States Coast Guard, have been generally approved for supporting and enforcing internationally agreed rules.

The lesson to be learned is that laggard governments have only themselves to blame if their flag ships are excluded from trading in certain regions, because they fail to comply *at least* with IMO standards. In other words, IMO standards are generally regarded as a 'passport' of universally accepted and reasonable regulations, thus allowing entry into coastal approaches and ports, *even where regional arrangements have been made*.

This understanding appears to have emerged clearly from the Paris meeting, in December 1980, of the thirteen European ministers responsible for maritime safety, together with representatives of IMO, the ILO and the European Commission. At this assembly the ministers reaffirmed clearly their conviction that, because of the international character of sea-trade, standards and rules in the field of maritime safety, pollution prevention and related social questions can best be established in the appropriate worldwide organizations, such as IMO and the ILO. Further details of this meeting are given in chapter IX.

There is, therefore, a complementary importance between the global and regional approaches in promoting ship safety and pollution prevention. Both are essential if the efforts are to be in any way effective, particularly since their effectiveness or success must depend upon acceptance by governments and the ship-owners who operate world-wide.

It is now perhaps clear that the impact of new technology upon one of humanity's oldest uses of the sea has produced a complex of difficult problems which it will require a great deal of effort, ingenuity and negotiation to solve if serious conflict with other uses is to be avoided.

Sources and Further Reading

Cohen, M., Travails of the Flying Dutchmen: Lloyds Standard Form of Salvage Agreement and the US Salvage Industry', *Marine Policy*, Oct. 1982, pp. 265–86.

Lowe, A. V., 'A move against substandard shipping', *Marine Policy*, Oct. 1982, pp. 326–30.

Nautical Institute, 'Memorandum on Maritime Safety', *Seaways*, May 1981, pp. 3–9.

Tribunal of Inquiry, *Report of the Disaster at Whiddy Island, Bantry, Co. Cork*, 1980, Dublin, Government Stationery Office (the *Betelgeuse* explosion and fire).

De Bievre, A., Memorandum on Shipping and the Environment, European Environmental Bureau, December 1981.

European Parliament, *Report drawn up on behalf of the Committee on the Environment, Public Health and Consumer Protection: on combating the effects of disasters where oil is released into the sea and reaches the shore*, Mrs A. Spaak, PE 65.851, Document 1-467/80.

Notes

1. These are required for compliance with the 1954 IMO Convention on Oil Pollution amended in 1969.
2. Compensation for damage caused by oil pollution is covered by two IMO conventions—the International Convention on Civil Liability for Oil Pollution Damage 1969 and the International Convention on the Establishment of an International Fund for Compensation for Oil Pollution Damage 1971. Both are discussed. Two further measures in this area are TOVALOP and CRISTAL.
3. *Explosions on Large Tankers and Combination Carriers 1974–1980*, Salvage Association, 1980.
4. Pearson, J., 'Shipping and the European Community', *Seaways*, July 1981.
5. Commission of the European Community. Proposal for a directive concerning the enforcement in respect of shipping using Community ports, of international standards for shipping safety and pollution prevention. Brussels COM (80) 360, 26 June 1980.
6. *International Legal Materials* (1982), pp. 1–30.
7. C.192/8 *OJ of the European Communities*, 1980.
8. O'Toole, M. 'The Future of Hydrography in Ireland', paper presented at a meeting of the Irish Society for Surveying & Photogrammetry, April 1982.
9. It is not, however, entirely clear whether this convention applies to the new 200-mile Exclusive Economic Zone. The Law of the Sea Convention which legislates such zones does not cover this point, but many north-west European states may not become parties to it, even though some have signed it (see chapter X).
10. *Oil Spill Intelligence Report*, vol. 2, nos. 1–7, 1979.
11. See also the numerous reports by UNEP on its Regional Seas Programmes.

VII

Defence

Introduction

This study as a whole is concerned with scientific and technical descriptions of the different uses to which the waters round the United Kingdom may be put, and the extent to which these uses may conflict. But such conflicts of function are twofold. First, there can be conflict arising from competition for commercial advantage between individuals or groups pursuing the same activity; and secondly there can be conflict between those using the same waters for different purposes. Legislation, and the means to enforce it, are both essential therefore in order to protect the weak from the strong, and to preserve resources and the environment for the common good. This implies authority, which in turn derives from sovereignty, a concept inseparable from extent of territory or territorial seas. Derogations from absolute sovereignty, as, for example, in adherence to international agreements regarding posts and telegraphs, or the rules for the prevention of collisions at sea, by definition confirm the fact of sovereignty, and the role of the nation state as the foundation of international order. National security, therefore, 'the preservation of the state against internal and external threats to its stability and independence', must be taken into account in studying conflicts of sea use, where the activities of the citizens of one sovereign power may impinge upon those of the citizens of another.

National security, as a concept, involves the preservation of public order, territorial integrity, and economic strength. All three elements interact continuously, and must be held in balance. The consent of the governed is hard to sustain if they are starved through overexpenditure upon arms, lacking which, however, the trade necessary for economic strength may be brought to a standstill by hostile action. In the case of the United Kingdom, the 'Defence of the Realm' is more intimately bound up with uninterrupted and orderly use of (in the words of John of Gaunt) 'the silver sea which serves it in the office of a wall, or as a moat defensive to a house against the envy of less happier lands'.

It should, however, be recognized that the era of *laissez-faire* at sea is over. The politics of abundance upon which our attitude to maritime matters was founded must give way to the politics of scarcity. If the object is to preserve freedom of operation where this remains vital for the common good, it is necessary to be prepared to exercise sensible authority where this has become indispensable to the maintenance of essential 'law and order'.

Defence forces are closely concerned with the offshore waters of the United Kingdom in two different but related ways. First, they are an agency—often a principal, always the ultimate agency—for enforcing the good order and security of the offshore zone in peace and war. Second, they require from time to time the use of parts of the area for trials, exercises and weapons practices, activities which could conflict with other uses.

The Legal Background

It will be necessary, in the following treatment of those two main aspects of defence activity, to make some assumptions about the international legal background for the future. The basis, it is believed, must be the convention[1] which has now been signed by the majority of nations at the United Nations Law of the Sea Conference. Either this will come into force as a codification of international law, or its main elements will be adopted in the practice of the vast majority of states and become customary law where it is not already so. Since defence forces not only use the sea but help to regulate it, there are very few of these main elements that do not affect defence in one way or another (for details see chapter X).

In internal waters, which lie shoreward of the baselines allowed by the convention (generally the low water mark, but straight baselines between points are allowed in certain cases), the coastal state has full national jurisdiction. Its laws apply to the extent where it can deny access, restrain departure, and take legal proceedings against foreign merchant ships or members of their crews. The immunities of foreign warships are, however, respected.

In the territorial sea, which a state may now declare up to a maximum of 12 miles to seaward of the baselines, the coastal state has sovereignty and may make laws and regulations covering a wide variety of matters: customs, fiscal and sanitary regulations, shipping lanes and traffic separation schemes, buoyage and pilotage, the preservation of the environment, and the general security of the state. There is, however, a balancing right in the territorial sea for ships of other nations: the right of innocent passage. This is defined generally as passage which is not prejudicial to the peace, good order, and security of the coastal state, and activities which constitute non-innocence are further defined. They include weapons practices, the operation of aircraft from ships, acts of espionage, and of course threats or use of force against the coastal state; but they also cover more mundane matters, such as anchoring or stopping where this is not justified in the ordinary course of navigation. The coastal state's criminal and civil jurisdiction over individuals in passing ships is severely limited. There are no separate restrictions on the innocent passage of warships, except that submarines must navigate on the surface and show their flag. There is no right of innocent passage for aircraft except for international straits which fall within the territorial sea, or seas, of coastal states. In international straits, even though these may consist entirely of the territorial sea of one or more countries, a more liberal regime called transit passage applies. While the coastal state or states may still make certain rules concerned with the safety of navigation and good order, including the establishment of sea lanes and safeguards against pollution, all users have freedom of navigation and overflight for the purpose of transit and may use their normal mode of operation; this is of course particularly important for submarines, which may (if the water depth allows) proceed submerged under the transit-passage regime, and for aircraft.

To seaward of the territorial sea, the coastal state's competences become more functional. They belong to three overlapping areas: the contiguous zone, the exclusive economic zone, and the continental shelf (see chapter X).

Regulation in Peacetime

The fishery protection task

The oldest-established regulating task in British waters is fishery protection. Indeed, the Fishery Protection Squadron claims an unbroken period of duty since 1379. No doubt there were many periods of relative ineffectiveness during those six centuries, and some of the political as well as operational misconceptions still contain lessons for today; there is, for example, some evidence that Charles I's ship-money fleet had fishery protection as one of its primary justifications. In any event, fishery protection is, round the coasts of England, Wales and Northern Ireland, a firmly established task of the Royal Navy; around the Scottish coast the responsibility is less clear-cut as the Department of Agriculture and Fisheries (Scotland) administers certain craft of its own.

The fishery regime that has to be enforced is now exceptionally complicated and is covered more fully in chapter V.

As can be deduced from the protracted negotiations, enforcement of the CFP will be not only an intrinsically difficult but also a politically charged matter. It has been made no easier by the emasculation of the North East Atlantic Fisheries Commission (NEAFC), whose Joint Enforcement Scheme allowed inspection of fishing vessels of all members by authorized agents of any member state. Now national forces have the job of enforcing EC-agreed compromise arrangements, often still disputed by individuals, within their own zones.

Enforcement requires finding out where fishing is taking place, the ability to visit, the power to inspect, and the capacity to arrest if an infringement is discovered. When it is considered that the EC countries bordering the North Sea alone owned more than 2,000 fishing vessels of over 100 tonnes in 1978,[2] and that a considerable proportion of these can be expected to be in the British fishing zone at any one time, it is clear that the task is a formidable one. Its purposes must be deterrent as well as corrective; the knowledge that there is a very good chance of being caught and penalized is perhaps the most one can hope to achieve.

To reach this minimum desirable state, three elements of the task can be identified: surveillance to establish where the fishing concentrations are, presence to deter possible transgressors, and active inspection and follow-up action to give teeth to the whole notion of enforcement.

The forces and agencies that are available to carry out this task will be described later. This is because they are not exclusively dedicated to fishery protection; they are, indeed, one of the stronger threads in what has been called the offshore tapestry, the whole business of the public management and good order of the sea areas round the United Kingdom.

Oil and gas rig protection

There are about a hundred oil and gas rigs and production platforms in the waters surrounding the United Kingdom. Safety zones are established in a radius of 500 metres around such installations, which are subject to the limited jurisdiction of the United Kingdom. The numbers of people employed on them vary from over a hundred on some to none on others.

Threats to these units fall into two categories. There are the common stresses of sea and weather, and misdemeanour or crime among those on board; and there are external threats from those who for whatever reason are opposed to the British offshore effort. It must be said, however, that the latter category has not been very obvious during the decade of exploitation of these resources; there have indeed been a few alarming incidents, and rather more vague threats, but no published evidence of anything like a sustained campaign.

Those who manage and operate the rigs are, clearly, responsible in the first instance for taking due precaution against both types of threat. Good order, normal vigilance and enforcement of the many structural and operating rules are clearly essential and there is much evidence that, after a somewhat anarchic start in the late sixties, the operations are now conducted in a manner that is itself a deterrent to any kind of serious dispute. But, clearly, accidents can occur and order break down, and either civil or military assistance may have to be called in.

In the first category of threat, accidents of any sort are more likely to require the involvement of defence agencies. Diving accidents are a particular case in point. Fewer will be the cases where rigs or their personnel are threatened by weather; in this case the rescue services, which are described below, will be involved. Drifting vessels have threatened rigs in the past; here again defence resources may be called in. In the event of serious misdemeanour on board an installation, of course, the services could be called in to aid the civil power, but this would be a rare occurrence.

So far as the second category of threat is concerned, the chief aim of any defence organization must be to deter it. Again, the risk of being caught must be maximized in the eyes of a potential wrongdoer. Surveillance is clearly a powerful aid, and random patrols of sufficient frequency will help to produce the necessary uncertainty. This framework needs to be backed up by a quick-reaction force with special skills of the sort needed in anti-hijacking and anti-kidnapping operations.

Traffic regulation

The International Regulations for the Prevention of Collisions at Sea have evolved steadily over the century. Their latest codification under the IMO is dated 1972. It incorporates a requirement to observe traffic separation schemes adopted by IMO,[3] by proceeding in the prescribed direction for that lane or, if crossing it, by doing so at right angles to the traffic flow.

There are about a dozen separate traffic separation zones around the British Isles. They all fall wholly or partially outside the territorial sea, which makes the problem of jurisdiction over foreign vessels a difficult one, and it will be made only marginally easier when the territorial sea limit is extended to twelve miles. Once inside the territorial limit a foreign vessel can, in theory at any rate, be ordered to observe the regulations; outside it, he can only be advised, enforcement being the prerogative of the flag state.

It should perhaps be gratifying that, in spite of the difficulties of policing the schemes, the proportion of 'rogues' going the wrong way in the Dover Strait is as low as 5 per cent and many of these are fishing vessels. There is no doubt, too, that the incidence of collisions is much lower since the schemes were introduced. But, as the *Niki/Texaco Caribbean/Brandenburg* disaster in 1971 showed, the penalties of non-observance are high and supervision of the schemes, to the maximum extent allowed by the law, is necessary.

Once again, surveillance is a necessary element. Also essential in this case where co-operation has to be requested rather than demanded, is a good and accessible information and advisory service. This implies well-organized communications. Finally, some form of physical enforcement may be necessary in extreme cases, either for British ships wherever they may be or for foreign ships within the British territorial sea.

Customs, fiscal and immigration regulations

In the United Kingdom these are in the hands of HM Customs, which has its own water craft in which it can visit ships. The vast majority of infringements occur on landing and are dealt with by normal procedures.

Defence forces exercise no jurisdiction in the usual course of events; they could be called in in the unlikely event of resistance to or assault on customs officers or their vessels, or in hot pursuit of offenders beyond the territorial sea.

Search and Rescue (SAR)[4]

Fortunately there is no need to discuss questions of jurisidiction in the context of search and rescue for those in distress at sea. It is well known that under the Geneva Convention on the High Seas, 1958, all who can should render assistance, whatever their nationality and whatever waters they are in.

In the United Kingdom the overall responsibility for maintaining a standing organization to deploy life-saving resources in case of accidents around the coast rests with the Department of Trade, and Her Majesty's Coastguard is the authority responsible for initiating and co-ordinating all civil maritime search and rescue measures. The area to which this responsibility extends, the UK Search and Rescue Region (SRR), is subdivided into six maritime SRRs each under a Maritime Rescue Co-ordination Centre. These have the function of allocating to any shipping casualty the appropriate SAR resources, which may be provided by the Royal National Lifeboat Institution, the Royal Navy, the Royal Air Force, the Coastguard itself, or any combination of these. RAF Rescue Co-ordination Centres perform a similar function in relation to aircraft casualties. Lloyds are informed of casualties and are responsible for notifying ocean-going tugs.

The resources concerned are the property of various agencies and the organization depends critically on excellent communications, both by telephone ashore and by radio at sea. There will always be the possibility of difficulty and uneven reaction when the command and control of forces is fragmented in this way. Any such loose organization is bound to encounter a number of obstacles to its smooth functioning; many of these, which are numerous in Britain, can be traced to the haphazard way in which the structure has grown up. There is, at any rate, no doubt about the courage and skill of those concerned in search and rescue; the record speaks for itself. Any radical reorganization or centralization might well cause a sharp drop in the individual character, and ultimately the spirit and expertise, of the component parts.

Pollution control

It must first be said that only a quarter of the total pollution of the marine environment comes from ships. The flag state has a responsibility to ensure that vessels flying its flag comply with the applicable international rules and standards, which include standards of construction and training as well as of operation (see chapter x). As is well known, this responsibility is not always effectively discharged, and indeed it is intrinsically difficult to discharge. Consequently the coastal state has powers in its territorial sea, and has been given powers in its exclusive economic zone, to take enforcement action in certain cases. In the territorial sea these extend to physical inspection when the coastal state has clear grounds for believing that any pollution laws or regulations have been violated. In the exclusive economic zone, a simple alleged violation may be dealt with only by requiring the vessel concerned to communicate its identity, port of registry and next port of call; a violation causing significant pollution may justify physical inspection; and a violation causing major damage to the marine environment may be followed by detention by the coastal state.

These rules are carefully graded and worded in the convention, but they are no doubt a source of anxiety to shipmasters who may, in many parts of the world, fear that they can be used in a discriminatory way. Even in a coastal state of impartiality and goodwill, the judgement and organization of the authorities is put under considerable pressure. There is a need for quick and accurate decisions on whether a violation is technical, significant or major, and subsequently on the action to be taken.

In the UK the responsibility for such action rests with the Department of Trade, which co-ordinates other agencies as necessary. But defence forces often become involved. In the case of casualties causing pollution, particularly, there has been no major incident in the past twenty years where Royal Navy and Royal Air Force units have not participated; while at the other end of the scale, oil slicks are more often than not reported by military aircraft. It is in the nature of vessel-source pollution that it occurs in a haphazard way, and it is open to question whether permanent anti-pollution patrols are a cost-effective way of deterring it, although they have been adopted by the Netherlands. However, the knowledge that a country runs a vigilant anti-pollution organization, able to react quickly to violations and to enforce the necessary boarding, inspection, and detention procedures, ought to be a powerful deterrent to the deliberate polluter.

Some considerations about enforcement vehicles

The functions of defence forces in the preservation of good order round our coasts seem to fall into three broad categories: gathering information; communicating instructions or advice; and enforcement. The ability to do all these, in an organized way with sufficient scope and frequency, will be a powerful deterrent to potential transgressors.

To fulfil their functions in the conditions of the UK's territorial waters and offshore zones, regulating forces will need certain characteristics. They will, first, need the capacity to *acquire data*. They will also need rapid and reliable *communications* with each other, with headquarters and with those whom they are trying to control. They will need *mobility*; the territorial sea is wide, the exclusive economic zone much wider. They will need *endurance*, otherwise their sortie rate will be uneconomic. They will need to be *weatherwise*; trouble is more likely in fog or bad weather, and transgressions do not stop at night. Finally, their *weaponry* will require great *flexibility* in application, since the principle of minimum force will apply even in those cases where coercion is allowable.

When these characteristics are looked at in the light of the vehicles that may be available—aircraft, ships, submarines, divers and fixed installations—all appear to have something to offer. The best mix will depend on the UK's geographical circumstances and finances.

First, it is certain that the most effective way of scanning the sea's surface is from high up. Radar-fitted aircraft are, therefore, high on the list of essential equipment of most coastal states. But visual identification of suspicious contacts will be necessary, and for this another aircraft, fixed-wing or helicopter, may well be more useful than the surveillance aircraft itself. For detailed radar surveillance of coastal waters, a shore installation may be better or cheaper than aircraft; even so, aircraft or surface craft for probe and visual identification will be highly desirable.

Surface ships become even more necessary if boarding is required, for though more and more merchant ships are becoming accustomed to being boarded by helicopters, they have to be not merely acquiescent but co-operative, and boarding from boats or small patrol craft is still a more certain method. Moreover, ships can remain on station for days, whereas aircraft cannot. On the other hand, ships are intrinsically slow, and control of a large sea area by ships means having either a large number of them or having the capability for a quick dash to the scene of action; there may be a place for the hydrofoil here, as indeed there may be a place for the airship in the field of long-endurance surveillance. Finally, if coercion is required, the surface ship is probably the best instrument, since it can command a greater variety of weapons than an aircraft and with greater discrimination. Guided missiles, for regulation work, will always be too stern a remedy; it is instructive to recall that no documented fishing case goes beyond the use of a 127 mm gun, and that was regarded by a (West European) tribunal as excessive. The ability to hit, and to miss with accuracy—so necessary in many situations—are two sides of the same coin and the shipborne gun provides it.

The need to safeguard sea-bed extraction industries raises requirements of a unique technical kind. The overall need for surveillance, presence, and patrol can certainly be met by aircraft and ships; but threats such as clandestinely fixed limpet mines, deliberate fracture of pipelines, and variants of the hijack, can be met only by more specialized measures. These include underwater patrols and inspections by either divers or small submersibles, and quick-reaction forces, specially trained, based ashore, and helicopter-equipped for rapid transport.

British Defence Organization for Offshore Regulation

The defence forces provided for the offshore task have grown quite rapidly in the last decade. The Royal Navy now has for this task sixteen surface vessels, a number of helicopters, and diving resources; the Royal Marines have a large company of over 400 men; the Royal Air Force has four long-range maritime patrol aircraft specifically provided, and a number of helicopters. It is sometimes not possible to assign precise numbers to the forces listed above, since some are provided for other tasks in addition to regulation. However, this is not the full extent of Service participation in the offshore tapestry, since general-purpose defence forces may be called in either to cope with particular large-scale emergencies or for patrols on an opportunity basis when they are passing through an offshore area of especial interest.

The forces provided for offshore regulation are described in more detail below.

Surface ships   Three classes of surface ship are now employed in offshore work. The earliest vintage are the 'Ton' class coastal minesweepers, built in the 1950s, 153 feet (46.6 m.) long with a complement of about 30. Built of wood to lessen their magnetic signature and therefore their vulnerability to magnetic-influence mines, these sturdy little diesel-powered ships have supplemented their war role by coastal fishery protection for many years. Seven are now under the command of the Captain, Fishery Protection Squadron, based in the Firth of Forth.

Under him come also the patrol vessels of the Island class, built from 1976 onwards. These were not quite the first custom-built patrol vessels—an inshore class was built in the early 1970s—but they were the first real successes of the offshore tapestry programme; 195 feet (59.5 m) long and of 1,000 tons standard displacement, they are trawler-shaped and stabilizers have improved their seakeeping. Two diesel engines, driving a single shaft, give them 16 knots. They have a complement of 39. There are at present seven such vessels.

Finally, two vessels of the Castle class (Offshore Patrol Vessels Mark 2) have recently been completed. These cost £10 million apiece, not very expensive by warship standards but much more expensive than any previous patrol vessel. They are, however, much larger than their forerunners, being 264 feet (81 m) long and having a speed of nearly 20 knots. Their most striking external feature is a large helicopter deck aft which can handle a helicopter the size of a Sea King for embarking stores or personnel or for fuelling. There is no provision for permanent stowage of a helicopter, however. Navigational and plotting equipment is computer-assisted and particularly accurate. Standard armament is a single 40 mm Bofors gun. The Castle Class has innate flexibility and could easily accommodate further weapon and sensor systems, though its basic crew of 50 is a limitation on the war-fighting roles it could be given.

Helicopters   Two kinds of helicopter are involved in the search and rescue services. The older is the Wessex 5, powered by two 1,250-shaft-horsepower Rolls-Royce Gnome engines, with a maximum take-off weight of 13,500 lb (6,136 kg). It can carry 15 people with ease and aircrews are fully trained in the difficult and often dangerous task of winching down to pick up people in trouble. The newer Sea King, operated by the Royal Air Force in a purely search and rescue role and by the Royal Navy as an anti-submarine aircraft that can be used for search and rescue, has two Gnome engines of an uprated type giving 1,660 shaft horsepower, and a take-off weight of rather over 10 tons. It can carry over 20 people, and its endurance is a great deal better than that of the Wessex 5. It is hard to say exactly how many helicopters are available in the search and rescue role since so many of them are doubling other tasks, but effectively at any one time the number round our long coastline runs into tens rather than single digits. In 1980, service helicopters were called out 1,223 times, and 858 people were assisted.[5]

Search and rescue are not the only tasks carried out by helicopters in the offshore zone. Apart from exercises and training, these versatile aircraft have investigated oil slicks, probed on behalf of fishery protection forces, carried troops to oil rigs, investigated transgressions of traffic regulation schemes, and transferred casualties from ship to shore, or to another ship for treatment. The future will provide equally diverse tasks for them.

Fixed-wing aircraft   Four RAF Nimrod aircraft are provided for the offshore role. This does not mean that there is a dedicated flight of our aircraft at any one time; simply that of the total Nimrod force a proportion of aircraft time equivalent to four airframes' worth is spent in activities such as fishery protection and the patrolling of oil and gas installations. The Nimrod is a large land-based aircraft with a typical endurance of 12 hours. It is designed for maritime reconnaisance and particularly for anti-submarine work, which accounts for a high proportion of its expensive and complex equipment. In the offshore role, however, its radar is the most important sensor; the Mark I Nimrod has an ASV-21D equipment, workmanlike but of a previous generation, while the Mark II has the much superior Searchwater radar with facilities to classify as well as locate surface targets.

The provision of fixed-wing aircraft illustrates in an unusually graphic way a dilemma of defence forces in offshore regulation. The Nimrod is a very expensive aircraft. It is not designed for the task, which could be done by much simpler aircraft such as the BAe Coastguarder or Britten-Norman Maritime Defender. But the introduction of these types would create new training, maintenance and spares requirements for the Royal Air Force, and moreover they would be of less use in war. These considerations would apply *a fortiori* to the use of airships. Another solution, to divorce the offshore regulation task from the fighting services altogether, raises the problems of command, control, communications, financing and support that have already been touched on. The provisions of Nimrods for the offshore task, imperfect as it may seem, has to be looked at in the light of these unpalatable alternatives.

Other defence forces   Quick reaction to an already developed threat to oil and gas rigs, or action to pre-empt a potential threat, is provided by Comacchio Company Royal Marines, 400-strong and stationed at Arbroath. Specially trained and frequently exercised in rig protection work, using helicopters or waterborne raiding craft as appropriate, they would certainly act as a deterrent to any would-be hijacker or saboteur.

Underwater surveillance is, of course, often conducted by the oil companies themselves, but Royal Navy divers carry out exercises on the rigs and with their comprehensive expertise can give most valuable back-up. A new Sea-bed Operations Vessel, HMS *Challenger*, has recently been launched. Equipped with all the latest paraphernalia of deep-sea diving and recovery, including a moon-pool for operating submersibles and very precise means of positioning, she will be available to help in offshore emergencies.

Finance   It has long been a Whitehall principle, much favoured by the Treasury and the lower-budget departments, that costs should 'lie where they fall'. In the case of the offshore tapestry, this arrangement was clearly inequitable towards the defence budget, which was predicated upon the forces needed to deter war, not on those to regulate the peace. In consequence, most of the running costs of the forces provided for regulation are now recovered from the Department of Energy and the Fisheries Departments.[6] The capital costs have, however, been borne up to now by the Ministry of Defence. This is about to change to a system whereby the capital costs of dedicated units are shared between the interested departments. Clearly the Ministry of Defence would not wish to lose its liability completely, because it feels that it is essential to have a final say in the bestowal of these forces, particularly in a time of crisis or war.

Deterring War

Britain maintains defence forces in order to deter armed attack on her vital interests. Her strategy is based on membership of the NATO Alliance, but she needs to be able to respond, herself, to threats that may develop at levels or in places where the Alliance cannot be expected to operate.

This strategy entails providing defence forces with a large degree of autonomy, capable of fighting (and therefore deterring) at all levels of combat against a variety of threats in widely separated areas. Readiness, as events in 1982 showed, is a necessary element in deterrence and both operational deployments and realistic training are therefore vital activities for defence forces.

In order to show how such activities bear on the coastal waters of the UK, it is necessary first to describe the sort of operations for which our maritime forces are designed.

Strategic deterrence

The reasoning behind the UK's maintenance of an independent strategic nuclear deterrent is stated in detail in government publications[7] and need not be reiterated here. Operationally, it entails keeping in a state of immediate readiness the ability to inflict on an aggressor damage that he would find unacceptable. This leads not only to calculations about targets and the number of warheads that it is necessary to deliver with certainty, but to assessments of the best vehicles to carry the missiles.

In 1962 the UK government decided that the Polaris system, based in submarines, was the best answer to the defence needs of the UK. Updated, it still provides the strategic deterrent. Four submarines are based at Faslane on the west coast of Scotland, and this force has maintained at least one boat on patrol, at readiness, continuously since 1969. Since they are well equipped with sensors, have great attention paid to their quietness in operation, and have no reason to indulge in manoeuvres that would give away their position, these submarines once in the ocean are very difficult to detect and even more difficult to trail for any length of time.

In spite of likely advances in Soviet anti-submarine warfare techniques, it appears that, given steady application of improvements in western technology, the Soviets would have no realistic hope of being able to count on destroying a submarine on patrol at a time chosen by them. In consequence, it has been decided that the next generation of strategic deterrent weapons should also be submarine-based. The delivery system chosen, the Trident D-5, is of very long range and of great warhead-power and accuracy—all probably more than the UK needs even into the 2020s, but preferred to the more exactly matched Trident C-4 for reasons of logistic commonality with the USA. In any event, the longer range gives the parent submarine more ocean in which to hide, thereby compounding the Soviet anti-submarine problem.

Every patrol must have a beginning and an end (they last 60 days or so), and it is here that the Polaris/Trident submarine is least comfortable. It is possible for the Soviet Union to station both intelligence-gathering trawlers and submarines just outside territorial limits; they will not necessarily be any more than a nuisance but they are certainly that, and the deployment of other British units may sometimes be necessary to minimize their nuisance value. Further inshore, the final approaches to Faslane must be negotiated on the surface, for the channels are not particularly deep and so are vulnerable to mining in times of tension or war. There is, therefore, a requirement for mine-countermeasures vessels able to keep the approaches open, and the new Hunt class—very expensive and constructed of glass-reinforced plastic—is well fitted for this task. Finally, servicing and storage facilities for missiles have to be located ashore; and it is obvious that it will be necessary to take some precautions in the sea area in the immediate vicinity of their depot.

It is worth pointing out that a nuclear-powered submarine, and indeed a nuclear weapon-carrying submarine, does not contaminate the water in which it lies or through which it passes. Indeed, the water going into a submarine is more radioactive than the water coming out of it, because of the built-in purifying systems. Naturally, very great attention must be paid to safety aspects in all stages of a nuclear submarine's operation, and the way in which the traditional hazards of the sea—fire, collision and grounding—may affect nuclear systems has to be closely studied. In fact, during the twenty and more years of nuclear submarine operation, all three of those hazards have occurred, but in none of the occurrences did the nuclear system give rise to any public danger.

General maritime operations

By far the bulk of Britain's maritime forces, however, is provided not for strategic but for all-level deterrence. This means not only being on the spot but, more importantly, being able to act; in defence planners' jargon, to maintain a presence, to counter aggression, and to escalate. Given this philosophy, it is not irrational to describe the activities of maritime forces by way of a Determinant Case which brings all their necessary functions into play. It is tempting to take the South Atlantic operations of 1982 as the determinant, and certainly the lessons to be learnt were many: not least that the British people still clearly expected their fleet to be capable of independent operations of war. But the case on which the comprehensive capabilities of that fleet must be founded is still the classic NATO contingency of a large-scale conflict in central Europe. It is not, we now well know, the only likely situation for a major conflict; on the contrary, it is a rather unlikely situation because of the deterrent paradox which says that the better you are at fighting a certain sort of war, the less likely is your opponent to embark on that kind of war. But in so far as such a conflict would be particularly damaging for the West, it is one that the West particularly wishes to deter, and consequently one for which it must be well prepared.

In such a conflict, Western objectives would include the continuing transfer of supplies running into several millions of tons from the USA to the European theatre of war; checking any Soviet advance in Norway; the deployment of many hundreds of thousands of men from the UK and the USA in Europe; and ensuring that strategic deterrent forces at sea remained secure. Without the use of the sea to achieve these aims, there would be no prospect of bringing the conflict to a successful conclusion. Anyone planning for a war so short that sea power is irrelevant is, in effect, planning to lose it.

But each use of the sea would be contested by formidable Soviet forces. The Soviet Northern Fleet alone could deploy some 90 tactical submarines, a quarter of them missile-armed and about half nuclear-powered; over 50 major surface units; and about 70 aircraft armed with air-to-surface missiles. The missiles are generally of long range, which sharpens the tactical problems. Soviet tactical doctrine particularly stresses the importance of getting in a heavy and co-ordinated 'first salvo'.

In these circumstances and against this threat, British maritime forces would have the following tasks:

Anti-submarine (ASW) protection for the NATO Strike Fleet in Atlantic waters   This task is laid upon the Royal Navy by the Supreme Allied Commander, Atlantic. It involves the provision of defence in depth against a highly sophisticated Soviet submarine threat. It entails the operation of fixed-wing aircraft and helicopters, surface ships and nuclear-powered fleet submarines. All require up-to-date sensors and weapons.

Offensive ASW Operations   In order to impose maximum attrition on enemy submarines in transit, and thus reduce the burden of direct defence of war and merchant shipping, submarines and long-range maritime patrol aircraft are required to operate well forward in the direction of enemy bases, closely co-ordinated and using all available data from ocean-surveillance systems.

Defence for merchant shipping   Experience of the past, and assessment of the present state of the maritime art, suggest that reinforcement shipping across the Atlantic will have to be closely organized and afforded protection against those enemy forces–air, surface and sub-surface–that will inevitably get through our forward defences.

Deployment of an amphibious force   The existence and readiness of such a force, able to support Allied Command Europe or the Island Commando, is a powerful bonding force in NATO, since it adds much to the confidence of allies on the flanks of NATO that they will be supported in an emergency. It requires specialized and highly trained commando forces with enough specialized amphibious shipping and supporting aircraft to ensure quick reaction to a swiftly building crisis.

Mine countermeasures   The maintenance of ports and their approaches in a mine-free state is a national responsibility. Soviet mine stocks are large and sophisticated and the units available for laying them are numerous and diverse. The Royal Navy needs minesweeping capability against deep and moored mines, and minehunting capability against shallow influence mines. An efficient watching, spotting and information organization is important in countering mine warfare.

Countering hostile surface ships   Now that so many surface ships are armed with offensive missiles, it is more than ever necessary to be able to take the offensive against them. The best vehicles for such operations are submarines, both nuclear and conventionally powered, and aircraft both land- and sea-based. Sufficient surface craft must be fitted with surface-to-surface missiles to provide a further line of defence.

Self-defence against missiles   Major surface units in all the situations described above must have the ability to defend themselves against anti-ship missiles. The methods used include active means (anti-missile missiles, guns) and passive means (chaff, electronic seduction).

Surveillance   This is a necessary element in war just as it is in peace. As well as aircraft, whose capacity for this task has already been mentioned, submarines can act covertly and gain much useful information. Combined with the satellite and other ocean surveillance systems available to NATO, such operations can build up a picture of potential and immediate threats that enables commanders to use resources to the best advantage. Reconnaissance, which is surveillance directed towards a specific objective, may use an even wider spread of means including sonobuoys laid from fixed- and rotary-wing aircraft, surface ships and organic fixed-wing aircraft probes.

Exercises and training

The tasks of maritime forces have been covered in some detail because they describe the activities for which such forces must train as well as the sort of forces the UK has. Much training concerns the individual and much can take place ashore; even operational conditions can be simulated ashore to a degree. This sort of training does not concern us here. But there can be no full replication of sea conditions ashore and it is absolutely necessary that much training and exercising takes place on, in and above the sea: for the individual, to acclimatize himself to conditions as close as possible to those he will find in action; for the team, so that it can find out how best to work together, and practise and develop the procedures by which it may produce a co-ordinated result; and for commanders, so that they become familiar with the limitations of their forces, the practices of their colleagues, and the ease or difficulty with which orders, instructions and information can be communicated. Frequent sea exercises are therefore necessary in order to keep defence forces ready to defend the realm, and so to deter aggression. The descriptions below cover four types of exercise: weapon firings, submarine exercises, minesweeping exercises, and large-scale exercises.

Weapon firings   An Admiralty Notice to Mariners reissued annually[8] says that 'firing and bombing practices . . . take place in a number of home waters' and that 'limits of practice areas in home waters are shown on a series of six small-scale charts called the PEXA series.'

These charts show that almost the whole of the sea round the United Kingdom, well beyond territorial limits, falls within the red, blue, or green sectors[9] of some firing danger area, which is, at first glance, startling information. The list of abbreviations appended to the chart runs to 24 different descriptions of exercises, all sounding lethal; the Notice to Mariners is slightly less detailed, singling out bombing practice, air-to-air and air-to-sea or ground firing, anti-aircraft firing, firing at fixed or floating targets or remote-controlled craft, and rocket or guided weapons firing.

However, a careful reading of the Notice to Mariners will give a less daunting impression. In fact the Firing Danger Areas are delineated to impose absolute geographical limits on their users. Once a practice is started, those users come under functional and strict regulations which may be called, for brevity, clear range rules. These put squarely on the range authority or firing units the responsibility for seeing that no vessel or person is endangered by the firings, and lay down rules for each type of firing which, if followed, will ensure that there is no such danger. For example, in anti-aircraft firings a broad arc, out to the maximum range of guns, must be clear of contacts during firing; in surface firings, where the rate of traverse of the gun is slower, a narrower arc either side of the gun's bearing needs to be clear. In the special case of long-range missile firings it is usual to employ a down-range vessel to report the range clear and, if necessary, warn approaching ships.

The point must also be made that these areas are only in intermittent use. Plans to use them are generally promulgated by local radio warnings or Notices, but of course these may not be received by all concerned and it is because of this, as well as of legal liability incurred, that the clear range rules are so important and so meticulously observed. However, a hazard which can be encountered in these areas is that arising from unexploded military devices left drifting or lying on the sea-bed.

Submarine exercises   The invaluable Annual Summary of Admiralty Notices to Mariners also gives information about submarines[10]. In fact, submarines exercising—even in the areas shown on the general charts—are more often than not at what is called 'safe depth', that is to say a depth at which no surface vessel even of deep draught could strike them. When a submarine is above safe depth it has a responsibility to make observations by periscope and by acoustic means at intervals to assure itself that it is causing no danger to itself or to other sea users.

It is when a submarine has just dived, or is about to surface, that it can be most vulnerable. On these occasions there is often a surface vessel in attendance, and smoke signals are released by the submarine at intervals to indicate where she is and what course she is on. Again, the ultimate responsibility for avoiding danger rests with the submarine, but other ships in the area can help by keeping clear and above all by keeping going: propeller noise is a good guide to the submarine commanding officer of where danger may lie.

Submarines on the surface are not always easy to see, because of their very low freeboard and the relatively small size of the conning tower. At night, their masthead and side navigation lights are very close together and may not give an adequate impression of the vessel's length; stern lights are placed very low indeed. At anchor, the statutory lights are displayed in the best available places, but it is not always easy for the observer to identify that they belong to a submarine. Some submarines are now equipped with an amber quick-flashing light to emphasize their presence. It should be noted, too, that radar echoes from surfaced submarines are likely to be much smaller than responses from surface ships of similar size and tonnage, because so little of the submarine is exposed to act as a reflector.

The years since the Second World War have not been free of submarine disasters, though there have been none in the Royal Navy for two decades and more. There is a comprehensive organization within the Royal Navy for dealing with them. There have been some more recent incidents, including one where a fishing boat in Irish territorial waters was towed by its nets by a submerged UK submarine and eventually sank. Fortunately the crew survived and compensation was paid. The rarity of such an occurrence in the busy waters surrounding the UK is perhaps a tribute to the care with which submarines are operated. However, it should be borne in mind that the penalties, in terms of both finance and operational flexibility, of introducing rigid regulations on either fishing or submarine areas to avoid the possibility of this sort of mishap would be much greater than the cost of an occasional incident.

Mine warfare exercises The areas in which practice minelaying and mine-countermeasures exercises may take place are laid down by Annual Notices to Mariners[11]. When any such area is to be brought into use for the laying of practice mines, notification is given by Navigational Warning. Since, however, the mines are harmless and non-explosive, ejecting when activated only a red, green, or white flare, non-receipt of these notices will do no more than cause a moment's alarm to the activator and a good deal of annoyance to the exercising forces.

There is one area in the Firth of Forth, some four miles across, which is in almost daily use because of its proximity to the main mine-countermeasures training base. The co-ordinates of this area, too are in the Notice to Mariners. Anchoring and fishing are prohibited in this zone, which lies within the dockyard port of Rosyth.

Ships engaged in minesweeping show special lights and shapes prescribed in the International Regulations for the Prevention of Collisions at Sea. These regulations add that 'it is dangerous for another vessel to approach closer than 1,000 metres astern or 500 metres on either side of the minesweeper'.[12] Mine-hunters are not so well protected by the regulations; they show the lights or shapes for 'vessels restricted in their ability to manoeuvre', and the small boats or dinghies from which they may operate divers show single white lights at night. Mariners are asked in the Notice to Mariners to navigate with caution in their vicinity.

Large-scale exercises   From time to time large-scale exercises under either national or NATO sponsorship, are held in the waters surrounding the UK. They are generally promulgated by Navigational Warning; the sea area may be delineated, but for major NATO exercises the whole of the north-east Atlantic may be involved. The principles on which these exercises are run are the same as for any other practice or exercise: that is to say, there is no restriction of other lawful users and the onus for the avoidance of damage or interference rests with the defence forces involved, subject always, of course, to the operation of the Regulations for the Prevention of Collisions at Sea. During such exercises, weapons may be fired, flares dropped, and ships, aircraft, and submarines manoeuvred. The exercises also generally attract the attention of Soviet surveillance forces, but a certain *modus vivendi* has been established in such cases. The message for all sea users is clear: 'there is no cause for alarm'.

Research, development and trials

A defence establishment as large as that of the UK is bound to require some research and development structure and some organization for conducting trials. In fact, the UK's defence research and development takes up an unusually large proportion of the defence budget, some 12–13 per cent. Whether this is all necessary is a matter for debate, but what is certain is that much of it is concerned with the sea and many of the activities connected with it have to occur at sea. A concentration of such facilities occurs off Portland and in Weymouth Bay: arrays to measure the noise made by ships, arrays to measure the magnetic influence of ships, a torpedo-testing range and a sonic reflector on which anti-submarine systems can be calibrated. All these are marked by appropriate buoyage. They do, without doubt, inhibit other maritime activities in this small area, and it is said that drilling for oil in the Bay was restricted as a consequence of them. On the other hand, there is no record of any traffic to and from Weymouth having been held up, nor of the Weymouth regatta being cancelled because of such activities.

A good deal of ordnance is also fired out to sea, in one place or another, for proving purposes; Shoeburyness is a particular example. Those places where it has systematically been deposited are, of course, well defined and marked on the charts. Cases naturally occur of unexploded ordnance outside these limits; the service authorities are quick to respond in cases where it is trawled up or otherwise becomes a danger. One notorious wreck, containing much unexploded unpleasantness, still lies off the coast in the Medway estuary; the controversy surrounding it and what (if anything) to do about it has been fully exposed in the Press. Most mariners would probably choose to play the percentages, let it be, and give it as wide a berth as they can.

Alliance aspects

Many of the exercises and practices that have been mentioned are carried out, in or over the waters adjacent to the UK, by the forces of our NATO allies. This is a reflection not only of the close co-operation between the maritime services of NATO, but of the part the UK plays as the principal European maritime partner in the alliance. In particular, the waters off Portland and the Clyde see a great deal of active participation by other northern European navies, which make use of the work-up and training organization and facilities there. All operate under the same set of rules for clear range and avoidance of interference with other sea users.

A price for deterrence

Any country requiring defence against external enemies has to pay for it. The strategy of deterrence and alliance that the UK has adopted is the most economical that can be sensibly devised, but because of the complexity of the threat it is not cheap in financial terms. To deter at all levels of conflict means to be able to fight at all levels, and that means diversity, which in turn means cost.

Inevitably, too, part of the price to be paid is in limitations placed upon other uses of Britain's offshore resources. It has been shown in this chapter that some areas have to be restricted and that others are used for activities which, however scrupulously conducted, can cause unease to other users. But every effort is made to keep the areas small, the impact light, and the safety at a maximum; and by careful negotiation, good planning, and meticulous observance of the rules this aim is generally achieved. One has only to contrast the British experience with the arbitrary imposition of large closed areas, both temporary and permanent, off the coasts of say the Soviet Union and Finland, to see how strongly the principles of free and equal use are upheld by the UK. It is, of course, to preserve these and other freedoms that our defence forces exist; the occasional unavoidable derogation from them in detail is a small price to pay.

Notes

1. The convention referred to in this chapter is A/Conf. 62/122, 1982.
2. Ian Scott in Watt, D. C. (ed.), *Greenwich Forum* V, Westbury House, 1980, p. 135.
3. International Regulations for the Prevention of Collisions at Sea, rule 10.
4. *Admiralty Notice to Mariners*, no. 4/82.
5. Cmnd. 8529–II, table 7.2.
6. Cmnd. 8212–II, table 7.4, notes.
7. Open Government Document 80/23.
8. Admiralty Notice to Mariners, no. 5, 1982, in the *Annual Summary of Notices to Mariners*.
9. Army, Navy and Air Force areas respectively.
10. *AN to M*, no. 8/82.
11. *AN to M*, no. 10 of each year.
12. International Regulations for the Prevention of Collisions at Sea, rule 27(f).

VIII

Discharges into the Sea and their Environmental Impact

Introduction

The vast majority of wastes created by human societies, whether discharged to the sea or to any other part of the environment, are eventually broken down by chemical or biochemical processes to simpler substances by the biogeochemical cycles responsible for the recycling of elements essential to living organisms. Some wastes are broken down and recycled quickly, others much more slowly, but whatever the timescale, the ultimate products of decomposition include the source materials for plant life which, in the sea as on land, are the ultimate food source for animals.

In most developed countries, water carriage systems have been developed to transfer material, initially directly to watercourses, and more recently to sewage treatment works prior to discharge. Thus the problem of controlling the environmental effects of waste disposal has become more and more concerned with protecting the aquatic environment. Recently, more effective legislation to control the volume and composition of discharges to inland waters has been introduced in most of western Europe concurrently with a trend towards larger industrial units requiring greater volumes of processing and cooling water. These factors have tended to increase the number and size of factories situated on estuaries and the coast where sufficient volumes of water have generally been available for the reception of effluents. In addition to material entering the sea from these coastal industries, the less readily degraded material from inland centres of population and industry are also introduced via rivers and the atmosphere and by marine disposal operations involving the controlled discharge of wastes from ships to designated offshore dumping areas. Operational or intentional discharges of oil from ships, the dumping of shipboard-generated litter or garbage, and accidents at sea causing loss of cargo also contribute to the sum of materials introduced by human activity. Continental shelf operations can also make a considerable contribution to such sources.[1]

Most wastes are complex mixtures containing substances which affect the environment in different ways and for different periods of time. In assessing the effects of wastes discharged to the marine environment, it is necessary to consider the various classes of material, such as oxygen-consuming substances, nutrients, metals, persistent organics, particulates, solid wastes, oil and radio-active substances; but for the purpose of assessing the amounts of pollutants discharged to various areas of the sea, it is convenient to consider more general categories of wastes such as sewage, industrial effluent, and river input, each of which tends to have a similar composition.

The Input of Pollutants to the Sea

Pollutants or contaminants[2] may enter the sea from ships, aircraft, pipelines, rivers, offshore platforms, or the atmosphere. Chiefly as a consequence of international agreements to limit the amounts of pollutants entering the sea, drawn up during the 1970s, much effort has been directed to attempting to quantify the total amount of material discharged from these sources. Discharges from pipelines usually consist of either an admixture of domestic and industrial effluent referred to as sewage, or industrial effluent alone. Similarly, discharges from ships may consist primarily of domestic sewage, oil bilge or ballast water associated with the cargo carried, or of solid wastes, particularly plastic packaging, or may include specific industrial wastes which are considered suitable for disposal at sea. Inputs from both rivers and the atmosphere consist of the more persistent materials resulting from man's domestic and industrial activities. The magnitude and distribution of the main inputs to the shelf seas are considered below. In most cases the data presented were gathered in 1976 by an international working group set up by ICES.[3]

Sewage

Sewage consists of a complex mixture of predominantly organic material discharged from domestic and industrial premises to the sewerage system. It contains large amounts of readily degradable organic matter and will exert a high oxygen demand on the receiving waters. The average person produces an amount of sewage daily which requires about 70 grams of oxygen to break it down and fully oxidize it and this is derived from the water.

Additionally, sewage contains appreciable amounts of solids, bacteria, nutrients and toxic materials such as metals and persistent organic compounds. Although complete information about sewage discharges to the shelf seas is not yet available, the majority of the discharges were included in the 1978 ICES report. From this it is possible to estimate that about 15,500,000 cubic metres per day of sewage are discharged directly to the European shelf seas from a population of about 37,300,000. The distribution and magnitude of these discharges are shown in figure VIII.1. Of this total some 10,600,000 cubic metres per day are discharged to the North Sea from a population of about 23,300,000. Other areas receiving

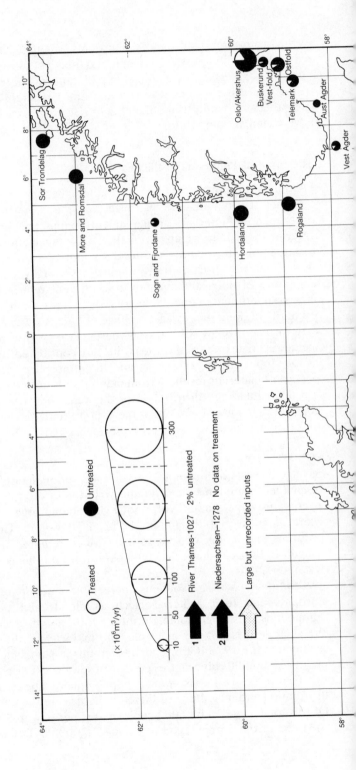

Treated ○   ● Untreated

(×10⁶ m³/yr)

10 50 100   300

River Thames–1027   2% untreated

Niedersachsen–1278   No data on treatment

Large but unrecorded inputs

1

2

Sor Trondelag

More and Romsdal

Sogn and Fjordane

Hordaland

Rogaland

Oslo/Akershus

Buskerud

Vest-fold

Telemark

Ostfold

Aust Agder

Vest Agder

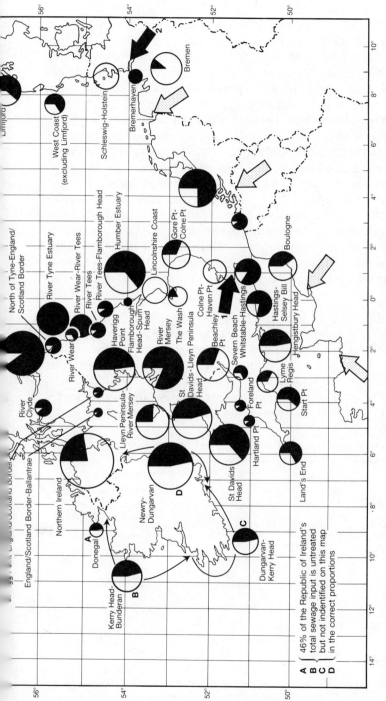

FIG. VIII.1. Sewage input to the sea (excluding dumping). From Lee, A. J. and Ramster, J. W. (edd.), *Atlas of the Seas around the British Isles*, MAFF, Directorate of Fisheries, Lowestoft, 1981.

substantial direct inputs are the English Channel and the Irish Sea. Estimates of the total amounts of sewage discharged from individual countries are given in table VIII.1. The degree to which these discharges receive treatment varies from country to country, and from region to region within each country, with generally a greater degree of treatment for discharges from areas of high population density or for those discharging to areas of particular biological importance. An indication of the degree of treatment may be obtained from a knowledge of the biochemical oxygen demand (BOD) of a particular effluent or the per capita BOD load discharged. Untreated domestic sewage will exert an ultimate oxygen demand of about 70 grams per person per day, and biological treatment will reduce this to about 15 grams per person per day. The figures given in table VIII.1 show that the majority of sewage discharged to the sea from Norway, Belgium and Iceland is untreated as the average per capita BOD load is greater than 60 grams per day. A greater degree of treatment in Denmark, Germany and Holland and the UK reduces the figure to between 40 and 50 grams per day, and in Sweden sufficient of the sewage is treated to reduce it to less than 30 grams per day.

Industrial wastes

As with sewage discharges, industrial wastes usually exert a significant oxygen demand on the receiving waters and can also contain solids, nutrients, and toxic materials. Additionally, many industrial effluents contain appreciable amounts of both vegetable and mineral oils. It is estimated that about 9,400,000 cubic metres per day of industrial wastes are discharged to the shelf seas, with about 7,500,000 cubic metres per day

TABLE. VIII.1. *Discharges of Mixed Domestic and Industrial Wastes to the Shelf Seas*

Country	Population millions*	Flow thousand cubic metres per day	Per caput Biochemical oxygen demand grams per head per day
Norway	2.13	682	64
Sweden	0.81	362	23
Denmark	0.93	392	53
West Germany	2.89	3907	47
Holland	2.20	310	41
Belgium	0.25	27	88
UK	24.96	8852	55
Ireland	2.98	896	51
Iceland	0.18	90	63
TOTAL	37.33	15518	

* i.e. discharging directly to the coast.

or 80 per cent entering the North Sea, particularly the shallow southern sector south of 54°N (see figure VIII.2). Other areas also receiving large inputs of industrial effluents are the English Channel and the Irish Sea.

River inputs

For many pollutants, particularly the more persistent or non-biodegradable materials discharged to inland waters, agricultural run-off such as fertilizers and pesticides, and most materials discharged to estuaries and fjords, river inputs appear to be the major pathway for their transfer to the marine environment. However, estimating the quantities involved is difficult, since in most cases there is a lack of understanding of how materials behave whilst passing through the freshwater/saltwater mixing zone; and also for many rivers adequate flow data are not available, though the publication by UNEP/UNESCO in July 1981 of a comprehensive report on river inputs to ocean systems has gone some way towards filling this gap. Little information is available on the transport of pollutants through estuaries but it has been established that substances may be accumulated in the sediments or lost to the atmosphere.[4]

In the absence of specific information on the behaviour of most pollutants, the assessments provided for the ICES working group have been made on the assumption that all the measured inputs will eventually reach the open sea. The total flow of river water into the shelf seas is estimated to be about 800,000,000 cubic metres per day of which about 600,000,000 cubic metres per day enter the North Sea principally from the river Rhine which discharges to the shallow southern sector. The distribution of the major river inputs is included in figure VIII.1.

Waste disposal from vessels

The intentional disposal of harmful or potentially harmful substances into the shelf seas from vessels has been regulated in north-west Europe by international law since the entry into force of the Oslo Convention in 1974.[5] Under this convention, the dumping of certain substances such as mercury, cadmium and many pesticides is prohibited, unless they occur only as trace contaminants in waste to which they have not been added for the purpose of disposal. Also, other substances such as arsenic, lead, copper, zinc and their compounds may only be discharged after an appropriate permit has been obtained, though in practice there are difficulties in attributing pollutants to the appropriate annexes of the convention.

In certain areas where centres of population and industry are situated near to coasts and estuaries, it has proved economically advantageous to dispose of sewage sludge and the wastes from some industries to the sea rather than to transport them considerable distances inland to suitable disposal sites. In addition, the dredging of harbours and waterways often results in the

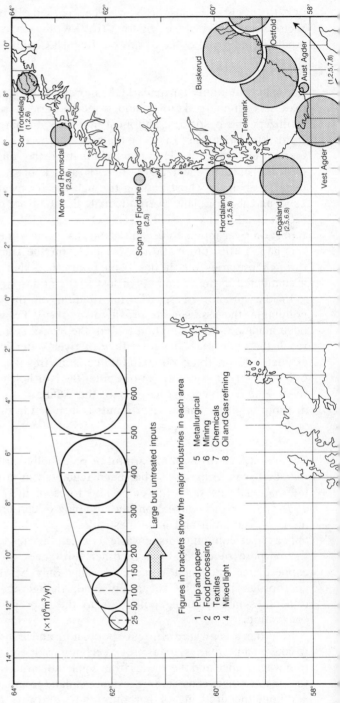

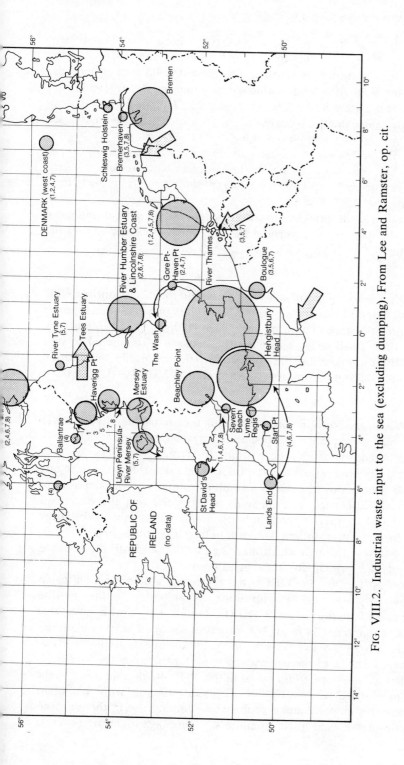

FIG. VIII.2. Industrial waste input to the sea (excluding dumping). From Lee and Ramster, op. cit.

transfer of material from inshore to further offshore areas in sufficient quantities to affect the water quality and sediment composition of the disposal area. The input of shipboard-generated solid wastes into the marine environment has been estimated as being in the region of 6.4 million tonnes per annum[6] A more recent study by Horsman,[7] based on an analysis of the waste dumped overboard by two merchant ships on long sea voyages, estimated that a minimum of 6,816,000 metal cans, 426,000 glass bottles and 639,000 plastic containers are dumped into the world's oceans daily. This has given rise, during the last decade, to increasing concern about the presence of solid wastes, notably plastic materials, in the marine environment.

Around the UK the principal locations where industrial and municipal sludges are dumped are in Liverpool Bay, the Firth of Clyde, and off the Thames estuary.

Particulate matter

From the ICES working group study, it is apparent that the majority of fine material discharged from vessels results from dredging activities. Further amounts enter the area as a result of sewage sludge disposal operations, mostly off the British coast, and from the disposal of industrial wastes, principally from titanium dioxide production. The magnitude and location of marine disposal operations are shown in figures VIII.3 and VIII.4.

Atmospheric inputs

Pollutants discharged into the air, or entering the atmosphere by the other pathways, may subsequently be washed out by rain, or deposited directly by a process known as dry deposition. It is only very recently that monitoring programmes have been established to determine the amounts of materials which enter the sea as a result of rainfall and dry deposition. The earlier David Davies Institute study of the North Sea also examined the role played in marine pollution by non-biodegradable substances deposited from the atmosphere. Deposition from the atmosphere is not an important pathway through which metals enter the sea, with the possible exception of lead, principally from car exhausts.

In north-west Europe, the OECD has conducted a detailed monitoring programme to measure concentrations of sulphur dioxide in the atmosphere, and in the UK the AERE, DAFS and MAFF have also carried out research in this field. The impact of so-called 'acid rain' on the regional seas is a topic of even less certainty, but the effects are not likely to be significant because of the capacity of seawater to buffer the acidity.

One other atmospheric trend noted in the 1972–82 decade was a slight increase in particulate matter in the stratosphere, with uncertain consequences for climate, and a probable continuing rise in the airborne dispersal of metals and toxic chemicals.[8] Once again, however, it is

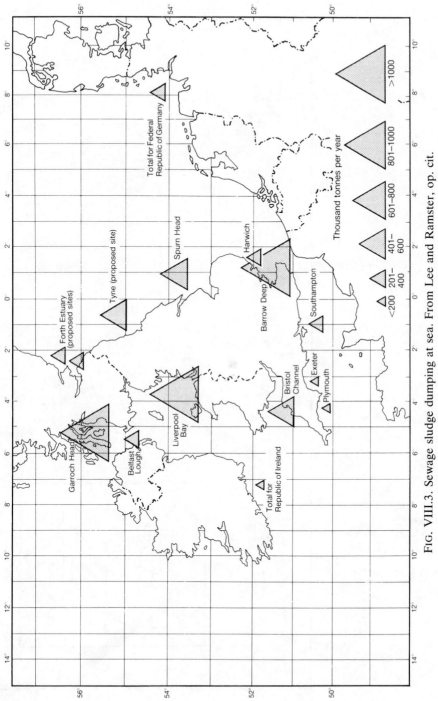

FIG. VIII.3. Sewage sludge dumping at sea. From Lee and Ramster, op. cit.

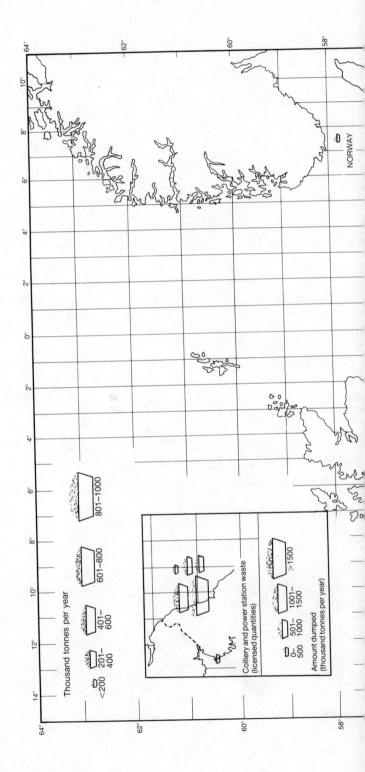

Thousand tonnes per year

<200   201–   401–   601–800   801–1000
       400   600

Colliery and power station waste
(licensed quantities)

Amount dumped
(thousand tonnes per year)

0–   501–   1001–   >1500
500 1000 1500

NORWAY

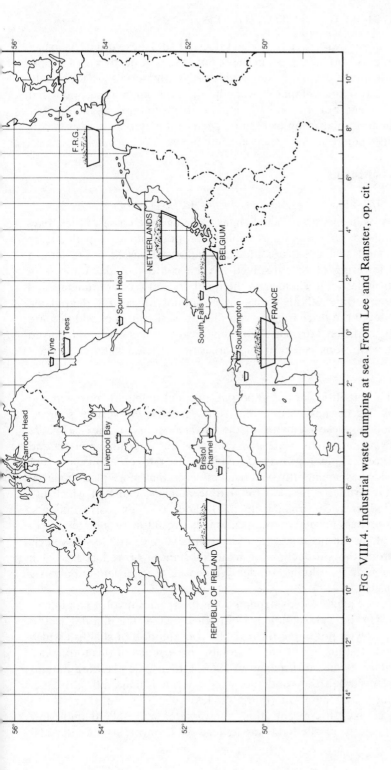

FIG. VIII.4. Industrial waste dumping at sea. From Lee and Ramster, op. cit.

impossible to state with certainty what effects, if any, these trends have had on the quality of surface waters in the regional seas of north-west Europe. Atmospheric inputs of readily degradable organic materials are thought to be insignificant when compared with the inputs from sewage, industrial wastes and rivers, but the limited amount of information available does suggest that atmospheric inputs of more persistent materials such as metals and pesticides could be significant in some areas.

The Effects of Inputs

Substances affecting the oxygen concentration of receiving waters

In bodies of water with restricted water exchange such as estuaries, bays and fjords, the discharge of appreciable quantities of material with a large oxygen demand, such as sewage and many industrial wastes, can result in a significant lowering of the dissolved oxygen content of the water with consequent undesirable changes in the numbers and types of animals and plants present. But, although very large amounts of readily degradable organic material are discharged to the shelf seas, the rates of addition are not usually sufficient to cause any significant reductions in dissolved oxygen concentrations except in small areas of restricted water exchange.

Nutrients

Considerable quantities of the important nutrient elements, nitrogen and phosphorus, are discharged into the shelf seas from the various sources. The addition of these elements to the surface waters of the sea where nitrogen levels in particular are generally low, has a fertilizing effect and results in greater plant growth. Providing the rate of addition is not excessive, this has a generally beneficial effect in that more plant material will be made available as food for marine animals, many of which are directly or indirectly consumed by man. The addition of excessive amounts, however, a process termed eutrophication, can result in very large growth or blooms of certain plant species which can have undesirable side effects resulting from the production of toxic substances or reduced oxygen concentrations if the blooms suddenly die once the nutrient supply has been exhausted.

The effects of algal blooms depend upon the species involved and upon their density in the water. Some toxic species, such as the dinoflagellates, can cause paralytic poisoning through the consumption of shellfish which have accumulated the organisms. A notable occurrence of this took place on the north-east coast of England in 1968. Other toxic plankton blooms cause problems when they undergo what is termed 'mass mortality', i.e. large numbers of them die more or less at the same time. As a consequence, oxygen concentrations in seawater may fall to quite low levels, particularly in sheltered areas, leading to mortality of intertidal animals. Both types of bloom have caused serious problems for mariculture operations.

In some localities, elevated nutrient levels are associated with abundant growths of green algae on the shoreline. These may subsequently become detached, and are then moved by wind and tidal currents to areas of deposition where, under the normal processes of decay, they may become a public nuisance.

River inputs are thought to be the largest contributors of nutrients to the area.

The effects of these inputs of nutrients to the sea have been reviewed by Topping[9]. Measurements of the concentration of nitrogen and phosphorous in the sea have been made for many years, revealing that higher levels exist in coastal waters near to known inputs. Individual sewage and industrial waste discharges seldom result in anything more than very local elevations of nutrient concentrations, but the major river inputs such as those into the southern North Sea and the Irish Sea have resulted in fairly large areas with concentrations higher than those found in more remote areas.

Metals

Natural weathering processes result in the transporting of large quantities of metals from the land into rivers and the sea. The present composition of seawater is a reflection of the amounts of metals and other elements added to the oceans and the processes which remove them to the sediments and the atmosphere. Almost all the naturally occurring metallic elements are known to be present in seawater at concentrations ranging from less than one part in one thousand million in the case of rare metals such as gold and platinum up to more than one part in a hundred in the case of sodium. The possibility of deleterious effects on marine organisms occurs when concentrations of metals are locally increased to levels greater than those normally present in seawater, for this will usually result in greater uptake by the organisms and can lead to interference with essential biochemical processes which are often dependent on certain concentrations of some metals, such as sodium, potassium, magnesium, calcium and iron.

The importance of the various metals from a pollution point of view is related to their toxicity and availability, as discussed by Wood.[10] Some metals such as sodium, potassium, calcium, magnesium, aluminium and iron are non-critical since, although they occur in relatively high concentrations and are easily taken up by organisms, mechanisms exist to ensure that harmful levels do not normally build up within the cells. Other elements such as titanium, niobium, gallium, and barium are known to be toxic, but are either very insoluble or do not exist in sufficient amounts for harmful levels to occur. The main problems from metals are associated with a third group including mercury, cadmium, lead, arsenic, silver, copper, and zinc which are very toxic and can be readily accumulated to harmful levels. Of these perhaps mercury and cadmium are of most immediate concern because of their high toxicity and the amounts in which they are discharged to the seas as a result of man's industrial activities.

Mercury   Estimates of the amounts of mercury discharged to the shelf seas suggest that the principal sources are rivers and marine disposal operations—primarily harbour dredgings, other sources being sewage discharges, industrial operations and the atmosphere. Relatively high concentrations (up to 0.2 parts per billion) have been detected in nearshore samples from the southern North Sea and the eastern Irish Sea, areas which are known to receive the main mercury inputs. These higher mercury levels are reflected in fish caught from these areas, but the levels are not thought to present a health hazard to people eating them.[11]

As mercury is included in the list of substances which it is prohibited under international conventions to discharge to the sea from either marine or land-based sources, and is the subject of European Community legislation, it is probable that mercury levels in areas with elevated levels will not increase and should, in time, decrease.

Cadmium   The input of cadmium to the shelf seas is principally from rivers, other sources being marine disposal operations (particularly of dredging spill), sewage, industrial operations and from the atmosphere. As with mercury, the high levels are found in the inshore waters of the southern North Sea and eastern Irish Sea. Around the Orkney Islands, high concentrations occur in fish and lobsters as a result of natural input, but, in general, the levels of cadmium in the waters of the shelf seas do not result in elevated levels in marine organisms except in one or two localized areas near to industrial premises using large amounts of cadmium. Cadmium is included in the list of substances which are prohibited from deliberate discharge to the marine environment and increasingly more effective control of the amounts discharged should ensure that existing levels do not increase, and decrease in the localized areas where elevated levels occur at present.

Lead   Estimates of the amounts of lead entering the area indicate that the major sources are marine disposal operations (including dredging), and river inputs and the atmosphere, with small amounts contributed by sewage discharges and industrial operations. A considerable amount of work has been carried out in recent years to try to determine whether the levels of lead in coastal seawaters has been raised by the entry, particularly via the atmosphere, of the lead which was blended with petrol as an anti-knock additive. Studies of the waters off California[12] have indicated that airborne lead forms a very important part of the total input of lead to the area and the provisional figures available for the inputs to the shelf seas are in agreement with this. It is likely that the lead concentrations of coastal surface waters have increased more than ten fold since the industrial revolution, but the significance of this increase for marine life is not known. Furthermore, most earlier measurements of lead in seawater were unreliable. There is, however, no evidence that present levels are exerting any harmful effects.

Copper   Copper discharged to the shelf seas comes primarily from the atmosphere, rivers and marine disposal operations, including dredging, with small amounts from industrial operations and sewage discharges.

The copper concentration of the majority of the shelf seas is less than 0.2 parts per billion although values of up to 2.0 parts per billion are found in the coastal waters of the southern North Sea and eastern Irish Sea. Copper is one of those metals which are required in small amounts by some organisms, but are toxic when present in excess. For most of the shelf seas, the copper concentrations are below the level of about 1 part per billion which has been demonstrated to cause a reduction in the rate of photosynthesis of marine algae.[13]

Where concentrations of copper are persistently above the usual levels, as in the Fal estuary, a population of marine organisms that are copper tolerant may develop.

Zinc   Estimates of the amount of zinc discharged to the shelf seas suggest that the primary sources are rivers, the atmosphere, industrial discharges and marine disposal operations, including dredging. A small amount comes from sewage discharges. As with the other metals, coastal waters of the southern North Sea and eastern Irish Sea contain relatively high concentrations, of up to 10 parts per billion. These latter concentrations are similar to those which have been shown to reduce the rate of photosynthesis of marine algae.[14]

A review of heavy metal contamination of the sea concluded that, with the exception of the Minamata mercury incident in Japan, there is no evidence that foodstuffs of marine origin have caused any permanent forms of metal poisoning.[15] It seems unlikely that the amounts of most metals being discharged to the shelf seas are leading to widespread pollution, but the levels of some metals present in some of the coastal waters may well be high enough to cause subtle ecological effects.

Persistent organic compounds

Technological development has continually provided mankind with the means of producing more and more chemical compounds, many of which do not occur naturally in any detectable amounts. A consequence of this has been the production, particularly over the last forty or fifty years, of a vast range of new chemicals to fulfil the needs of medicine, agriculture and industry. Many of these compounds, such as those used in pest control, have been temporarily useful in increasing the yield of a number of crops and in controlling disease; others such as the polychlorinated biphenyls (PCBs) are used by the manufacturers of certain electrical equipment. However, the introduction of these materials into the environment as a result of their manufacture, use, and disposal has resulted in consequences, associated with their chemical stability and persistence, which were not foreseen. In particular, deleterious effects have resulted from the widespread use of pesticides, such as DDT, and PCBs.

Organochlorine pesticides   The majority of pesticides belong to a group of compounds which consist of organic molecules containing a number of chlorine atoms. Perhaps the best known of these is DDT, which has been used since about 1940 to combat a number of disease-spreading insects. As with other pesticides, DDT is also toxic to other organisms if it is accumulated in sufficient quantities. Once introduced into the environment, DDT is broken down only very slowly by naturally occurring bacteria and then only to equally persistent derivatives such as DDE which is also appreciably toxic to a variety of organisms. Other pesticides of particular concern because of their persistence in the environment are aldrin, dieldrin, and endrin. Increasing concern about the environmental effects of persistent pesticides has resulted in the introduction of strict controls on their manufacture, use and disposal.

As a result of the data gathered in order to apply the marine dumping conventions, it is possible to estimate that the amounts or organochlorine compounds discharged from vessels is about 100 kilograms per day. Data for the amounts entering the sea from other sources are more difficult to come by although, from the pattern of usage, it is probable that inputs from rivers are significant as also are those from the atmosphere.

The precise effects of the present levels of organochlorine compounds in seawater and marine organisms are not known. It has been shown that very small amounts can decrease the photosynthetic capacity of unicellular algae, but it is not known whether levels of these substances in the environment actually reduce the primary productivity of the sea to any significant extent. There are only a few examples of mortalities associated with discharges of organochlorine compounds to the shelf seas,[16] but it is likely that the amounts accumulated by birds and possibly also seals have proved harmful, particularly during times of stress when the animals draw upon the fat reserves where the compounds are accumulated.

Polychlorinated biphenyls (PCBs)   Unlike the chlorinated organic compounds used for pest control, PCBs have not been deliberately introduced into the environment but have become widely distributed as a result of their manufacture, use and disposal. They are extremely stable compounds and have been used for a number of industrial applications including electrical transformers, hydraulic fluids, lubricants, adhesives, and printing inks. Since their implication in a number of marine pollution incidents became apparent in the 1960s, their use has been very strictly controlled and releases to the environment much reduced. However, their great stability means that it will be a very long time before the amounts already present are significantly reduced. Analyses of marine organisms have shown PCBs to be ubiquitously present at concentrations greater than those of the organochlorine pesticides. Estimates of the amounts entering the shelf seas are incomplete. The atmospheric input to the North Sea is thought to be about 2 kilograms per day, that from UK marine disposal operations about 1.6 kilograms per day. The magnitude of the other inputs are not at present known. The effects of the observed levels of PCBs in marine biota are difficult to assess; the levels usually found do not seem to have a profound effect on organisms in good condition, but under conditions of stress when fat reserves are mobilized, the concentrations of PCBs which are produced could have detrimental effects. The deaths of large numbers of sea birds in the Irish Sea in 1969 was probably associated with high contaminant levels, particularly PCBs, combined with adverse weather conditions and various unknown factors such as failures of food sources and, possibly, infectious diseases.

Solid wastes, packaged chemicals, and munitions

The most obvious impact of solid wastes in the marine environment is the aesthetic degradation of coastal amenities, particularly beaches used for leisure and recreational purposes. Ecological impacts have also been identified; living organisms have ingested solid wastes or become entangled in them, sometimes with fatal results. For example, sea-birds have lined their nests with scraps of fishing net and inadvertently killed their offspring when they subsequently became entangled in it. Antarctic and northern fur seals have been injured following entanglement in the remains of fishing gear in both the north and south Atlantic oceans. Nylon monofilament gill-nets in particular, since they are non-biodegradable, continue to catch fish after being discarded for periods of up to two years.[17] Because they are tight and much less costly than those of natural fibre which they have replaced, monofilament nets are used in areas where in the past such use was avoided because of their probable loss or damage.

Economic damage by other solid wastes includes the fouling of fishing nets or ship's propellors, the blocking of water-intake pipes and damage to ships following collisions with metal drums or wooden pallets at sea.[18] Human injuries include foot lacerations from the ring-pull tabs of drinks containers or other sharp edges of metal or glass items washed ashore. Human health hazards arising from encounters with packaged hazardous chemicals, discarded drugs or medicines and munitions have also been identified. Contrary to popular scientific belief, there is no evidence to show a widespread accumulation of specimens of domestic and commercial packaging in the marine environment of north-west Europe. The available evidence suggests that most plastic bottles become enbrittled and break up into small fragments within two or three years following manufacture and disposal at sea. However, as plastics packaging is a major constituent of litter found in both terrestrial and marine environments, attempts are being made to enhance further its degradability. On the north-east coast of England, the dumping of colliery waste has despoiled a number of beaches.

In the UK some coastal local authorities regularly collect and remove solid wastes from their beaches. Some beach cleaners have been developed from agricultural machinery such as ground-nut harvesters. In other areas, notably east Kent, local authorities have organized beach cleaning competitions. However, it is highly improbable that beach cleaning operations will substantially reduce the quantities of solid wastes on beaches. The few available resources, in terms of manpower and equipment, have to be deployed in small areas used intensively by holidaymakers in order to justify expenditure. Consequently, the great majority of beaches are ignored.[19]

Prevention is the direct approach to the control of marine pollution by solid wastes from ships. At the present time, the routine disposal of shipboard-generated solid wastes at sea is not an offence under national or international maritime law. Annexe V of the International Convention for the Prevention of Pollution from Ships (MARPOL) 1973, as modified by the 1978 protocol, does contain provisions regarding the disposal of shipboard-generated solid wastes and the prevention of this type of marine pollution. Unfortunately, the effectiveness of these proposed measures is questionable because, although MARPOL is now in force, it is so for only a few states and:

(a) Annex V of MARPOL is an optional rather than obligatory annexe, and this distinction may considerably delay the widespread application of its provisions;
(b) it will be difficult if not impossible, to enforce the proposed regulations governing the disposal of garbage at sea if they enter into force: this will depend on the bona fides of the parties;
(c) It has yet to be established whether ports can provide the necessary facilities for the disposal ashore of ship-board-generated solid wastes and whether waste disposal or storage systems can be relatively easily installed on ships.

Most packaged hazardous chemicals washed ashore are believed to originate from losses of ships' deck cargoes during adverse weather. Parts of southern England situated close to major shipping routes are particularly vulnerable in this respect. The *Aeolian Sky* incident, when thousands of packages of chemicals were washed ashore onto the beaches of southern England, raised questions on the international procedures for reporting such incidents and the subsequent arrangements for establishing liability and compensation for packaged cargoes lost at sea.[20] It has since been suggested that the IMO Cargo Loss Reporting Scheme, at present a recommended procedure, should be made compulsory. If this were done, there would be greater success in alerting coastal authorities to the possibility of beach pollution by such cargoes, thus enabling them to take adequate precautionary measures to safeguard the public. Since at the present time there are no recognized provisions for compensation for injuries to people or for the cost of cleaning the beaches, what is required is an international convention on liability and compensation for damage caused by packaged chemicals lost at sea. IMO's Draft Convention on Compensation for Pollution by Chemicals and Hazardous Materials does not cover packaged chemicals. At a conference in November 1981, the representative of a major container shipping operation revealed that of the random 15 per cent of dangerous-goods freight containers inspected at a large UK terminal prior to each vessel sailing, about 35 per cent were deficient in some way as regards labelling, documentation and securing.[21]

It is also only too easy for an unscrupulous operator to pack hazardous cargo into a container or trailer and not to declare it. Undeclared dangerous substances can also be shipped as a result of genuine human error. In the UK, under the Merchant Shipping (Dangerous Goods) Regulations (1981), it will be possible for penalties to be imposed on shippers of improperly documented, packaged or labelled dangerous goods. In Sweden and Holland, it is a legal requirement that ships' crews be provided with emergency response information to cover the cargoes being carried.

A wide range of munitions are regularly recovered from the marine environment following accidental losses or deliberate dumping in the past. Occasional fatalities and injuries have resulted from human encounters with munitions, usually following attempts to dismantle them. Sub-aqua divers and treasure hunters using metal detectors are particularly at risk.[22]

Marine disposal of unwanted munitions in British coastal waters is now regulated by the Dumping at Sea Act 1974. The Ministry of Agriculture, Fisheries and Food (England), the Secretary of State (Wales) and the Department of Agriculture and Fisheries (Scotland) are responsible for implementing this Act in relation to loadings taking place in the United Kingdom ports. Authorization is not given for the dumping of munitions in British coastal waters. When there is no practicable method of dealing with these materials on land, they are now dumped in deep water in the Atlantic Ocean.

Oil

In contrast to most of the pollutants considered in this section, oil is not toxic, but it is of significance because of the very large quantities which enter the sea as a result of many small incidents and occasional large ones. Oil pollution is a phenomenon which has affected the marine environment—as natural seeps of oil from the sea-bed and into rivers—since the formation of oil deposits hundreds of millions of years ago.

With the increase in the amount of oil transported around the world during the past fifty years, the amount introduced into the marine environment has also increased, and the effects on marine biota have become more apparent. Prior to any of the major oil spills which made news in the 1960s and 1970s, enough oil was entering the sea to cause the oiling and subsequent death of a small but significant number of sea birds. However, this was regarded as a relatively insignificant problem and it was not until several major spillages occurred in the late 1960s and offshore production increased in the 1970s, that systematic studies of the effects of oil pollution of the sea began.[23] As a result of these investigations much is now known about the effects of oil spills and repeated low level discharges on coastal communities and in estuaries, but much less about the possible effects of the lower concentration to which open sea organisms are subjected.

Oil reaches the marine environment in a variety of ways. Tanker wrecks and oil-well blow-outs are the spectacular incidents which alert the world's press and are usually regarded as the major sources. In fact, the majority of damage stems from apparently insignificant discharges from ships of all kinds—including ballast washings from tankers—from offshore installations and from land-based sources. Accidental spillages are also attributable to human error, be it ignorance, faulty equipment or sheer apathy. Cowell's figures for the north-west European shelf estimated that 1,600 tonnes are from fresh-water sources, 550 tonnes from the atmosphere, 900 tonnes daily from tanker operations, 470 tonnes daily from refineries and 55 tonnes daily from offshore installations. 370 tonnes per day are attributed to major shipping casualties. Oil pollution today follows a pattern very closely associated with the density of shipping and tanker traffic using the sea lanes around the continental shelf of Europe. The major route for the traffic runs along the west and north-west coast of France, and through the Channel to the major ports in the southern North Sea. The volume of oil carried along this route now exceeds three million tonnes annually.

In the North Sea, the loss of oil-well control, such as a blow-out, is an ever-present risk. The Ekofisk blow-out of 22 April 1977, in the Norwegian sector of the North Sea, caused widespread alarm at the time, but later investigations could not detect that any lasting ecological damage had resulted from the estimated 30,000 tonnes of oil spilt during the incident. North Sea oil field operators now have to submit oil spill contingency plans to their governments and these must include a list of essential elements for dealing with oil pollution. However, each operator is responsible for dealing with the oil pollution, although monitored by the responsible government agency. A total of 86 spills were reported to the UK Department of Energy in 1980, consisting of approximately 1,120 tonnes. A single incident, where a pipeline snapped, accounted for 980 tonnes of this.

Although oil is included in the list of substances which are not permitted to be discharged from ships, aircraft, platforms, or land-based sources, under the terms of the London, Oslo and Paris conventions, the original control of the main source of oil pollution at sea is exercised under the terms of an earlier IMO convention covering vessel sources, agreed in 1954. This convention was amended in 1969 to introduce stricter controls. MARPOL, in 1973, and the protocol of 1978, which is now in force, introduced *inter alia* stricter controls over all discharges. But offshore operators are permitted by government in exceptional circumstances to discharge small amounts of oil during operations. In 1980, 20 platforms discharged 157 tonnes of oil under this exemption, in concentrations of less than 50 parts per million. One of the most significant developments in reducing the amount of oil discharged to the sea has been the introduction of the load-on-top system for tankers. A report by the Central Unit on Environmental Pollution suggests that this reduces the amount of oil discharged to the sea by some 5,500 tonnes per day.[24] However, shore reception facilities are still not available in many ports and therefore tank washings are still discharged at sea, so that the vessel can load immediately on arrival at the terminal. Other means of reducing operational oil pollution include crude oil washing, clean ballast tanks and segregated ballast tanks. Better operation of oil refineries has also reduced the amount of oil lost to the environment. For refineries situated in Europe, it is estimated that the oil lost has been reduced from 260 tonnes per day in 1969 to about 80 tonnes per day in 1976.[25] The current input of oil to the North Sea resulting from oil production operations is estimated to be about 2 tonnes per day. Increasing exploitation of the reserves will probably increase this amount to about 7 tonnes per day by 1985.[26]

Many studies have been made on the effects of oil pollution on marine organisms. Laboratory tests have shown that low concentrations of petroleum hydrocarbons are lethal to a wide range of plants and animals or impair their physiological function. In the natural environment, spilled oil causes casualties, but these are usually rapidly made good. More prolonged damage may follow oiling of beaches or contamination of the sea-bed. Salt-marshes appear to be rather fragile environments and may be severely damaged by repeated oil pollution.

Public concern has been expressed above all over the continuing loss of sea-birds from floating oil. Species most affected are diving sea-ducks and auks (guillemots and puffins) which congregate in enormous numbers offshore of most North Sea coasts in winter. A small oil slick floating through such a congregation of birds can cause a disproportionately large death toll and it is not necessarily the major oil spills that have the most serious consequences for sea-birds. Summer breeding colonies, particularly numerous in northern Scotland, the Northern Isles, and on the Norwegian coast are vulnerable to oil pollution in summer, but so far have been rarely affected. Estimates are inevitably imprecise, but several tens of thousands of sea-birds are probably killed annually by oil pollution in the north-eastern Atlantic. Auk colonies in the south and south-western parts of the British Isles and in Brittany, already in decline probably as a result of climatic change, have been seriously affected by repeated oil pollution losses. More northerly colonies, on the other hand, have shown a substantial increase in strength in recent years.

Offshore and onshore cleaning costs are borne by both local and national ratepayers who seldom recover the costs as fines on offenders. The very large increases in fines reflect both government and public attitudes towards those who are caught.

The nature and size of the oil threat was examined by the Royal Commission on Environmental Pollution in 1981.[27] This report constitutes one of the best summaries of all that is known about oil pollution and it comes to the conclusion that oil pollution causes short-term damage to the coast and to marine life, that its immediate consequences are potentially serious, but that it entails no permanent threat to the marine environment. The report also examined very closely the attitudes of the relevant UK government departments to oil pollution and the overall effectiveness of the country's oil spill response system. Both were found to be lacking in effectiveness.

Arrangements for dealing with large oil spills were also criticized. In particular, the Royal Commission considered that there had been a misplaced emphasis on the effectiveness of dispersants and that the division of responsibilities between the Department of Trade and local authorities for action at sea and in inshore waters or on shore, was inimical to dealing with a major spill effectively. It recommended that a strengthened Marine Control Unit (in the Department of Trade) should assume overall control of oil spill counter-measures, liaising with local authorities.

Radioactivity

The discharge of radioactive substances to the marine environment is a complex issue which presents a number of serious problems, and which therefore requires more detailed treatment here. In addition, the problems of radioactive waste disposal have become inextricably mixed, or even confused, in the public mind with other major issues such as the use and siting of nuclear weapons, nuclear disarmament, and the social and political impact of nuclear power generation. Radioactive materials are a naturally occurring component of the marine environment, and thus marine life has always been subject to radiation exposure from this source as well as from cosmic radiation. Additional quantities of radioactive materials have been added to the seas as a result of man's activities since 1946 when the first quantities of radioactive waste were dumped in the ocean.

Inputs to the shelf seas arise from the activities of the nuclear power industry, power stations and fuel reprocessing plants, and military establishments servicing nuclear-powered submarines. Of these sources, the fuel reprocessing plants account for by far the largest inputs. Data from Britain, where the largest reprocessing plants are situated, show that over 96 per cent of the total radioactivity discharged arises from these sources, principally the Windscale (now called Sellafield) plant in Cumbria.[28]

The other principal pathway through which radioactive materials enter the sea is by ocean dumping. In general this is outside the scope of our study, but could affect the continental shelf and coastal waters through the transport of radioactivity by ocean currents or by biological mechanisms, or as a result of an accident to a vessel carrying material to a dumpsite.

Discharges to coastal waters

The introduction of radioisotopes to the seas of north-western Europe from industrial installations began in 1952 with discharges from the Windscale works into the Irish Sea. This plant reprocesses the spent fuel rods from nuclear power stations in Britain and other countries including Japan. Highly radioactive wastes are stored in rolled stainless steel tanks on land since they must be kept isolated from the environment for hundreds of centuries. Intermediate level wastes are dumped at sea, while the low level wastes are disposed of in special waste disposal sites (solids) or piped directly to the sea (liquids). The other European nuclear fuel reprocessing plant at Cap de la Hague, on the coast of France, commenced discharging radioactive waste into the English Channel in 1967.

Nuclear power stations also produce radioactive wastes in addition to the spent fuel. These wastes result from corrosion of the fuel rods while they are stored in cooling ponds, and include sludges and radioactive liquids and solids. Most of the material is taken to Windscale, however, and is not discharged directly. Britain has about 20 nuclear reactors in operation; several more planned or under construction, and there are likely to be increased quantities of corrosion products awaiting disposal from the new reactors.

As a result of the discharges from Windscale, levels of caesium-137 in the Irish Sea are now around 50 times those found in the Atlantic to the west of Ireland; and near the outfall they are several hundred times as high. Other radioisotopes discharged include caesium-135, ruthenium-106, zirconium-95, strontium-90, cerium-134 and niobium-95. The discharges mix with seawater and are transported through the Irish Sea in a westerly and northerly direction, leaving via the North Channel and moving in a well-defined path northwards along the west coast of Scotland. The radionuclides can then be traced around the north of Scotland, into the North Sea and across to the coast of Norway. In fact, their distribution has provided information on the pattern of residual currents in the Irish Sea and North Sea. In contrast, the discharges from Cap de la Hague can be traced only over a much smaller area.

Other nuclides discharged from Windscale are retained in the top few centimetres of sea-bed sediments within a few miles of the point of discharge. These include plutonium-241 and its decay products americium-241 and neptunium-237, which are among the most biologically hazardous of materials. Over the past decade increasingly large and uncontrolled (i.e. not subject to authorization) discharges of plutonium-241 have taken place, and it has been estimated that a total of 381,527 curies had been discharged to the Irish Sea by the end of 1980. This represents around a quarter of a tonne of material which will continue to be radioactive for a very long time. This cumulative amount represents an extremely serious yet relatively unknown problem, for there is very little information about the specific effects of these radionuclides.

Impact of coastal discharges

All radionuclides discharged from nuclear installations add to the background radiation attributable to naturally occurring radionuclides, but some are more important from an environmental point of view because they can be concentrated in organisms or sediments, and cause greater increases in radiation to critical groups living near the discharge or eating particular organisms. Long-term monitoring of the discharge from the Windscale plant has shown that the main pathways whereby man is exposed to the radiation contained in the discharge is through the consumption of fish and shellfish, from the consumption of seaweed, and through external exposure to material retained on the foreshore sediments.

Marine organisms too may be directly harmed by radioactivity, but natural mortality of marine biota is so great that it is impossible to differentiate between effects caused by exposure to ionizing radiation and those caused by other agents, including chemical pollution or changes in environmental conditions. Our lack of knowledge in this area has been used to justify further research aimed at identifying the effects of low-level radiation, and at considering the consequences of these effects in terms of the stability of whole ecosystems.

Monitoring and control

Because of concern about the possibly harmful effects of artificially produced radioactivity to the environment in general, the discharge of all radioactive material has always been strictly supervised. In the case of the shelf seas, the control of radioactive discharges from land-based sources is the subject of national legislation which takes into consideration, where necessary, international obligations, such as those of EC countries under the Euratom Treaty of 1957 not to affect adversely the interests of others in the course of handling radioactive materials for peaceful uses. Control is also exercised under the terms of the Paris convention, administered by the Paris Commission.

As the amount of radioactivity discharged to the shelf seas is predominantly associated with fuel reprocessing activities, principally those at Windscale, a considerable amount of work has been carried out to determine the extent of the influence of the discharges, and to develop sensitive monitoring techniques. So, far, no demonstrably harmful effects on marine life have been noted, but the elevated levels of radionuclides have given rise to serious concern among public interest groups and the environmental movement.

Ocean dumping

Some 130,000 tonnes of intermediate level wastes have been dumped in the European Atlantic Dumpsite, 380 nautical miles off the south-west coast of Ireland. Strong currents occur at the dumpsite, vertical mixing and upwelling may also be taking place and there is evidence of a movement of surface water towards the coast. The British nuclear industry began sea dumping in 1949 and was soon followed by Germany, Italy, Switzerland, Belgium, Holland, Sweden, and France. Following considerable international opposition, however, including a UN resolution, the amount of waste dumped in the sea was gradually reduced during the 1960s. Germany ceased dumping in 1967; Italy, France, and Sweden in 1968; the US in 1970; and Holland in 1982. Since then, only Britain, Belgium, and Switzerland have continued; and Britain has increased the amount dumped to 92 per cent of the total. Since 1971, the European Atlantic Dumpsite is the only site in the world where ocean dumping of nuclear waste has continued to be permitted. Use of this site was suspended in 1983.

The wastes are packaged in steel drums, filled with concrete or bitumen, and it is likely (from tests conducted by the US Atomic Energy Commission) that about one-third of the barrels become crushed during descent. Concrete blocks, in which some of the waste is packaged, also disintegrate, some at depths of less than 500 feet. Inspection of barrels *in situ* on the sea-bed showed that 25 per cent of those tested were damaged, and therefore leaking radioactivity.

The control of this dumping rests with the Consultative Meeting convened by IMO under the London Dumping Convention (LDC) and with its secretariat, and with the Oslo Commission relating to that convention. While the quantities of waste dumped at this site appear to present less of a pollution hazard than, for example, the radioactive discharges from Windscale, it is clear that the long-term hazards cannot be discounted. The Royal Commission on Environment Pollution, reporting on nuclear power and the environment in 1976, concluded that the existing analysis which defined the limits for ocean dumping did not offer a secure basis for large dumping operations in the future. The commission also expressed concern about the lack of a clearly formulated policy for the disposal of intermediate level solid waste, and criticized the policy of accumulating more highly active solid wastes at Windscale with a view to eventual ocean disposal. No decision, however, has yet been taken to alter this policy.

Some further unresolved issues

All areas of the nuclear industry have an excellent record of safety, and in general the hazards may be compared favourably with those common to any major industry. This situation reflects the considerable care which has been taken to ensure that radiation has been contained. Nevertheless, although the IAEA has set safety standards, there is still much public concern about the methods of disposal of radioactive substances. In relation to naturally occurring radio-nuclides, the contribution from man-made sources is still very small, and no detrimental effects have so far been found. The distribution of long-lived radionuclides in the marine environment, and their movement into the atmosphere, on to land, or via any other pathway to reach human beings is, however, a serious cause for concern, not least because these substances will be present in our seas for tens of thousands of years to come. The issue is clearly an emotive one, and its resolution is made more difficult by inadequate communication between the general public, environmentally concerned groups, and those with a vested interest in the nuclear industries. Underlying this difficulty is the disagreement among scientists about the precise effects of exposure to low levels of radiation and, in relation to this study, about what are safe levels of discharge to the marine environment. Under such conditions, rational management of the resources (including the use of the sea for the disposal of radioactive wastes in a manner *proven* to be safe) becomes impossible; and the levels of discharge deemed 'acceptable' reflect to a considerable extent the political pressure exerted and weight of argument advanced. A considerable amount of further scientific research is required—both radio-ecological and general environmental—and it is necessary that this should be carried out by multidisciplinary teams whose independence is guaranteed.

Alternatives to Discharging

The alternative of land-based surface or underground storage has been mentioned in connection with radioactive waste. But this alternative solution applies also to other industrial and domestic wastes. Our real problem, therefore, is not whether marine discharges are acceptable, but whether they have consequences more or less serious than the alternatives available. Such alternatives include, where appropriate, recycling, incineration, biological degradation, landfill, burial in underground storage and, all too frequently, illicit discharges to watercourses. There is no general solution; each source of waste needs to be examined individually, and the impact of each alternative assessed in detail. Economic factors will have a significant effect on the choice taken, but these can be changed (for better or worse) by setting the standards or conditions for each type of operation so as to make it more or less costly. Hence government policy is a powerful instrument for determining the eventual fate of the material to be disposed of.

The Role of the European Community in Marine Pollution Control

One of the most significant developments in marine pollution in north-west Europe has been the emergence of the European Community as a focus for concern and action to protect the marine environment. The concern really begins with the adoption of the first Environmental Action Programme in November 1973.[29] The development of a Community interest in environmental issues provides an extra institutional and political dimension to the forces involved in the negotiation and implementation of an anti-pollution regime for north-west Europe's shelf seas. The principal question to emerge from its achievements is whether or not the EC's involvement has extended beneficially, or has merely duplicated, the broader international regime based on other sources, such as the global and regional conventions.

But one major weakness of the Community as a regional actor in the politics of marine pollution control, particularly as far as the North Sea is concerned, is that membership does not include Norway and Sweden. A more serious political obstacle is the fundamental conflict between Britain and most other member states in respect of the steps necessary to reduce pollution from land-based sources, a conflict which reflects similar disputes in the Oslo and Paris conventions. This conflict has acted as a severe constraint upon the attempt to give practical substance to the declared objectives of the aquatic environment directive. The Community's emphasis on harmonization in order to ensure fair competition, which was enshrined as a basic principle of environmental policy in the 1973 environment action programme, makes it difficult to get agreement on common policies for all environments irrespective of their physical differences. Variations in the degree of involvement of member states in activities constituting an environment hazard also complicate the political process; British and Norwegian dominance of the offshore industry reduce the likelihood of an effective Community policy in this area, although the European Parliament has not been reluctant to offer advice on measures to reduce oil pollution of the sea from the offshore industry.

Commission proposals and Council decisions have tackled a wide range of individual pollutants, sources of pollution (land-based and vessel-source), and sections of the total marine environment, for instance waters for sea-bathing, the Rhine basin and the high seas. It is, none the less, useful to distinguish two main phases, which are not mutually exclusive, in the Community's treatment of pollution issues. From 1972 to 1976, the Council, the Commission, and member states struggled to reach agreement on both the general and operational principles which would provide the basis of a specifically Community regime. The climax of this phase was the adoption of the extremely important—but compromise—aquatic environment directive in May 1976. The attempt to apply the general objectives of the aquatic environment directive to particular pollutants, especially from land-based industrial sources, comprises one major element in the development of the Community's anti-pollution regime.

The second phase began somewhat hesitantly with the Community's reaction to the Bravo blow-out in the Ekofisk field in March 1977, and emerged conclusively (in response to the *Amoco Cadiz* disaster) as a declaration by the European Council at the Bremen Summit in July 1978, in which control of oil pollution of the sea was identified as a major objective of the Community.

The Framework of Community Policy Making

The Treaty of Rome does not make any direct references to the environment because environmental issues generally were not perceived as a major public policy area when the European Community came into being in 1958. The political pressures favouring a Community environmental policy became decisive at the beginning of the 1970s. The legal basis for such a policy was found in several sections of the Treaty of Rome, including:

(a) *the preamble*, which proclaimed 'the constant improvement of the living and working conditions of their peoples' to be an 'essential objective' of the member states;

(b) *Article 2*, which uses phrases such as 'a harmonious development of economic activities' which were subsequently interpreted as necessitating 'an effective campaign to combat pollution' when member states sought a legal basis for the first environment action programme in 1973.

The most controversial principle to emerge from the action programme was its view on the link between national policies and the Community's policy: 'Major aspects of environmental policies in individual countries must no longer be planned and implemented in isolation. On the basis of a common long-term concept, national programmes in these fields should be co-ordinated and national policies should be harmonized within the Community.'

The enlargement of the Community's policy-making sectors to include the environment led to the institutional innovation of an Environment and Consumer Protection Service, which subsequently became a Directorate General (DGXI). Marine pollution is one of the responsibilities of DGXI; others include water pollution in general, air pollution and noise.

The Political Outlook for the Community's Environmental Role

As the underlying principles and the operational bases of a potential Community anti-pollution regime began to emerge in the 1970s from the first and second Environmental Action Programmes and a variety of Council and Commission publications, it was interesting to speculate about the particular contribution which could be expected from the Community given its political characteristics. Three features of the Community's political system suggested that its assumption of a role as an environmental protection agency might turn out to be the most significant step in the development of an effective regime for Europe's regional seas.

The first significant aspect of the Community's entry into environmental politics was the establishment of the Commission as a forceful proponent of protective measures. The Commission is the source of the legislative proposals whose fate is decided under the Community political system by the Council of Ministers. Though the Commission works closely with member states and its proposals reflect an awareness of what members will or will not accept, the Commission possesses considerable leeway when it initiates policy studies leading up to the formulation of specific proposals. In contrast to the *ad hoc* nature of most international decision-making in relation to environmental issues, the Commission's Consumer and Environmental Protection Directorate can be considered as a standing conference on all aspects of the Community environment. The Commission's environmental role is potentially most significant in the area of land-based sources of marine pollution which are the most difficult to regulate effectively at the international level.

The second aspect of the Community political system which could be expected to influence the development of a marine anti-pollution regime lies in the nature of Community decisions. The directives of the Council of Ministers are legally binding upon member states. This feature of Community decision-making explains the frequent intense confrontations between member states which have characterized the meetings of the Council of Environmental Ministers, which perhaps has acted more as an intergovernmental than as a supranational institution. Once the Council adopts environmental rules, both the Commission and the Court of Justice may be involved in ensuring that such rules are effectively implemented by member states, thus giving the Community's environmental regime a greater enforcement potential than is typical of international institutions.

The third significant factor that affected the Community's role in dealing with marine pollution was that the Community's environment included not only the Continental shelf seas of north-west Europe, but also the Mediterranean and Baltic Seas and the fresh-water environment. Thus, heavily polluted rivers such as the Rhine and the Po, and enclosed seas such as the Mediterranean and Baltic, had to be taken into account. Member states confronted by the problems of pollution in these waters insisted upon a uniform environmental policy applicable throughout the Community's aquatic environment.

The Development of Community Policy for the Marine Environment

The Community's policy for the marine environment is to be found in a variety of pronouncements which range from the generalities expressed in point eight of the declaration emerging from the first summit of the enlarged Community in 1972, to the specific obligations accepted by member states in directives adopted on particular pollutants such as waste from the titanium dioxide industry. The preliminary objectives of the Commission and the member states are to be found in the two action programmes adopted in 1973 and 1977,[30] and these are further developed in the third action programme, adopted in February 1983.

The roots of future controversy over the direction and substantive content of the Community rules were established in the first action programme's commitment to 'standardization or harmonization of the methods and techniques for sampling analysis and measurement of pollutants', to quality objectives 'determining the various requirements an environment must meet', and to standards including emission standards. Point five in the programme's description of 'Action to Reduce Pollution and Nuisances' (part 1, title iii, chapter 1) picked out three particular industries, including the paper and pulp and titanium dioxide industries, whose pollutants were deemed sufficiently harmful to merit investigation in the first phase of the programme. Point eight identified three 'zones of common interest' requiring 'the introduction of special measures and procedures'; the zones included marine pollution and pollution of the Rhine basin. It is clear from the first action programme that land-based sources were regarded as the most appropriate area of marine pollution as regards the development of a specifically Community regime. It was acknowledged that other sources (sea transport, deliberate dumping, and exploitation of the sea-bed) required wider fora. The Community was well aware in 1972–3 of the significant enlargement of the regional and global regimes then taking place.

None the less, the action programme did envisage a Community role in combatting marine pollution from sources other than the land. The role was to be mainly one of complementing the measures adopted under regional and global conventions with the emphasis, as usual, on harmonizing any national rules adopted by member states to implement conventions. The programme envisaged the 'application of a uniform system of licensing in the Community' in respect of national measures to implement the Oslo Dumping Convention. Prophetically, the first action programme did point out that 'Western Europe, because of its fragmented coastline and especially since it is the main crossroads for shipping, has a greater interest than any other area in the world in effective action being taken on a world scale against the dangers inherent in the transport of oil'.

The Aquatic Environment Directive

In 1975–6, when the Community's institutions began the task of converting the objectives and principles of the first environmental action programme into practical measures against pollution, it quickly became clear that widely divergent views existed. In particular, Britain differed from the other member states over the principal method of achieving the objectives in the Commission's draft directive 'on the reduction of pollution caused by certain dangerous substances discharged into the aquatic environment of the Community'.

The Commission had proposed *emission standards* as the principal method of achieving Community objectives, i.e. direct controls over the concentrations of specific pollutants to be allowed *into* the aquatic environment (inland surface waters, territorial waters, internal coastal waters and ground water). The same physical restrictions would be imposed throughout the Community in the concentration of offending substances to be discharged from shore-based installations. Britain alone was prepared to veto the Commission's proposal as it stood, preferring instead environmental *quality standards*, i.e. controls over the amount of contamination permitted *in* (as opposed to the amount of pollution allowed into) the Community's aquatic environment. The principle of a quality objective allows the amount of pollutant to vary according to the capacity of the marine environment to absorb it without 'deleterious effects'. So far as disposal is concerned, the UK is in a geographically advantageous position as compared with the majority of its European partners. A compromise was reached at the December 1976 meeting of the Environment Council. Subject to Commission approval member states would be permitted to choose between quality objectives and emission standards.

A start was made in implementing the aquatic environment directive by selecting five substances as requiring priority treatment, namely, aldrin, cadmium, dieldrin, endrin, and mercury. When subsequently the Commission decided to draw up proposals for the control of aldrin, eldrin and dieldrin, (three halogenated organic compounds used as pesticides and listed in the 'black list' of prohibited pollutants as originally drawn up under the Oslo and Paris conventions in article 2 of the aquatic environment directive), two draft directives were required, one dealing with emission standards, the other with quality objectives. The requirement was criticized by the European Parliament's Environment Committee, which 'would have preferred a uniform system for the entire Community, but does not feel that it is now in a position to question the wisdom of the 1976 decision'.[31]

These draft directives were discussed at the Environment Council meetings in 1979 and 1980. No agreement was reached and the matter was referred to the Committee of Permanent Representatives. In June 1979 the Commission prepared further draft directives to regulate discharges of mercury by the chlorakali electrolysis industry. Once again the choice between emission standards and quality objectives permitted by the aquatic environment directives has led to an impasse at Council level concerning the rules to be applied to any new establishment in member states choosing quality objectives. Article 3 of the proposed directive would permit member states to authorize new establishments to operate only if they were to use the best technical methods available for preventing pollution. Britain is opposed to any such rule on the grounds that it is unnecessary if quality standards are chosen. France is the leading advocate of the view that the most modern techniques should be required in all new plant irrespective of the choice made between emission standards and quality objectives. It is clear that the compromise which permitted the adoption of the declaratory aquatic environment directive did not solve the underlying conflict between Britain and most of its partners in the Community. Britain relies on the argument that its favourable marine environment, which justified the quality objectives option, should still permit cost differentials between Britain and other member states.

The slow progress achieved in building a Community regime to curb land-based sources of marine pollution is underlined in the case of mercury discharges by the fact that the Commission's proposals relate to only one-third of the sources of mercury discharges. The proposals do not cover mercury discharges by dentists, laboratories, or the electrical appliance and instrument industry.[32] Nevertheless, the Council did eventually adopt a directive relating to mercury discharge in March 1982.

In February 1981 the Commission sent the Council its proposals regarding cadmium. At its December 1982 meeting, the Environmental Council reviewed these proposals thoroughly, but did not reach a decision, preferring to instruct subordinate Community bodies to continue their examination of the Commission's proposals.

Titanium Dioxide Waste

The titanium dioxide industry was specifically identified in the initial environmental action programme as requiring study in the first phase of implementing the programme. Two draft directives relating to the disposal of titanium dioxide waste have been proposed by the Commission. The first proposal was adopted, after considerable amendment, in February 1978.[33] The Council received the second proposal in December 1980. The titanium dioxide waste directive emphasizes the decentralized nature of the Community policy implementation system. The directive leaves the evaluation of 'deleterious effects' in the hands of member states. The contents of the national programmes leading to the 'eventual elimination' of pollution from the industry were left to be negotiated at a later date. It can, therefore, be argued that the first titanium dioxide directive belongs in the category of declaratory instruments.

The directive does commit member states to monitor the impact of such dumping and discharge as is allowed. The next step in the development of a regime to control titanium dioxide pollution is contained in the Commission's proposals for a directive 'on methods for the surveillance and monitoring of the environments affected by waste from the titanium dioxide industry'. At its June 1982 meeting, the Environmental Council approved the Commission's proposals.

Not until there is uniformity in surveillance and monitoring procedures is it likely that there will be progress towards vigorously applying similar standards restricting the amont of titanium dioxide waste permitted to enter the Community's marine environment.

Oil Pollution and the Broader Regime

The task of giving practical substance to the principles of the aquatic environment directive might have remained the dominant approach to the problem of marine pollution but for the spate of oil pollution incidents which began with the Bravo blow-out in the Ekofisk field in April 1977.

Subsequent incidents involving oil tankers such as the *Amoco Cadiz* (March 1978) and the *Betelgeuse* (January 1979) intensified the political visibility of marine pollution and stimulated the Community's institutions to consider the question of developing an appropriate Community response.

The European Council declared prevention of oil pollution of the sea to be a major Community objective at its April 1978 meeting in Copenhagen. The European Parliament's Environment Committee was unimpressed by the activities of the Council and the Commission in the following two years, characterizing the Community's record as 'one of declaration of high intent in the wake of oil disasters, with an unwillingness to follow up with concrete measures once the memory of the disaster fades'. What is clear from both the 'concrete' steps already taken by the Council to implement the aquatic environment directive and the fate of 'measures' so far proposed by the Commission in pursuit of polluters at sea (described below) is that the pace of Community action is extremely slow.

Following the Bravo blow-out in the Ekofisk field, the Commission prepared in June 1977 a number of measures designed to prevent or reduce oil pollution of the sea. The measures included:

(a) establishment of a data bank on the means currently available for dealing with accidental discharges of oil;

(b) the development of research programmes into chemical and mechanical technologies for coping with oil spills;

(c) the appointment of a group of experts to examine recent instances of accidental oil pollution;

(d) exhorting member states to implement effectively the Bonn agreement, and, in respect of the Mediterranean, the Barcelona protocol.

The Council took no decision on the Commission's post-Ekofisk attempts to stimulate action because, according to one insider's view. 'the Council never had the time to examine' the proposals.[34]

The Council's reaction to *Amoco Cadiz* almost twelve months after Ekofisk appeared much more positive, due in part to the embarrassing (or shaming) proximity of the disaster to a European Council of Heads of Government. The Copenhagen Summit on 7–8 April 1978 invited the Community's institutions to take appropriate measures regarding:

(a) the implementation of existing international rules, especially those regarding minimum standards for the operation of ships;

(b) the prevention of accidents through co-ordinated action on the part of member states, e.g. compulsory shipping lanes, control over sub-standard vessels;

(c) search for and implementation of measures to combat pollution.

The summit declaration, under the impact of the circumstances of *Amoco Cadiz*, focussed attention on shipping as a principal source of oil pollution. The first two sets of areas of decision envisaged for the Community, i.e. implementation of existing rules and co-ordination of actions by member states, belong to the Community's role as an adjunct to the global and regional regimes which already exist to tackle the problem of oil pollution of the sea. The Community can function as an additional force pushing for speedier ratification and more effective implementation.

The initiative taken at the Copenhagen summit permitted the Commission to transform its various existing proposals into a draft action programme 'on the control and reduction of pollution caused by hydrocarbons released at sea'. The draft programme was deemed satisfactory by the Environment Council at its May 1978 meeting and was then formally adopted by another European Council meeting in Bremen on 26 June 1978.[35]

This draft programme and the process of implementation emphasizes the highly decentralized and bureaucratic nature of Community decision-making. Despite the 'major objective' status of the problem of preventing and reducing oil pollution at sea, the process of decision-making in fulfilling that objective (i.e. the flow of ideas on how to proceed) has been outwards *from* the Commission *to* the Council rather than *from* the member states, galvanized by incidents such as the *Amoco Cadiz* disaster, *to* the Commission: hence the slow progress, as not all members support the extension of the role of the EC.

The draft action programme is significant because it highlights the approaches to combatting oil pollution at sea which the Community institutions consider to be appropriate or feasible in the light of the contribution of other sources to the overall regime such as IMO and the various regional conventions. The Community is also involved in the development of the broader regime in its links with institutions established under the Paris and Oslo conventions and the Bonn agreement. The Commission is a member of the Paris commission and an observer of the Oslo commission—its attendance at meetings of the Oslo commission is increasingly necessary because there is much common ground between Oslo and Paris.

The pace of establishing links between the Community and elements of the broader regime is, however, somewhat leisurely. In December 1978 the Council agreed *in principle* to a directive authorizing the Commission to negotiate the Community's accession to the Bonn agreement. In May 1980 the Commission took part as an observer at the fourth meeting of the contracting parties to the Bonn agreement (which dates back to 1969). In May 1981 the Council finally authorized the Commission to negotiate the Community's accession to the Bonn agreement.

The Council has adopted a number of directives which focus on various aspects of shipping as a source of marine pollution. It has recommended that member states sign and ratify a number of conventions on safety, viz. SOLAS (1974), the SOLAS protocol (1978) and MARPOL (1978). Council recommendation 79/114/EEC suggested that member states sign the 1978 International Convention on Standards of Training, Certification and Watchkeeping for seafarers by 1 April 1979, and ratify it not later than 31 December 1980. Directive 79/115/EEC dealt with pilotage in the English Channel and the North Sea. Member states were asked to ensure the availability of 'adequately qualified deep-sea pilots' to ships which might require them. Member states were also required to take steps to ensure that vessels flying their flag used only adequately qualified pilots. The directive dealt only with qualification of pilots, not with circumstances in which pilots must be used. Directive 79/116/EEC laid down 'minimum requirements for certain tankers entering or leaving Community ports'. These requirements, to be applied to all oil, gas, and chemical tankers over 1,600 gross registered tonnes, include notifying port authorities of details such as nature of cargo and 'any deficiencies or incidents which may decrease the normal safe manoeuverability of the vessel'. A tanker check list to be handed to a pilot was included in an accompanying annexe.

On 25 June 1980, the Commission submitted to the Council a proposal for a decision establishing a Community information system for preventing and combatting oil pollution of the sea. The Commission classified the information required under three headings:

(a) a permanent inventory of staff, equipment and products for combating oil pollution of the sea, and a compendium of national and regional contingency plans;
(b) a compendium of the properties of hydrocarbons liable to pollute the waters of member states:
(c) a Community oil-tanker file.

The Commission established on 25 June 1980 an Advisory Committee on the Control and Reduction of Pollution caused by Oil discharged at Sea, to be composed of representatives of member states.

The slowness of the development of a Community anti-pollution regime is again indicated by the year-long interval between the Commission's proposals for the information system and the approval *in principle* of two features (no mention of the oil tanker file) by the Environment Council on 11 June 1981. This was described as the first measure put forward under Council Resolution of 26/6/78.

On 21 April, 1981, the Advisory Committee on the Control and Reduction of Pollution caused by Hydrocarbons discharged at Sea held its first meeting in Brussels. The main business was described as 'sounding out views on the organization of measures to combat oil pollution in the member states'. This committee met again on 7–8 July. Business consisted of 'an initial exchange of views on the advisability of Community-type approval for dispersants and the value of technical recommendations concerning the mechanical means for combating the pollution of the sea by hydrocarbons'.

Third Action Programme

In February 1983 the Council formally adopted a Third Action Programme (1982–6) for the Environment, which included a potentially significant change of direction in the philosophy behind the Community's approach to environmental issues. The Community's environmental efforts under the broad umbrella of the first two action programmes concentrated on developing a legal regime consisting of Council directives aimed at various sources of pollution or at particular pollutants. The third action programme hints at an additional tactic, namely, Community expenditure based on specific budgetary allocations to environmental objectives. The rather leisurely pace of the Community's environmental efforts are repeated in the third action programme's comment that the 'Commission has proposed the inclusion in its preliminary draft budget for 1982 (admittedly symbolic) amounts for these purposes'. Two areas of proposed expenditure were identified—the development of 'clean' technologies and the protection of environmentally sensitive areas.

It seems likely that Community expenditure, like Community legislation, will, as a strategy for attacking environmental problems, develop somewhat slowly.

Notes

1. UNCLOS gives six such sources. See p. 292.
2. GESAMP's definition of 'pollution' distinguishes between a pollutant which causes adverse effects and a contaminant which either does not or has not been shown to do so.
3. ICES *Input of Pollutants to the Oslo Commission area*, Co-operative Research Report no. 77, 1978.
4. DSIR, 'Effects of polluting discharges on the Thames Estuary', Water Pollution Research Technical Paper no. 11, HMSO, 1964: Head P.C., 'Discharge of nutrients from Estuaries', *Marine Pollution Bulletin 1*, 1970, pp. 138–40.
5. The London Convention of 1973 is also applicable here. For further details of these see chapters X and XI.
6. Mathews, W., in *Assessing Potential Ocean Pollutants*, National Academy of Sciences, Washington DC, USA, 1975.
7. Horsman, P. V., 'The amount of garbage pollution from merchant ships. *Marine Pollution Bulletin* vol. 13, no. 5. 1982, pp. 167–9.

8. Holdgate, M. W., Kassas M., and White, G. F., 'World Environmental Trends between 1972 and 1982', *Environmental Conservation* Volume 9, no. 1., spring 1982, pp. 11–29.

9. Topping C., 'Sewage and the Sea', in Johnston, R. (ed.) *Marine Pollution*, Academic Press, 1976, pp. 303–51.

10. Wood, J. M., 'Biological cycles for toxic elements in the environment', *Science, NY*, vol. 183, 1974, pp. 1049–52.

11. MAFF, 'Survey of mercury in food: Working Paper on Monitoring of foodstuffs for Mercury and other heavy metals, first report, HMSO, 1971.

12. Burnett, M., Ng., A., Settle, D. and Patterson, C. C., 'Impact of Man on coastal marine ecosystems, in Branica, M., and Konrad, Z. (edd.), *Lead in the Marine Environment*, Pergamon Press, 1980, pp. 7–13.

13. Davies, A. C. and Sleep, J. A., 'Copper inhibition of carbon fixation in coastal phytoplankton assemblages', *Journal of the Marine Biological Association UK*, vol. 60, 1980, pp. 841–50.

14. Davies, A. C. and Sleep J. A., 'Photosynthesis in some British coastal waters may be inhibited by zinc pollution', *Nature* 277, 1979, pp. 292–3.

15. Bryan, C. W., 'Heavy metal contamination of the sea' in Johnston, op. cit. n. 9., pp. 185–302.

16. Bourne, W. R. P., 'Seabirds and Pollution', in Johnston, op. cit. n. 9, pp. 403–502.

17. Lilygreen, V. and Meade, B., 'Fish stocks under pressure from nylon monofilament gill-nets', *Marine Pollution Bulletin*, vol. 13, no. 8, 1982, pp. 263–6.

18. Matthews W. in *Assessing Potential Ocean Pollutants*, National Academy of Sciences, Washington, DC, 1975.

19. Dixon, T. R. and Dixon, A. J., *Marine Litter Surveillance at two sites on the Western Cherbourg Peninsula and West Jutland Shores of the English Channel and southern North Sea*, 1980, Marine Litter Research Programme, stage 2, Keep Britain Tidy Group, Brighton.

20. '*Aeolian Sky* Packaged Chemicals Pollution Incident', *Marine Pollution Bulletin*, 12 (2), 1981, pp. 53–6.

21. *Hazardous Cargo Bulletin*, vol. 3, no. 1, January 1982, pp. 12–14.

22. Dixon, T. R. and Hawksley, C. *Litter on the Beaches of the British Isles*, report of the first National Shoreline Litter and Refuse Survey sponsored by the *Sunday Times*, Watch and Keep Britain Tidy Group, 1980, Marine Litter Research Programme: Stage 3.

23. See in particular: Royal Commission on Environmental Pollution, *Eighth Report: Oil Pollution of the Sea*, HMSO Cmnd 8358, 1981.
    Cowell, E. B., *Data presented to a European Parliamentary Hearing in Paris*, 4 July 1978. Bourne, op. cit. n. 16.

24. Central Unit on Environmental Pollution. *Accidental Oil Pollution of the Sea*, Pollution Paper no. 8, HMSO, 1976.

25. CONCAWE, *The environmental impact of refinery effluents: CONCAWE's Assessment*, report no. 1, 1980.

26. Read, A. D. and Blackman, R. A. A., 'Oil Pollution of the Marine Environment', *Marine Pollution Bulletin*, 11, 1980, pp. 44–7.

27. Royal Commission on Environmental Pollution, op. cit. n. 23.

28. Department of the Environment, Scottish Office, and Welsh Office, *Annual Survey of Radioactive Discharges in Great Britain*, HMSO, 1979.
29. *Official Journal of the Communities* (OJC), 112, December 1973.
30. *OJC*, 139, 13 June 1972.
31. Working Document 1-54/80.
32. Working Document 1-55/80.
33. DIR 78/176/EC in *OJL* 54, 25 February 1978.
34. Nagelmackers, H., 'Aftermath of the *Amoco Cadiz*', *Marine Policy*, January 1980.
35. *OJL* 194, 19 July 1978.

IX

Development and Conservation on the Coast[1]

Introduction

From prehistoric times the coast has provided food and living areas for mankind. Places where shellfish could be gathered and fin-fish trapped or netted, and where the sandy soil provided easily worked agricultural land, were centres for primitive settlement. Travel by sea was the link between such coastal communities, and also the avenue along which invaders came, to colonize, conquer, or become assimilated. Islands, exposed headlands, and in some places sea-cliffs, were choice sites for the establishment of defensive positions against invasion. Some of these promontory, island, and cliff forts may still be seen today, for example, at the Old Head of Kinsale, Dun Aengus in the Aran Islands, and Dunvegan on Skye.

As trade and commerce grew, creeks and inlets developed as focal points. Major cities and ports were built on estuaries, where there was deep sheltered water. Improvements in engineering allowed the construction of totally new harbours and the extension of existing ones. In Victorian times, the steam train and the rise in popularity of the seaside holiday introduced a new element: mass recreation. Industry began to compete for space with holiday camps, and the travellers' enjoyment of the seaside was accompanied by the discharge of large quantities of raw sewage.

Today, industry continues to demand extensive coastal sites, creating pressure on estuarine and coastal wetlands and intertidal areas. The existence of large urban agglomerations, increasingly mobile working populations, and greater leisure time, has enabled recreational development to spread to coastal areas previously considered too remote or unsuitable for the temporary or permanent accommodation of large numbers of people.

Mankind has only recently come to realize the finite limitations of the coast as a place to live, work, and play, and as a source of valuable materials. This realization has come with overcrowding, overdevelopment in some areas, and the destruction of valuable resources by misuse of this unique environment. More than 50 per cent of the population of the USA lives in the states bordering the Great Lakes and the sea coasts, and the percentage is increasing. In many developing countries, 75 per cent of economic activity takes place in coastal areas; in a number of small island states this percentage may rise to 90 per cent. As well as causing congestion in parts where space is limited, this level of economic activity can have adverse effects upon the exploitation of other coastal resources. Sewage disposal from large urban settlements has significantly enriched some semi-landlocked coast waters and has destroyed shellfisheries; industrial wastes have caused fish kills and have reduced sport and commercial fishing: while oil and solid wastes have reduced the potential value of beaches for recreation and tourism.

Human society has not consciously decided to wreak this destruction. It has come about as a result of an exponential growth in human activities on the coast in the absence of proper planning or management. These processes are continuing, and although vigorous attempts are being made in a few places to stem the flow and conserve what is valuable, reversal of the process is proving very difficult. The rising human population, with its attendant industrial and commercial activity and resulting wastes, is one of the most critical coastal problems. The degree of misuse has been so great as to threaten on a world-wide scale the survival of certain particularly vulnerable natural habitats and some plant and animal species. Some conservation areas have been established, and a number of successes in this field will be described later, but as pressure for development increases, the opportunity to establish adequate additional nature reserves is rapidly disappearing. The management of coastal areas must be given high priority since, following the loss or destruction of vulnerable habitats, their repair or reinstatement is extremely difficult and may in reality prove impossible.

Previous chapters of this study have explored individual offshore resources, all of which affect the coastal lands and shallows in one way or another. This chapter concentrates on activities whose main impact is on the coast rather than in the seas, such as urban and industrial development, recreation and tourism, and the use of the coast for education and research. It is on the coast that much of man's interaction with the sea takes place. Conservation of natural resources is necessary not only for their direct use as food or raw material, but also for their intrinsic merit: their contribution to the maintenance of the global ecosystem and to man's well-being. New strategies for the resolution of conflicts of use are desperately needed. The offshore resources described earlier, as well as the coastal resources discussed here, must be taken into account in planning an overall strategy. Existing planning controls leave much room for improvement, and some possible changes will be explored.

But before considering the impact of human activities on the coast, some definitions are necessary.

The Coastal Zone and Coastal Resources

Coastlands are zones of interaction between the sea and the land. Mud-flats and salt-marshes, beaches and rocky shores are alternately covered and exposed by the tides. Sea-cliffs and sand-dunes are open to the influence of salt spray and storms. Coastal waters are influenced in many ways by their proximity to land. Despite the great differences between their various maritime and marine habitats, their plants and animals share the problems of an unstable and constantly changing environment.

Nevertheless, while the above description may be accurate, and may illustrate the variety of coastal habitats, it does not constitute a definition. Indeed defining the coastal zone has proved a problem for some considerable time; there is no generally agreed-upon and acceptable definition in a legal sense. In the USA for example, where the term 'coastal zone' originated, definitions of the landward boundary ranged from 300 feet inland of mean high water mark to a 5 mile wide strip.[2] The seaward limits of the coastal zone are equally ambiguous and arbitrary. On the whole it is not possible to establish precise boundaries, either landward or seaward of the high water mark, because of the differences among the various authorities claiming jurisdiction at local, national and international levels. A useful definition adopted by a coastal zone management workshop at Woods Hole, Massachusetts in 1972 referred to the coastal zone as the 'band of dry land and adjacent ocean space (water and submerged land) in which land ecology and use directly affect ocean space ecology, and vice versa'.[3] The coastal zone is therefore a band of variable width which borders the continents, their offshore islands and inland seas. Functionally, it is the interface between land and water where great interchanges of materials and energy take place.

The landward boundary is necessarily vague. The ocean affects climate far inland from the sea; and in the other direction, pollutants discharged far upstream will eventually reach estuaries and the sea. The seaward boundary is easier to define scientifically; coastal waters differ chemically from those of the open sea, even in areas where the impact of human activities is minimal. Generally, coastal water can be identified at least to the edge of the continental shelf but the influence of major rivers may even extend beyond this. The coastal zone management workshop referred to above defined the seaward boundary of the coastal zone as the line beyond which man's land-based activities no longer have a measurable influence on the chemistry of the water or the ecology of marine life.

In discussing coastal resources we can for the most part avoid the need for a precise spatial definition by adopting a more functional approach based on whether or not the resource is primarily dependent on coastal lands (including wetlands) or shallow inshore waters. The classification of resources used so far in this study has been based on:

(a) exploitation of non-living resources (raw materials and energy);
(b) harvesting of naturally occurring living resources (for food and raw materials);

(c) cultivation of living resources (primarily for food, but potentially also for chemicals and pharmaceuticals);

(d) using the sea for transportation;

(e) utilizing the waste-absorbing and dispersing abilities of coastal waters.

However, in order to emphasize the increasing extent to which the coast is used to satisfy human needs, and the close connections between planning for more rational exploitation of coastal resources and the planning process generally, it is also necessary to consider coastal resources in terms of 'human habitat'. The coast provides resources for the following human activities: settlement and food production; commercial and industrial development; tourism and recreation and education and research. This chapter, therefore, begins with interactions of these human activities on the coastal environment and continues with an evaluation of existing and potential coastal planning and conservation strategies.

The Impact of Human Activities on Coastal Resources

Settlement and food production

The coast is a major area for human settlement; two-thirds of the world's population lives in coastal settlements, and more than half of the world's cities with a population of over one million (including the five largest) are situated on the coast or on estuaries. Throughout history, mankind has preferred to settle on the coast for a number of reasons, such as the availability of a wide range of food, the moderate climate, transportation and commercial advantages, and frequently the presence of suitable land for building. More recently, new factors have added to the attraction of the coast: the development of industrial complexes around ports, recreational space, the growth of water sports, and the fashion for spending holidays and retirement in a warm coastal climate. In the process, very large areas of the coast have been urbanized, especially around estuaries. Relatively few constraints on buildings have had any effect, and engineers have become skilled at overriding both natural and man-made constraints on coastal zone development.

Overall, the extent of Britain's urbanized coastline can be judged from the results of a survey carried out by the National Trust in 1963. Of the 4,800 kilometres (3,000 miles) of coast around England and Wales, 1,600 kilometres were already built on beyond redemption. Another 1,600 kilometres were found to be without scenic value, partly because of the uninteresting topography, partly because of insensitive developments. While these developments were not technically ineradicable, they were so extensive as to eliminate all practical hope of rehabilitation.

Coastal urbanization has been accompanied by the use of the sea for waste disposal. By far the greatest volume of waste discharged into the sea is domestic sewage, which on the coast is almost invariably untreated or given only primary treatment (that is, screened or comminuted before discharge). Sewage discharges may create a public health hazard through contamination of the environment and various food resources. Bivalve shellfish in particular concentrate bacteria and viruses, or harbour the often highly persistent eggs of parasitic worms. Where sewage is present in large quantities the bacterial action exerted on it reduces the oxygen concentration of the water, which can exclude higher organisms such as fish, or in extreme cases all other form of life. Historically, many coastal populations have been dependent upon locally collected shellfish or fish as a major component of their diet. Fortunately the relationships today are less direct, but some coastal communities still rely on inshore fishing for their livelihood, and the processing of the catch is frequently a basis of local industry. All too often, the response to pollution from domestic wastes is to prohibit fishing, rather than to treat the wastes. Moreover, where the discharge is visible or malodorous, or causes algal bloom, an amenity problem may also arise.

Agriculture as well as settlement has contributed to the destruction of coastal habitats. The reclamation of estuarine intertidal areas has been carried out for centuries; quite low embankments are usually enough to prevent flooding since much of the marshland reclaimed is covered only during spring tides. Furthermore, the shelter from wave action provided by the estuary enables simple earth embankments to survive. However, the result is often the destruction of extensive maritime habitats, particularly winter feeding grounds for migrant waders, sea-duck and shore-birds.

Large areas of land have been reclaimed from the sea in Holland and to a smaller extent on the east coast of England. More than half of the territory of the Netherlands now lies below sea level, and a complex system of barrages is required to protect it from flooding. The most recent major flooding took place in 1953, when winter gales caused the inundation of some 2,000 square kilometres of arable land in the south-west Netherlands, drowning 1843 people in the process. Following the disaster, the Dutch Parliament launched the Delta Plan, under which it was proposed to strengthen the entire Dutch coastline and to close off all the estuaries in Zeeland completely from the sea, with the exception of the Western Scheldt which had to remain open to allow access to the Belgian seaport of Antwerp. Closure of the Eastern Scheldt, the last in the Delta Plan, was due to be completed in 1978, but a protest movement by nature conservation groups, fishermen and shellfish breeders succeeded in getting the original plan changed. The fishermen feared that the closure of the estuary would destroy the valuable molluscan and shrimp fisheries which thrived in the reasonably unpolluted water. The revised plan now includes a storm-surge barrier to replace the dam originally planned, and is expected to be completed during 1985. The barrier will normally allow reduced tidal movement in the estuary, but during periods of storm it can be closed to prevent dangerously high water levels from occurring within it.

Nevertheless the impact on the environment will be significant, especially on two major estuarine habitats: salt-marsh and intertidal flats.[4] The area of salt-marsh will be reduced by nearly 60 per cent and the intertidal flats by 45 per cent. The latter will have major implications for the present role of the Eastern Scheldt as an important feeding ground for migrant and wintering wading birds. Most importantly, the use of the barrier for storm-surge control or to prevent the entry of, for example, an oil spill, could have significant ecological effects depending on the timing and duration of closure. If a tanker spill occurred in the North Sea during the summer, and the tidal barrage was closed at low tide to prevent entry of the oil, calculations show that the estuary would become anoxic in a matter of days, while the intertidal flora and fauna could suffer heavy losses by drying out. Thus, by preventing oil pollution, ecological damage would occur through lack of oxygen in the intertidal zone. Alternatively, if the barrier had to be closed at high water, in winter particularly, for example to protect mussel-beds from frost damage, the feeding grounds of waders would remain covered, and the birds spending winter there could suffer severe mortality.

In Britain, the reclamation and destruction of estuarine wetlands has proceeded more slowly, but is still a cause for concern. Under UK law, ownership of the land extends in general only to the high water mark; below this, the sea-bed is usually owned by the Crown, and permission for any developments must be obtained from the Crown Estate Commissioners. Nevertheless, many salt-marshes which were covered by high spring tides have now been enclosed and converted to pasture or arable land. Coastal lagoons have been filled in, often with domestic refuse. Sand-dunes have also been reclaimed. Even the less dramatic changes associated with agricultural improvement–for example drainage, application of herbicides, and reseeding to convert poor pasture to grass ley for silage—may destroy rare and valuable habitats. Very often the threat arises not so much from major developments (these are usually the subject of public enquiries), but from large numbers of minor changes.

One factor contributing to this problem may well be the exemption from planning controls of changes relating to the use of land for agriculture. Engineering works associated with agricultural development are also exempt. If control by local planning authorities could be extended to these developments or, better still, if all such developments came under the aegis of a comprehensive coastal resources plan, then protection for coastal and estuarine habitats could be improved.

A number of other uses of the coast are directly related to local lifestyles and livelihood. Seaweed collected on the coast has long been used as a valuable source of nutrients and as a soil conditioner. In Shetland, sheep are fed on foreshore seaweeds. At the present time both attached and storm-cast algae are gathered on the west coasts of Ireland and Scotland and in Norway, where they form the basis of local industries. However, there are fears that where the cutting of seaweed is practised on a commercial scale, as is proposed in Orkney, increased erosion and damage to lobster breeding could occur. Sea-sand was traditionally used as a bedding for animals and a soil conditioner in many coastal communities, particularly in the nineteenth century. Mixed with seaweed or animal manure it provided a deep man-made soil in coastal districts and allowed intensive arable farming to take place on what would otherwise have been very poor land. Sea-sand was also extensively used as a building material in many coastal areas, but its removal from beaches led to such erosion of the shore and, in some cases, destruction of sand-dunes, that the practice has largely been halted. Local cutting of marram grass for thatching, fodder, and cattle bedding is still practised on the south and west coasts of Ireland to a minor extent. The cutting of marram grass can have serious detrimental effects upon the sand-dunes where it helps to stabilize the sand and a number of dune areas have had to be protected from cutting by orders made under section 36 of the Land Act 1936.

Commercial and industrial development

The distinction between the use of the coast for living space and its use for commercial and industrial development is not clearly definable. Rather, as the activities required to support coastal communities diversify, they become increasingly commercialized. Similarly, as urbanization takes place, the number and variety of industrial undertakings increases. These in turn become more complex with technological development.

In general, the coast is an attractive location for five major types of industry:

(a) port-associated industries that benefit from low-cost transportation by water of bulk raw materials or products;
(b) merchant shipping and ship-building industries;
(c) industries that use seawater for cooling or process purposes;
(d) industries that depend directly on the marine environment for their raw materials; and
(e) industries that are beneficially located near centres of population, but that are dependent on water, access to the sea, shipping or marine raw materials.[5]

As a result of industrial or commercial growth, many coastal settlements have become adapted to a particular function: the fishing ports of eastern England, for example; the oil port of Aberdeen; the short-sea passenger and freight ports of Dover, Fishguard, and Holyhead; and the ship-building and heavy engineering port of Barrow-in-Furness. Other cities and conurbations embrace highly developed and complex economic bases; examples of cities with a wide range of industrial and commercial activities, and a record of vigorous recent growth, include Hamburg, Rotterdam, Southampton, and Cork. Despite the fact that some major ports are suffering economic difficulties and even decline, there can be little doubt that in future the coastal areas of Europe are likely to fare better economically than inland areas with fewer locational advantages.

The relationship between industry and urbanization has, of course, been two-way. As mentioned above, the growth of coastal settlements provided the markets, the infrastructure and the focal points for the establishment of industry. On the other hand, the expansion of industry and commercial activities has accelerated the process of urbanization as a result of the need to provide housing, social facilities and services for industrial workers. A substantial number of European cities with over 250,000 inhabitants are situated on the coast, and in their vicinity are those parts of Europe with high population densities. Census results and population distribution maps demonstrate the effects of the locational advantages to be found on the coast for generating urban growth.

Less developed locations with deep and sheltered water in areas formerly considered too remote are now often key areas for economic and industrial growth promotion; such 'development areas' include the Cromarty Firth (Scotland) and the Shannon estuary (Ireland). In the case of the Cromarty Firth, the Highland Regional Council has an active policy of attracting industry to the area, while around the Shannon estuary the efforts of the Industrial Development Authority and the Shannon Free Airport Development Corporation have resulted in several large industries being established.

In other areas, however, coastal industry has been declining or suffering severe constraints on expansion and development. The United States Commission on Marine Science, Engineering and Resources produced in 1969 a list of existing and future coastal industries, which is reproduced in Table IX.1.

Most sectors of the fishing, merchant shipping and ship-building industries are seen as in decline in the United Kingdom, and with some notable exceptions this also holds true for the rest of Europe. In some areas coastal fisheries have continued to expand, although the deep-sea fishing industry has declined generally, and several deep-sea fishing ports are seriously concerned about their prospects of survival. The recent recession in the merchant shipping industry has also caused severe economic problems in traditional shipyards whose future is now uncertain even with large-scale government support.

The operation and fortunes of ports and harbours have also changed markedly as a result of new technologies, such as containerization and the

TABLE IX.1. *Existing and Future Coastal Industries*

	Type	Example
Existing Industries	Mature, healthy and growing	Oil and gas, food processing and packaging, chemical extraction from seawater, mining of sand, gravel, sulphur, fisheries, surface marine recreation.
	Early stages of growth	Desalination, bulk and container transportation systems and associated terminals, aquaculture, fresh water and estuarine underwater recreation.
	Mature, but static or declining	Most segments of fishing, ship-building, merchant shipping.
Future Industries	Near-term promising (where near-term is less than 15 years)	Mining of placer minerals, oils and gas beyond the continental shelf, continental shelf sand and gravel.
	Long-range	Sub-bottom mining (excluding sulphur), aquaculture, open ocean deepwater mining, power generation from waves, currents, tides and thermal differences.

increasing size and draught of vessels. Ports such as London and Liverpool have had to redevelop to meet these changing needs, with considerable social, economic and environmental consequences. The number of workers engaged in the loading and discharge of ships has suffered drastic reductions, the economic and social life of the dockland areas has declined, and extensive acreage of dockland has become disused, abandoned and derelict. Some schemes to develop these dockland sites for new industry or for leisure and recreation have been successfully completed in London. In Liverpool various dockland rehabilitation schemes are underway. To encourage economic regeneration, a number of the traditional ports, including London, Merseyside, and Clydeside, have in the last few years been declared 'enterprise zones'. Industries moving to these zones receive grants and concessions on rates.

Other ports, by contrast, have expanded their traffic significantly: for example Felixstowe, Dover, the Forth ports, and Waterford. Most spectacular of all has been the development of new terminals for the transhipment of North Sea oil. Sullom Voe in Shetland, Flotta in Orkney, and Aberdeen (as an oilfield service port) have experienced rapid growth and significant problems. Petroleum refining and associated petrochemical plants are also concentrated on the coast. Large modern coastal refineries are more likely to survive the present difficulties arising from excess refining capacity. Within the last few years, several planning applications to construct new refineries on the coast have been made, while older inland refineries are threatened with closure.

The construction of ports and establishment of industry often involve radical physical change to the configuration of the coastline. Sea and harbour walls, jetties, and groynes are all direct forms of physical change. They are functional designs to enable harbours to operate, roads to remain open, and factories and construction sites to exist in safety. The influence of such structures is generally felt over a wide area. The speeds and patterns of currents may be altered and allow the deposition of sediment. The character of local habitats, both terrestrial and aquatic, is frequently changed, yet the importance of working with nature wherever possible, by encouraging natural processes, has only gradually been realized: low-angle slopes, for example, have largely replaced the vertical wall; surfaces are rough and permeable so as to dissipate wave action and reduce backwash. Unfortunately, much of the coastline of Britain is surrounded by earlier, rigid structures that can be shown to have contributed to beach erosion, and to have caused geomorphological side-effects along adjacent coastlines.

Reference has already been made to coastal reclamation schemes. These are frequently aimed at industrial as well as agricultural use. The scale of engineering works is constantly growing. Modern techniques now enable barrages and embankments to be constructed in deeper and more exposed areas, enabling long estuaries and shallow coastal sites to be cut off from the sea. Such enclosed areas can then be either reclaimed, or allowed to remain filled with water for the purpose of tidal power generation or for the storage of fresh water with ancillary recreational uses. In all of these uses, even where the habitats and environment remain aquatic, the existing ecosystems are altered and the connection between the estuary or enclosed shallow-water marine area and the sea is broken.

An increasing number of tidal barrage schemes for power generation have been or are under construction. In Britain, the possible environmental effects of the proposed Severn Barrage have been the subject of detailed study, but a great deal of uncertainty still surrounds the extent of these effects. The ecological consequences of tidal barriers generally may be more far-reaching than is often thought, while active management of the tidal regime for flood prevention or other purposes will introduce additional potential ecological problems. No two estuaries are the same, thus making scientific progress in estuarine studies very slow. In the UK a number of estuarine studies carried out under the aegis of the Natural Environment Research Council have paved the way to providing a generalized appreciation of estuarine problems. The European Commission has also funded a comprehensive estuarine programme aimed at the development of a system of harmonized criteria for assessing estuarine quality under different degrees of industrial and urban pressures.

The generation of electric power from fossil fuels or from nuclear sources requires large amounts of cooling water, and for this reason power stations have also tended to be sited on the coast or in estuaries. The dispersion of the warm water from these utilities has not caused significant harm to local flora and fauna, largely because the sites have been chosen for their capacity to achieve the required amount of dilution. Of much greater concern has been the disposal of radioactive effluent from nuclear stations and from the associated fuel reprocessing facilities at Sellafield and Cap de la Hague. There has been increasing public disquiet about the safety, long-term integrity, and economic viability of nuclear power plants. The warmed cooling water from both nuclear and fossil-fuelled plants has in fact proved a valuable resource for increasing the growth rates of plants, fish, and shellfish in adjacent horticultural or aquacultural enterprises. Unfortunately the use of power-station cooling water for fish farming development has been restricted to one or two locations, even though significant potential exists for its more widespread use.

Another 'industrial' use dependent on a coastal location, preferably isolated, is military use. Defence establishments occupy sizeable stretches of coast in parts of the British Isles. Large beach complexes are often involved. For example, in Scotland, Morroch More on the Dornoch Firth is used as a bombing range, and Luce Sands in Wigtown District is used for bombing and weapons training. Other coastal locations are used for firing ranges. Some of the sites are of outstanding scientific interest. The degree of impact arising from military use varies considerably. In some respects the environment is protected, due to the exclusion of recreation and other forms of land use. However, military use can be very damaging. Although on firing ranges the amount of earth moving and other change effected may be fairly slight, on bombing ranges such as Luce Sands large expanses of dune terrain have been levelled and grassed over to facilitate the retrieval of weapons.

One new type of industrial activity located on coastal sites which has given rise to a great deal of concern, particularly in Scotland, is the construction of oil production platforms for use in the North Sea. These construction projects are very large relative to the area of their socio-economic and environmental impact, they require large numbers of workers over a short time-scale, and there is considerable uncertainty about the future demand for their products. It is, therefore, difficult for the local authorities to plan the necessary infrastructure, and services. The effect of such projects on other resources has primarily been through the labour market; skilled and semi-skilled mechanics, local construction workers, equipment operators, diesel engineers and others are likely to find jobs on the construction projects at attractive wage levels, thereby causing a labour shortage among local firms. Wage levels tend to rise all round and the survival and economic competitiveness of traditional resource-based industries is threatened. Additional spending and investment in infrastructure in the local area will to some extent diminish the problem, but will not eliminate it completely. Moreover, concern has been expressed about the compatability of these major construction projects—with their long hours, shift-working and six- seven-day working weeks—with the traditional rural lifestyles, based on agriculture, fishing, and tourism, onto which they have been grafted. Furthermore, migration to construction sites may accelerate the depopulation of the most peripheral areas. But while large numbers of workers are required, there has also been a persistent tendency for unemployment rates to equal or exceed initial levels after the project becomes fully operational. The combination of returning emigrants, reduced emigration of school leavers, and outside workers who wish to remain in the area can raise serious unemployment problems when the construction phase of a single large project ends.

One possible benefit which may accrue to the locality, provided that the project is oriented towards the exploitation of marine resources, is an increased awareness of the more locally available coastal resources, which could be exploited. Welding, mechanical and boat-handling skills acquired or perfected on the large-scale construction project can be adapted to the development of inshore fishing, mariculture or small-scale boat building and marine engineering. However, such follow-on developments are unlikely unless encouraged by government aid and by the existence of willing investors.

A large-scale coastal construction project can, therefore, have a significant impact, detrimental and beneficial, on the region around it, on local lifestyles and on the exploitation of other marine resources. As well as increasing wage levels and creating spending power, it can also put pressure on the local infrastructure and cause subsequent unemployment. Opportunities for new productive investment are increased, but traditional industries may suffer. The question of whether the impact will be largely beneficial or detrimental will depend to a major extent upon awareness, foresight and planning by local, regional and central governments.

The effects of traditional industries, which benefit from being located near centres of population, but are not necessarily dependent on proximity to the sea, can also be significant. Their main impact on the coastal environment is through effluent discharges. However when discussing the environmental consequences of these discharges, it is more useful to consider the nature of the effluent than its source.

Industries such as brewing, distilling, wood-pulping, and some branches of the chemical industry discharge wastes containing large quantities of organic material with effects similar to those of domestic wastes. Short-lived wastes, such as acids, alkalis, cyanides, phenols, chromate, and ammonia, are toxic but are fortunately usually rendered innocuous fairly rapidly by dilution or by chemical conversion in the sea to non-toxic compounds. Inert solids cause greater problems. Colliery wastes, pulverized fuel-ash, and waste from potash mining are dumped in coastal waters off the north-east of England, and china clay waste has been discharged off the south coast of Cornwall. The effect of these siliceous wastes is to increase the turbidity of the water and cover the sea-bed with a fine deposit. The increased turbidity reduces light penetration and seaweed growth, and the particulate matter harms filter-feeding animals such as sponges and bivalve molluscs. Persistent, non-degradable wastes such as heavy metals and organohalogens are yet more damaging, as we discussed in chapter VIII. Finally, petroleum wastes can cause severe local damage. The toxic constituents of petroleum oils kill plants and animals, and where the discharge is continuous, as in the vicinity of refineries, recovery is prevented.

Tourism and recreation

The coast has for a long time been a prime focus for tourism and recreation, and there is little sign of its importance diminishing. J. Allen Patmore's classic study *Land and Leisure* states that 'the coast is Britain's most important resource from a recreational point of view'[6] No part of the British Isles is further than 120 kilometres from tidal water. British seaside holidays have suffered a relative decline in recent years, but the coast still satisfies a very large part of the total demand for outdoor recreation, because it is accessible to most of the population for day trips.

In terms of the impact on the coastal environment, the location and timing of recreational activities are important factors. A great deal of the pressure on the coast continues to be taken in the summer season by the large urban resorts and by camping and caravan sites covering a small percentage of coastline. A majority of people obviously enjoy holidaying together in large numbers. At the same time, there are few parts of the coast which can now be said to be underutilized because of the mobility brought by the car.

Coastal development for recreation and tourism began on a serious scale during the inter-war period. The more fortunate built themselves holiday homes by the sea; others took advantage of the development of long lines and heavy agglomerations of mostly wooden shacks which had been built with little regard for the resulting deterioration in landscape quality. Much of the east and south coasts is affected by this shack development, for example the Norfolk coast from Cromer to Great Yarmouth.

Such visual intrusion is an obvious impact of tourism and recreation on the coast. There is inevitably conflict between the development of car parks, cafes, caravan sites, tenting sites, and so on, and the continuing enjoyment of open spaces and scenic beauty. Cars are a particular problem, with both visual and practical implications. The aim of most people would appear to be to get their cars as close to the beach as possible. The result is 'rows and rows of gaily coloured metal boxes disfiguring the landscape'.[7] Cars in particular also contribute to the erosion of dune systems. The only solution to serious erosion problems is to relocate car-parking inland and restrict public access by fencing or erecting artificial walkways. The sheer numbers of holiday-makers also damage the flora and fauna of dune and intertidal habitats simply by trampling. Although such damage is evident in various parts of the country, the worst-affected areas are in the south-west of England, which has particularly rich flora and fauna but where a considerable part of the coastline supports an active tourist trade.

Specific recreational activities have specific effects; moreover, the activities interact, and may conflict with each other. There is, for example, strong evidence of damage to sandy and muddy beaches by bait-digging. Immature forms and other invertebrates can be killed by being left exposed at the surface. The holes created can be a hazard to children and horse-riders, may undermine moorings, and eventually could lead to beach erosion. The excessive collection of shellfish and of benthic organisms by skindivers also gives cause for concern. Water sports, which are generally increasing in popularity, may be a nuisance to others; water ski-ing may be unpopular with bathers and sea-anglers. Although few water sports appear to have serious ecological implications, the wash from fast boats may swamp birds' nests and erode salt-marshes. Furthermore, the construction of facilities such as marinas and slipways causes the destruction of existing habitats.

In recent years a variety of planning mechanisms and management techniques to resolve or at least mitigate these problems and conflicts have been adopted by local authorities, public bodies and others. These will be described and discussed later.

Education and research

The value of coastal resources for educational and research use is less obvious than their value for settlement, agriculture, industry, and tourism, but is none the less significant. One of the outstanding characteristics of the coastline of the British Isles is its extraordinary length, which totals about 19,500 kilometres. The variety of physical and ecological conditions is proportionately large; for example, the beach, dune, and machair resources of the Highlands and Islands of Scotland have been called 'unique in Europe'[8] since no other country boasts so much diversity in one regional setting. Geology, physiography, and climatic conditions all offer great contrasts, and combine to cause great variations in ecological habitats. Some aspects of British coastal ecology are important on a global scale. The northern half of the British seaboard, for example, has important sea-bird resources, a·major survey of which is at present being undertaken for the Nature Conservancy Council. Numerous species of migrant wildfowl and waders spend part of the autumn or winter on British estuarine mud-flats, sand-flats, or coastal wetlands and the numbers of these species wintering in Britain are often a significant proportion of the total European or even world population. Destruction of these birds' habitats—by reclamation, for example—threatens nothing less than the genetic diversity of the global ecosystem. For these and other reasons the World Conservation Strategy recognizes the environmental significance of northern coastal Britain, and identifies it as being inadequately protected.[9]

Britain has a long tradition of field studies in the coastal zone, and in some areas education and field research have themselves had a direct adverse impact on the environment studied. Carelessness, disturbance of habitat—by trampling, overturning stones, or frightening birds—and unnecessary collection of specimens are the main problems. There is evidence that this has resulted in some depletion of flora and fauna, and the concern of the Nature Conservancy Council is shown by the publication of a code of behaviour entitled *The Seashore and You.*[10]

However, it is to be hoped that the positive repercussions of education and research more than outweigh any adverse impact. Teaching, ideally, encourages increased environmental awareness, and strengthens the voluntary conservation movement. Research highlights the need to establish conservation areas, conduct impact studies, and carry out further research. There is a growing realization among biologists and other marine scientists of the important role played by near-shore shallow waters and intertidal zones in the maintenance of the biological productivity of coastal waters. Such shallows act as nursery areas and sources of nutrient for many economically important offshore species. They are also, as we have argued, of inherent physical and ecological value.

Coastal Planning and Conservation Strategies

As pressures for various human activities, developments, and land uses grow, it is becoming increasingly apparent that coastal resources are finite, just as the coast itself is finite. Pressure on available space has increased, and so have the number of conflicts between competing uses. The role of the planner is to reconcile these conflicts of use, and to conserve and gain the optimum use of resources. This section reviews some of the mechanisms and management techniques which have been used so far. As coastal planning has been approached somewhat differently in England and Wales, Scotland, and Ireland, separate attention will be given to each area. The problems of all three areas are common, however. Peculiarities of ownership, anomalous and ill-defined boundaries, archaic legislation, confusion as to responsibilities, and lack of co-ordination are among the factors which have made attempts at comprehensive planning or management of the coast exceedingly difficult.

England and Wales

There was little widespread appreciation of the problems of coastal development until the inter-war period, and it was only in 1947 that the Town and Country Planning Act came into effect. This, however, gave powers that were adequate only to control development in a negative sense; no positive and concerted action was apparent until the 1960s. In 1963 the Minister of Housing and Local Government expressed concern at the diminishing coastal resource at a time of increasing pressure for recreational and leisure activities. Government circular 56/63 advocated stricter developmental control and asked all coastal-planning authorities to institute a special study of their coastal areas. This was followed by a series of Regional Coastal Conferences organized by the then National Parks Commission during 1966 and 1967.

In a parallel movement, the National Trust was attempting to save the finest stretches of coastline through the more practical approach of acquiring either the land itself, or restrictive covenants. A survey identified some 1,568 kilometres (980 miles) of Britain's coast that were still of outstanding beauty and almost undamaged by developments, largely because of inaccessibility. 'Enterprise Neptune', a campaign launched by the National Trust in 1965, resulted in the purchase of 200 kilometres by 1971. The campaign was justified by the belief that statutory designations, such as National Parks, failed to provide proper defences against despoliation. In Pembrokeshire, for example, the designation of the coast as a National Park has been interpreted by some groups as a commercial opportunity to exploit an increasing tourist influx, to the detriment of the environment.

In 1970, however, a new designation was suggested. The Countryside Commission, which replaced the National Parks Commission after the 1968 Countryside Act, issued a report entitled *The Coastal Heritage*,[11] which included specific proposals for the definition of 'heritage coasts'. The principal qualities possessed by the proposed heritage coasts were to be their unspoilt character, their exceptionally fine scenery, and their heritage features. Forty-three stretches were considered as possessing these requirements, but actual designation was left to the discretion of the local authorities concerned. By 1979, thirty-three heritage coasts had been designated, covering 1,734 kilometres of coastline.

There is a strong emphasis on management within heritage coasts. The aims have been to develop practical techniques for conserving undeveloped coasts, by, for example, the employment of wardens, interpretive services and management plans, and the provision of the appropriate recreation facilities such as coastal footpaths and country parks. Three proposed heritage coasts—Suffolk, Dorset, and Glamorgan—were selected by the Countryside Commission as pilot schemes. Each was provided with a full-time officer and grant aid. In many respects the heritage coast concept has been successful. It is flexible. It promotes co-operation between landowners, residents, amenity groups and local authorities, and facilitates local involvement. In many instances, it has achieved marked physical improvements. The only serious disadvantage of the heritage coast concept has been its limited scope. It has concentrated primarily on recreation, but only in selected, relatively remote areas, not in resorts. To a lesser degree it has been concerned with conservation, but in a general, not a specifically scientific sense. A still wider range of coastal problems, such as the removal of eyesores, and marine industrial areas, have not been tackled at all. Although these wider problems were dealt with in *The Planning of the Coastline*,[12] a parallel report to *The Coastal Heritage*, the findings were never developed by the Countryside Commission, within whose mandate they lie. Instead various other bodies have taken planning and conservation initiatives, with varying degrees of success.

There never has been a co-ordinated national policy for resort planning. Our resorts still accommodate the majority of coastal visitors but there is growing concern for their architectural, social, and economic futures. In particular, the traditional seaside resorts such as Scarborough, Great Yarmouth, and Llandudno have suffered some decline in recent years. They are single-industry towns that have high seasonal unemployment, low wage rates and unbalanced populations. Competition from foreign resorts has taken a heavy toll. There is a need to broaden the employment base to reduce dependence on the tourist economy. At the same time the physical fabric of seaside towns has suffered from lack of investment. Many seaside towns have valuable heritages of Georgian, Victorian, and Edwardian architecture, but modern preferences are for self-catering accommodation in chalets or caravans, so the older property in some cases is no longer in use, or is inadequately maintained. Some of the more favoured and enlightened local authorities are attempting to conserve their resorts' identity and at the same time to revive and spread their trade over a longer season by refurbishing existing facilities for conference use. For example, Scarborough is extensively refurbishing its Victorian Spa with the aid of grants from the English Tourist Board, the Historic Buildings Council, and the European Community. There remains great scope for similar planning and conservation work in other resorts.

Conservation of the coast from a scientific point of view has been the responsibility of the Nature Conservancy (a branch of the Natural Environment Research Council) and the independent Nature Conservancy Council which replaced it in 1973. The work of these two bodies has shown a growing interest not only in sea-cliffs and sand-dune systems, but also in the foreshore and indeed the offshore marine environment.[13] Vulnerable and ecologically important areas have been designated as National Nature Reserves (NNRs) and Sites of Special Scientific Interest (SSSIs). A comparatively high proportion of these areas are coastal in location. NNRs are specially managed for conservation purposes; where other uses conflict, they are excluded. SSSIs are somewhat less important, and are not specially managed.

Legislative changes brought about by the 1981 Wildlife and Countryside Act will have implications for coastal nature conservation. The committee stages prior to the passing of the Act highlighted several controversial issues. The possibility of extending planning controls to the countryside was raised and rejected. The Royal Town Planning Institute, in its submission to the House of Lords, recognized undesirable aspects of agricultural improvement, such as the removal of hedges, walls, moors, marsh dykes, and wetlands, but did not consider formal control a realistic proposition. The arguments against formal control are that it would be too bureaucratic, and that in any case serious problems exist only in certain parts of the country.

Another issue raised was the question of management agreements. Previously it has been common for National Park authorities and the Nature Conservancy Council voluntarily to negotiate management agreements with land managers to regulate the use of land in return for financial and other benefits. Under the new legislation, if a farmer is refused grant aid by the MAFF because of objections on conservation grounds, the authority objecting has a duty to offer to enter into a management agreement, and to provide compensation. This new provision may be very expensive and sets a legal precedent which worries conservation groups.

A beneficial provision of the Act is the notification procedures for SSSIs. The Nature Conservancy Council is required to notify landowners and occupiers of the existence of such areas and to specify what operations might harm their features of interest. In return, owners and occupiers have to give three months' notice of any plans to carry out such operations.

But the most significant provision of the Wildlife and Countryside Act with regard to the coastline is that it makes it possible for the first time to establish *statutory* Marine Nature Reserves. Many other countries already have statutorily protected marine reserves, and Britain has for some time been in danger of lagging behind. A major purpose of these reserves will be to protect representative offshore areas with specially interesting marine flora and fauna or other features, but they will also be important for education and research. The Nature Conservancy Council is empowered to propose the establishment of the reserves in which certain activities such as fishing, sports, building operations or even access may be restricted. Plans to designate a reserve must be confirmed by the Secretary of State for the Environment, and there are provisions for a public inquiry to be held into objections. Nine non-statutory reserves already exist, and extensive surveys over the last few years have led to the preliminary identification of a number of other sites worthy of conservation. These include areas round small islands such as Lundy, mainland coastal areas with rocks and sand such as around Start Point in Devon, low-tide sand flats as in the Isles of Scilly, tidal rapids such as the Menai Strait, and inlets such as the Helford River in Cornwall.

Coastal planning for industrial and related uses in England and Wales is even less developed than other types of coastal planning strategy. There is no national overview of preferred conservation zones and preferred development zones such as exists in Scotland (see below). The statutory planning powers of local authorities—development planning (the drawing up of structure plans and local plans) and developmental control—are strictly defined, and more negative than positive in nature. Environmental impact assessment (EIA) of major industrial developments is not a formal requirement, although its use is increasingly being encouraged.[14]The scale of potential industrial developments is vast, however. If, for example, the proposed new generation of nuclear power stations materializes, they will almost certainly be located mainly on coastal sites. Billions of litres of cooling water will be required daily by each station. It is very difficult for planners, in the absence of an integrated policy for the users of the coastal zone as a whole, to approach such forms of development pressure in a rational and comprehensive way. An additional problem is that British planning powers are almost non-existent below the low water line, where an increasing amount of industrial activity is occurring, such as dredging, oil and gas development, sewerage disposal and dumping. Local and regional planning, both conceptually and practically, has tended to use the coast as a boundary, and a confused one at that. The powers of some authorities extend from the land to the high water mark, others to the low water mark encompassing the tidal zone, and still others are bounded by mean tide levels.

Scotland

Much of what has been said about coastal planning and conservation strategies in England and Wales also applies to Scotland, but some aspects differ.

There are no heritage coasts in Scotland. Instead there are forty National Scenic Areas, over half of which are on the coast. These were defined by the Countryside Commission for Scotland's 1978 report, *Scotland's Scenic Heritage*.[15] The bulk of the areas, the report states, 'are not under severe recreational or other specific pressures at present'. No measures are yet available to protect the National Scenic Areas, although the Countryside Commission for Scotland suggested that certain classes of planning application should require notification (to the Secretary of State for Scotland), and that there should be management agreements for the conservation of scenic resources between land managers and the commission.[16] Practical management, as exists on the heritage coasts, has never been proposed, because many of the National Scenic Areas are remote and sparsely populated.

Nature conservation provisions for Scotland are basically the same as for England and Wales. A high proportion of NNRs, SSSIs, and suggested Marine Nature Reserves are in Scotland.

Both agricultural and industrial developments may threaten the Scottish coastal environment. The potential for conflict between agriculture and nature conservation is illustrated by an experiment in comprehensive planning—the Integrated Development Programme (IDP) for the Western Isles. Funded jointly by the DAFS and the EC, the programme attempts to alleviate a wide range of social and economic problems, such as unemployment and emigration, by means of grants for agricultural improvement, fish farming, tourism, craft industries, and other activities. Many interests, including those of the Nature Conservancy Council, are represented on the programme's steering committee. Already, however, there is controversy over the environmental effects of the project. Some conservationists argue[17] that a disproportionate amount of money has been earmarked for agricultural intensification: by means of amalgamation of holdings; rearrangement of common grazing; drainage, herbicide application, and re-seeding. This, they fear, will destroy the rare machair habitat where the beaches and areas behind them are formed from ancient shell-sand, bringing an unusual alkaline fertility, and supporting a remarkable flora and fauna. Conflict between the Nature Conservancy Council and the government agricultural agency has been predicted.

By far the greatest impact on the Scottish coast in recent times has been that of the North Sea oil and gas industry. National policy guidance on oil-related development in Scotland was issued by the Scottish Development Department in 1974, in the document entitled *North Sea Oil and Gas: Coastal Planning Guidelines*.[18] The main guidelines took the form of identifying 'preferred development zones' and 'preferred conservation zones'—a policy of concentration of developments rather than dispersal. The guidelines provided a sensible, though fairly modest basis for a planning strategy designed to protect coastal amenities while expediting the exploitation of North Sea oil. However their effectiveness has been criticized in a number of respects[19] They were issued long after the first major developments took place, and the 'preferred development zones' coincide closely with those areas in which development was already occurring. They thus appear to be a rationalization for what has occurred rather than a framework for forward planning. There are instances of development being permitted within 'preferred conservation zones', such as the Loch Kishorn platform construction yard. Finally, the guidelines do not provide for evaluation of alternative sites, or for environmental impact assessment of proposed developments.

In the more practical aspects of dealing with the environmental effects of the oil industry on the coast, Scotland and the UK as a whole have taken a lead. Contingency planning for the control of oil pollution, for example, is very advanced. A communications network round the coasts provides an early-warning system for oil slicks. Oil rigs, ships, and aircraft report the occurrence or sighting of oil spills to the various authorities which need to be alerted. The polluting company is generally held responsible, but where no source is apparent or the polluter is unable to respond adequately, the Marine Pollution Control Unit of the Department of Trade takes any necessary action. Local authorities take similar action in inshore waters and on the coast. These executive authorities have contingency plans which ensure a rapid response, and include consultation with interested bodies such as the DAFS and the Nature Conservancy Council, who advise on the best action to be taken. A great deal of expertise now exists in coping with accidental oil pollution in ecologically sensitive environments.

Another field in which expertise has been developed is environmental restoration. Coastal sand-dunes traversed by pipeline landfalls have been restored, so as to be almost invisible, at several points on the north-east Scottish coast.

In both the control of oil pollution and the restoration of sand-dunes, as well as in other circumstances, environmental impact assessment, including baseline studies of existing conditions, monitoring of actual effects, and evaluation of the accuracy of impact predictions (auditing) has proved worthwhile.

Ireland

The main legislation concerning planning and development in Ireland is the Local Government (Planning and Development) Act 1963. Its provisions, in principle, are similar to those of British planning legislation, with development planning and development control being undertaken by local planning authorities. The responsibilities of central government bodies are considerably different, however. *Bord Failte Eireann*, the National Tourist Authority, has responsibility for both the development of tourism and the conservation of the environment: an unusual and possibly contradictory combination of roles. *An Foras Forbartha*, the National Institute for Physical Planning and Construction Research, has duties including physical planning at a national level, and the conservation of areas of scientific and educational interest.

In 1968 *Bord Failte* and *Foras Forbartha* jointly commissioned a National Coastline Study from a firm of planning consultants.[20] The approach used in the study was quite different from any used in Great Britain. The objectives of the study were to provide advice in formulating a national development and investment programme in coastal areas, to guide local authorities in development planning and development control, and to assist

Bord Failte in the formation of policies for the development of tourist and recreational facilities around the coast. The scope of the study was thus very wide-ranging. Development was seen as any change in existing use; and conservation as the attempt to achieve harmony and stability in the use of natural resources. There was thought to be 'no necessary conflict between the aims of conservation and development' given a consistent and comprehensive approach.[21]

A national strategy for the development and conservation of the coastline was drawn up. This involved an examination, first, of existing land uses such as agriculture, fishing, settlement, and tourism. Each of these was recognized to be changing or expanding in various ways due to factors such as technological or organizational change. A detailed survey of the coastline revealed particular problems, and their distribution. The pressure on beaches, for example, was found to be most serious on the east coast; land speculation and high land prices were thought to contribute to the spread of development; and the spread of development was identified as weakening the service role of existing villages. In the strategy itself, coastal areas were classified according to landscape type and scientific interest. For each category, prescriptive management statements were formulated. Proposals included the encouragement of some types of tourism, but not others; the establishment of coastal easements for public access and commerce; scientific research on problems of erosion; the designation of exceptional landscapes for protection; and the protection of agricultural interests on good agricultural land. The Irish coastal strategy is not a statutory document, and cannot be enforced, but it does, as intended, provide useful general guidelines for coastal development. To date (1983) it is the only holistic coastal planning strategy in the British Isles.

Coastal Zone Management: Regional and International Perspectives

Having examined in some detail the impact of human activities on the coastline and the strategies so far adopted to optimize the use of coastal resources, it is possible to draw some tentative conclusions.

There has been repeated reference to the confusion existing over the jurisdiction of public authorities in the coastal zone. It is worth emphasizing the extent of this confusion. A study by the Nature Conservancy Council and the Natural Environment Research Council[22] of legal provisions relating to the coastal zone indicates that different bodies, boundaries and legislation govern all the following aspects: ownership, access, collecting, fishing, navigation, coast protection, mines and quarries, and pollution. There is no area defined in law as the coastal zone and treated as an integrated whole. As uses have developed, regulatory arrangements have been employed in an *ad hoc* manner. Not only are the different uses tending to become conflicting ones, but the regulatory controls themselves are not systematic.

The same study goes on to identify further problems. There is, it states, no integrated policy for the users of the coastal zone as a whole, based upon an overall development plan; nor is there a single public authority with overall or even primary responsibility. There are no uniform mechanisms whereby claims for new uses can be evaluated or priorities between different uses determined. Although clearly recognizing the problem, the study unfortunately fails to suggest adequate solutions, presumably because proposals for radical new legislation—which would almost certainly be required—lay outside the remit of the study group. None the less, the need for unified 'coastal zone management' (an American term now in general usage) is increasingly being acknowledged. This is an expression not only of the absolute increase in development pressures on the coastline, but also of the 'growing awareness that the coastline is a resource of national importance, while decisions relating to the planning and development of the coastline have at least until recently been made almost exclusively at the local level'.[23] Local councils and small communities have been unable to stand up against strong and often economically-advantageous development, and serious conflicts of use. If coastal resources are to be developed in the best interests of the state as a whole, new, positive, strategic planning measures are required.

The coastal zone management concept is much better developed in parts of Europe and North America than in the British Isles. In Brittany, for example, there is a regional coastal planning strategy, which combines physical and socio-economic objectives in the belief that physical and economic planning can no longer be divorced. In Norway each county is required to formulate a 'shore-plan', and development is prohibited within 100 metres of the high water mark. Sweden has extensive data on coastal environmental conditions, and a comprehensive National Physical Plan forms the framework into which regional and other plans are fitted. The Netherlands has excellent, far-sighted regional coastal plans, and Belgium has established a coastal advisory body, the Consultative Commission for the Littoral Zone. In the USA the Coastal Zone Management Act of 1972 recognizes that there is a 'national interest in the effective management, beneficial use, protection and development of the coastal zone'. It requires states to prepare management plans which set out, at the state level, objectives, policies and standards to guide public and private uses of lands and waters in the coastal zone. This general trend towards increasing national or regional intervention, in an integrated fashion, in the field of coastal resource management, has also been endorsed by international bodies such as the Commission of the European Communities[24] and the Organization for Economic Co-operation and Development.[25]

How could coastal planning in the British Isles be improved? A number of options are available to the governments concerned. Most important is the need for a national plan for the coastline, giving a broad strategy and guidelines for development. Only in Ireland has this so far been attempted. There is also a need for a co-ordinating body to formulate general regional policy for coastal land use and to regulate the activities of interested public bodies. Thirdly, there is a need for an information base containing coastal data of all kinds, to be used in future decision-making. Finally, specific practical measures that have proved worthwhile in other countries should be considered. The prohibition of development within a shore zone 100 metres or more in width, for example, might be a good idea. Any new measures adopted need to be as straightforward as possible, in order to simplify rather than increase the existing confusion and bureaucracy. However, there can be little doubt that new planning and management procedures dealing specifically with the coastal zone as a whole are urgently required.

Notes

1. This chapter focuses largely on aspects of the subject illustrated by experience in Great Britian and Ireland, but it can be extrapolated to cover the basic problems encountered in analagous situations in north-west European states.
2. Ketchum, B. H. (ed.), *The Water's Edge: Critical Problems of the Coastal Zone*, MIT Press 1972.
3. Smies, M. and Huiskes, A. H. L., 'Holland's Eastern Scheldt Estuary Borriee Scheme: Some Ecological Considerations', *Ambio*, vol. 10 no. 4., 1981, pp. 158–65.
4. Smies and Huiskies, op. cit. n. 3.
5. Ketchum, op. cit. n. 2.
6. Patmore, J. A., *Land and Leisure*, Penguin, 1970.
7. Wheeler N., 'Our Coastline: the Last Frontier' *Journal of the Royal Town Planning Institute*, 66, 1980, 154–6.
8. Ritchie, W. and Mather, A. S., *European Beach Complexes*. University of Aberdeen, 1976.
9. International Union for Conservation of Nature and Natural Resources *et al.*, *World Conservation Strategy*, 1980.
10. Nature Conservancy Council, *The Seashore and You*, 1977.
11. Countryside Commission, *The Coastal Heritage*, HMSO, 1970.
12. Countryside Commission, *The Planning of the Coastline*, HMSO, 1970.
13. Nature Conservancy Council and Natural Environment Research Council, *Nature Conservation in the Marine Environment*, 1979.
14. Clark, B. D. *et al.*, *A Manual for the Assessment of Major Development Proposals*, HMSO, 1981.
15. Countryside Commission for Scotland. *Scotland's Scenic Heritage*, 1978.
16. Ibid.
17. Rose, C. and Bradley, C., 'Good news for the crofter is bad for the corncrake', *Guardian*, 26 August 1982.

18. Scottish Development Department, *North Sea Oil and Gas: Coastal Planning Guidelines*. HMSO, 1974.
19. Manners, I. R., *Planning for North Sea Oil: The U.K. Experience*, University of Texas at Austin, 1978.
20. *National Coastline Study*, 3 volumes, *An Foras Forbartha*, 1973.
21. Martin A. *et al.*, 'A conservative strategy for the Irish coastline', *Elkistics* 1974, 74–80.
22. Nature Conservancy Council, op. cit. n. 13.
23. Wheeler, N., *Our Coastline: the Last Frontier*, op. cit. n. 7.
24. Commission of the European Communities, *Integrated Management of the coastal areas of the European Community*, ENV/465/78-EN, 1978.
25. Organization for Economic Co-operation and Development, *Recommendations of Council of 22 October 1976 on the principles relating to the administration of the coastal zones*, 1976.

X

International Organization and Legislative Change

PART 1: GLOBAL CO-OPERATION: THE THIRD
UNITED NATIONS CONFERENCE ON THE LAW OF THE
SEA (UNCLOS III)

Background to the Conference and the new Convention

At the time of our North Sea Study, the Third United Nations Conference on the Law of the Sea (UNCLOS III) had only just begun. We concluded that in view of the number and complexity of the issues before it, its outcome was both remote and uncertain. We did not, therefore, embark upon any detailed analysis of the proposals then under discussion. The conference had been convened in 1970 by the UN General Assembly, which instructed it to produce a single treaty dealing with 'ocean space as a whole'.[1] It was to cover all the issues relevant to the law of the sea, not only those dealt with in the 1958 Geneva conventions, but also several others including deep sea-bed mining in the areas beyond national jurisdiction which the General Assembly had declared to be 'the common heritage of mankind' to be exploited only for the benefit of mankind as a whole under an international regime to be established.[2] The conference first met in 1973 and by 1981 had produced the sixth version of a non-binding single negotiating text. At the tenth session in 1981 this was designated 'The Draft Convention on the Law of the Sea' and issued in the conference's legal document series.

Even now, though the conference adopted the draft with some revisions as a final convention on 30 April 1982, its eventual ratification, especially by north-west European states, remains uncertain. One hundred and thirty states (including France, Japan, and all the Scandinavian states) voted in favour of adopting the text, four (USA, Israel, Turkey and Venezuela) voted against, and 17 states (including the UK, West Germany, Italy, Belgium, Luxembourg and the Netherlands) abstained. Moreover, when it was opened for signature on 10 December 1982, only 117 states (plus Namibia and the Cook Island territories, which were specially designated in the convention as qualified parties) signed it out of the 160 states which had at times participated in UNCLOS III. The signatories included the USSR and Eastern European states, but several important industrialized states which are involved in international deep sea-bed mining consortia did not sign, including the United States, Japan (though it is likely to sign later) and, in north-west Europe, Belgium, the FRG, Italy, Luxembourg, and the Netherlands. Denmark (also a member of the European Community) along with the other Nordic countries signed the convention, as did land-locked Austria and Switzerland.

This is especially significant to our study since, after a long struggle, the European Community had been successful in securing the insertion of articles in the final convention which allowed the Community as such to sign and adhere as a full party in its own right. However, the relevant articles (article 305(1)(f); 306, and annex IX, especially articles 1 and 2) provide that international organizations of an economic character which have competence in issues covered by the treaty must fulfil two conditions before they can sign: first, a majority of their members must also be parties; secondly, on signing, the organization must make a declaration that it has competence concerning the issues covered by the convention, specifying the issues concerned and the extent of its competence. These conditions now pose serious problems for the Community; the European Commission considers that the Treaty of Rome, as interpreted by the Court of Justice, requires it to sign. Certainly, Community competence is now accepted in relation to fisheries, though there continues to be dispute over the legal basis and scope of the Community's competence in some environmental matters. Since five members of the Community have so far signed the convention and five have not, it remains to be seen whether the Community as such will be able to sign.

The convention remains open for signature for two years. Original signatories can become members of the Preparatory Commission (Prep. Com.) established by the UNCLOS Final Act (which the United States signed, among others). After two years, states can still accede to the convention, but by then it will be too late directly to influence the direction of the Prep. Com. though non-signatory member states may hope to influence it indirectly through their allies. They might also act through the Community if it is enabled to become a party, i.e. should another member state sign the convention.

A highly complex and confusing legal situation has now emerged as a result of the UNCLOS outcome. Signature of the convention signifies little more than an endorsement of the convention's articles, objects, and general principles and a possible willingness to work in good faith towards securing ratification. It does not formally bind the signatory state to ratification or the application of specific articles. States generally become bound only following the deposition of a formal instrument of ratification; it may, in the case of such an elaborate and often innovatory treaty, take several years for states to introduce the necessary enabling legislation at the national level. Even then the treaty does not enter into force, under its terms, until one year after the sixtieth ratification has been deposited. It is impossible to predict how long this will take. By June 1983 the treaty had been ratified by only three states, including Jamaica, which was designated as host nation to the International Sea-bed Authority.

The treaty is very much a 'package deal' and one that has to be ratified whole; no reservations (except minor ones permitted under specific articles) can be made. However, it is possible that additional parts of it may become accepted into customary international law since non-signatory or ratifying states are likely to adopt such parts as they accept into national law or practice; the lengthy negotiations secured general consensus on a number of important provisions and sections of the convention. It is impossible to predict with any certainty which these might be, but the concept of an Exclusive Economic Zone is certainly one, even if its precise jurisdictional content might be disputed. President Reagan in early 1983, in an effort to bring about the kind of regime *outside* the new treaty that the US would like to see, issued a proclamation of a US 200-mile EEZ.[3] It is in very general terms, avoids repeating the language of the treaty and specifically omits proclaiming US jurisdiction over scientific research. The US is, however, willing to accept other states' claims, as long as they have reasonable access agreements with the US. The US is to keep a 3-mile limit for its territorial sea, but will recognize other claims to a limit up to 12 miles. The US hopes by these means to ensure that the residual high-seas freedoms protected by the convention are accepted into customary practice and that, in particular, the right of transit passage through international straits is guaranteed. It remains to be seen whether the five member states of the EC which have not signed the convention will follow the American example. Without such supporting practice, or at least acceptance of US moves, it cannot yet be said that Reagan's proclamation is more than a non-binding unilateral act so far as the creation of new international law is concerned.

While it remains impossible to say which states will finally sign and ratify the convention, what is certain is that it will have a profound effect on the development of the law of the sea affecting all uses of the waters of this area, whether or not all north-west European states ratify it. Some parts of the treaty, such as the 200-mile fisheries jurisdiction, have already been put into effect on the basis of the consensus arrived at during the prolonged negotiations and evidenced in the series of negotiating texts. Others are likely to be similarly implemented and gradually to enter into customary international law, in the absence of any treaty obligation. Some of these are identified below. Moreover, it should be noted that the failure to reach consensus on the whole package means that there is a serious risk that some states (which have already declared 200-mile territorial seas, such as Argentina) will also reject the convention. Argentina may reassert rights over international straits in their new 12-mile territorial seas.

Even if the treaty does enter into force for all north-west European states, which may take some years, it is important to realize that because of the vast number of issues and of participants, the provisions are often of a very general nature, conferring on states parties the duty or power subsequently to develop specific laws, regulations, practices or recommendations by a variety of means—bi- or multi-lateral agreements, *ad hoc* diplomatic conferences, and through 'appropriate' international organizations at the global, regional, or sub-regional levels. These powers, though wide, are not unlimited. The convention frequently restricts them by requiring that 'due regard' be paid to the rights or interests of other states, or that the rules applied be those 'generally accepted'.[4] We can thus expect many years of law-making activities in the area of our study, that many jurisdictional boundaries (both horizontal and vertical) will be delimited and that numerous accommodations of rival interests will have to be arrived at in order to regulate activities. In this process existing international organizations at all levels will have an important role to play, especially as fora for the identification and accommodation of special interests.

The 1982 Law of the Sea convention establishes, in terms which are frequently deliberately ambiguous, a holistic regime, based on an integral package, for all areas of the seas: the surface waters; the water column; the continental shelf; and the deep sea-bed beyond. The preamble asserts the parties' consciousness that 'the problems of ocean space are interrelated'. The convention lays down a jurisdictional framework for virtually all the uses of the seas including navigation, exploitation of living and non-living resources and of the water itself, disposal of wastes, military uses, and scientific research. It also includes rules for the preservation of the oceans from pollution and for the conservation of living resources. The preamble further states that the parties are 'desiring to settle all issues' concerning the Law of the Sea, 'but affirms that matters not governed by the convention will continue to be governed by international law'.

It is not possible to describe in detail the 320 articles and 8 annexes which make up the convention, but it is necessary for the purposes of our study to outline the nature of the regime proposed and to identify its possible applications in north-west European waters. It is based on an interleaved series of jurisdictional zones so intricately and numerously layered as to be reminiscent of the cake known as a *mille-feuille*; some of those are extensions of zones already known to international law, others are new. It is not a cake that can be cleanly cut. The package treaty contains a large number of intertwined individual packages concerning, for example, powers to regulate scientific research, deep sea-bed operations, passage through straits, and conservation of the marine environment.

For states parties the new convention will technically supersede the four existing Geneva conventions (article 311);[5] its preamble proclaims that it is laying down 'a new and generally acceptable law of the sea'. For non-parties to the new treaty, however, and for areas covered by the Geneva conventions which are not included in the new convention, the former will remain valid; they are not in any event rendered totally obsolete and can still be referred to as a source of international law to which in many respects the new convention is closely related. None the less, there are important changes, not least that whereas the 1958 conventions provided only 5 jurisdictional zones, the new convention introduces over 40 distinctive legal maritime areas, as well as a large number of new legal relationships and legal actors. It also establishes new grades of coastal, flag, port, and other states' rights in areas such as the territorial sea and the new EEZ. It is important to realize that the new convention aims at introducing a form of distributive justice in the extent to which it carefully provides for states to share the benefits and obligations of using their jurisdictional zones. With or without ratification of the convention, north-west European states in the coming decade will be obliged to reach a balance favourable to their own interests within the framework set by the following provisions:

The Territorial Sea,[6] Innocent Passage,[7] and Contiguous Zone[8]

The convention permits every state to extend the breadth of its territorial sea to a limit of 12 nautical miles, thus enabling better enforcement and application of national and international laws; pending conclusion of the convention, the UK, like the US, retained a three-mile limit though it announced that it intended to adopt a 12-mile limit. Baselines are almost the same as in the Geneva convention.

Innocent passage is, however, redefined to include twelve activities which render it non-innocent, including any act of serious and wilful pollution. The coastal state cannot hamper innocent passage, but it can take the 'necessary' steps in its territorial sea to prevent non-innocent passage. All ships are given the right of innocent passage; no exception is mentioned for military vessels, though submarines and so forth are still required to navigate on the surface and warships which do not comply with the coastal state's laws concerning passage can be required to leave immediately. Had the requirement concerning submarines, which follows the Geneva Convention, been observed by the UK, the sinking of the trawler *Sharelga* in the Irish territorial sea by a British submarine which became entangled in her nets might have been avoided.

A corresponding increase to 24 miles is made in the breadth of the contiguous zone, in which some functional jurisdiction such as customs and immigration can be enforced, though not all European coastal states (including the UK) currently assert such zones.

International straits and transit passage[9]   In straits used for international navigation as defined in the convention, a right of unimpeded transit passage is guaranteed, since a 12-mile territorial sea results in enclosure within the national jurisdictional limits of one or more states of over 100 straits, (including the straits of Dover) which are less than 24 miles wide, removing them from high seas freedom of navigation. Coastal states will be allowed, however, to designate as necessary sea lanes and prescribe traffic separation schemes conforming to generally accepted international regulations, though the straits' states must refer these to the competent international organization (IMO). The UK and France were particularly concerned that this provision should achieve a balance between the interests of coastal and ship-owning states.

The Exclusive Economic Zone (EEZ)[10]

The EEZ is a radical new concept: an area beyond and adjacent to territorial sea in which the coast state can exercise a prescribed bundle of rights and jurisdictions. It must not exceed 200 nautical miles measured from the baselines of the territorial sea; the convention also governs the rights and freedoms exercisable in it by other states.

Its legal status is ambiguous: it is a shared zone so far as its waters are concerned but it is not high seas; the Convention's high seas provisions apply only to 'parts of the sea that are *not* included in the exclusive economic zone, in the territorial sea, or in the internal waters of a state, or in archipelagic waters (emphasis added), yet residual high seas freedoms still apply in it.

The coastal state will exercise a carefully graded package of jurisdictions; it has, not sovereignty, but, 'sovereign rights for the purpose of exploring and exploiting, conserving and managing the natural resources, whether living or non-living, of the sea-bed and subsoil and the superjacent waters, and with regard to other activities for the economic exploitation and exploration of the zone, such as the production of energy from the water, currents and winds'. It has non-exclusive jurisdiction 'as provided for in the relevant provisions of this convention', with regard to: artificial islands, which have not hitherto been covered by global treaty installations and structures; marine scientific research (under part xiii); the protection and preservation of the marine environment (under part xii); and other rights and duties in the Convention. Other states, whether coastal or landlocked, continue to enjoy the freedoms of navigation and overflight, laying of submarine cables and pipelines and 'other internationally lawful uses of the sea related to these freedoms' such as those associated with the operation of ships, aircraft, and submarine pipelines, and compatible with the convention. They in turn must have due regard to the coastal state's rights.

Fisheries[11]

General provisions

Part V of the convention dealing with the EEZ lays down a detailed regime for fisheries. The coastal state determines the total allowable catch (TAC) and its capacity to harvest it. If it decides that it does not have the capacity to take it all, it *must* give access to the surplus to other states, based on agreements laying down terms of fishing which can cover: licensing; species to be caught; quotas; fishing areas; age and size of fish; information on fishing vessels; research programmes; placing observers or trainees on board; landing the catch in the coastal state; joint ventures; transfer of technology and training; enforcement. Factors which need to be taken into account in allocating access include: the significance of the resource to the coastal state; requirements of developing countries; and the need to minimize economic dislocation in states whose nationals have habitually fished in the zone or which have made substantial efforts in research and identification of stocks.

Land-locked states in the region or sub-region must be given access to the surplus, but agreements are necessary to determine this. Access for land-locked and geographically disadvantaged states (LLGDS) is limited, especially for developed ones. Clearly the European Community will take care of Luxembourg's interests, but the position of Switzerland and Austria is problematic. However, these and other articles give the land-locked a legal interest in north-west European waters. They result from the pressure exerted at UNCLOS by a group of over 50 LLGDS led by Austria.

Chapter III described the extent to which states in north-west Europe have already implemented by unilateral legislation the 200-nautical-mile jurisdictional limit for fisheries (not other EEZ rights), though not in terms identical to that of the convention. Although the European Community's Common Fisheries Policy prevents member states from unilaterally determining the TAC in their zones and reserving to themselves all the TAC within their harvesting capacity, it does enable uniformity in conservation measures. But some of the factors required to be considered by the convention appear to have been disregarded in the EC's common access regime, which gives preference to member states and has paid limited attention to minimization of economic dislocation: fishing by third parties has been either discontinued (for example, the eastern bloc states) or reduced (for example Norway), albeit sometimes on a reciprocal basis (Spain and Portugal).

The convention requires coastal states to promote the optimum utilization of fisheries including highly migratory species (for which article 64 makes special provisions), though marine mammals are excepted from this requirement.[12]

Coastal states must, however, take into account the best scientific evidence available to ensure through proper conservation and management measures that the maintenance of the living resources in the exclusive economic zone is not endangered by overexploitation; as appropriate, the coastal state and competent international organizations, whether sub-regional, regional or global, must co-operate to this end. Measures must aim at a maximum sustainable yield (MSY) as qualified by relevant environmental and economic factors, including the economic needs of coastal fishing communities and the special needs of developing states, and taking into account fishing patterns, the interdependence of stocks, and any generally recommended international minimum standards, whether sub-regional, regional, or global. Effects on associated or dependent species must be considered, and states must provide and exchange scientific information and data relevant to conservation through competent international organizations, whether sub-regional, regional or global; for instance in the European area these would be the European Community, the NEAFC, ICES, and the FAO.

Special provisions

Common stocks, highly migratory species, and marine mammals   There are special provisions concerning co-operation in the management of common stocks (article 63), highly migratory species (article 64)—which are identified in an annexe (very few are found in European waters) and subject to requirements of both conservation and optimum utilization based on direct co-operation or use of organisations—and marine mammals (article 65), which are excepted from optimum utilization and can be regulated by coastal states more strictly than under the EEZ articles. States must co-operate in the conservation and development of these stocks and, in the case of cetaceans in particular, must work through the appropriate international organization (generally the International Whaling Commission). Not all European states are parties to the International Convention for Regulation of Whaling—Denmark, France, Iceland, the FRG, Netherlands, Norway, Sweden and the UK are parties; Belgium and Ireland are not. The UK in 1981 banned all taking of cetaceans in its 200-mile FZ, but Denmark (Faroes and Greenland), Norway, and Iceland still harvest some whales. Denmark and Iceland have not lodged objections to an IWC decision to protect all species of whales currently regulated by the IWC after 1985/6 though Norway has done so; the Faroes are disputing Denmark's decision.

Anadromous species   These are stocks of species such as salmon, which spawn and are nurtured in the freshwater rivers of one state, then migrate in maturity to the sea, through that and other states' zones and also on to the high seas, where the doctrine of freedom of fishing permits their taking by all states whether or not the states concerned have contributed to research, restocking, and other necessary conservatory measures. Close co-operation is essential for the preservation of these anadromous species. In north-west Europe this has not yet proved achievable, and although a Convention on Conservation of the Salmon Stocks in the North Atlantic was adopted early in 1982, establishing the North Atlantic Salmon Conservation Organization (NASCO), it has not yet been signed or ratified by all states concerned in this fishery. Particular problems have been the increasing catch of salmon on the high seas by the Faroe Islanders (Denmark) and the massive increase in catches of capelin, on which the salmon feed.

Article 66 introduces an innovatory concept into international law, namely the preferential right of the state of origin of anadromous stocks, its consequent right to determine the TAC, and an accompanying requirement that fisheries for such species, other than in exceptional circumstances, be conducted only in waters *landward* of the EEZ limit unless this would result in economic dislocation for other states. It states that 'states in whose rivers anadromous stocks originate shall have the primary interest in and responsibility for such stocks' and 'shall ensure their conservation by the establishment of appropriate regulatory measures' in all waters landward of the EEZ's outer limit for fishing of the stocks.

Fishing beyond the EEZ limit must then be the subject of consultation between the states concerned 'with a view to achieving an agreement on terms and conditions of such fishing giving due regard to the conservation requirements and needs of the state of origin in respect of these stocks. Economic dislocation must be minimized and affected states given special consideration, enforcement of regulations being by agreement between the parties. States into whose EEZ anadromous species migrate must also co-operate with the states of origin in conservation and management, and states of origin and other states fishing must 'make implementing arrangements where appropriate through regional organizations'.

There will be many problems of interpretation, including devising a method for identifying the country of origin of salmon caught in the high seas. The North Atlantic Salmon Convention, discussed in chapter V, shows that the UNCLOS created an awareness of the seriousness of the problems in relation to the maintenance of salmon fishing, and that agreement is possible.

Catadromous species   These are species such as eels which spend most of their adult lives in fresh water, but return to the sea in order to spawn. The young elvers then make their way back into rivers and streams where they grow to adulthood before undertaking their spawning migration.

Article 67 of the convention provides that states in whose waters such species spend most of their life cycle shall have responsibility for their management and shall ensure the ingress and egress of migrating fish. Harvesting is to be conducted only in waters landward of the outer limits of the EEZ; if the species migrate through other EEZs, management and harvesting must be regulated by agreement between the states concerned.

Sedentary species   Article 68 of the convention withdraws these species from all application of the EEZ articles, leaving them to be regulated, as under the Geneva Convention on the Continental Shelf, as resources of the shelf, subject to part vi, article 77 of the new convention. This provides that the coastal state exercises sovereign rights over them for purposes of exploration and exploitation, and specifically repeats that if the coastal state does not exploit them, no one may do so without its express consent. Sedentary species are still defined as 'living organisms which, at the harvesting stage, either are immobile on or under the sea-bed or are unable to move except in constant physical contact with the sea-bed or subsoil'.

The confusion engendered by discrepancies between this legal definition and the biological facts and scientific definitions (it is unclear, for example, which crustaceans are included) is perpetuated, as also is the failure to require that such resources be conserved since the removal of these species from the EEZ regime not only frees the coastal state of the requirement to determine a TAC and allow other states access to any surplus to its own harvesting capacity, but also exempts it from any obligation to take account of scientific advice, to prevent overexploitation by proper conservation and management measures, to co-operate with competent organizations to this end, to promote optimum use and to maintain qualified MSY, related to interdependence of stocks and environmental factors. It is, however, possible for north-west European states to ignore this legal distinction and to co-operate in conservation measures through the European Community and ICES as appropriate, and there is evidence in the light of present practice that they will do so. Introduction of EEZs or FZs, should provide the opportunity for a more holistic approach to conservation of living resources.

Artificial Islands, Installations, and Structures[13]

In the EEZ the coastal state can erect, authorize, and regulate the construction and operation of artificial islands for all purposes, and erect installations and structures for purposes provided for in article 56 and for other economic purposes. It can also erect other installations and structures subject to various terms and conditions. These provisions fill a gap in current treaty law where there is no specific provision covering artificial islands.

The Continental Shelf[14]

Part VI of the draft convention, which deals with the continental shelf, does not change substantially the jurisdictional regime laid down in the Geneva convention as described in our North Sea study, but it does greatly enlarge the concept and outer limits of the shelf (the LLGDs did not succeed in efforts to limit it geographically) since article 76 defines it as follows:

The continental shelf of a coastal state comprises the sea-bed and subsoil of the submarine areas that extend beyond its territorial sea throughout the natural prolongation of its land territory to the outer edge of the continental margin, or to a distance of 200 nautical miles from the baselines from which the territorial sea is measured where the outer edge of the continental margin does not extend up to that distance.

This definition follows the approach of the International Court of Justice in 1969 in the North Sea Case (analysed in our earlier North Sea study)[15] relating the shelf to natural prolongation, a decision much criticized[16] since it leaves the outer limit uncertain, to be decided by reference to criteria of geology and geophysics rather than distance or exploitability as in the Geneva convention. Moreover, the above definition, by awarding also a 200-mile shelf to all states whether or not they have a geographical continental shelf, makes superfluous the EEZ provisions concerning coastal states' rights to sea-bed resources. Articles 56 and 76 in fact award areas of the deep sea-bed to states with little or no actual shelf, whereas article 76 specifically excludes the deep ocean floor with its oceanic ridges from the shelf.

Article 76 removes the open end to the shelf limit left by the Geneva convention by requiring coastal states to establish the outer edge of the continental margin beyond 200 miles from the baselines by drawing either a line based on fixed points related to the thickness of sedimentary rocks near the foot of the continental slope, or to fixed points up to 60 miles from it, the points being defined by latitude and longitude co-ordinates and the slope foot by the point of maximum change in gradient at its base. The outer limit must not exceed either 350 nautical miles or 100 miles from the 2,500-metre isobath; on submarine ridges the outer limit must not go beyond 350 nautical miles, unless the submarine elevations are natural components of the margin (e.g. plateaux, rises, caps, banks, spurs).

A Commission on the Limits of the Continental Shelf is established in annex ii, consisting of twenty-one experts in geology, geophysics, or hydrology acting in a personal capacity, for the area beyond 200 nautical miles. It will consider data and so forth submitted by coastal states concerning these outer limits and make *recommendations* to them in accordance with the limits prescribed in article 76, and, in co-operation with competent international organizations, will provide scientific and technical advice, if requested by coastal states concerned. Coastal states will *have* to submit to the commission particulars of limits and supporting evidence when they proceed towards establishing outer continental shelf boundaries, at least within ten years of the entry into force of the convention.

These procedures will introduce a formidable new body into the north-west European network of maritime commissions. Its influence is difficult to gauge at this stage; much will depend on the acceptability of its advice in the light of all the preliminary work already undertaken in this area and the importance of the as yet undetermined boundaries to national interests.

Jurisdiction over the shelf and its resources is generally comparable to that under the Geneva convention, though there are some changes, including that shelf rights do not affect the 'legal status' of the superjacent waters (article 78), and that in respect of the areas beyond 200 miles coastal states shall make payments or contributions in kind, through the Authority for the Deep Sea-bed Area, to be shared out by it among states parties. As payments only begin five years after joint production, they may be an incentive to hasten depletion.

The provisions for delimiting the EEZs and shelves of opposite and adjacent states (failing agreement) are vague, ambiguous, and unsatisfactory, reflecting the failure to achieve consensus for either equidistance or equitable principles as the exclusive rule, despite the exhaustive examination of the Geneva convention and customary rules in both the North Sea Case and Anglo-French Channel Arbitration.[17]

Article 83 non-committally provides that delimitation, 'shall be effected by agreement on the basis of international law, as referred to in Article 38 of the Statute of the International Court of Justice, in order to achieve an equitable solution . . .'

This will contribute little to the settlement of the several potential continental shelf disputes in north-west Europe concerning the western approaches off Ireland and the United Kingdom; the island of Rockall between Ireland, the UK, Denmark and possibly Iceland; and in undelimited parts of the straits of Dover. The above formula leaves unresolved the status of offshore islands and other geographical features as 'special circumstances' in delimitation. Moreover, the problem concerning the delimitation of the Rockall Bank, from which Rockall Islet (a small uninhabitable rock which is part of the British Isles, although 180 nautical miles west of the outermost islands of the Hebrides) protrudes, is compounded by article 121 which provides that 'Rocks which cannot sustain human habitation or economic life of their own shall have no exclusive economic zone or continental shelf,' thus preventing use of Rockall as a base point. It has, in fact, already been used by the UK as a base point for delimiting its fisheries zone in 1977. The UK and Ireland are preparing for arbitration of this dispute; the former is likely to argue that Rockall Bank is geologically part of the natural prolongation of UK land territory.[18]

Enclosed or Semi-enclosed Seas[19]

Although these provisions would seem to be particularly relevant to our study, after very general definitions they merely urge that states bordering such seas, in broad terms, should co-operate for certain specified purposes (exploitation of living resources, protection of the marine environment, scientific research), trying to do so through 'appropriate' regional organizations. North-west Europe is, as we shall see, exceptionally well provided with relevant global and regional organizations. Ratification of the LOS convention would provide the occasion to re-examine their efficiency and interrelationships.

The High Seas[20]

The regime based on the four freedoms buttressed by the Geneva conventions is continued, in modified form, with the additional freedom to construct artificial islands and installations, and the freedom to conduct scientific research, subject to the rights laid down in part XI for the deep sea-bed area. The high seas are reserved for peaceful purposes; flag state duties are specified (improving enforcement) and hot pursuit for EEZ and continental shelf violations is permitted as well as from the territorial seas and contiguous zones. Various duties concerning conservation of living resources are also detailed.

The Deep Sea-bed Area[21]

This area is defined as 'the sea-bed and ocean floor and subsoil thereof' beyond national jurisdiction, and it and its resources, including the polymetallic nodules, are declared 'the common heritage of mankind'. They are therefore removed from claims to sovereignty and vested in mankind as a whole on whose behalf the International Sea-bed Authority (ISA), established by the convention, must act. The ISA is to consist of an assembly, a 36-member executive council (based on representative interest groups) and a secretariat (based on a sea-bed disputes charter). An enterprise is to be set up—an organ of the ISA which will directly execute activities in the area alongside states and state-sponsored companies contracted to the ISA.

The ISA is given wide powers to conclude contracts, regulate exploitation and rates of production, and distribute revenues derived from royalties and so forth. It is these provisions, coupled with representation on the council and requirements for providing finance and technology for the enterprise, which led the US to vote against the text of the convention and several EC states to abstain and then not to sign. The north-west European deep sea-bed is unlikely to prove profitable for mining in the foreseeable future, but companies taking part in international mining consortia are registered in Belgium, France, West Germany, the Netherlands, Italy, and the UK. As the above provisions are an essential part of the package deal, they are highly relevant to the question of the treaty's ratification by these states, three of which have already enacted unilateral legislation to enable licensing of deep sea-bed mining companies after 1988 and two of which have legislation in progress.[22] The convention does now provide for investment protection for pioneer miners, the establishment of an interim commission and, to encourage US participation, it more or less guarantees the US a seat on the council.

Protection and Preservation of the Marine Environment: The Six Sources of Marine Pollution[23]

General provisions

Part xii of the convention dealing with the above issues contains some of the most effective provisions which progressively develop both the application and the enforcement of the law for these purposes. As so many treaties and international institutions already exist in north-west Europe which directly or indirectly are concerned to protect the marine environment from all sources of marine pollution, part xii offers a yardstick for measuring the present regime against future international standards. Moreover, part xii is regarded as based on a wide consensus so that even if the treaty does not enter into force, or is not widely ratified, this part of the text is likely, in time, either to become part of customary international law as it gradually enters into state practice, through national laws, or to be adopted in regional or global treaties. Its innovatory provisions are among the most important parts of the convention for north-west Europe.

For the first time at a global level the convention enunciates the obligation of *all* states (including the land-locked) to preserve the marine environment and to take the necessary practicable measures to prevent pollution from all sources. It specifically provides for six sources: land-based; exploitation of sea-bed resources (of the continental shelves); activities in the Deep Sea-bed Area; ocean dumping; the atmosphere; and vessels. The convention prescribes actions based on agreed measures for all these sources, though the kind of action varies with the source, but for all these sources development of global and regional rules and standards, taking account of internationally agreed rules and standards, is required, as is their re-examination as necessary. States are required to proceed to this end through *ad hoc* diplomatic conferences and international organizations. Development of the appropriate laws is, however, left more to coastal states in the case of land-based and sea-bed sources, while in the Deep Sea-bed Area the International Sea-bed Authority will develop the rules—machinery is provided for this in part xi. Whatever the source, there is no doubt that international organizations, at global, regional and sub-regional levels, will play a major role in the future in both developing and harmonizing these standards and rules. Although the convention lays down a comprehensive international duty to protect the seas, it does not emphasize the need for a holistic approach in controlling pollution, i.e. for the controls for the different sources to be inter-related to restrict the intermingling and possibly dangerous interaction of pollutants from, for example, land-based discharges and dumping, from vessels and from the atmosphere, from the sea-bed, and the Area or other combinations. In some areas, such as the semi-enclosed seas and straits of north-western Europe, effluents from all six sources may commingle.

It is not possible to examine the LOS treaty's marine pollution articles in detail, but there are some innovatory proposals which north-west European states will understandably wish to develop, bearing in mind the consensus which was reached on them.

Ocean dumping[24]

There exist both a global (the 1972 London Convention on Ocean Dumping) and a regional (the 1972 Oslo Convention on Ocean Dumping in the North Atlantic) convention, both of which are in force and to both of which the UK and several north-west European states are party; both cover various forms of hydrocarbon and other dumping. One improvement introduced by the LOS Convention which will greatly strengthen the effectiveness of these two conventions is that the coastal state's approval will be required for dumping not only in its territorial sea, as at present, but in its EEZ and on its continental shelf, which will include the whole of the continental margin.

Pollution from the atmosphere[25]

As well as establishing and enforcing national laws, states are required to try to establish global and regional rules to prevent such pollution of their airspace and for their vessels and aircraft. Until very recently these were non-existent, but in November 1979 the UN Economic Commission for Europe (ECE) succeeded in concluding the first convention to prevent atmospheric pollution, the Convention on Transboundary Air Pollution.[26] It is not yet in effect, but it is an encouraging development as much marine pollution, including hydrocarbon pollution, emanates from this source.

Vessel-source pollution[27]

The provisions for vessel-source pollution constitute a highly complex effort to balance the rights of coastal states to make and enforce regulations in their territorial seas and EEZs with the rights of flag states to innocent passage and freedom of navigation. Part xii follows the logical approach that the coastal state's powers to regulate and enforce are wider the nearer to its shores an offending incident occurs. Noteworthy new provisions include:

(a) *Reporting-in*[28]   States *must* (not merely 'must try to') establish international rules and standards for prevention of pollution from this source acting through competent international organizations or general diplomatic conferences, and must also promote the adoption of routeing systems to avoid accidents. On France's initiative, following the *Amoco Cadiz* disaster, the convention's requirements were tightened up in order to improve: the opportunities for identifying and inspecting sub-standard vessels; requirements relating to port entry and the harmonization of reporting-in to states participating in regional arrangements; the availability of information on the port of destination of vessels traversing the territorial sea, and whether such vessels conform to the entry requirements of that port.

(b) *Special areas*[29]   In the EEZ, coastal states can generally establish only pollution prevention laws which conform to international standards, established through conferences and organizations. However, in particular defined areas of the EEZ which, for oceanographic, ecological, resource protection, or traffic utilization reasons require special mandatory standards, or where existing international ones are inadequate for the special circumstances, higher standards may be imposed by coastal states. There may be several areas in north-west European waters which conform to these criteria. It has already been suggested that the North Sea should be so regarded, even on the basis of the limited criteria of the IMO Oil Pollution Convention (as amended).

   In such areas the coastal state may establish special laws and regulations after: submitting its proposals and the necessary evidence to establish the special character of the area to the competent international organization for special areas (not designated, but likely to be IMO); securing its approval; allowing for the various procedural delays and requirements which would enable states affected to adjust to the new requirements. Any additional laws can relate only to discharges and navigational practices, not to design, construction, manning, or equipment of foreign vessels, which are subject only to international standards.

(c) *Ice-covered*[30] *and 'fragile' areas*[31]   Special provisions are also made for vessel-source pollution in ice-covered areas, which might apply to parts of Greenland. The convention also requires states generally to take the necessary measures to protect and preserve rare or fragile ecosystems as well as the habitat of depleted, threatened or endangered species and other forms of marine life.

(d) *Enforcement by flag states*[32]   Procedures are complex, depending on the location of the violation. Primary responsibility remains with the flag state and its duties are spelled out in the convention; these include the ensuring that all necessary certificates are carried on board, prevention from sailing of sub-standard vessels, immediate investigation of violations of international standards, and the taking of proceedings when appropriate, irrespective of where an offence occurs or where the resulting pollution manifests itself.

(e) *Enforcement by port states*[33]   Progressive provisions, not yet in general existence under present international law and for the introduction of which a treaty is essential, permit that if a ship is *voluntarily* within a port or offshore terminal the 'port state' can investigate discharges which have taken place on the high seas and which violate international standards and can take proceedings when justified. If the discharge occurred in the waters, including the EEZ, of another state, the port state cannot take proceedings unless either that state so requests, or the resultant pollution is likely to damage the waters of the port state. Port states must investigate vessels causing violations in the waters of other states on their request. They must also, if requested, subsequently transfer records and proceedings to that state. Port states can also, in the circumstances described below, take action for offences committed in their coastal waters.

(f) *Enforcement by coastal states*[34]   When vessels *voluntarily* enter ports and offshore terminals, coastal states can take proceedings for violations of national laws conforming to international standards when the violation has occurred within their territorial sea or EEZ. They can physically inspect vessels if there is clear evidence that an offence has occurred within their territorial sea. However, if there is clear evidence that an offence occurred in the EEZ, the violating vessel can at first only be asked to give information on its identity, registration and other details. If there is then clear evidence of a violation of applicable international rules and that this 'has resulted in a *substantial* discharge causing or threatening *significant* pollution of the marine environment' the coastal state may physically inspect the vessel in the EEZ to check the veracity of the information given. Only if there is then objective evidence that a vessel navigating the EEZ or territorial sea of the coastal state has committed '*a flagrant or gross violation*' of the international standards, resulting in '*discharge causing major damage* or threat of major damage to the coastline or related interests of that coastal state or resources within its jurisdiction' can that state detain the vessel or take proceedings against it. Even then the coastal state must allow the vessel to proceed if acceptable bonding or other financial procedures are complied with. Moreover, all the procedures for verification, inspection and so forth are subject to detailed safeguards set out in the text, which also are a progressive development of enforcement powers not available under present international law.[35]

Marine Scientific Research[36]

Although this part of the text gives to all states and competent international organizations, irrespective of their geographic location, the right not fully recognized in the Geneva convention to conduct marine scientific research, the right is made subject to the rights and duties of other states under the convention.[37] This subjects research to considerable coastal state control in the new EEZs, on the continental shelf and in the territorial sea, restricting freedom of research in areas previously regarded as the high seas, though the new convention does prescribe freedom of research for the remaining high seas area. Scientists have expressed considerable alarm at the proposed restrictions since the adoption world-wide of EEZs will account for 37 per cent of the ocean surface. Many of the most interesting scientific problems relate to coastal regions, which, because they are relatively shallow, are also easier and cheaper to work in. US oceanographers carry out about 50 per cent of their research within 200 miles of foreign shores; hence the guarded terms of President Reagan's statement concerning scientific research which accompanied his declaration of an US EEZ.

Coastal states are given the right to regulate, conduct and authorize research in their EEZs and on their continental shelves on terms laid down in the convention. A balance between the rights of the coastal and foreign researching states is struck, however, in the following provision in article 246 (3), though ambiguities remain:

Coastal states shall, *in normal circumstances*, grant their consent for marine scientific research projects by other states or competent international organizations in their exclusive economic zone or on their continental shelf to be carried out in accordance with this convention exclusively for peaceful purposes and in order to increase scientific knowledge of the marine environment for the benefit of all mankind. To this end, coastal states shall establish rules and procedures ensuring that *such consent will not be delayed or denied unreasonably*. [Emphasis added]

Even before adoption of the convention, refusals of consent were reported to be increasing, partly for political reasons, but sometimes due to bureaucratic failures even in north-west Europe.[38] The convention does, however, specify four instances (presumably the 'abnormal circumstances') in which states can withold consent—if a project relates to natural resource exploitation, involves drilling into the continental shelf, construction of artificial islands or the like, or contains inaccurate information, or the researcher has outstanding obligations to the coastal state from a previous project. Various other safeguards are also provided—consent can be implied if four months after a research request was received the coastal state has not taken action. Balancing this are requirements that the researching state fulfils certain conditions—allowing coastal state participation, sharing data with it, and so forth.

All states and organizations must promote research and provide favourable conditions for it by concluding agreements. Dispute procedures are provided, subject, however, to certain reservations. Research in the Deep Sea-bed Area is open to all states but only in conformity with the provisions of part xi of the convention, namely for peaceful purposes, for the benefit of mankind as a whole, and alongside the International Sea-bed Authority itself.

Even with the balances struck, the new regime seems likely to restrict research; if introduced in north-west Europe, its effects may be mitigated by channelling research through ICES since consent given to programmes of international organizations is assumed to represent coastal state consent.[39]

Settlement of Disputes[40]

Part xv of the LOS convention requires states parties to settle disputes between them concerning the convention by peaceful means according to the UN Charter (article 33), but the convention also establishes means of its own including use of conciliation procedures laid down in an annexe, or of compulsory procedures including a new International Tribunal for the Law of the Sea and special arbitration tribunals of experts qualified in fisheries, protection and preservation of the marine environment, marine scientific research and navigation, and pollution from vessels and by dumping. These procedures will, of course, only exist between states parties to the convention.

Final Clauses[41]

The convention will enter into force twelve months after the sixtieth ratification. No reservations or exceptions can be made to it except as provided under specific articles of the convention. Amendments are, however, possible, but only from ten years after the treaty's entry into force, following specific procedures laid down in the convention. The UK's statement that it hoped the Preparatory Commission (in which, because of its non-signature of the convention it will not be a voting member although its signature of the conference's Final Act allows it to attend as an observer) would be able to make sufficient changes in the sea-bed mining regime and regulations to enable it and other non-signatories to sign, seems unrealistic. The Preparatory Commission now has powers to amend the substance of the convention and spent most of its first meeting at Montego Bay in March 1983 rent by disagreements on the election of its chairman and choice of meeting-place; no progress was made on the regulations and the US did not participate in the Preparatory Commission. This does not bode well for the UK Government's hopes. Under article 155, the deep sea-bed regime is subject to review after fifteen years by a review conference, which five years later can decide by a two-thirds majority vote to amend or change the system. This is another provision especially objectionable to the US, which sought a veto.

A provision of exceptional importance for north-west European states is that the Law of the Sea convention shall prevail, as between states parties, over the Geneva conventions. A complex situation will develop if only some states in the north-west European area become parties to the UNCLOS treaty; it is clearly important to the European Community, for the reasons outlined earlier, that all its members should become parties once one member has done so. However, adverse effects are to some extent modified by the provision that the new convention will not alter the rights and obligations of states parties which arise from other agreements *compatible* with it and which do not affect the enjoyment of other states parties of their rights or the performance of their obligations under the new convention.

Conclusion

Ratification of the new Law of the Sea convention would have considerable impact on north-west European waters: its jurisdictional extensions, the complex nature of rights and duties within the new jurisdictions, the improved opportunities for enforcement, and the radical development of the deep sea-bed regime create a new legal order of the oceans.

If the integrated treaty package does enter into force in Europe, it will be important that it does so in as harmonized a manner as possible. Existing organizations will have to work to ensure this: a patchwork of jurisdictions, rights and obligations could lead to many confrontations, especially if the new settlement procedures for disputes are not applicable. It is difficult, in the light of the final vote and signatures, to predict at this stage either which European states will ratify or which parts of the text will enter into customary law; in any event, undoubtedly many parts will do so, such as the pollution prevention provisions; the fisheries provisions have already done so. New regional agreements may be required for these and other purposes.

The convention makes innumerable references to the need for international organizations to develop new rules, standards, practices and recommendations. It does not itself establish a new body or specifically allocate the risks to existing ones. It is, therefore, necessary to examine existing appropriate organizations to assess their preparedness for the new tasks.[42]

PART 2   GLOBAL CO-OPERATION: GLOBAL INTERNATIONAL ORGANIZATIONS

The LOS convention refers to the need to establish new bodies when they do not exist for particular areas or purposes. Our North Sea and Celtic Sea studies drew attention to the legal and organizational problems to which the multifarious conflicting uses of these areas give rise. These problems are magnified in relation to the larger area covered by this study, which includes the English Channel. The need for international co-ordination and harmonization of national laws to enable rational management of internationally used waters in the best long-term interests of all is intensified as modern technology advances. The international and UK legal regimes based on the Geneva conventions and customary law were fully discussed in our previous studies.[43] The changes that might ensue from adoption of the LOS convention have been discussed above. It remains to examine the changes that have developed through the organizations established for achieving them. In the rest of this chapter the most relevant bodies operating at the global level will be examined; the following chapter will evaluate the work of the plethora of regional bodies concerned with uses of the north-west European seas and sea-beds.

Although there are a large number of international organizations which are concerned in various activities in north-west European waters, none has a leading or co-ordinating role; nor, because of the particularization of their tasks, is any one appropriate to be designated as such a lead organization. Global organizations, however effective, are not suited to this regional role almost by definition, although the scope of the United Nations Environment Programme (UNEP), as will be seen, would seem prima facie to make it an appropriate body to overview the environmental aspects of the regime. The following analysis of leading relevant global bodies covers their structures, organs, powers and programmes. It will, it is hoped, stimulate and facilitate consideration of the options available for constructing any new organization or organizations which may be required; existing organizations have frequently provided models, even if only partially, for the range of subsequent bodies established in north-west Europe.

Shipping and Offshore Installations

The International Maritime Organization (IMO)[44]

Role and relation to other bodies   IMO, which has 125 members, is the specialized agency of the United Nations for shipping. Its objective is to facilitate co-operation among governments on technical matters affecting international shipping in order to achieve the highest practicable standards of maritime safety and efficiency of navigation. It has a special responsibility for safety at sea, and for the protection of the marine environment through prevention of pollution of the sea caused by ships and other craft, defined in some circumstances to include offshore platforms. It also deals with legal issues concerning international shipping and with the facilitation of international maritime traffic, and provides technical assistance to developing countries.

One of IMO's most important roles and *modi operandi* is that it is responsible for convening any necessary international conferences on shipping issues and for drafting the relevant international conventions, agreements, recommended practices and codes relating to these subjects. It also performs functions relating to other conventions, such as the 1972 London Convention on Ocean Dumping, for which it acts as a secretariat, and convenes consultative meetings as provided in the treaty. Shipping is essentially an international business. Most European and Nordic states register vessels which ply their trade world-wide; conversely north-west European waters are traversed by ships of all nations, many of which do not enter the territorial seas and ports of the particular states in whose waters they commit violations of international and national law. IMO's standard-setting role and the machinery it provides for the adoption of conventions and so forth to render these standards binding internationally is thus exceptionally important to orderly regulation and protection of the waters in an area of semi-enclosed seas and international straits subject to heavy traffic. This is widely recognized and IMO commands the confidence of all states in the area.

IMO co-operates with other international agencies on such matters and co-ordinates its activities with other specialized agencies of the UN, its subsidiary bodies and commissions; it reports to the UN's Economic and Social Council and sends details of its programmes to the UN secretariat, which transmits them to other appropriate bodies. IMO also takes part in bodies within the UN system specifically established to promote co-ordination since many other UN agencies, such as the UN Development Programme, the UN Conference on Trade and Development, the International Labour Organization, and the United Nations Environment Programme, are interested in various aspects of shipping. In 1976 IMO and UNEP concluded a Memorandum of Understanding aimed at strengthening links between them in combatting marine pollution, one result of which was the establishment of a Regional Oil-Combatting Centre for the Mediterranean; no such initiative has been taken for north-west European waters. IMO, the FAO, and the ILO have formed a Group of Experts to deal with the safety of fishing vessels and IMO is a joint sponsor of GESAMP (Group of Experts on the Scientific Aspects of Marine Pollution, which includes seven agencies).

IMO and the ILO also, in 1968, established a Joint Committee on Training, augmented in 1974 by a formal understanding that proposals arising in either organization concerning international marine training, qualifications and certificates would be examined by the committee in an advisory capacity. More recently, IMO convened a conference, again in association with the ILO, which led to the adoption in 1978 of a Convention on Standards of Training, Certification and Watchkeeping. The Convention will come into force in April 1984. The topic had not been subject to treaty regulation before, but in the light of the growing awareness that human error is a major contribution to marine pollution accidents and incidents, it has become a matter of concern to both IMO and the ILO. The same concern has led to the establishment by IMO of a World Maritime University in Malmö, Sweden, for advanced maritime training, particularly for the benefit of developing countries.

Organs IMO's main organs are its Assembly, Council, and Maritime Safety Committee (MSC). Over the years other bodies have been set up, such as the Marine Environment Protection Committee (MEPC), a Legal Committee and a Committee on Technical Co-operation. These have been established as the need was perceived. There is also a Facilitation Committee patterned on the model of the International Civil Aviation Organization. The assembly, in which all member states participate, is the supreme governing body, deciding the work programme, approving recommendations made by IMO, and its budget, based on an agreed assessment scale related partly to members' registered tonnage and partly to the UN scale. The assembly meets biennially, elects the IMO council and approves the appointment of the Secretary-General. The council of twenty-four member states is elected for a two-year term, generally meets biannually, and acts as the governing body between assembly sessions. At present it includes four north-west European states, namely France, West Germany, Norway, and the UK.

The MSC includes all member states and deals with all aspects of safety at sea. Sub-committees deal, *inter alia*, with safety of fishing vessels; aids to navigation; construction and equipment of ships; rules for preventing collisions at sea; bulk and dangerous cargoes; standardization of training, watchkeeping and qualifications of officers and crew; and other safety-related matters. The other committees are open to all member states; their work is backed by the widely respected IMO secretariat, whose headquarters are in London. The secretariat is the focal point for liaison with bodies interested in these fields; over forty non-governmental organizations, representing technical, legal and environmental interests, also have consultative status with IMO and play an important part in directing its attention to new areas.

Recent IMO conventions   IMO has now adopted a large number of conventions, many of which were described in our North Sea study. Recent disasters have prompted increased activity to improve vessel safety and prevent pollution, and enough have occurred in north-west European waters for serious concern to be voiced in many European organizations (especially the European Community) about the need to augment IMO's global approach and to solve the problem of the use of substandard vessels. Amongst the disasters during the period 1977–81 were the Ekofisk Bravo blow-out off Norway; the grounding of the *Amoco Cadiz* off Brittany and the *Christos Bitas* off Wales; the *Esso Bermuda* oil spill off Scotland; the *Eleni V* collision off the English coast; the *Betelgeuse* explosion off Ireland; the *Andros Patria* explosion off France; the wreck of the *Tanio* in mid-English Channel; the Thistle field pipelines leak off the UK; the spill off Scotland by the *Scenic*, and in Rotterdam harbour by the *Energy Concentration*. As mentioned in chapter VI, these, coupled with many similar disasters elsewhere,[45] have prompted increased attempts to improve vessel safety and prevent pollution by the tightening up of international regulations on the standard of ships.

Since our 1974 study, IMO has adopted the 1975 amendments to the Load Lines Convention of 1966, and a protocol to the 1974 Safety of Life at Sea Convention (SOLAS). This requires, *inter alia*, that some vessels be fitted with inert gas systems, that some have radar and remote steering gear control systems, and that surveys and inspections should be increased and improved by the introduction of unscheduled inspection and annual mandatory surveys. SOLAS came into force only in May 1981, two years after its target date and the protocol entered into force on 1 May 1981, having been ratified by the fifteen states constituting not less than 50 per cent of the total GRT of the world's merchant shipping required to bring it into force. It does not apply to all ships.

In 1978, a protocol was also added to the 1973 International Convention for the Prevention of Pollution from Ships (MARPOL), which also covers all offshore installations and emissions, enabling parties to it to avoid being bound by annexe ii to MARPOL for three years from the entry into force of the protocol. Compliance with this annexe, which detailed discharge criteria and measures for control of pollution caused by noxious liquid substances carried in bulk, and which required, *inter alia*, that residues of some 250 listed substances be discharged only into reception facilities, presented difficulties for most states, thus delaying the entry into force of MARPOL, required ratifications being the same as for the SOLAS protocol. The MARPOL protocol, which entered into force on 2 October 1983, requires states to fit some new and old carriers with segregated ballast tanks or provide crude oil washing for carriers over 40,000 d.w.t.

Both the International Convention on Civil Liability for Oil Pollution Damage 1969 (CLC) and the International Convention on the

Establishment of an International Fund for Compensation for Oil Pollution Damage 1971 (Fund convention) are now in force[46] (from 19 June 1975, for 47 states, and 16 October 1978, for 23 states, respectively). In 1976 protocols to both were adopted to enable substitution of a unit of account based on the Special Drawing Rights (SDRs) used by the International Monetary Fund (IMF), enabling more account to be taken of variations in exchange rates. The Fund convention adds a new body to those operative in European waters—the Fund assembly—serviced by a secretariat headed by a director. The Fund has now dealt with several claims for compensation for pollution damage resulting from ships in cases where the protection afforded by the CLC is inadequate.[47] A review of the limits of these conventions is under consideration in IMO's Legal Committee, as are other improvements: extension to damage caused by unladen ships and non-persistent oils; extension of their geographical scope to damage outside the territorial sea; redefinition of the 'preventative measures' compensatable; definition of 'pollution damage'; and compensation for damage caused by unidentified ships.[48] IMO is planning for 1984 a Convention on the Civil Liability of Ships Carrying Hazardous and Noxious Cargoes, a subject on which, in spite of its importance and urgency because of the increased trade in these substances, no conventions currently exist, even at the regional level.[49]

By 1976 IMO had concluded two more important treaties: a Convention on Limitation of Liability for Maritime Claims which will replace the 1957 Brussels convention when it comes into force, considerably raising the limits for claims, and a Convention on the International Maritime Satellite Organization (INMARSAT) which establishes a new maritime communications system based on satellite technology with the aim of improving maritime communications. INMARSAT consists of an assembly, council and directorate headed by a Director-General, and is located in London. This convention entered into force on 16 July 1979 and operations began on 1 February 1982. There are thirty-nine member states, including all the north-west European coastal states. Procedures for the settlement of disputes are provided.

Also adopted in 1977 was the Torremolinos Convention for the Safety of Fishing Vessels, the first in this field. Its entry into force requires ratification by 15 states owning 50 per cent of the world's fishing fleet of such vessels. Only two further ratifications are required to bring it into force.

As mentioned earlier, the International Convention on Standards of Training, Certification and Watchkeeping for Seafarers was adopted in 1978, following the *Argo Merchant* and the *Amoco Cadiz* disasters. This provides standards for deck, radio and engineering activities, laying down principles for the keeping of navigational and engineering watches, and minimum requirements for the certification of masters, chief engineers, mates, radio officers and operators, and crew members. Requirements for maintenance and updating are included. An important innovation is that the certification requirements must be applied as may be necessary to ensure that no more favourable treatment is given to ships who fly the flag of a non-party than is given to ships entitled to fly the flag of a party. This seems to require enforcement against non-parties unilaterally, an innovatory extension; it remains to be seen how north-west European states will interpret it, but the Hague Memorandum referred to in chapter IX indicates that they will make discreet use of this power.

In 1979 IMO adopted a Code for Construction and Equipment of Mobile Offshore Drilling Units,[50] laying down non-binding guidelines. This was followed in 1980 by the adoption of Conclusions Concerning Working Conditions in the Oil Industry, including offshore activities.[51]

Although IMO is obviously the lead organization for shipping in the area of our study, and is expanding its activities, the ILO and some regional organizations, such as the European Community, the Council of Europe and the OECD, have begun to interest themselves in the subject of prevention of pollution, use of flags of convenience and of substandard ships. This illustrates the dissatisfaction in Europe with the slow pace at which IMO conventions are adopted and enter into force, and with the weaknesses in enforcement, by coastal states in their territorial seas or the flag state or both. Although recent conventions are introducing new enforcement techniques, for example, port state inspection of standards, not only are the relevant conventions slow to enter into force, and then not for all states, but the innovations are cautious and limited, reflecting both the need to obtain the consent of shipping states and the reluctance of states fundamentally to change existing international law, or shipping practice, or to provide adequate means of enforcement (see below).

Entry into force: target dates and tacit amendment procedures IMO Conventions usually stipulate conditions which must be fulfilled before they can enter into force, which ensures that at least some of the most important shipping states are party to them, but which means that on average they take between five and eight years to achieve the necessary ratifications. The 1978 SOLAS and MARPOL protocols were adopted before either of the basic treaties was in force. IMO has attempted to speed up these processes by setting target dates for entry into force, for example for the 1974 SOLAS, but these have tended to pass without the desired effect being achieved.

Many technical conventions need frequent amendment, but as most of IMO convention amendments come into force only after a certain specified percentage of contracting states have accepted them, the number of acceptances required rises as the convention attracts more ratifications and more acceptances are thus needed than were necessary to bring the original convention into effect, causing long delays. IMO has, therefore, devised a tacit amendment procedure, used for the Convention on International Regulation for Preventing Collisions at Sea 1972, the 1974 SOLAS convention and MARPOL 1973. Such amendments enter into force at a particular date unless objections are received prior to that date from a specified number of parties; for example, SOLAS amendments are deemed accepted two years after their communication to contracting governments unless objected to by more than one third thereof or by those owning not less than 50 per cent of the worlds GRT. This has already speeded up the amendment process.

Enforcement   IMO has no powers to enforce its conventions; this is left to the signatories, which, as the accidents show, do not always effectively carry out their responsibilities, especially as flag states. IMO has tried to improve this situation as far as is possible within a broadly based organization dealing with vital international and national shipping interests. Its advances have inevitably been marginal as regards obligations which are wholly for states to enforce. Under some conventions, such as SOLAS and MARPOL, certificates are required to be carried on board to show that the vessels have been inspected and met the convention's standards; in certain circumstances states into whose ports such vessels enter can detain vessels which do not conform to their certificate if they represent a danger to passengers or crew. MARPOL provides for a form of innovatory port state jurisdiction: an administration which is informed of a violation and is satisfied that sufficient evidence is available to enable proceedings to be taken, shall cause them to be taken under its law if the offending vessel enters its port; if the offence reported has occurred in another state's jurisdiction, the port state can either take proceedings itself or pass on the details to the flag state so that it can institute proceedings.

However, before MARPOL entered into force, north-west European states resorted to other arrangements based on the Hague Memorandum of Understanding[52] concluded between the administrations of eight North Sea states (Belgium, Denmark, France, FRG, Netherlands, Norway, Sweden, UK), as later approved and extended by the European Community. These did not go as far as the port state jurisdiction proposals in the UNCLOS text or in MARPOL. The original eight states agreed to co-operate on a uniform basis, in enforcing, by port inspection, in *all* their ports, existing internationally agreed standards as laid down in various IMO and ILO conventions and recommendations, not all of which were in force at the time.[53]

In order to achieve real improvement in the deficiencies of enforcement, it is important that, when it enters into force on 2 October 1983, MARPOL should enter into force for all north-west European states so that full advantage can be taken of its port state jurisdictional and regional reporting provisions (the same may be said of the need for the UNCLOS convention to enter into force). At present, Denmark, France, West Germany, Norway, Sweden, and the United Kingdom are contracting states. IMO's role is central and important for laying down standards and rules of prevention of vessel-source pollution in north-west European waters, but its necessarily global approach results in many inadequacies as far as fully effective protection of this area from pollution is concerned. There is certainly scope for supportive action by other bodies, especially regional ones, to develop effective means of enforcement such as the Hague Memorandum and Community actions, and to encourage implementation of the LOS convention.[54]

The International Labour Organization (ILO)[55]

Objectives and procedures   The ILO's objective, within its overall purpose of building up a code of labour standards to improve the social and economic well-being of working people everywhere, is to establish better conditions of maritime labour. Special machinery has been instituted within the ILO for this purpose. The ILO is unique in that its member states are represented on a tripartite basis: delegations are composed of representatives from government, employers and labour, and its governing body is similarly constituted. It meets at an annual conference to consider conventions and recommendations on labour questions. When adopted, these conventions have a special status, different from that of IMO conventions. They become instruments of the ILO and must be presented to national legislatures for ratification. They do not become binding on individual member states, but states put them before their parliaments and report annually on their progress to the ILO. Governments which do not observe conventions which they have ratified can be reported by the non-governmental delegates to the International Labour Office, which can establish a commission of inquiry to investigate the omissions; results are communicated to the defending government concerned, which can appeal to the International Court of Justice.

Organs   The ILO, which has over 150 members, is a specialized agency of the UN and relates to other specialized agencies and to the UN through the UN's Economic and Social Council in the same way as IMO. It has three organs: the annual International Labour Conference, a governing body of 48 (24 government members, 12 employers' members and 12 workers' members), and the International Labour Office, its secretariat. The conference consists of national delegations of four members (two appointed by government, one by the employers, and one by the employees' associations). A move to establish a separate Maritime Conference was rejected when the organization was established in 1919 and instead maritime matters are allotted occasional special conferences backed by a permanent Joint Maritime Commission (JMC), an 18-member committee of seafarers and employers which ensures that maritime matters are given specialized attention before being brought before the maritime sessions. Because of the JMC's composition, its work 'has above all been realistic; it has indeed been a highly successful means of international co-operation designed to further the interests of the merchant navies of the world rather than the narrower purposes of individual countries . . . The ILO officials responsible for maritime questions have always been knowledgeable, forward-looking and anxious to advance the seafarers' interests'.[36] However, the recent Convention on Training and Watchkeeping was concluded through IMO, not the ILO, and is subject to IMO procedures although the ILO co-operated in the conference which adopted it.

The 32 conventions and 26 recommendations adopted by Maritime Sessions up to 1978 are known informally as 'the Seafarer's Code'. At the twenty-third JMC Session in 1980 the ILO considered formal adoption of such a code and examined model legislation for seafarers. In spite of the strength of the institutions and procedures, however, the record of ratification by north-west European states, among others, is not good. Non-maritime states, which can attend the Maritime Sessions (but not the preceding Joint Maritime Preparatory Conferences), find no need to ratify; some early conventions were inadequate and poorly drafted, others are complex and present national legislative problems; states also fear loss of competitive advantage if they adopt higher standards.

Relevant ILO conventions and recommendations   Several ILO maritime conventions are relevant to the improvement of operating standards on ships, an essential element in the avoidance of human error. Relevant conventions cover the Minimum Age of Seafarers; Officers' Competency Certificates; Wages, Hours of Working and Manning at sea; Certification of Able Seamen; Crew Accommodation on Board Ship; Prevention of Occupational Accidents to Seafarers; Continuity of Employment of Seafarers; Annual Leave with Pay for Seafarers; and Minimum Standards in Merchant Ships. The last three were concluded in 1976; the last is one whose requirements will be inspected under the Hague Memorandum of Understanding. It requires that certain personnel are certificated for their posts, although it does not provide for enforcement.

Among other, particularly relevant, ILO recommendations are those which derive from the industry's demands for more highly trained mariners equipped with the technical skills necessary for new developments in giant oil tankers, bulk carriers (OBOs), chemical carriers (LNGs and LPGs), the use of container ships and roll-on/roll-off vessels. The ILO has also responded to the industry's demands for comprehensive training, adaptation, and requalification programmes for both officers and ratings, and has issued many guidelines for the necessary vocational training in an industry which hitherto has too often been based on casual labour.[57] If all its recommendations in these fields were implemented by all its member states, the problems of flags of convenience and of substandard ships would be eliminated.

The ILO has also directed its attention to the fishing industry and the need for new skills and abilities. Requirements under new laws promulgated to establish 200-mile FZs have added to such problems; compliance with them requires skill and accuracy. The ILO, *inter-alia*, has adopted conventions on Fishermen's Competency Certificates, on Crew Accommodation and on Vocational Training, but as yet has not succeeded in laying down a comprehensive 'Fishermen's Code', though it has passed a number of resolutions which include plans for training and safety.

Finally, the ILO has now also studied and reported on standards for workers on offshore platforms,[58] following the Ekofisk disaster. Like IMO, the ILO has sought to expand its activities as technology advances.

Enforcement   The problem posed by ILO conventions is that, despite the special procedures, they are not widely ratified because of the economic costs. Compliance with them all could raise operating costs of ships by at least 30 per cent, a cost many owners find impossible to bear, particularly during the recessions in the fishing and tanker industries, and with growing competition from new flags and UNCTAD's endorsement of the 40–40–20 formula for sharing trade between coastal and maritime states.[59] Thus, though many north-west European states ratify the relevant conventions and apply them to their own flag ships, their shipowners often use flags of states outside the region, or charter foreign vessels. European states, therefore, through bodies such as the UNCLOS, the European Courts and the Council of Europe, and arrangements such as the Hague Memorandum, are endeavouring to take regional action to improve the operating standards of vessels entering regional waters and to encourage foreign flag states to take a more responsible attitude to maritime standards.

The ILO usually provides general guidelines, leaving states some leeway in the methods of compliance; poor states can then fulfil recommendations according to their means. However, this method has not been demonstrably successful in the past and is not likely to have much more success in the immediate future.

In its 1976 Convention on Minimum Standards for Merchant Ships, therefore, the ILO, like IMO, introduced new techniques. Article 1 requires states parties to ensure that their national laws are 'substantially equivalent' to various parts of fifteen conventions, including IMO conventions, listed in an annexe; the implication is that a ratifying state does not need to ratify these other conventions, nor is ratification of them implied by adherence to the new convention. The 1976 convention also provides for limited port state inspection. However, it does not enter into force until 10 states owning 25 per cent of the world's GRT have ratified it.

Relationship to other organizations   It is clear that the interests of the ILO and IMO overlap. At the ILO conference at which the Minimum Standards Convention was adopted, some states thought the subject was outside the ILO's competence and IMO indicated that it believed the primary responsibility for promoting maritime safety and the adoption of regimes concerning substandard vessels lay with itself. It added that it would co-operate with the ILO in drafting maritime instruments, but these should remain in the respective spheres of competence of the two organizations. There is a joint ILO–IMO Committee on Training and a formal understanding that all relevant proposals will be scrutinized by it and that conferences on such topics will be convened jointly or with the direct participation of the other organization, as was the 1978 conference. When in 1976, during discussion of an ILO Report on Substandard Vessels, particularly those registered under flags of convenience, the Netherlands proposed that the two agencies should reach some accommodation on their competences, the ILO referred to this committee and the full consultations carried out with the IMO secretariat and other organs.[60] There is little doubt that many governments regard IMO as the organization most suited to discussing all shipping matters, both because of the ILO's political difficulties and because of its tripartite representation, but in fact the ILO has more experience of the human factors involved. Continued close co-operation is essential.

However, the fact remains that north-west European states' efforts to improve ship standards are thwarted by the framework of international law based on the primacy of flag state jurisidiction and the need for ratification of conventions before they bind states: European states are thus pursuing other techniques to compel observance and improve regional enforcement. The European Community's role is discussed later. The Hague Memorandum approach is one that could also be extended to other conventions.

Fisheries

The Food and Agriculture Organization (FAO)[61]

Objectives   The FAO, which has 144 members, is a UN specialized agency and has close working relationships with others. All states of north-west Europe, including Luxembourg and Austria, are members.

Its role in north-west European waters, however, is limited since its aims are not purely maritime—it was established to fight poverty, malnutrition, and hunger. Fisheries are only a part of its strategy. It aims to ensure that the maximum sustainable yield of fisheries is everywhere achieved or maintained, supported by conservation as necessary, based on the best scientific advice concerning the methods of achieving MSY, and that fisheries are developed to optimize food potential. The FAO has particularly directed its attention to the optimum development of the living resources within the new 200-mile Fisheries Zones, especially in developing countries, and to promoting the establishment of regional fisheries organizations or supporting those already in existence. It continues to play a role in European waters in support of these aims and frequently criticized the more disastrous policies of the old NEAFC.

Organs   The FAO's members usually meet biennially in Rome to decide on its work programme. A council of 49 states meets annually as an Interim Governing Body; the Committee on Fisheries (COFI), which is open to all member states, is one of the committees which report to the council. A 3,000-strong secretariat, headed by a director general and including a fisheries department, is located in Rome, in regional offices and on field projects. The budget is voted by the Governing Conferences and paid by all member states in shares related to their gross national product. The FAO publishes many useful studies and reports related to fisheries (for example, one examined new fishery legislation implementing the 200-mile zones)[62] and a *Yearbook of Fishery Statistics* which includes the European area, but it is through COFI that most work relevant to European fisheries is done. COFI's terms of reference require it to review the work programmes of fisheries organizations and their implementation, to conduct periodic general reviews of fishery problems of an international character, and to fulfil other tasks.

It can make appropriate recommendations, report to the council and tender advice to the director general. Numerous sub-committees and working groups have reported on particular problems (for example, the Advisory Committee of Experts on Marine Resource Research (ACMRR) which has a large number of working parties related to it and also advises other UN bodies and programmes such as the IOC)[63] and COFI's annual assessment of the work of regional bodies has included the European Community and the NEAFC. No progress, however, has been made on COFI's other task, which is to consider the desirability of preparing and submitting to member states a global international convention to ensure effective international co-operation and consultation in fisheries on a world-wide scale. Linkage between regional fisheries and other related bodies thus remains *ad hoc* and informal, often conducted through secretariats, by sending observers (for example, by the EC and FAO to the old NEAFC, the IWC and ICES), or by using a member state which is representing other bodies to represent the FAO as well.

The international aspects of the FAO's work bring together the global experts in these fields, and have important application to management of fisheries and evaluation of the factors affecting yield in the waters of north-west Europe. The FAO has no direct role in fisheries in this region, but as all north-west European member states of the FAO take part in COFI, those regulating these fisheries can evaluate them in an international perspective and benefit from shared knowledge when developing fishery policy; the primary role in formulating and enforcing regulations remains, however, with the regional bodies.

Environmental Protection

The United Nations Environment Programme (UNEP)[64]

Objectives UNEP was established by the UN, following the Stockholm Conference on the Human Environment in 1972, as an institutional arrangement within the UN system. It aims to promote international co-operation in the environmental field; to keep under review the world environmental situation; to ensure that environmental problems of wide international significance receive appropriate consideration by governments; and to promote acquisition, assessment and exchange of environmental knowledge.

Organs UNEP consists of a governing council of fifty-eight states elected by the UN General Assembly to decide its environment programme; a small secretariat of about 100 people to serve as a focal point for environmental action and co-ordination with the UN system, headed by an executive director elected by the General Assembly; and an Environment Fund based on voluntary contributions to finance environmental programmes. This is, however, very short of money and the executive director regards it as inadequate for the fulfilment of UNEP's priority programmes. The Stockholm Conference Declaration of Principles and its Action Plan, which included 109 recommendations, were referred to UNEP.

UNEP could assume an overview role for preservation of the marine environment of north-west Europe, except that its programme is broad, its resources, of both personnel and funds, restricted, its headquarters, in Nairobi, distant, and its main object is the provision of technical help to developing states. It cannot, therefore, comment on critical detailed problems; and it is subject of course to global political and economic pressures.

Programme Another limitation on UNEP's regional role is that its programme is global, comprehending many problems other than the marine, although it has made the oceans one of its priority areas.[65] None the less, UNEP has a regional centre in Geneva which promotes its successful Regional Seas Programme and Action Plans,[66] and though north-west European seas are not part of this programme, it participates in the work of various bodies in the region.

UNEP has also established a global Earthwatch Programme, based on Global Environmental Monitoring (GEMS) and an information retrieval system (Infoterra) in which north-west European states participate. UNEP, moreover, gives priority to protection of endangered species, including marine species such as cetaceans. It has also concerned itself with prevention of pollution, including that from offshore operations,[67] embracing liability and responsibility for them, and has developed principles and guidelines for the use of states' natural resources.[68]

In order to make the most of its limited funds, however, UNEP tries to assist existing programmes rather than launch new ones, seeing itself as a catalyst, stimulator, and co-ordinator of other programmes, and drawing attention to the complexity and intersectoral aspects of environmental problems as part of the global problem. There certainly appears to be a need for some organization to promote these values and considerations in north-west European waters.

UNEP reports annually on 'the state of the environment', drawing attention to the major environmental issues requiring the attention of policy-makers and the public. This report is lengthy, concerning itself more with the broader global problems than detailed regional ones. Attention has, however, been drawn to such aspects of environmental pollution as the problems arising from fossil fuels, proliferation of nuclear reactors, the introduction of vast numbers of new chemicals, and the effects of science and technology on the oceans. The effects of marine pollution on food chains have also been highlighted; hence the Regional Seas Programme, one of UNEP's most successful initiatives. UNEP has stressed that there *are* 'outer limits'; that growth within the finite earth cannot continue for ever; that mankind must become aware of the 'public services' provided by the environment and its interrelationships; that an understanding of their intricacies is essential to solving the problems.

The regional seas programme   UNEP has developed a strategy to preserve the marine environment in areas of the world where the seas are particularly vulnerable to pollution.

Work has been most advanced in the Mediterranean area: the Barcelona Convention for the Protection of the Mediterranean Sea against Pollution[69] has been in effect since 1978, together with its protocol on Co-operation in Combatting Oil Pollution of the Mediterranean by Oil and other Harmful Substances in Cases of Emergency.[70] States, on ratifying, were required to adopt either this or a protocol on Control of Ocean Dumping. The EC and thirteen Mediterranean (developed and developing) states have ratified the Convention. In addition, in 1980, the EC and twelve Mediterranean states signed a protocol on control of pollution from land-based sources, and in 1981 the EC and 16 states approved a $12-million three-year programme to improve the environmental quality of the Mediterranean. Initially UNEP provided secretariat facilities for this convention.

There is no comparable integrated plan for UNEP involvement in the north-west European area. Nor perhaps has it been necessary since Europe led the way by adopting the Oslo Convention on Dumping in 1972, the Paris Convention on Land-Based Pollution in 1974, and the various other regional agreements specific to north-west European waters that are described in the next chapter. Should it be thought that a co-ordinating framework convention *is* still required for this region, UNEP would be well placed and qualified to advise and initiate the necessary conference. It would, however, be an exception to the UNEP action plan strategy under which the framework precedes the specific protocols, and in order to take account of the progress already made in north-west Europe, it would have to be in a very different form and terms.

The comparable Helsinki Convention for the Protection of the Marine Environment of the Baltic Sea[71] is not a UNEP convention; it established its own commission on entering into force. The only north-west European states to have ratified it are Denmark and the Federal Republic of Germany. The European Community is not a party, and it tried to discourage these two states from ratifying, on the grounds that some of the activities covered were the exclusive responsibility of the Community.

Fisheries   UNEP takes a considerable interest in conservation and the effects of pollution on fisheries, in accordance with its perceived role of pointing out the cross-sectoral and interdisciplinary nature of these problems, but it has not included fisheries conservation in its action plans. It supports the FAO's efforts to establish and advise regional fisheries bodies and recently collaborated with the FAO in producing a Draft Action Plan for the Conservation of Marine Mammals.[72]

Scientific Research

The United Nations Educational, Scientific and Cultural Organization (UNESCO): the International Oceanographic Commission (IOC)[73]

Objectives   UNESCO, as its name suggests, has 'somewhat amorphous and wide responsibilities';[74] production of and co-operation in research is part of its activities, and it assists research and technology in developing countries, as well as in specialized fields. It supports independent bodies in these fields, one of which is the IOC.

Organs UNESCO has a secretariat staff of about 4,000 at the Paris headquarters; a 34-member executive board generally meets biannually and a general conference biennially. It also has an extensive regional organization based on 8 regional offices. Unfortunately it has been much criticized for ineffectiveness, its aims being regarded by many as too diffuse and ill defined; the IOC, however, is one of its more successful enterprises.

The International Oceanographic Commission (IOC) [75] The IOC was established to promote scientific research in the world's oceans. Its members are states. The number of developing states which are members has increased and this is having some effect on the direction of IOC activities, for example in helping such states to develop their capacity to explore and exploit rationally the marine environment. The IOC promotes many co-ordinated programmes for scientific investigations, several of which impinge on north-western European waters, for example GIPME (Global Investigation of Pollution of the Marine Environment), and IGOSS (Integrated Global Ocean Station System). Particular attention has been paid to morphological charting of the sea-floor in conjunction with the International Hydrographic Organization.

The IOC has appreciated the need to adapt its role to the needs of the changing ocean regime, including the complex multi-lateral arrangements required for successful prosecution of scientific research, since many states are beginning to implement the proposals in the LOS convention which require that the consent of the coastal state be sought for certain kinds of research within 200-mile zones, in the territorial sea, and on the continental shelf.[76] The IOC has also emphasized the risks arising from man's slow response to the possible development of irreversible damage to the marine environment arising from the increases in certain marine pollutants.[77]

IOC members support a trend towards regionalization in order to improve its effectiveness at local levels; it has begun to establish regional secretariats though not yet in the north Atlantic area, as the emphasis is on provision of training, education and aid where most needed.[78]

Many IOC programmes indirectly affect north-west European waters, requiring data collection and assessment, for example, as part of the global co-ordinated plan: the GIPME programme includes work by ICES, and the Oslo and Paris commissions.[79] The IOC also maintains MEDI, the Marine Environmental Data Information Referral System, as part of UNEP's Infoterra data. North-west Europe is recorded in this system, alongside that of other regions.[80] The IOC also assists the FAO to gather information on fisheries; to this end at its eleventh session in 1979 the IOC assembly called on member states to establish national ASIFIS (Aquatic Science and Fisheries Information System Centres).

The Group of Experts on the Scientific Aspects of Marine Pollution (GESAMP)   This group, sponsored by seven UN agencies,[81] consists of scientific experts nominated by the sponsoring agencies to act in their individual capacities. Outside scientists can be called in to augment its working groups and it is attended by observers from other international bodies such as ICES. It provides the factual scientific information necessary to develop international and national laws and standards, and advises on the identification of pollutants of broad international significance as well as on the development of specific anti-pollution programmes within the UN system. For example, it has facilitated the production of the annexes to the London Dumping Convention, the 1973 MARPOL and others. It also evaluates the International Maritime Dangerous Goods Code. It has various working groups concentrating on, *inter alia*, the effect of offshore developments on the marine environment. Its work has included consideration of toxicological problems; the development of GIPME and pollution monitoring; review of methods of treating sewage and industrial wastes; radioactive waste disposal at sea; the development of coastal water criteria; interchange of pollutants between ocean and atmosphere; removal of harmful substances from waste water; monitoring of biological variables related to marine pollution. GESAMP has identified a need for more uniformly available information on the potential hazards posed by certain substances, and has set up working groups on dispersion of waste disposal in the deep sea, on criteria for identifying sensitive sea areas, and on the marine pollution implications of ocean energy exploitation.[82]

The 1977 UN Stockholm Conference on the Human Environment (UNCHE) particularly asked GESAMP to re-examine annually and revise as required its Review of Harmful Chemical Substances with a view to elaborating further its assessment of sources, pathways and resulting risks of marine pollutants. GESAMP has thus played a respected and crucial role in developing and stimulating pollution prevention measures throughout the area of our study within almost all the bodies referred to in it.

Conclusion

Not all global bodies with an interest in our region have been discussed—the World Health Organization (WHO), for example, has an interest in water quality standards—but the most relevant have been examined. Although all have an important role to play, none appears to be fitted to fulfil an overall co-ordinating role for all activities and commissions in the area. IMO, though it has a large secretariat and is popular with governments in the region and active and effective up to a point, suffers from the primary disadvantage that its concerns are limited and do not include the wide range of activities covered by existing regional commissions, as will be seen in the following chapter. Also IMO has difficulty in securing effective enforcement of its conventions, and the conventions themselves have various inadequacies, as several regional bodies have observed. The ILO has similar advantages and disadvantages, with the additional drawback that its tripartite structure makes it less popular with governments than IMO; its constitution and scope make it unfitted to co-ordinate measures to prevent pollution and conserve fisheries.

For these purposes UNEP is more appropriate than either the ILO or IMO; its aims are close to those which a regional co-ordinating body might adopt, and though its headquarters are far from Europe, it does have a regional office in Geneva from which its regional seas programme is promoted; this office has built up considerable expertise on regional problems and approaches. Moreover, all agencies with projects affecting the environment have agreed to designate UNEP as their 'contact' or 'focal point'. The FAO has set up an Environment Programme Co-ordinating Unit to facilitate contact with UNEP, but not all agencies are so well equipped. UNEP's present facilities are, however, inadequate for the north-west European tasks and its work on fisheries is subordinate to the efforts of the FAO, which itself is based in Europe. To encourage UN agencies to work towards integration of activities, UNEP holds many bilateral meetings with them and various medium-term programmes have been developed. There has been a visible improvement in inter-agency relationships following regular consultations convened by the UN's Administration Co-ordinating Committee, though both its and the agencies' separatist and isolationist policies have been much criticized in the past, as was pointed out, for example, by Evan Luard who, in an extensive study of UN institutions, concluded that institutional changes alone may not be enough to bring about a more co-ordinated system in the UN 'family' of agencies itself; other agencies need to be regarded as partners not rivals.[83] Environmental protection, however, does seem to foster a better climate for co-operation.

Before considering whether UNEP should be encouraged to play some co-ordinating role in north-west European waters, however, it is necessary to examine the extent to which this ground is already occupied by existing regional bodies. This is dealt with in the following chapter.

Notes

1. GAOR 2750 (XXV), adopted 17 December 1970.
2. GAOR 2749 (XIV), adopted 17 December 1970.
3. Proclamation dated 10 March 1983.

4. An interesting analysis of the new convention has been provided by Philip Allot in an unpublished paper delivered to a meeting of the British branch of the International Law Association in Cambridge, UK, on 15 May 1982. He regards it as 'not a codifying instrument but a supreme legislative act of true sophistication comparable to the UN Charter or the EEC treaties,' adding that 'it is a new form of international law being increasingly used: a legislative act constituting an administrative law process. States are asked to enact subordinate legislation in accordance with the principles of administrative law.' The treaty confers the necessary *powers* for this, but also lays down meticulously drafted *'power modifiers'*. (Quotations based on author's notes, emphasis added.)

5. Fully described in ch. iv of Sibthorp, M. M., *The North Sea: Challenge and Opportunity*, Europa, 1975.

6. Draft convention, part ii, articles 2–16.

7. Ibid., articles 17–32.

8. Ibid., article 33.

9. Part iii, articles 34–45.

10. Part v, articles 55–75.

11. Part v, articles 61–8 esp.

12. Article 65.

13. Article 60.

14. Part vi, articles 76–85.

15. Op. cit. n. 5, p. 91, n. 27.

16. E.g., Brown, E. D., 'The North Sea Continental Shelf Cases', 23 *Current Legal Problems*, 1970, pp. 187–215; Friedman, W., 'The North Sea Continental Shelf Cases—a Critique', 64 *AJIL*, 1970, pp. 229–240; Grisel, E., 'The Lateral Boundaries of the Continental Shelf and the Judgment of the ICJ in the North Sea Continental Shelf Cases', 64 *AJIL*, 1970, pp. 562–93.

17 *Arbitration between the United Kingdom of Great Britain and Northern Ireland and the French Republic on the Delimitation of the Continental Shelf*, Decisions of the Court of Arbitration dated 30 June 1977 and 14 March 1978; Cmnd. 7438.

18. Brown, E. D., 'Rockall and the limits of national jurisdiction of the U.K.', 2 *Marine Policy* no. 3, 1978, pp. 181–211; ibid. no. 4, pp. 275–303.

19. Part ix, articles 122–3.

20. Part vii, articles 86–115.

21. Part xi, articles 133–173.

22. The Federal Republic of Germany, France, and the United Kingdom; Italy and Belgium have legislation in progress; the USA and USSR have also enacted it.

23. Part xii, articles 192–237.

24. Articles 210 and 216.

25. Articles 212 and 222.

26. UN Convention on Long-range Transboundary Air Pollution, Geneva, 11 November 1979, xviii *ILM* (1979), pp. 1442–56.

27. Articles 211, 217–21; see also section 7 on safeguards, articles 223–33.

28. Article 211 (3).

29. Article 211 (6).

30. Article 234.

31. Article 194 (5).
32. Article 217.
33. Article 218.
34. Article 220.
35. Articles 223–33.
36. Part xiii, articles 238–65.
37. Article 239.
38. Smith, P. J., 'The Scientist in Deep Water'. See also Wooster, W. S., 'Research in Troubled Waters; U.S. Research Vessel Clearance Experience, 1972–1978, *Ocean Development and International Law* pp. 219–39.
39. Article 247.
40. Part X, articles 227–97 and annexes V (Conciliation), VI (Statute of the International Tribunal for the Law of the Sea), VII (Arbitration) and VIII (Special Arbitration Procedures). It should be noted that the coastal state is *not* required to submit certain disputes concerning marine scientific research and some fisheries disputes (relating to sovereign rights to the living resources of the EEZ) to compulsory dispute settlement. Disputes concerning the exercise of the freedom of the seas and preservation of the marine environment can otherwise be submitted, but no mention is made of disputes concerning boundary delimitation; by implication these are excluded, except for the ambiguous role of recommendations by the Boundary Commission. For a critical analysis of these procedures see Brown, E. D., 'Dispute settlement', 5 *Marine Policy*, 1981, pp. 282–5.
41. Part xvii, articles 305–20.
42. Kingham, J. D. and McRae, D., 'Competent International Organizations and the Law of the Sea', 3 *Marine Policy* 1979, pp. 106–32. This gives a comprehensive analysis of organizations concerned with the law of the sea and the effects of the convention upon them.
43. *North Sea*, op. cit. n. 5, pp. 85–157 and Sibthorp, M. M. and Unwin, M. (ed.), *Oceanic Management: Conflicting Uses of the Celtic Sea and other Western UK Waters*, Europa, 1977, pp. 147–67.
44. For full details, see *IMCO and its activities*, IMCO, 1978. All the conventions referred to in this section are summarized in that publication. See also *The International Conference on Tanker Safety and Pollution Prevention 1978*, IMCO, 1978.
45. For details of these and other accidents, see ACOPS *Annual Reports* for 1977, 1978, 1979, 1980, 1981.
46. From 19 June 1975 and 16 October 1978 respectively.
47. For details, see ACOPS *Annual Report* 1980, s. 7.1, pp. 29–30.
48. *Draft Report of the Legal Committee on the Work of its Forty-eighth Session*, IMCO Doc. LEG/48/W.P.5, 3 March 1982.
49. Substantive work has now been completed on a draft Convention on Liability and Compensation in connexion with the Carriage of Noxious and Hazardous Substances by Sea (HNS Convention) which will be considered at a diplomatic conference in the near future; *IMO News* no. 2 1982, p. 1. The substances to be covered, however, remain an unresolved issue; they will be limited to those carried in bulk. The scope of its application, i.e. whether it should be limited to damage caused in the territory (including territorial sea) of contracting states, is also unsettled; ibid.

50. *Code for Construction and Equipment of Mobile Offshore Drilling Units* (MODU Code), IMO, 1980.

51. *Safety Problems in the Offshore Industry*, ILO, 1980.

52. The 1978 Hague Memorandum has been replaced by a Memorandum of Understanding on Port State Control signed by fourteen West European states on 26 January 1982 (xxi *ILM*, 1982, pp. 1–30). The fourteen states are Belgium, Denmark, Finland, France, Federal Republic of Germany, Greece, Ireland, Italy, Netherlands, Norway, Portugal, Spain, Sweden, and the UK.

53. The eight states agreed to apply in *all* their ports (i.e. not only North Sea ports) chapter i, regulation 19 of the 1960 SOLAS Convention; the 1974 SOLAS Convention; article 21 of the 1966 Convention on Load Lines; Procedures for and Guidelines for the Control of Ships set out in IMCO-MSC Circular 219, 20 December 1976, various ILO standards and the ILO Merchant Shipping (Minimum Standards) Convention 1976. These enable inspection in port, *inter alia*, of: age of crew; certificates of competency; food and catering; medical certificates; crew accommodation; accident prevention equipment. No information, however, has been published on incidence of inspections or numbers of deficient vessels identified.

54. COM (78) 587, *OJ* no. C284/5, 28 November 1978; Council Resolution setting up an Action Programme for the European Communities on the Control and Reduction of Pollution Caused by Hydrocarbons Discharged at Sea; *OJ* vol. 21, 8 July 1978, p. 1; see also *Europe* no. 2531 (NS) 4 October 1978, p. 9.

55. For the ILO's role in maritime affairs, see Price, J., *A Tribute to Fifty Years' Work for Seafarers: the International Labour Organization's Seafarers' Code*, Merchant Navy and Airline Officers Association (undated); also *Winds of Change*, pub. ILL, 1971. For a summary of relevant ILO conventions see Birnie, P., 'The Legal Regime for Prevention of Collisions and Strandings of Vessels Carrying Hazardous and Noxious Cargoes', Annexe to report of House of Commons Trade and Industry Sub-Committee of the Expenditure Committee on *Measures to Prevent Collisions and Strandings of Noxious Cargo Carriers in Waters Around the United Kingdom*, 12 January 1979, vol. I, HMSO, pp. 105–11.

56. Price, op. cit., n. 55, p. 7.

57. See for example ILO report V (2) (1976). 'Substandard Vessels, Particularly Those Registered under Flags of Convenience'; 'Consideration of an International Seafarers' Code and of Model Legislation Concerning Seafarers', JMC 23rd Session, Geneva, October 1980; 'An International Seafarers Code', JMC 23/3/a; 'Compilation of Models for Maritime Labour Legislation', JMC 23/3/b; 'Employment Conditions of Seafarers Serving in Ships Flying Flags other than those of their own Country', JMC 23/2; 'Social Security and Employment Conditions of Seafarers Serving in Flags of Convenience Vessels', JMC 23/1.

58. *Safety Problems in the Offshore Industry*, ILO, 1980.

59. For the problems raised by this see Pender, R. R., 'UNCTAD Provisions in Relation to the Bulk Trade, *Greenwich Forum vi, 'World Shipping in the 1990s'*, Records of a Conference at the Royal Naval College, Greenwich 23–5 April 1980, edited by Ranken, M. B. F., Westbury House, 1981, pp. 19–34.

60. ILO Report V (2), 1976, op. cit. n. 57.
61. See generally *FAO: What it is and what it does: how it works*, FAO undated; *Directory of FAO Statutory Bodies and Panels of Experts*, 1974.
62. Moore, G., *Legislation on Coastal State Requirements for Foreign Fishing*, FAO Legislative Study no. 21, FAO, 1981.
63. *Directory of FAO Statutory Bodies*, op. cit. n. 62, p. 47.
64. See generally *The United Nations Environment Programme: A Brief Introduction*, UNEP, 1975; for a report on UNEP's 1981 Session, including oceans issues, see 7 *Environmental Policy and Law*, 1981, pp. 138–45; and for a critical analysis of UNEP's performance to date, see Scharlin, P., 'The United Nations and the Environment: After Three Decades of Concern Progress is Still Slow', XI *AMBIO*, 1982, pp. 26–9.
65. UNEP 3rd Session. Proposed Programme, UNEP/GC/31; 11 February 1975, pp. 33–8: the oceans.
66. For progress on Action Plans, see *The Siren*, UNEP pub. on the Regional Seas Programme. For an analysis of regional pollution conventions, see 'The role of regional agreements in the protection and preservation of the marine environment from pollution', report of British Branch Committee on the Law of the Sea in report of the International Law Association's Fifty-Eighth Conference, Manila 1978, pp. 325–6.
67. 'UNEP—Offshore Mining and Drilling—Contingency Planning', *Environmental Policy and Law*, 1980, pp. 114–16.
68. 'UNEP's Draft Principles for the Conduct of States in the Conservation and Harmonious Utilisation of Natural Resources Shared by Two or More States, UNEP/IG/2/2, 8 February 1978, pp. 11–14; xvii *ILM* (1978) pp. 1098–9. The principles are in very general terms; some states consider that some of them are already part of international law, others dispute this; none the less, as the UN General Assembly has circulated them to member states for consideration, these states must in good faith consider them and decide what action is required.
69. Convention for the Protection of the Mediterranean Sea, Barcelona, 16 February 1976, xv *ILM*, 1976, pp. 285–310.
70. Protocol for Protection of the Mediterranean Sea Against Pollution from Land-based sources, done at Athens, 17 May 1980, 6 *Environment Policy and Law*, 1980, pp. 144–7. For analysis, see Dobbert, J.-P., 'Protocol to Control Pollution of the Mediterranean, ibid, pp. 110–16.
71. Convention for the Protection of the Marine Environment of the Baltic Sea Area, done at Helsinki, 22 March 1972, xiii *ILM*, 1974, pp. 544–610.
72. *Global Plan of Action for the Conservation, Management and Utilization of Marine Mammals* (FAO/UNEP project no. 6502–78102), FAO, 1981.
73. For the work of the IOC, see UNESCO's *IMS* (International Marine Science) *Newsletter*, nos. 1–30 (1973–1982).
74. E. Luard, *International Agencies: The Emerging Framework of Interdependence*, Macmillan, 1977, p. 186.
75. The IOC was founded in 1961, and by 1980 had 103 member states; from 1973 it has met under new statutes permitting it to act as a focal point for the development and co-ordination, in association with other international organizations, of programmes for the scientific investigation of the oceans and related services.

76. UNESCO, *IMS Newsletter*, no. 17, December 1977, p. 1.
77. In Goldberg, E. D., *Health of the Oceans*, IOC, UNESCO, 1976. Current information on and effects of five major marine pollutants (halogenated hydrocarbons; radioactivity; heavy metals; petroleum hydrocarbons; litter) were reviewed. The report aroused controversy.
78. Ibid, p. 8.
79. In reviewing regional programmes, IOC's working committee for GIPME noted that considerable progress had been made in this region; *IMC Newsletter*, no. 22, June 1979, p. 1.
80. A MEDI pilot catalogue is published by the IOC; see also IOC's *Manual for monitoring of oil and petroleum hydrocarbons in marine waters and on beaches*, 1977.
81. The group is jointly sponsored by IMO, the FAO, UNESCO (IOC), WHO, the WMO, the IAEA, and the UN, but is organized by the IOC.
82. *IMS Newsletter*, no. 25, 1980, p. 2.
83. For detailed criticism of the ACC, see Luard, op. cit. n. 75, pp. 269–86, 312–13. It has a sub-committee on marine affairs; for details see *IMS Newsletter*, no 18, 1978, pp. 1 and 8. It deals, *inter alia*, with implications of, and developments in, science and technology related to use of the sea; interaction between uses of the sea as reflected in the functions of UN organizations, examination of the implication of major decisions and resolutions of UN organizations as they affect marine affairs. The FAO maintains an activity register, and a serious attempt is being made to meet the need to harmonize activities and increase co-ordination in order to introduce systematic linkage between concerned agencies at the earliest possible planning stage. The trend towards regionalization of the law of the sea is also under attention.

XI

International Regional Co-operation

PART 1: REGIONAL CO-OPERATION: COMPREHENSIVE ORGANIZATIONS

Introduction

Our previous studies—on the North Sea, and the Celtic Sea and Western Approaches—have drawn attention to the legal and organizational problems to which the multifarious conflicting uses of the seas give rise. The need for co-ordination of activities in these waters was stressed, including the need to view the problems comprehensively, balancing the needs of all competing uses to enable essential economic activities to be carried out in harmony, within a general scheme, based on international harmonization of national laws in order to achieve rational management of uses of an international body of water in the best long-term interests of all users. For this, it was emphasized, 'the law provides the guidelines. It provides the framework, it provides the obligations.'[1]

In our North Sea study we suggested that there was a clear case for trying to solve that area's problems on a regional basis;[2] a similar solution might well be applicable to the extended area of the present study.

It is not proposed to study further the detailed national and international legal regime which was explained in our North Sea study, since the fundamental framework, apart from fisheries, has not changed, although it has been embellished by some new conventions and many detailed national orders implementing, for example, the various acts enabling exploitation of the continental shelf and fisheries. Major developments will be noted in the context of the relevant organizations. Our North Sea study concluded that the law has difficulty in keeping up with technological change: north-west European organizations have been struggling to increase the pace of their adaptation to scientific advance. We shall try to measure their success.

Since our earlier studies, several commissions then merely provided for have become effective and new sub-regional bodies have been set up. Taking into account other existing and well-established bodies, it will be seen that there is now a wide and varied range of concerned regional agencies. These can be divided into two kinds: those that are comprehensive in membership and scope, such as the EC, the Council of Europe, and the OECD; and those that are functional but with broad regional membership, such as the Oslo and Paris Commissions on Ocean Dumping and Prevention of Land-based Pollution respectively, and NATO. There are, however, many other specific conventions and agreements, both multi-lateral and bilateral, which establish limited commissions for specific purposes—for instance, the Oslo, Paris and Straddle Field Commissions. Only comprehensive bodies are candidates for an expanded co-ordinating role, but it is necessary to examine briefly the other bodies since it is their multifarious activities that a wider based organization might need to overview. The three potential 'lead' organizations are very different in concept and powers, as will be seen.

The Council of Europe

The Council of Europe was established on May 5 1948 with the aim of achieving 'a greater unity between its members for the purpose of safeguarding and realizing the ideals and principles which are their common heritage and facilitating their economic and social progress'.[3]

The Council now has twenty members. It has two major organs: the Committee of Ministers[4] (with various subordinate bodies) which meets in closed sessions, and the Parliamentary Assembly[5] which meets in open sessions; the Council's Statute states that the latter is the deliberating organ and the former that which acts on behalf of the Council.

The Committee of Ministers[6]

The Committee considers the action required to further the aims of the Council—the conclusion of conventions or agreements and the adoption by governments of a common policy with regard to particular matters. It can ask member governments to inform it of the action taken by them on its recommendations. The subject areas of co-operation are stated in broad terms: economic, social, cultural, scientific, legal and administrative matters.

The Committee proper meets twice yearly for a one-day session. Few important political decisions are taken. Ministers seldom try to co-ordinate a common policy, but they discuss matters of European co-operation and other political questions. Much of their authority has been delegated to special deputies who take decisions in their name. Important new conventions, however, are opened for signature on the occasion of Committee Meetings; more than ninety of these have been adopted, as well as hundreds of recommendations, some of which affect our study. There is a continuous monitoring and follow-up through several main committees, numerous sub-committees and working groups on which member states are represented by their appropriate experts. Their work is co-ordinated by the Deputies.

The Parliamentary Assembly

The Assembly can discuss but not decide: it relies on publicity for the effect of its efforts. Parliamentarians see their task as limited to influencing people and promoting action; thus 'they become imaginative, expansive and outspoken. They promote bold ideas and visions, which are forwarded to the Committee of Ministers for action'.[7] Ministers do not always act on these ideas. There is therefore a built-in latent conflict between the two bodies.

The Assembly's recommendations on fisheries and oil pollution exemplify this. In its report on European action to prevent oil pollution of waters and coasts, the Assembly commented: 'Our survey of the many proposals and warnings addressed to governments by the Parliamentary Assembly and their very limited success is hardly calculated to inspire excessive optimism when the time comes to make proposals on joint action to prevent oil pollution of our coasts and seas. It may not, however, be a waste of time to persevere, taking advantage of the sense of urgency created by recent accidents'.[8] The report recommended, inter alia, that states should co-operate in order to preserve their common heritage of living resources in the seas, and considered that the Council of Europe was the most appropriate and effective forum for this purpose.

However, it has been suggested that the Council has lost much of its momentum and sense of identity in recent years. Much of this decline can be attributed to the institutional development of the European Community, including direct elections to the European Parliament, and its gradual assumption of responsibility in fields previously left to the Council. On the other hand, it is interesting to note that the EC adheres to the Council's conventions.

Relations with the EC and other bodies[9]

In view of the above, and because of the dangers of duplication as well as of rivalry, it is clear that there is a considerable need for close consultation and a degree of co-ordination between the Council and the Community. To some extent this is provided by the membership of ten countries of both organizations. Two more Council members, Spain and Portugal, will become members of the EC in 1986. In addition, a Council Liaison Office has been established in Brussels and the President of the Community's Council of Ministers provides a personal report. None the less, the Council's Committee of Ministers has concentrated on defining its own role in the evolution of European co-operation and in instigating studies of the problems which have often led to more practical inter-governmental co-operation. A recent example is the protection of the environment, including the marine environment, which it stimulated *before* the EC adopted its first Action Plan for the Environment in 1973, by organizing a

Nature Conservation Year in 1970. In its oil pollution report, the Assembly noted that EC action was justified by its own powers and economic interests at stake, but thought its geographical scope was too limited since pollution was a threat to *all* the coasts of Europe, and concluded 'Herein lies the need for concerted action by the Council of Europe.'[10]

Thus in 1979 the Council adopted a Convention on the Protection of Wildlife and Habitats in Europe,[11] which includes marine species, and the Assembly has recommended support for the Economic Commission for Europe of the UN 1979 Convention on Long-Range Trans-boundary Pollution.[12] In 1981 it supported a European Island Region Conference, organized by the Conference of Local and Regional Authorities in Europe and the Conference of Peripheral Maritime Regions, aided by the Council of European Municipalities and the International Union of Local Authorities. The Conference discussed, amongst other things, problems of fisheries and environmental protection.

Obviously there is still some duplication of effort, not only between the Council of Europe and the Community, but also with other bodies: the Council's work on vessel-source and river pollution, flags of convenience and fisheries, for example, overlaps that of the EC, IMO, ILO, FAO, and Oslo and Paris commissions. Each body doubtless has its champions. It has been said, for example, of the Council of Europe that it 'is probably the one organization which is least guilty of duplication . . . one of the purposes of [its] Work Programme was that the Council of Europe could make sure that it would only take up a new field of endeavour if it were certain that no other organization was active in that field'.[13] Other organizations lacking work programmes sometimes use the Council of Europe's as a shopping catalogue.

The very broad mandate of the Council of Europe, its expanded and flexible work programmes and its comprehensive European membership, make it a body worthy of consideration for an overviewing and co-ordinating role in European waters. Two hundred and sixteen non-governmental organizations have consultative status with it, joining their work across national frontiers to influence the Council, *inter alia*. The Brussels-based European Environment Bureau (EEB), described later, co-ordinates those with an environmental interest. The Council's powers, however, are weaker than those of the Community—it cannot bind its member states unless they ratify its conventions—but it is the oldest and most broadly based of European institutions. Given the political difficulties encountered by the Community in harmonizing maritime laws and policies, the Council may be a more appropriate body for the achieving of harmonization: it remains 'a force at the service of a political will'.[14]

The Assembly advocated in its report on oil pollution the establishment of another international agency to provide a central institutional framework for the co-ordination of existing organizations and governments for the protection of European maritime and coastal zones. It noted that, since European seas represent a shared waterway like the Rhine, the complexity of the problems involved necessitated the establishment of a flexible permanent co-ordinating and co-operative body of European states, like the Rhine Commission. This should collect and disseminate information; survey maritime waters and transmit the information thus gained; draw up contingency plans for maritime basins; enable co-operation and participation with other bodies for the Baltic and Mediterranean. It would be a body to combat 'the slow death of our seas . . . the cradle of our way of life and of our civilization'.[15]

A role as co-ordinator of the maritime roles of its member states and regional bodies would certainly give the Council of Europe a practical focus. However, the European Community is unlikely to relinquish its developing environmental roles. A way forward might be for the two institutions to undertaken joint activities in marine environmental affairs through a specialized agency, and to intensify co-operation and information exchanges in common fields.[16]

The European Community[17]

Eight of the ten member states of the European Community border north-west European waters; of the twelve bordering states only four—Norway, Sweden, Iceland, and Greenland (Denmark)—are not in the EEC, though these omissions are significant for the purposes of our study. This, coupled with the Community's powers to bind member states' conduct, makes the organization potentially one of the most useful and effective for regulating maritime activities. Unfortunately, differences between member states have often made political agreement elusive and it has thus not been able to fulfil its potential as harmonizer of conflicting ocean uses. The European Community is 'cast in the classic mould of international organisations', yet at the same time it is unique because of the deep involvement of its institutions in matters traditionally within the control of an individual state. The institutions also have the capacity to make rules directly and automatically binding not only on the member states themselves, but also on individuals and corporate bodies within them, and so to penetrate their internal as well as external legal relations.[18]

Objectives

Apart from the very general objectives set out in the preamble to the Treaty of Rome, including closer union among European peoples, promotion of economic and social progress, concerted action to ensure steady expansion, balanced trade and fair competition, and reduction of differences between regions, article 2 of the Treaty lays down the basic aims: harmonious development of economic activities throughout the Community, continuous and balanced expansion, increased stability, accelerated living standards, and closer relations between member states. These are to be achieved by creation of a common market and the progressive approximation of the economic policies of the member states. The first method requires the protection of the freedom of movement of goods, persons, services, capital, and related payments, the right of establishment and rules governing competition, for which purposes the Community has used its law-making powers. The second method is expressed in much more general terms requiring policy-making rather than law-making, and gives more scope for application of the treaty to wider fields such as the environment.

Detailed treaty objectives include adoption of a common agricultural policy (including fisheries) as required by article 3 (d) and which resulted in the problems described in chapter V.

Organs

The Treaty of Rome provides for an Assembly (now known as the Parliament), a Council of Ministers, a Court of Justice and the Commission, with the following powers:

The European Parliament The treaty provides for the European Parliament to exercise advisory and supervisory powers only. It is not, therefore, a legislative body; it cannot raise taxes; it does not control the executive, that is, the Council of Ministers—though it can reject the Community's budget (it did so in 1979) and exercise some control over administration. However, since May 1979 it has been the only body which is directly elected. The move to democratic elections greatly enhances its importance as a political forum and opens up the possibility for it to play a more influential role.

As the Parliament's powers, based particularly on articles 137–44 of the Rome treaty, are so general and are limited to advice and supervision, it does not face the strong political pressures and need for compromise which restrict the decision-making body, the Council of Ministers. Like the Council of Europe's Assembly, the European Parliament has been able to be much more forward looking and controversial in investigating and expressing its views upon a wide range of subjects, including marine affairs. The exercise of the Parliament's powers requires an absolute majority of votes cast; in its advisory function it can express opinions and make recommendations whenever it considers it necessary.

The Treaty of Rome also requires that the Parliament is consulted in certain instances before the Council adopts the proposals submitted to it by the Commission. In fact the Council now consults the Parliament on nearly all important issues. The Commission also informally sends the texts of all its proposals to Parliament in advance. The Commission can amend its proposals in the light of Parliament's decisions, but it is not bound to do so. The Council, acting unanimously, can modify the proposal to take account of parliamentary comment if the Commission does not do so.

Parliament's influence varies with the subject matter. It has tended to have more effect on social rather than fisheries policy—notwithstanding the activities of the Danish MEP Mr Kent Kirk immediately prior to the final agreement on a Common Fisheries Policy in early 1983—since the CFP has involved complex and practical negotiations and compromises. It has been more influential on urgent issues of oil pollution, preservation of the living resources, and so forth, though the influence of committee reports to some extent depends on the reputation of the committee concerned and its rapporteur. One notable report was that drawn up for the Committee on Regional Policy, Regional Planning and Transport on the best means of preventing accidents to shipping and consequential marine and coastal pollution, and on shipping regulations.[19] It proposed a European coastguard service to supervise common fisheries measures, controls on shipping, anti-pollution measures, marine scientific activities, and search and rescue, and discussed ideas for a marine police force, a European agency to collate states' information derived from their marine pollution plans, and for a disaster prevention organization.

The Parliament has real supervisory powers over the Commission, which it can censure and even dismiss, albeit only *en bloc*. This is a power found in no other international organization, but obviously it cannot be used lightly. None the less, the Parliament can supervise the regular activities of the Commission by asking written questions and this it frequently does. Written questions can also be directed to the Council of Ministers and to the Conference of Foreign Ministers, that is to say, to ministers meeting outside the formal framework of the Treaty of Rome; questions and replies are published in the Community's *Official Journal*. During parliamentary sessions, oral questions, often with short debates, can also be addressed to the Council or Commission, thus enabling the Parliament to comment on a broad range of topical issues. It has consistently pressed for broader powers, but has received them so far only in relation to the budget.

The Parliament has closer links with the Commission than with the Council, the decision-making body. Moreover, the Parliament discusses Commission proposals well in advance of the Council's final decision, indeed at the same time as the Council's working groups are formulating that decision. Its impact on the public is blunted in consequence. Various proposals have therefore been under discussion in the Parliament which would enable it to impinge more on the public's consciousness. Moreover, its legal powers as an institution of the Community have, in general, received remarkably little attention, and it is possible that there could be significant development of its role, either by adapting existing treaty provisions or extending them. The Parliament could, for example, fulfil a wider supervisory role over European waters than at present.[20]

The Commission   The Commission consists of fourteen Commissioners appointed by the member states, but who thereafter are independent of their national governments. The Commission acts as a *collegium*, accepting collective responsibility for its acts, but in practice individual Commissioners are allocated specialized responsibilities, such as agriculture (fisheries). Each Commissioner is backed by a cabinet of officials, comparable in some respects to a ministerial private office staff, and a general Commission staff of about 9,000 (including well over 100 interpretors and translators) with roughly equitable representation from the member states.

The Commission's task is to ensure the proper functioning and development of the common market. It supervises the application of the treaties and Community rules, formulates proposals for decision by the Council of Ministers, and participates in the Council's decision-making processes, exercising any powers delegated to it by the Council or the Treaty. Its powers have been succinctly categorized as: initiator and co-ordinator of Community policy; executive agency of the Community and guardian of the Community treaties.[21] It regards itself as the primary motor for further integration within the Community and tries to inculcate a Community spirit. It also assesses whether actions and policies are 'communautaire'; it must ensure that Community provisions are applied.

Member states are bound by the treaties, as are enterprises operating within them, and the Commission can take action against those defaulting on Community obligations. It can proceed either informally or, if this fails, it can resort to formal procedures which, if compliance remains lacking, can lead to the issue being referred to the European Court of Justice, which can give a binding judgment on the matter. These are altogether stronger procedures than are available in other organizations, even though the Court has no means of enforcing its judgment on states—it is left to them to accept the treaty obligation to comply. Defaulting enterprises, however, can be fined or otherwise penalized by the Commission.

The Commission plays a major role in working out detailed policies to achieve the general aims of the Treaty. Our chapters on fisheries and pollution illustrate the difficulties involved for the Commission in evolving proposals which are both 'communautaire' and acceptable to all the Council members. None the less, it is one of the most important roles of the Commission and one in which it is most active. After all, article 189 of the Treaty of Rome provides for the power which distinguishes the Community from all the other organizations mentioned in this section: it can legislate, and the formal power to initiate this rests with the Commission.

Moreover, not only does the Commission have responsibility for initiating proposals, it is intimately involved in the decision-making process and the search for acceptable compromise solutions. However, the role of the Commission in both areas has been affected by the trend towards intergovernmentalism and away from the supranationalism which inspired it.

The Commission can also be given powers to enforce Council decisions, as has been done in the case of fisheries and environmental protection, as well as ensuring that treaty rules are applied in particular cases. For certain agricultural and fisheries questions, the Commission also chairs management committees on which national governments are represented. Commission proposals have to be submitted to the Council only if a qualified majority of the Committee disagree with them. However, the Council and the member states have refused many of the calls for more power to be delegated to the Commission.

In addition, the Commission has the responsibility, either alone or in conjunction with the Presidency of the Council, of representing the Community in a wide range of international negotiations with, for example, third countries on fisheries access agreements; or on the increasing number of international bodies such as fisheries and pollution control commissions, although its status on the latter varies.

Finally, the Commission administers four Community funds within the Community budget, of which the European Agricultural Guidance and Guarantee Fund and the European Regional Development Fund are of particular relevance to our study, since they can be used to enable the restructuring of, *inter alia*, the fishing and shipping industries.

The Council   The Council of Ministers is the Community's principal decision-making body. It is composed of one representative of the government of each member state, and varies depending on the subject matter for discussion at a particular meeting. Each member state acts as President of the Council for six months in rotation. In addition, since 1974 the heads of government have met three times a year in summit meetings, known as the European Council. It takes its most important decisions by unanimous vote, although most decisions could be taken by a qualified majority. Two exceptions of particular importance are decisions on new members and on policies not specifically called for by the treaties. Article 235, for example, under which several proposals in the environmental field have been adopted, requires unanimity. Since the Luxembourg compromise of 1966, the practice has prevailed that the Council will not impose a decision by qualified vote on a member state on an issue which that member considers to be of vital national interest. In fact the Council almost always aims at unanimity, which tends to slow down the decision-making process. Indeed, some problems, such as that of budgetary contributions, appear to be virtually insoluble.

Considerable attention has inevitably been focused on improving the Community's decision-making, including, of course, greater use of majority voting. The Presidency of the Council of Ministers has, for example, taken on a very much more important role in mediating between the member states and in drawing up acceptable package deals—roles previously undertaken by the Commission. In addition, the trend towards intergovernmentalism has been reinforced by the role of the European Council which often lays down broad lines of policy. The Commission and Council of Ministers have then the responsibility of attempting to implement these. Decision-making in the Community will not be eased with further enlargement when Spain and Portugal are finally admitted. Such difficulties must cast some doubt on the Community's potential for co-ordinating the work of other institutions relevant to north-west European waters.

The European Court of Justice   This is another unique institution among international organizations. It is based in Luxembourg and is composed of eleven judges appointed for a six-year period by the mutual agreement of member states of whom the judges are, however, independent. The Court's functions are to:

(a) annul any measures taken by the Commission, the Council of Ministers, or member states which are incompatible with the treaties. The procedures can be initiated by Community institutions, member states, or individuals directly concerned;

(b) pass judgment at the request of national courts on the interpretation or validity of Community laws; if the case cannot be resolved by the national courts, they can request an interlocutory judgment from the European Court.

The Court heard 323 cases (including 99 interlocutory ones) in 1981 and passed 149 judgments, including several fisheries cases relevant to this study. The Court is proving a valuable body, determinative of the Treaty, and interpreting it broadly, as in the fisheries cases. Its judgments are binding.

Articles in the Treaty of Rome on which expansion of community activities related to north-west European waters might be based

The Treaty of Rome has a number of fairly general provisions which are open to interpretation and thus give the Commission an opportunity to propose developments of policies and regulations in fields not specifically covered by the Treaty and in ways not specifically required by the Treaty. For example, when in 1973 the heads of state and government of EC member states invited the institutions to establish an environmental policy, the Commission looked at a number of articles as a legal basis for this policy including the preamble, article 2, article 84 (2), article 100 and article 235. These have been analysed elsewhere[22] and the matter is discussed in our chapter on pollution. The UK House of Lords Select Committee on the EC has been critical of the Commission's view that these articles, especially article 2, *require* it to develop an Action Programme for the Protection of the Environment.[23]

This committee emphasized that the Commission's resources and staff are always likely to be small in relation to the scale of environmental problems and expectations and suggested development of a *strategy* (which would take about two years to prepare) which integrated aims, policies, assumptions, and methods with the Community's capacity for action, and which could take account not only of the work of member states but also of the activities of international bodies, such as the OECD and the Council of Europe. It expressed concern about the Commission's approach to pollution control and its large back-log of work, and recommended that EC anti-pollution measures should alter in character and scale, with the Commission integrating resource and environmental policies and encouraging and helping industrialists (under the OECD 'polluter pays' principle adopted by the Community) to assume greater responsibilities for pollution control. The late 1970s, when many Community policies were under review and when three countries had applied for membership, was regarded as particularly ripe for the necessary changes of strategy, to define more clearly Community level action such as transfrontier issues. The mere preparation of such a strategy, it was contended, would result in many gains—'it could be used to foster public awareness of the shared interest in the European heritage and thus be a force for unity . . . it will only be by mobilizing the hearts and minds of the peoples of Europe that the Commission's ambitious goals can be fully realized.'[24]

The House of Lords committee thought the Commission needed to improve links with scientific and professional bodies in the Community, to improve scientific data, to find ways of collaborating with industrial and commercial bodies, and to foster links with representative NGOs, at both Community and international level. It recommended the setting up of a new Community fund for environmental objectives, and the promotion of information dissemination. It further recommended that the community's research and development programme should be reviewed to meet the needs of the proposed environmental strategy, and that the Environment and Consumer Protection Service (CEPS) should be strengthened so that it could assume greater authority 'by enhanced capacity for leadership, consultation and monitoring of measures adopted'. This has since become a directorate general. The Committee also suggested that wise use of directives would greatly facilitate the realization of EC environmental policies and programmes and ensure a position of international leadership. However, it remains to be seen whether, in a time of recession and political rivalry, the EC is capable of making the integrated response required. The problems described in chapter VII do not augur well for radical reform, although the upgrading of CEPS into the status of a directorate is a step in the right direction.

A basic problem in creating a leading role for the EC in the field of our study remains that of linking its actions to those of non-member states. The problems of north-west European waters are generally holistic. CEPS maintains regular direct contact with international organizations such as the UN, ECE, UNEP, and OECD and with many non-member states. These contacts are mostly on a formal basis through exchange of letters relating to the biannual exchange of information on matters of mutual interest, though there are also joint research projects with non-member states on various scientific topics within the framework of a committee of senior national officials, known as COST, (Coopération Scientifique et Technique). Rather than creating new linking mechanisms, it might be possible to build upon these linkages through an enlarged CEPS. However, a number of member states consider that some Community measures have had the effect of limiting their freedom both to take stricter measures and to co-operate fully and freely with non-member states (in the case of Denmark with its Scandinavian partners in the Nordic Council). Others, including the UK, think the Community approach to environmental controls is often too rigid and uniform, taking too little account of sub-regional variations, and those with energy-rich continental shelves are anxious to discourage Community interest in the development of their national regimes.[25] The blow-out of the well head on the Ekofisk Bravo platform in the Norwegian sector of the North Sea in 1977 stimulated the Commission's interest in developing member states' laws to prevent such disasters.

There is no doubt that a more generous interpretation of treaty articles referred to than that given by the House of Lords committee would enable the Community to take an even more active role than it does in harmonizing regulation of activities and resources in north-west European waters, if that were politically possible, but our chapters on fisheries and pollution indicate the problems. There are now also many other bodies concerned and it would be inadvisable to increase the overlap. Despite this, the European Community has its attractions as a possible co-ordinating body: it has powerful mechanisms and institutions, and is active in relevant fields. Some co-ordination with non-member states already takes place in fisheries conservation.

A consultation procedure for Community member states has been in existence since September 1977, established by a decision of the Council of Ministers,[26] based on article 84 (2). Its objective is to facilitate co-ordination of the action taken by member states in international organizations, through consultation and exchanges of information between member states and the Commission on shipping matters, developments in relations between member states and third countries, and on the functioning of the international agreements concluded on these issues. This could be extended across a wider range of issues—pollution, conservation and other problems. It has also been suggested that the Community could give legitimacy to a regional policy on shipping safety and pollution prevention because it has competence and should therefore be represented in appropriate global organizations, particularly IMO and especially where regional arrangements affect the operation of international sea trade.[27] By the same token, the Community can become party to some conventions in its own right, enforcing them by directives and other means.[28]

The Nordic Council[29]

Objectives

The Nordic Council of Ministers includes only one member of the European Community. It was established in 1953 between Denmark, Iceland, Norway, and Sweden as a body through which the respective governments could co-operate. Finland acceded in 1953 and since 1970 the self-governing territories of the Faroes and of the Aaland Islands have had their own representatives on it. In including non-state entities it differs from both the European Community and the Council of Europe, though the former makes some special arrangements.

Co-operation is based not only on cultural affinities and shared values of law and government, but on the practical and economic advantages of sharing tasks and efficiently exploiting common resources. Joint work takes place at a variety of levels, public and private, without formal agreements, though the overall framework was eventually put on a formal basis by the 1962 Helsinki Treaty of Mutual Co-operation (revised in 1971) which expressed the desire of the Nordic states to reinforce their close community of interests, to adopt uniform rules in as many fields as possible, and to maintain and develop a greater degree of co-operation in the legal, cultural, social, and economic fields and in relation to communications and the environment. Thus Nordic co-operation shares with ICES the unusual distinction of being based for years on informal arrangements, the subsequent treaty merely symbolizing and helping to intensify on-going co-operative efforts, a contrast to most arrangements in which the treaty aims at originating co-operation, with actual attainment of this aim being uncertain.[30]

Organs

Nordic co-operation takes place through the Nordic Council of Ministers, serviced by an Oslo secretariat and a cultural secretariat in Copenhagen and also a Nordic Council which acts as a link between the Nordic parliaments.

The Nordic Council of Ministers   This is the body of co-operation for Nordic governments, responsible not only for co-operation between themselves but also between them and the Nordic parliaments' co-operative body, the Nordic Council. Resolutions of the Nordic Council of Ministers bind governments if adopted unanimously, though some also need parliamentary approval. Ministers participating in Council meetings vary according to the question in issue, as in the EC.

The Nordic Council   The Nordic Council is the oldest co-operative body, meeting annually for one week, and providing a forum for co-operation between the parliaments and the governments. It takes the initiatives and spurs on co-operation in ways similar to the European Parliament and the Assembly of the Council of Europe. It makes recommendations both to the Council of Ministers and to governments, and oversees their execution, and acts in other ways.

It is composed of 78 members elected by the respective Parliaments, and about 40–45 non-voting government representatives nominated by the respective governments. Elected members are divided into five Standing Committees (Legal, Cultural, Social and Environmental, Communications, Economic) which prepare Council business, meeting inter-sessionally, as also do the Council's two permanent Committees on the Budget and on Information. Between sessions, the Presidium functions as the Council's supreme body, dealing with current business aided by the secretariat in Stockholm and the national secretariats.

The Nordic Council of Ministers (for Co-operation) holds regular discussions with the Presidium and also (through specific ministers) consults the Standing Committee, but large numbers of recommendations remain uncompleted, with no action taken. Though the Nordic Council is more successful here than the Council of Europe[31], some observers consider that the resources and knowledge necessary to produce concrete, rather than general, results are lacking in the Nordic Council and that real benefits are modest, mostly concerning border regions. The Nordic Council generally is said to be more concerned with analysis than with action.

Unlike those of the Council of Ministers, Nordic Council recommendations are not binding, but as they often have the support of about 30 Nordic parliamentary parties they carry considerable weight, leading to national parliamentary and government action. One important co-operative activity has been rendering laws of Nordic countries mutually compatible, unifying them to the extent possible by common programmes of legislation in designated areas.

Relations with other organizations

It is realized that interconnections are increasing and problems have become harder to solve—co-operation has had to be enlarged. Nordic

Prime Ministers meet more frequently; there is increased bilateral co-operation, though Nordic co-operation is *not* treated as foreign policy. More controversial areas, including energy and the environment, are increasingly tackled, contradicting 'the common belief that Nordic co-operation is merely concerned with the various non-salient and politically less essential issues'.[32]

The assumption that Denmark's entry into the EC would weaken Nordic co-operation, making the region wholly dependent on the larger body, has proved incorrect; rather 'the challenge presented by the EC seems to have provided a stimulus for a strengthening and intensification of the Nordic co-operation process',[33] while at the same time bringing about co-operation with the EC to some extent. Denmark has taken very seriously its role as a bridge between the two organizations.

The Council also co-ordinates some of its activities and programmes with the other major bodies, such as the Council of Europe (the two have had a Joint Committee since 1975) and the OECD, not only by official contacts, exchange of reports, and so forth, but also by exchange of observers at meetings and attendance at conferences organized by the others.

The Organization for Economic Co-operation and Development (OECD)

The OECD, whose headquarters are in Paris, is not 'comprehensive' in the way that the three organizations so far referred to are, and thus cannot seriously be considered as a lead organization for the purposes of our study. Its concerns are exclusively economic, yet it plays an important role in economic co-operation and it must therefore be integrated into any co-ordinative system for European waters. It has twenty-four member states, including all north-west European states and industrialized states on both sides of the Atlantic (Canada and the USA are members, as is Japan); Yugoslavia also participates in certain aspects of its work. As in the EC, member states maintain permanent delegations.

Objectives

The OECD reflects recognition of the interdependence of the industrialized world. Its economic aims are set out in its treaty: to promote economic growth, to help less developed countries both inside and outside its membership, and to encourage trade expansion world-wide; the methods of achieving these are detailed in article 2. Relevant to our study is that members undertake to 'promote the efficient use of their economic resources' and 'in the scientific and technological field promote the development of their resources; encourage research and promote vocational training'.

Organs

The organs consist of a council (the decision-making body), an executive committee of 14 Members, a secretariat, and other committees (10 at present) on specialist topics, which are advised by working parties and expert groups; these include committees on the environment, energy, fisheries, and scientific and technological policy.

There is also an autonomous International Energy Agency (IEA) of 21 states co-operating in energy programmes and research, and a Nuclear Energy Agency which, *inter alia*, encourages harmonization of policy and practices in radioactive waste management.

The OECD council can bind members (except as otherwise provided) but this requires mutual agreement. It has no duty to harmonize its members' laws, but provides a broad forum for crystallization of principles which can be adopted into laws.[34] The OECD has become a leading proponent of the need for international co-operation and a leading actor in stimulating it realistically, through a variety of techniques.

Programmes

Inter alia the OECD is concerned with:

The Environment National environment policies and their economic implications are analysed (including shipping) and guiding principles adopted.[35] Proposals for assessing and improving environmental quality are made;[36] environmental and health hazards of chemical products are examined; advice is given on waste disposal;[37] environmental implications of producing energy from various sources are assessed. A major programme concerns analysis of transfrontier pollution problems and proposed solutions.[38] The OECD developed principles governing this and also the Polluter Pays Principle (PPP), adopted by the European Community for liability.[39] Though criticized by some in relation to limited liability ceilings in the IMO conventions and the possibility of passing the charges on to consumers, the PPP has been influential.

Following the *Amoco Cadiz* stranding, the OECD hosted a seminar on Economic Consequences of Oil Spills at which a large number of papers brought together the current state of scientific research on oil pollution impacts and the economic aspects,[40] an important advance enabling better evaluation of the kind of damage occurring, including environmental consequences, and methods of assessing and compensating for it.

Fisheries It reviews policy developments; promotes adaptation to changing economic conditions; forecasts production and marketing, and promotes co-operative research. It also produces annual fisheries statistics of member states.

Science and technology It promotes much research, confronting the scientific and technological policies of member states, and assesses the social consequences of technological developments.

Relations with other organizations

The OECD relates closely with other organizations. A supplementary protocol specifically states that representation of the European Community in the OECD is to be determined by the institutional provisions of the EC treaties—and that the Commission shall take part in the work of OECD. A second protocol establishes that the OECD has legal capacity in the territory of contracting parties according to the relevant instruments in the case of each contracting party; and article 5 of the main treaty allows the organizations to enter into agreements with members, non-member states and international organizations.

The North Atlantic Treaty Organization (NATO): the Committee on the Challenges of Modern Society (CCMS)[41]

NATO also is not strictly a comprehensive organization since its declared aim is the establishment of a military alliance for defensive purposes in the regions covered by its membership (which, like OECD's, is wider than our study area), but in 1969 its council established the CCMS to examine methods of improving inter-allied co-operation in the creation of a better environment in their societies,[42] though stressing the need to avoid duplication of the work of other bodies.

The CCMS has produced several reports to improve member states' environmental protection including reports on coastal water[43] and inland water pollution;[44] environmental and regional planning,[45] and many aspects of air pollution.[46] It also holds technical meetings, for instance on air pollution modelling.[47] The CCMS' unusual procedures are of particular interest to our study. Pilot studies are initiated—groups of interested member and non-member states and international organizations are led by a 'pilot country', the studies being financed and organized by individual states. The studies do not undertake long-term research, but lead to speedy adoption of resolutions and recommendations by the council to initiate action. All pilot studies and their documentation are open. Follow-up reports on implementing measures must be submitted by member states for two years following their completion.

Members, non-members (including the Nordic Group), organizations and private industry have all been increasingly interested in participating in pilot studies and all member states have now taken part in some. The approach is successful because it enables direct working exchanges between scientists and engineers, focuses on well-defined practical projects and permits exchanges across all organizational and political boundaries, providing a 'real medium of technology transfer and institutional change'.[48] However, there has been some criticism: it is alleged, for example, that it has tried to tackle too 'political' subjects; that it encroaches on other bodies, and that it lacks central purpose, resulting in relegation of reports to bureaucratic niches. It has been suggested that CCMS be removed from NATO and opened to all comers or moved to the private sector or used as a basis of East–West working activities.

Paradoxically, that the CCMS was born out of NATO seems to have facilitated wide participation, but prevented its purposes being taken seriously; its studies still lack high-level political backing and 'the status quo is not unlike a talented cast waiting for a challenging play'.[49] It cannot be expected that any government is currently aiming at giving it a central co-ordinating role in north-west European waters.

PART 2: REGIONAL CO-OPERATION: FUNCTIONAL ORGANIZATIONS

Introduction

Since our previous study, not only have several specific commissions then provided for but not in effect (such as the Oslo Dumping and Paris Land-based Pollution Commissions) come into being, following the entry into force of their constituent conventions, but new ones have been instituted, some sub-regional. There is now a considerable network of bodies whose activities impinge on the uses of north-west European waters. However, there is still no overarching co-ordinating commission or committee even for the pollution prevention commissions which have proliferated in the region, despite the fact that, as we have established in the first part of this chapter, none of the comprehensive regional bodies fulfils this role. Whether or not this is a serious deficiency in the system for managing or protecting the waters in question cannot be decided until we have examined this web of smaller agencies. Their activities can be surveyed under three major headings related to the main purpose—scientific research, prevention of pollution, and fisheries—although, of course, as with the comprehensive organizations there is some overlap of functions and interests.

Scientific Research

The International Council for the Exploration of the Sea (ICES)[50]

ICES was founded informally by scientists in 1902. Its objectives are to promote and encourage research and investigations for the study of the sea, particularly living resources; to draw up the required programmes; to organize the necessary research and investigations; and to ensure publication or dissemination of the results of research carried out under its auspices. Its objectives are thus very wide since the study of the sea could, in the absence of dispute procedures, cover anything which might reasonably be said to impinge upon it without frustrating the general aims of the convention. But ICES has a co-ordinating, not a managerial, role. It has no powers to decide the usage of the information it gathers, though it can come to conclusions and make recommendations concerning problems researched. It has no regulatory role, but has been active in drawing members' attention to the need for management actions.

ICES has eighteen members[51] (including EC and non-EC states bordering its area and 4 which do not), is now based on a convention concluded in 1964,[52] and is open to any state approved by three quarters of the existing parties. Its activities are limited to the Atlantic ocean and its adjacent seas, interest being especially concentrated on the north Atlantic. ICES headquarters are in Copenhagen; Denmark has granted it the same privileges and immunities as UN organizations. Its membership, constitution and area of interest make ICES a regional body, but as it is a scientific organization, used by its members both for scientific collaboration and as a scientific debating forum, its field of interest can be delineated in scientific rather than purely geographic terms. Only 49 per cent of its members' fishing catches, for example, come from the ICES area.[53] Its work for the fisheries commissions and other commissions, however, is only part of its wider activities.

Organs   The staff of ICES is small,[54] its main work being through closed committees of national delegates. The council meets annually, and takes its decisions by vote (each party having one vote); they are executed by a bureau,[55] which also prepares the budget, convenes meetings, and carries out other tasks entrusted to it by the council. Council meetings can be attended by delegates and their experts, invited observers from non-member states and international organizations, and guests and scientists invited personally.

In 1977, ICES changed its committee structure to meet the needs of the emerging new ocean regime, the increase in the council's membership to cover both sides of the north Atlantic and the scientists' requirement of more time for discussion.[56] Much of the Fish Committee's time had been occupied in advising the NEAFC and the Baltic Sea Fishery Commission; the twenty or so fishery assessment groups were henceforth to report directly to a new Advisory Committee on Fishery Management (ACFM), the renamed NEAFC–ICES liaison committee which reflects the 200-mile zones and EC interest. Committees on mariculture and on marine environment quality, handling the scientific aspects of marine pollution, were established and were indicative of ICES new interests and growing role; several others were changed, such as the Plankton Committee which was transformed into the Biological Oceanography Committee in order to study also food-chain dynamics and energy transfer.[57] They are supported by working groups, an important link in the ICES system. Scientific papers can be read and criticized in committees, a most useful procedure in the marine environment information system, which attracts wide participation.[58]

Work programmes on fisheries   For a detailed discussion of ICES' work in the fisheries field see chapter V.

The new Advisory Committee on Fisheries Management (ACFM) advises the EC on request[59]—the Community's own Scientific and Technical Committee on Fisheries liaises closely with ICES, which can also, through its working groups, evaluate the effect on fisheries of other activities in the area such as polluting industries and sand and gravel extraction.[60] In its second report, the working group on sand and gravel extraction pointed out, *inter alia*, the lack of international law and standards in that area, the deficiencies in existing national laws, and the need for a uniform code of practice (the Netherlands submitted a draft code) and for information exchange; it also made various recommendations.[61] This report prompted considerable national activity; it had particularly stressed the need for continued dialogue between fisheries scientists and administrators, especially concerning the new ocean regime.[62]

The ACFM's advice is often undermined by the unsubstantiated assumptions it has to make on management caused by the frequent lack of agreement on Total Allowable Catch (TAC), by distribution, and by other uncertainties,[63] not least differing degrees of enthusiasm with which member states fulfil their obligations to transmit information. None the less, its recent reports have been both comprehensive and valuable.

Work programmes on marine pollution   ICES first began a co-ordinated study of the inputs of pollutants into the North Sea in 1968,[64] which revealed many gaps in our knowledge of the type and quantity of pollutants discharged and their ecological effects. Following the adoption of the Oslo and London Dumping conventions in 1972, it undertook a more detailed survey with special reference to the level of pollution found in food fish which was published in 1974.[65] Following its publication, ICES reconstituted its Working Group on Pollution, which now works in the area of the Pollution Baseline and Monitoring Studies in the Oslo Commission and ICNAF (now NAFO). In order to advise the commission adequately it extended its studies and began to improve the data base,[66] excluding, however, radioactive substances, which it left to be dealt with by specialized bodies, such as the International Atomic Energy Agency and the European Nuclear Energy Agencies. The resultant report disturbingly concluded that, dumping apart, 'there are serious limitations in the accuracy and comprehensiveness of the data presented',[67] which made comparisons of sources difficult. Much more work was needed; such incomplete raw data could not be assessed in relation to distribution of pollutants or contamination levels in specific areas.[68] In 1972 ICES had also established an Advisory Committee on Marine Pollution (ACMP),[69] responsible for providing member governments *and* any intergovernmental body for the control of pollution requesting it, with scientific information and advice on marine pollution generally in the area, and its effect on living resources and their exploitation. Interested intergovernmental bodies include the EC, IMO, the Commission of the Oslo Convention on Ocean Dumping (OSCOM), and the Paris Commission for Prevention of Pollution from Land-based Sources (PARCOM), all of which have made use of ICES for these purposes. ICES' work was vital to their development. The ACMP's 1980 report covered intercalibration and intercomparison activities concerning cadmium, lead and PCBs in biological materials, and petroleum hydrocarbons in these materials and in sediments.[70] It proposed continuance of these studies, despite those of the IOC, because they are wider and also meet its commitments to the Helsinki Commission (for the Baltic) and OSPARCOM relating to their monitoring programmes.[71]

The ACMP has pointed out the need to monitor uncontaminated areas for comparison, and to study further the atmospheric pathways, incineration at sea, and deep ocean dumping. On biological monitoring it approved a paper for submission to OSPARCOM on the processes controlling contaminant movements in its area, though it has not found any one monitoring technique adequate—rather it recommends a 'suite' of techniques considered in ICES reports. Its interests extend to other fields—short- and long-term effects of oil spills and blow-outs; and the effect of pollution on marine mammals.[72]

Co-operation with other organizations   ICES necessarily co-operates with many organizations such as the NEAFC, FAO, IMO, EC, and the Helsinki, Oslo, and Paris commissions. It meets OSPARCOM officials to identify overlaps in coverage and avoid duplication, but has accepted a work programme advised by their Joint Monitoring Group for both commissions. ICES also collaborates with the Baltic Sea Fishery Commission, working in both cases through its ACFM, thus enabling intermingling of stocks to be assessed and the areas' problems compared.[73] It is notable that ICES recommendations continued to be applied through bi-lateral negotiations even after EC members withdrew from the NEAFC during 1977/8. Wise exercise of the new jurisdiction in 200-mile zones still requires use of international machinery if stocks are to be preserved.

ICES collaborates with the FAO on the basis of a formal exchange of letters in 1967[74]—there are many joint enterprises:[75] with UNESCO mainly on problems of physical oceanography and marine pollution;[76] with WHO and the WMO in studies; with UNEP (in its Regional Seas and other programmes); with SCOR (Scientific Committee for Oceanographic Research) in particular pollution areas studies; but such co-operation is neither regular nor institutionalized.

Conclusion The best method of organizing the best scientific advice has been debated. Choices appear to be for the organization concerned itself to employ scientists; for it to use scientists provided by member states, other experts being co-opted *ad hoc*; for an independent organization to be used; and for an intermediary mechanism to connect the scientific with the functional organization. Opinion seems to be divided as to which is the best method.[77] The ICES system of using 'national scientists', but keeping their meetings and advice apart from particular organizations, leaving the organizations to request advice, seems to have worked and to continue to work very well, though recently some criticism, hinting at the beginning of the politicization of ICES, has begun to be voiced. Its advice is widely and deservedly respected, as its continued use in the changed and changing regime of north-west European waters by all bordering states shows. It has proved both eminently flexible and able so far to maintain its distance from political argument and influence during what has been an unsettled and difficult period in its area; it must continue to be an essential link in the mechanism for managing and protecting north-west European waters. It remains to be seen, however, how quickly and fully its members and other regional bodies implement its recommendations. Its importance is enhanced by adoption of the LOS treaty since, as described in chapter X. that provides for a consent regime for scientific research in the new 200-mile EEZs. If the states of north-west Europe introduce these provisions, especially if only some do so, validation of research programmes by ICES will remove many of the potential difficulties and delays inherent in the new regime.

Prevention of Pollution

Multilateral commissions and conferences
The LOS treaty provides for six sources of pollution as we saw in chapter X. In North Western European waters five of these have been provided for (the exception is the Deep Seabed Area) by either commissions, conventions or continuing conferences as follows.

Ocean dumping: the Oslo Commission (OSCOM) The Oslo Commission, established under the 1972 Oslo Convention for the Prevention of Marine Pollution by Dumping from Ships and Aircraft, is primarily concerned with direct dumping from ships, aircraft and offshore platforms of wastes generated onshore.[78] These pollutants are categorized according to their harmfulness to the marine environment by allocating them to annexes requiring different treatment, enforced through a licensing system. This system is discussed and its problems analysed in chapter VIII.

The commission of all twelve members exercise overall supervision of the convention's implementation, reviews its sea area's condition, the effectiveness of measures adopted, the need for new measures, makes recommendations for amending the annexes and discharges other functions. It receives and reviews records of permits issued and pollutants dumped, and defines standard procedures for this. The parties to the convention must enact prescribed measures into their national laws and permits, and enforce them by national means. Although the area of application is limited, the convention is open to any other *states* (not organizations; accession by the EC would therefore require adoption of a protocol by unamimous vote).

Parties pledge themselves to take all possible steps to prevent pollution as defined in the convention, to harmonize their policies, to establish complementary research programmes in co-operation with international bodies, and to promote measures against pollution from oil, other noxious cargoes and radioactive materials. The small, underfunded OSCOM secretariat, which is shared with PARCOM and also services the Bonn Agreement described later, is a major instrument in maintaining co-operation with other organizations and between these three bodies; it receives and disseminates the information and reports. OSCOM and PARCOM meet both separately and jointly in sequence each year.[79]

A few other international bodies attend the meetings as observers, but it is questionable how effective this method of linkage is. OSCOM is particularly related to IMO[80] (that body being responsible for the London Dumping Convention), but IMO and OSCOM have identified areas in which duplication has occurred[81] and recently both have expressed concern at the effects of lead.[82] As monitoring is a most likely field of duplication, OSCOM has proposed a joint group of experts and organizational assignment of tasks, and the OSPARCOM joint monitoring group is a result of them.[83] There is a lack of information about dumping outside the OSCOM area[84] though pollutants from it intermingle; this exposes a limitation in the regional approach, but SACSA (OSCOM's Standing Advisory Committee for Scientific Advice) rejected an IMO proposal for a joint group of experts of the London, Oslo and Barcelona Dumping Conventions to avoid duplication in the reviewing of annexes.[85]

The Oslo and London Dumping Conventions see their relative roles in a different light[86]—the former seeing itself as 'the real working level' dealing with specifics, with the global convention's role being more general and restricted mainly to co-ordination and the creation of awareness of the problem, whereas the latter envisages for itself a more authoritative role, reviewing regional progress, though leaving administrative detail to OSCOM. The London Convention meetings are attended by many agencies as observers[87] including NGOs; OSCOM's few observers exclude NGOs and the UK would prefer to reduce even these (thus avoiding the interactions).[88] It must be asked, however, whether IMO is right in its views on the role of the London Convention;OSCOM does seem to be the best forum for practical regional work and so far as its activities need overview and co-ordination, it would seem to be more appropriate that this should be done regionally in connection with other regional conventions related to the other sources of marine pollution[89] referred to below (though taking account of the London Convention's progress and pronouncements and IMO conventions on vessel-source pollution generally) in order to achieve a more holistic approach.

However, IMO initiated a meeting of the representatives of secretariats of pollution prevention conventions.[90] It established the global responsibilities on lines similar to OSCOM's view, and recommended contracting parties to endorse these guidelines,[91] and to establish a small inter-sessional task force to prepare a detailed long-term strategy for the London Convention to the year 2000, in consultation with regional bodies. This was augmented by UNEP's Third Inter-Agency Meeting on Regional Seas in 1981 to which the secretariats of *all* global and regional marine environment conventions were invited in order to review co-operation.

Meanwhile the Oslo Commission, as well as considering interpretation of the terms referred to and categorization of pollutants, has also by resolution given a liberal interpretation to its definition of 'dumping', recommending that disposal of debris from offshore oil related activities should not be regarded as a 'normal' discharge but as an act of deliberate disposal. Parties are now urged to take and enforce all necessary steps to reduce dumping of bulky waste from these operations into the sea, though not all have fully co-operated.[92] MARPOL, it should be observed, applies to discharges from offshore platforms, but the London Dumping Convention does not—it expressly excludes all disposals related to sea-bed activities. There should thus be no confusion between the two dumping conventions on this account and the new Law of the Sea Convention extends coastal state jurisdiction under both.

Land-based pollution: the Paris Commission (PARCOM) This commission was established on 6 May 1978, under the 1974 Paris Convention on Prevention of Pollution from Land-based Sources.[93] As we have seen, it shares the OSCOM secretariat, meets jointly with it, and participates in several joint working groups, for instance the Joint Monitoring Group and Hydrocarbons (Oil Pollution) Sub-Group, as well as having its own Technical Working Group. Its role is similar in many respects: overall supervision of the same convention area and the effectiveness of measures adopted; advising on new measures which are applied and enforced nationally; recommending amendment of the annexes of controlled pollutants, and other specified tasks. The Paris Convention does not, however, provide for accession by states other than those originally participating, although it did allow the EC to accede.

The commission proceeds by unanimous vote in adopting measures, but can adopt them, in the absence of consensus, by a three-quarter majority vote (the measures then bind only states approving them).[94] Within the area of its competence the EC can exercise the number of votes equal to the number of its member states party to the convention, but cannot vote for individual member states which cast their own vote separately (because they take a different view of the proposal at issue from other EC members) and vice versa.

Parties accept the duty to co-operate and to co-ordinate measures in various ways: integrating planning policy to protect the environment; complementary and joint research and monitoring programmes (taking account of those already in existence internationally); and information exchanges.[95] The EC under its treaty must work to harmonize member states' laws, and has done so, issuing the directives and resolutions referred to in our pollution chapter to implement the Paris Convention, but obviously this has led to some duplication of effort and discussion, and there are some discrepancies in approach.

Like OSCOM, PARCOM is struggling with definitional problems, because of the economic as well as scientific implications of terms such as 'persistent oils', 'eliminate', and so forth, but the parties have interpreted its application to 'man-made structures', widely to include offshore oil installations,[96] which are now subject to the PARCOM recommended discharge standards.[97] This led to a possible overlap and confusion with the 1973 MARPOL provisions which defined ships to include offshore platforms and laid down more stringent discharge standards for 'special areas' than those recommended by PARCOM. For technical reasons newer platforms will not be affected, but meanwhile PARCOM has the possible divergency under review,[98] in conjunction with IMO.

The 1978 Hague Conference on Safety and Pollution Safeguards in the Development of North-West European Offshore Mineral Resources drew attention to these organizational responsibility problems concerning the setting of standards for discharges. It called on the Paris Commission, inter alia, to give priority to drawing up specific standards regarding the discharge and disposal of polluting substances deriving from offshore exploration and exploitation in so far as they did not already exist. Both the EC and PARCOM have been faced with the same divergence of views—as related in our pollution chapter—concerning the establishment of marine environment pollution standards—the UK preferring achievement by establishment of environmental quality objectives, other states seeking to establish uniform emission standards. Like the EC, PARCOM resolved the problem by compromising on a parallel approach—for five years parties can adopt either approach.[99]

Obviously, both OSCOM and PARCOM work; the questions are whether they work well enough and whether they integrate with other bodies successfully and so avoid duplication. There have been political difficulties; working groups appear to have been affected by this in that reports are belated because they sometimes attempt to find the compromises more properly left to the commission. PARCOM's Technical Working Group is now to try to resolve technical and scientific problems, identifying and evaluating their political consequences, but leaving decisions to PARCOM. It is clearly difficult for scientific committees to avoid pressures for political compromise—succumbing to them, however, can lead to disasters as happened in the early history of the International Whaling Commission. It could do so here if allowed.

Vessel-source and offshore pollution: the Bonn[100] and Nordic Agreements[101] for co-operation in dealing with pollution of the North Sea by oil The Bonn Agreement (1969) provides for co-operation in remedial action whenever oil pollution presents a 'grave and imminent danger' to the coast and related interests of the North Sea states party to the agreement. There is no commission, but a working group (with rotating chairmanship) considers the operational, scientific and technical aspects of oil spill response.[102] Since the Ekofisk blow-out, parties have agreed that its terms apply to offshore oil pollution as well as vessel-source. The agreement divides the North Sea into zones (which do *not* correspond to shelf sectors)[103] allocated to the responsibility (for monitoring) of one or more states; states are not required to deal with slicks, but can be called on by other parties to help.

After a dormant period, with only *ad hoc* meetings, the parties revived the agreement and asked the secretariat of OSPARCOM to service it on a repayment basis; the costs are currently shared.[104] This development is further evidence of the creeping bureaucratization of European seas.

The Nordic Agreement of 1971 is similar, but parties are required to maintain equipment to deal with significant slicks and to aid other parties to investigate violations in 'adjacent' waters.

Offshore pollution: conference on safety and pollution safeguards in the development of north-west European offshore mineral resources This conference of nine regional states[105] perhaps most nearly meets our study aims of improving co-ordination over north-west European waters, yet it lacks any regularity, has no permanent institutions and is almost unknown except to a narrow circle of official *cognoscenti*. It has held four meetings *ad hoc*: the first in London in 1973; a second in Oslo in June 1977; a third in the Hague in November 1978. A fourth meeting planned for 1980 to consider construction regulations for offshore installations (especially mobile ones) was postponed, but finally held in Oslo in May 1982. The next conference is planned for 1984 in London. Secretariat facilities have been provided by the host state though the OSPARCOM secretary acted as reporter for the 1978 meeting.

Until the 1982 conference, working groups (WG) led by individual countries took place between meetings: WG i on Environmental Matters Affecting Offshore Operations was chaired by the UK, WG ii on Offshore Facilities by Norway, and WG iii on Personnel Safety, Health and Welfare by the Netherlands. The meetings have made some progress;[106] the 1973 meeting, for example, led to the 1976 Civil Liability Convention (see below) and made recommendations on discharges to be implemented later by PARCOM;[107] the 1978 meeting adopted a resolution on offshore operations requiring international bodies such as OSPARCOM to give priority to setting discharge and waste disposal standards for these and also recommended avoidance of duplication of the work of existing bodies and better co-ordination between them in the area.[108] OSPARCOM acted on this resolution and prepared a report for the 1982 conference in Oslo. The 1978 conference also reiterated the need to harmonize laws in all fields and to identify the most appropriate topics for study; a large measure of agreement having now been achieved. The 1982 meeting achieved agreement on a number of issues and the 1984 meeting is charged with finalizing those standards on which agreement was not reached in 1982. The working groups have been disbanded and their work is being carried out by a British secretariat in preparation for the 1984 meeting. As conference proceedings and WG reports are not publicly available,[109] it is difficult to evaluate its progress, and its work is largely overlooked even by some informed observers in the field.[110]

Meanwhile recent disasters and critical appraisals have stressed the need for the urgent review of regulations, procedures, and practices in this field.[111] It might be advisable to institutionalize this conference, basing it on the OSPAR secretariat with regular meetings, publishing reports and ventilating data and conclusions to a wider critical audience. At present the conference seems uncertain what form or weight to attach to its conclusions; it seems unlikely to promote further treaties; adoption of non-binding codes of practice or guidelines would appear to be more likely.

1976 Civil Liability Convention for Offshore Oil Pollution Damage: Committee for Amendment of the Limits of Liability   This committee has not yet been established since it depends on the entry into force of the 1976 Convention of Civil Liability for Oil Pollution Damage Resulting from Exploration and Exploitation of Sea-bed Mineral Resources,[112] initiated by the above conference. Although all twelve participating states signed the convention, none has yet ratified it.[113] The convention provides for a committee, composed of two representatives of each state party, to be established to consider amendment of the liability and required insurance limits. It would be convenable at the instance of any state party which thought these limits had become inadequate or unrealistic. Decisions would be taken by an affirmative vote of at least three-quarters of the parties, but the committee would be able only to *recommend* new limits, though parties would be presumed to have accepted them if they had not, within six months, notified the depositary to the contrary.

Bilateral commissions

The Ekofisk Pipeline and Frigg, Murchison, and Statfjord Straddle Field Agreements   Several deposits of oil or gas traverse median lines between the UK and Norwegian North Sea sectors established by the agreements listed in our previous study.[114] These have led to further agreements for so-called 'straddle fields', to establish bilateral commissions as a framework for consultation between the UK and Norwegian Governments: commissions have been established for the Frigg (1976),[115] Statfjord[116] and Murchison[118] (1979) median-line fields. For economic reasons, these fields are developed and exploited as a single unit: the treaties are unitization agreements.

The 1973 Ekofisk Agreement[118] provided for a pipeline from that field to have its landfall in Teeside, UK. This subjects the pipeline to concurrent UK and Norwegian jurisdiction, to the Norwegian licensing system under its whole length, but to UK licensing also only in the UK sector. All the pipelines are, if possible, to be subject to uniform safety standards.

The three straddle field agreements each institute a consultative commission of six people (three from each state) with broad remits in identical terms: to facilitate the implementation of the agreement, whilst considering matters referred to it by the governments, subject to such further arrangements as may be agreed upon by the governments from time to time. No secretariat or budget is provided; each state bears its own costs and the costs of hosting the meetings. The agreements provide for joint inspection,[119] prevention of pollution of the marine environment or damage by pollution to coastlines, shared facilities and amenities, including vessels and fishing gear of either state. Each state retains jurisdiction over installations in its sector, but must consult on uniform safety and construction standards; some installations straddle the boundary. The commissions, meeting annually (more frequently if necessary) in London, Oslo, or Paris, deal with such matters as division of reserves, safety regulations, emergency procedures, employment, and prevention of pollution. Commissioners are supplemented by advisers according to topics discussed, which are mostly confidential. In the Frigg Field Commission, after execution of the first task of provisionally allocating and reviewing reserves, topics discussed have included harmonization of regulations and enforcement.

It has proved difficult in practice to harmonize laws which, until the agreement was concluded, had been allowed to diverge. Subject to harmonization, both states apply their own laws on the installations respectively registered with them. Problems increased once the field came into production including the application of employment laws on installations traversing the median line; the surveying of the position of the platforms since some were incorrectly located; the requirements of third parties using the field's facilities to transport gas from the field to other landfalls; the undesirability of flaring off gas. The delimitation of the 500-metre safety zones also gave rise to peculiar problems since the safety zone of one Norwegian platform could not be completed wholly within the Norwegian sector. Each state eventually agreed to permit the other to complete any safety zones in the other's sector. Neither the Frigg nor the other commissions maintain direct links with IMO, the ILO, the EC or OSPARCOM or other bodies. In the UK, the Department of Energy relies on internal liaison between its divisions and other departments, and on inter-departmental committees and private contacts.[120] Negotiations with other states concerned are co-ordinated by an official in the Department of Energy's Petroleum Directorate.

Even though mutual inspection is provided for, enforcement presents problems to which attention has been drawn elsewhere.[121]

The Frigg Field Agreement is unusual in one respect, however: article 28 provides procedures for settling disputes concerning its interpretation and application.[122]

These bilateral agreements are the most advanced co-operative agreements so far discussed. It seems that the smaller the number of parties, the greater the degree of effective and binding joint measures possible, though even here the commissions do not deal with matters of high political interest such as taxation policies or commercial, contractual, and other industrial matters which in governments' views are best left to themselves or to the oil and gas companies.

Private Arrangements: Industry Compensation Agreements

The oil industry, in the absence of effective intergovernmental agreements, has itself introduced private compensation schemes, which are part of the organizational regime of north-west European waters:

OPOL's Offshore pollution liability agreement 1975[123]

Pending the entry into force of the Civil Liability Convention, this is the only offshore compensation scheme. Companies voluntarily participating in OPOL accept strict liability (originally up to $16 million per incident, since raised to $25 million) for pollution damage[124] and for the cost of remedial measures when injury has resulted from an escape or discharge of oil from offshore exploration or production operations in the sectors of north-west European states (excluding Belgium). The agreement has been amended several times.[126] It is administered by an Offshore Pollution Liability Association instituted for this purpose. Liability is strict but not absolute (i.e. there are some exemptions). Pollution victims can elect not to resort to OPOL but to seek legal remedies. There is no limit (within the $25 million) to victims' claims against OPOL parties; both individuals and public authorities can claim, though the type of damage compensatable is unclear: it may by definition be limited to provable economic loss.

UK Fisheries and Offshore Oil Consultative Group 1975 (FOOCG)[127]

This voluntary scheme aims at compensating fishermen for damage to fishing vessels and gear caused by debris discharged from offshore installations which cannot be attributed to a specific culprit oil company (a problem the Oslo Commission also has under review). The group, established in 1974, consists of representatives of oil companies, the fishing industry and relevant UK government departments. After discussion of problems and information exchanges, the oil industry provided a small fund, on an *ad hoc* voluntary annual basis, to compensate fishermen for certain kinds of the above damage.

A remarkable unofficial system for administering the fund has been set up by the fishermen, a representative committee of whom settles claims after testing them against a set of self-imposed principles developed by the committee. It now meets claims for both damaged gear and lost fishing time (oil companies originally objected to inclusion of the latter), but not for hull damage which is covered by compulsory insurance. Fishermen contend that their excess at least should be paid; they also argue that they should be compensated for loss of access to traditional fishing grounds.[128]

The scheme applies only to UK registered vessels. Norway operates its own and different scheme for its sector.

Tanker owners voluntary agreement concerning liability for oil pollution 1969 (TOVALOP)[129]

TOVALOP supplements the IMO Convention on Civic Liability for Oil Pollution Damage. Tanker owners party to it agree to compensate for the removal costs only of oil pollution up to US $1,000 per gross registered ton or $10 million (whichever is the lesser), but only if (a) the oil pollutes or causes grave and imminent danger of pollution to coastlines, (b) the tanker owner is negligent, (c) the claimant is a government. TOVALOP has recently been revised, but is still in force despite the entry into force of the IMO Convention, as gaps remain. It is administered by the Tanker Owners Committee.

Contract regarding an interim supplement to tanker liability for oil pollution 1971 (CRISTAL)[130]

CRISTAL supplemented the 1969 Civil Liability Convention and TOVALOP by providing compensation of up to $30 million per incident ($36 million from June 1978) for both governments and individuals, in circumstances where a tanker owner would be liable under the 1969 convention, beyond that convention's and TOVALOP's limits of liability pending entry into force of the Fund Convention. It has not yet lapsed, though the latter is in force, but services areas where it does not yet apply. It was revised in 1978 to bring it more into line with the Fund Convention.

Other non-governmental organizations

So many old and new non-governmental organizations in all states bordering the area have increasingly concerned themselves with the conservation and pollution problems of north-west European Waters and their resources that it is not possible to detail their activities individually. In the UK, concerned bodies include the Royal Society for the Protection of Birds (RSPB); the Advisory Committee on Pollution of the Sea (ACOPS; there is a corresponding Nordic Union for the Prevention of Oil Pollution of the Sea); the Institute of International Environment and Development (which has a US office); the Conservation Society; Friends of the Earth (which also exists in several other bordering states). The activities of these and other European NGOs are now co-ordinated by the European Environmental Bureau (EEB) described below, but several are also involved with or are represented in some of the other bodies. All have taken an increasing interest in maritime affairs.[131]

The oil industry itself has established a large number of bodies to co-ordinate the activities of oil companies in various fields in the UK and elsewhere.[132] These include the Institute of Petroleum (IP) which produces codes of practice for the industry; the Petroleum Industry Association (UKPIA), which provides financial support for the IP; the Oil Industry Exploration and Production Forum (E & P Forum), which represents companies in matters relating to exploration and drilling and other related oil and gas activities and has, *inter alia*, reviewed discharges from offshore production platforms into the marine environment;[133] the UK Offshore Operators Association (UKOOA), which represents all companies acting as operators in production licensing areas on the UK continental shelf;

the International Petroleum Industry Environmental Conservation Association (IPIECA) of international oil companies and petroleum industry associations, which is concerned with the impact of the industries on the marine environment; the Oil Companies International Marine Forum (OCIMF) representing the oil industry as shippers and maritime transporters of crude oil and petroleum products. Some of these bodies have special links, and sometimes also observer status, with international organizations such as UNEP, IMO, and UNESCO (IOC), as well as working closely with each other and other bodies, including ACOPS, as the occasion requires.

Comprehensive NGO organization: the European Environment Board (Bureau Européen de l'Environment)[134]

The EEB, established in 1974 with a secretariat in Brussels, is a coalition of sixty leading non-governmental organizations concerned about the European Community's environment. Its broadly defined purposes are educational and scientific, including protection and conservation of the environment and better use of resources, especially in the EC. It makes recommendations and submits them to appropriate authorities. Its executive committee meets in Brussels and other European states; workshops, conferences and other meetings are also held throughout Europe, often in conjunction with other organizations.

In 1981 a workshop was held in London on shipping and the environment, at which several innovatory proposals were made,[135] particularly concerning improved enforcement of vessel-source pollution measures. Another workshop on deep sea-bed mining briefed members of the European Parliament's Environment Committee on the environmental implications of this activity.[136]

The EEB liaises closely with the European Community; it published comments, for example, on the Commission's proposals for shipping,[137] taking the view that, despite IMO's, role the EC, with its supranational powers, had good reasons to tackle these matters, and could impose co-operation on its members, thereby eliminating any 'power vacuum' that might arise from the failure of governments to exercise their jurisdiction. In 1981 it also commented on the Commission's proposals concerning titanium dioxide poisoning,[138] and has since convened a conference in Brussels to discuss all the environmental implications of the LOS Convention and the unsettled outcome of UNCLOS III.

Through the delegates attending its meetings, the EEB is building a network of contacts with them and their organizations, increasing mutual information exchange, adding to the register of environmental organizations in Community states (over 2,000 are listed) and intensifying contacts with invited bodies in non-member countries (in particular Austria, Sweden, and Switzerland). Several US organizations have also attended, and Spanish contacts are being formed preparatory to Spain's accession to the Community.

The EEB provides a unique non-governmental forum for the European public, to whom measures taken by all the other bodies mentioned in this study are eventually directed; none of the other bodies described does this, although the Netherlands Nord Zee Werkgroep have recently outlined a plan for a wider NGO and governmental forum. A better solution, rather than proliferating generalist bodies, might be to strengthen, support and expand the existing work of the EEB in the maritime field at the NGO level. If its work is practical and valuable, it can be fed into the appropriate existing bodies so that the European public can play its full rightful role in linking the measures to preserve its shared maritime environment and resources.

Conclusion

It will come as a surprise to many that there are so many bodies involved in this area of study, especially in the preservation of the marine environment. Even so gaps remain, and much is left to interpretation and development through national laws. Considerable progress has already been made in the operation and linking of regional bodies and conventions affecting our study area. There is organic growth in both respects, but the shoots are extending somewhat riotously and require both pruning and trellising. Many of the duplication and interrelationship problems stem from the fact that so many organizations were seeded at random, outside any containing organizational fence, and that once this has been allowed to happen it is extremely difficult to replant them inside any one framwork. The various organizations are now so flourishing, in such diverse varieties, that it would be difficult for any comprehensive regional body such as the Council of Europe, the European Commission, or the Nordic Council to overview them all, yet a comprehensive regional organization would have more practical and close interest in fulfilling such a role than the relevant global ones. However, in the absence of any initiative being taken by one of the comprehensive regional bodies to co-ordinate their activities at an early stage—before these functional organizations were allowed to proliferate—the global organizations, in particular IMO and, to a lesser extent, UNEP, have stepped in to fulfil the task and it may be that once again the ground is largely occupied. There are, none the less, possibilities for further co-ordinative action which need study in depth. These are considered in our final chapter.

Notes

1. Sir Francis Vallat, in Sibthorp, M. M. and Unwin, M. (edd.), *Oceanic Management*, Europa, 1977, p. 147.
2. Sibthorp, M. M., *The North Sea: Challenge and Opportunity*, Europa, 1975, ch. vi, pp. 210–45.

3. Knut Fydenlund, 'The Committee of Ministers', *Forward in Europe* no. 3, 1977, p. 90.

4. Ibid. pp. 9–14.

5. See Czernetz, Karl, 'The Parliamentary Assembly', *Forward in Europe* no. 4, 1975 pp. 58–9, and Frydenlund, op. cit., n. 3. It has been suggested that the Assembly would be more effective if it halved its output; Karesek, F., *Forum*, no. 3, 1979, p. 3, says, 'less would in fact be more'.

6. Frydenlund, op. cit. n. 3.

7. Frydenlund, op. cit. n. 3, p. 10.

8. 'Parliamentary Assembly Report on European Action to Prevent Pollution of Waters and Coasts', C. E. Doc. 4199, 28 September 1978, p. 22.

9. Frydenlund, op. cit. n. 3, pp. 11–12; see also Leo Tindemans, 'Relations between the Council of Europe and the European Communities', *Forward in Europe* no. 3, 1976, pp. 5–6.

10. 'Parliamentary Assembly Report', op. cit. n. 8, p. 23; see also pp. 22–4.

11. Convention on the Conservation of European Wildlife and Natural Habitats, done at Berne, 20 July 1979.

12. Convention on Long-Range Trans-Boundary Air Pollution, done at Geneva, 13–16 November 1979.

13. Frydenlund, op. cit. n. 3, p. 14.

14. Thorn, Gaston, 'The Council of Europe', *Forward in Europe*, no. 2, 1976, p. 5.

15. Parliamentary Assembly Report, op. cit. n. 8, pp. 23–4.

16. Tindemans, op. cit., n. 9, p. 5.

17. For an outline of EC institutions and powers, see Mathijsen, P. S. R. F., *A Guide to European Community Law*, 2nd ed., 1975; Lasok, D. and Bridge, J. W., *Law and Institutions of the European Communities*, 2nd ed., 1976.

18. Lasok and Bridge, op. cit., n. 17, p. 107.

19. 'Report on I: The best means of preventing accidents to shipping and consequential marine and coastal pollution; and II: Shipping regulations', rapporteur Lord Bruce of Donington, Eur. Parlt. Working Docs. 1978–79, Doc. 555/78, 15 January 1979. See esp. conclusions and recommendations pp. 28–33; opinions of committee on the environment pp. 34–9; and on agriculture, pp. 40–8.

20. See Prescott, John (UK, MEP), in *Powers of the European Parliament*, London Information Office of the European Parliament, December (1978), p. 38, and the 1972 Vadel 'Report of Working Party Examining the Problem of the Enlargement of the Powers of the European Parliament', *Bulletin of the EC*, Supp. 4, 1972.

21. Lasok and Bridge, op. cit., n. 17, p. 112.

22. Cremona, Marise, 'The Role of the EEC in the Control of Oil Pollution', 17 *Common Market Law Review*, 1980, pp. 171–89.

23. House of Lords Select Committee on the European Communities, 22nd Report (1978); see also its 5th Report (1979–80) on the EC Environment Policy. p. ix. The Committee considered that the purposes of the Rome Treaty are confined to the economic sphere and that none of the articles provided a legal basis for an environmental policy; moreover there were many limitations, particularly of staff resources, which indicated that a more general *strategy* would be preferable.

Mastellone, C., 'The External Relations of the EEC in the field · of Environmental Protection', 30 *ICLQ*, 1981, pp. 104–17.

24. House of Lords Select Committee Report (1978), op. cit., p. xxxv. The Committee arrived at its conclusions after receiving evidence from a wide range of bodies including the Association of County Councils, British Ecological Society, Chemical Industries Association, Confederation of British Industry, Council for Environmental Conservation, European Environmental Bureau, International Institute of Environment and Development, National Water Council, Nature Conservancy, the Royal Society, and the Royal Society for the Protection of Birds.

25. These problems have been exhaustively discussed in Mason, C. (ed.), *The Effective Management of Resources: International Politics of the North Sea*, F. Pinter, 1979, *passim*.

26. de Bievre, A., 'Memorandum on Shipping and the Environment', prepared for the European Environmental Bureau, Brussels, 1982, p. 4, in which the possibilities of EC action at IMO are discussed.

27. Ibid.

28. Four directives concerning seawater partially implementing the Paris convention on land-based pollution exist: on the quality of bathing water; on dangerous substances discharged into the aquatic environment; on waste from the titanium dioxide industry, and on the quality of water for shellfish. Other directives incidentally reduce land-based pollution and thus marine pollution, mostly concerned with waste disposal, e.g. of waste oil, PCBs and PCTs, toxic and dangerous wastes. See also Council studies commissioned following the *Amoco Cadiz* stranding, measures concerning carriage of hydrocarbons by sea (on pilotage; entry conditions for tankers in Community ports; ratification of relevant pollution conventions) and the declaration on harmonization of vessel inspection, in 'Progress Made in Connection with the Environment Action Programme and Assessment of the Work Done to Implement It', COM (80) 222 final Brussels, 7 May 1980; and 'Prevention and Control of Pollution and Protection of the Marine Environment: The Actions Undertaken by the European Community', in Watt, D. C. (ed.), *Greenwich Forum V: The North Sea: A New International Regime?*, Westbury House, 1980, pp. 215–18.

29. See generally *Nordic Cooperation*, Praesidium Secretariat, Stockholm, 1978 and Nordic Council of Ministers Annual Reports, esp. 1979 and 1980: Anne, Leif, 'Regional Policy Objectives of the Nordic Countries', in *Nordic Council: Instruments and Achievements*, Nordic Council Secretariat, 1979, pp. 41–56; Milas, Rene, 'Les Institutions de la Coopération Nordique', ibid., appendix; Koester, Veit, *Nordic Countries Legislation on the Environment with Special Emphasis on Conservation—a Survey*, IUCN, 1980.

30. Bengt Sundelius, 'Nordic Co-operation: a dead issue?', *The World Today*, July 1977, pp. 275–82, at p. 282.

31. By 1977 the Nordic Council had put into effect about 60 per cent of its then 638 recommendations, examined another 20 per cent and rejected only 20 per cent, whereas the Council of Europe had put only 30 per cent of its 940 recommendations into effect by 1979 (40 as conventions, 150 as resolutions of the Council of Ministers, 100 as decisions).

32. Sundelius, op. cit. n. 30, p. 275.

33. Ibid. p. 262.
34. Article 18(b) of OECD rules of procedure provides that recommendations are 'submitted to the Members for consideration in order that they may, if they consider it opportune, provide for their implementation'.
35. *OECD and the Environment*, OECD, 1979, pp. 21–22; this book covers OECD acts and declarations in the field, and provides a bibliography; see also report on *The State of the Environment in OECD Member Countries*, OECD, 1979.
36. Ibid. pp. 51–62.
37. Ibid. pp. 63–74 and 136–45.
38. *Legal Aspects of Transfrontier Pollution*, OECD, 1977, an international code of behaviour, based on the accepted principle of non-discrimination, and that of equal access rights, enabling victims to bring actions in the courts or administrative tribunals of the polluting state. See Smets, H., 'The OECD Approach to the Solution of Transfrontier Problems', in Nowak, J. (ed.), *Environmental Law*, Brit. Inst. Int. and Comp. Law, London, and Ocean Pub. Inc., NY, 1976, pp. 3–11.
39. See op. cit. n. 35, pp. 63–74, and *The Polluter Pays Principle*, OECD, 1975.
40. Proceedings of this seminar were published as *The Cost of Oil Spills*, OECD, 1982.
41. For details see *NATO Facts and Figures*, NATO Information Service, 1971; *NATO Handbook*, NATO Information Services, 1975, pp. 21–2.
42. NATO's treaty purposes include creation of stability and well-being, elimination of conflict in international economic policies, and encouragement of collaboration. Article 9 enables its Council to establish any necessary subsidiary bodies.
43. Coastal Water Pollution: Pollution of the Sea by Oil Spills, CCMS, no. 1.
44. CCMS, no. 36.
45. CCMS, no. 17.
46. CCMS, nos. 7, 12, 15, 114. Other topics covered include advanced waste water treatment, disposal of hazardous substances, rational use of energy.
47. Tenth International Technical Meeting on Air Pollution Modelling and its Application, CCMS, no. 108, 1979.
48. Van Ward, P., Kendall, G. R. and Breese, J. C., 'Ten Years of CCMS—The Record and Future', part i, *NATO Review* no. 6, 1979, pp. 12–17; part ii, *NATO Review* no. 1, 1980, pp. 17–19; see also Allen T., 'Marine Research', *NATO Review* no. 1, 1977, pp. 12–19; Ozdas, S. M., '20 Years of Scientific Co-operation', *NATO Review* no. 4, 1978, pp. 16–21.
49. Van Ward, etc., op. cit. n. 48, part ii, p. 18.
50. See *General Information on the International Council for the Exploration of the Sea*, by the General Secretary (Tambs-Lych, H.), January 1972.
51. Belgium, Canada, Denmark, Finland, France, FRG, GDR, Iceland, Ireland, Netherlands, Norway, Poland, Portugal, Spain, Sweden, UK, USSR, USA.
52. Convention for the International Council for the Exploration of the Sea, 1964; pub. 1974, vii *ILM*, 1968, p. 302.
53. ICES Statistical Area (North) is comparable to FAO's NE Atlantic Area and is larger than the old 1959 NEAFC Convention Area; for purposes of collecting information, ICES divides its area on a grid system, each 30 miles square being

alloted a number in relation to which information is supplied. This enables a detailed picture of the fisheries and environmental factors to be built up.

54. In 1979 it had only a General Secretary, a Hydrographer, a Statistician, an Environmental Officer, 17 full-time officials and some part-timers.

55. Consisting of the President, a First Vice-President and 5 other Vice-Presidents.

56. UNESCO-IMS *Newsletter* no. 17, December 1977, pp. 1 and 8.

57. There are five main ICES Standing Committees (Finance; Consultative; Advisory Committee on Fisheries Management (ACFM); Advisory Committee on Marine Pollution (ACMP); Publications) and twelve Area and Subject Committees* (Fishing Technology; Hydrography; Statistics; Mariculture; Marine Environment Quality; Biological Oceanography; Demersal Fish; Pelagic Fish; Baltic Fish; Shellfish; Anadromous and Catadromous Fish (Anacat); Marine Mammals (especially seals and whales). For details, see *General Information*, op. cit. n. 50, pp. 5–7.

58. This enables contact between basic and applied scientists and contributes to the foundation of marine science as well as to the understanding of practical aspects; *General Information* op. cit. n. 50; ICES has participated in the surveys of the Icelandic/Faroe Ridge (the 'Overflow' Expeditions); the CINECA Project and the Rheno, JONSDAP and BOSEX-77 (Baltic) Experiments. It enables research that might otherwise present political difficulties.

59. See Tambs-Lych, H., 'Monitoring Fish Stocks; the Role of ICES in the NW Atlantic', 2 *Marine Policy*, 1978, pp. 127–32; Ramster, J. W., 'Development of Co-operative Research in the North Sea: The origins, planning and philosophy of JONSDAP 76', 1 *Marine Policy*, 1977, pp. 318–25; Parrish, B., 'The Future Role of ICES in the Light of Changes in Fisheries Jurisdiction', 3 *Marine Policy*, 1979, pp. 232–7.

60. The working group on the sand and gravel industry identified four areas of concern including damaging effects on fisheries, fishing gear, spawning grounds and habitats; 'Report of WG on Effects on Fisheries of Marine Sand and Gravel Extraction', *ICES Co-op Res. Rep, no. 46.*, March 1975. Second Report of the ICES WG on Effects on Fisheries of Marine Sand and Gravel Extraction', *ICES Co-op. Res. Rep. no. 64*, April 1977. The industry has published a reply. ICES had already drawn attention to the speculative nature of assessment because of the lack of adequate research, etc.

61. *Inter alia*, that there should be no dredging in spawning grounds until the effects are better understood; WG Second Report, op. cit. n. 60, pp. 14–15.

62. IMS *Newsletter* no. 24, (written 1979–80), p. 12.

63. NEAFC, 18th Report, 1979, p. 1: it emphasized the continuing lack of information, drew attention to the problem neglected by UNCLOS III that in the NE Atlantic in particular major fish stocks are distributed through more than one national 200-mile zone, and that therefore 'the first priority in dealing with fully exploited stocks of the shared resource category should be to establish a system of joint overall management of the resource in its entire distribution'.

64. *ICES Co-op Res. Rep.*, Series A., no. 13, 1968. It was based on incomplete answers to a questionnaire sent to members.

65. The results of this 'International Study of the Pollution of the North Sea and its

Effects on Living Resources of the North Sea and Their Exploitation' were published as *ICES Co-op Res. Rep.* no. 39, 1974. Coasts had been divided zonally and data elicited on effluents such as nutrients, metals, organochlorine pesticides, PCBs.

66. New questionnaires were despatched seeking information on more pollutants discharged via five pathways directly into the sea as by pipelines; rivers; the atmosphere; dumping; other sources, e.g. incineration. Again not all states responded. By 1977 there were still no data at all on the Oslo Convention's southern section.

67. *ICES Co-op Res. Rep.* no. 39, 1974, p. 16. See also pp. 15–18 and annexe I, p. 56. Industrial and sewage data were incomplete, the former often absent or indistinct (e.g. zinc and mercury); the quantity of such inputs and the types and amounts of potentially harmful substances in them needed much research.

6ᵠ. Ibid, p. 18.

69. It includes the Chairmen of the Hydrography, Marine Environment Quality and Biological Oceanography Committees and co-opted scientists (nine in 1979), selected in their personal capacity as experts in a relevant field.

70. *ICES Co-op. Res. Rep.* no. 103, March 1982.

71. ACMP also considered a draft report on the 1978 Co-ordinated Monitoring Programme on concentrations of selected heavy metals and organochlorine residues in certain fish and shellfish; the UK had not provided data.

72. Following ACMP's work on marine mammals, ICES adopted a resolution inviting members to study the problems identified; C. Res. 1979/4:19.

73. For details see Tambs-Lych, op. cit. n. 59.

74. Between the Director General of FAO and the President of the ICES Council.

75. Joint publications (reports of Working Groups and Symposia); joint meetings and symposia; joint courses, ICES also works with FAO Commissions (e.g. CECAF and EIFAC). Observers are exchanged at meetings; mutual consultation takes place; secretariat officials meet.

76. Through joint working groups and publications; co-operation in data collection and exchange at the planning stage; exchange of observers at meetings; mutual consultations; contacts between secretariats.

77. Alternative methods were fully ventilated in a correspondence between Gulland J. (FAO), and Joseph, J. (ITTC) in *Marine Policy*; See 2 *Marine Policy*, 1975 pp. 161–3 and 2 *Marine Policy* 1978, pp. 239–40. Gulland favours fisheries commissions to be without their own research staff, thus enabling the widest possible international criticism of data and advice. Joseph prefers the commission to have its own research staff as a more timely method of getting research done and making appropriate recommendations.

78. Done at Oslo, 19 February 1974; in force 5 September 1976, Cmnd. 4984; the 12 members are Belgium, Denmark, Finland, France, FRG, Iceland, Netherlands, Norway, Portugal, Spain, Sweden, United Kingdom. The EC has observer status; ICES has not. For details see Henderson, H. (ed.), *Oil and Gas Law: The North Sea*, pp. 1.0032–1.0033, 1.0045–1.0046.

79. In 1981 OSCOM's 7th Annual Meeting took place from 10–12 June; OSPARCOM's Joint Meeting from 12–13 June, and PARCOM's 3rd Meeting from 17–19 June—all in Brussels serviced by the same secretariat.

80. Through document exchanges, exchange of observers, the Joint Working Group on Incineration, some harmonization of reporting procedures.
81. E.g. definition of key conventional terms such as 'trace contaminants', 'harmless', 'non-toxic', 'significant amounts'; development of the legal framework for incineration at sea; establishment of prior consultation procedures; review of annexes.
82. This is not on annexe i (totally banned from dumping) of either convention.
83. OSCOM has made progress in this area with ICES.
84. Only 24 of the 44 states that had ratified the London Dumping Convention by 1977 had supplied information.
85. 'Relations with other Organizations: Meeting of Representatives of the Consultative Meeting and of Regional Organizations on the prevention of marine pollution', IMO, Doc. LDC.VI/60, p. 3, 6 October 1981. Inc. annexe 3, statement by UNEP; Report of Sixth Consultative Meeting, IMO, Docs. LDC. VI/12, 10 November 1981.
86. OSCOM sees the regional convention's role as: creation of a specific legal framework for a particular geographical region taking into account local circumstances, requiring a regulatory body; review of the condition of the marine environment based on monitoring, leading to applicable measures; determination of noxious substances of *regional* concern. The global convention would establish overall policy and principles applicable globally, from which regional agreements would draw inspiration and guidance; it would establish the *international* framework for dumping only in regions not covered by agreements and regulate dumping of wastes of *international* concern, e.g. radioactive waste. The London Convention however, sees itself as having the overview role for regional bodies and providing the linkage between marine environmental protection bodies whether global or regional, but does accept that if a regional agreement imposes more stringent conditions than the global and states are parties to both, they must implement the more stringent measures. cf. 'Co-operation with the London Dumping Convention and Other Organizations Concerned with the Prevention of Marine Pollution,' OSCOM VII/8/2-E, and 'Relationship of the Oslo Convention to the London Dumping Convention', letter from Sasamura, Y., IMO, 12 March 1981. For an independent view of the roles of the two conventions, see Norton, M. G., 'The Oslo and London Dumping Conventions', 12 *Marine Pollution Bulletin*, 1980, pp. 145–9.
87. E.g. UNEP, Baltic Commission, IAEA, OECD (NEA), ICES, EC, Greenpeace International.
88. See OSPAR 11/11/1-E (1980) para. 57. Only one observer attended the joint OSPARCOM Meeting—ICES; cf. similar attitudes evinced at the Fifth Meeting of the Contracting Parties to the Bonn Agreement on Oil Spills, in following section.
89. The Paris Commission (land-based sources); the new Sea-bed Authority (deep sea-bed sources); the 3 Straddle Field Commissions, the NW European Safety etc. Conferences (continental shelf sources); ECE and OECD (transfrontier and atmospheric sources); EC (various sources).
90. Letter to Hayward (Secretary, OSCOM) from Sasamura (IMO), loc. cit.

n. 86. The Oslo, Paris and Helsinki Commissions accepted the offer; UNEP also attended.

91. Including encouragement of development and review of regional agreements; regulation of wastes contributing to the over loading of the ocean's resilience to pollution; provision of necessary linkage with other pollution bodies and of a forum for information exchange. Parties to the London Dumping Convention approved these responsibilities, Norton, op. cit. n. 86, p. 149.

92. Article 19 (2) of the Oslo Convention defines 'ships and aircraft' to include 'floating craft whether self-propelled or not and fixed and floating platforms' but dumping (Article 19 (1)) covers only 'any *deliberate* disposal of substances and materials into the sea by or from ships or aircraft *other than*: (a) any discharges *incidental to or derived from the normal* operations of ships and aircraft and their equipment' (emphasis added to indicate ambiguous terms). The measures now to be taken to control offshore bulky waste dumping are defined in an annexe to the resolution. For further details, see Henderson op. cit. n. 78, at pp. 1.0032–1.0033. Response in reporting actions taken pursuant to the resolution has, however, been rather poor, though Norway has made considerable efforts. The UK was prepared to exchange information in SACSA on the understanding that regular reports were not *required*, but doubted whether the matter came within the Convention; Report of Sixth Meeting of Oslo Commission, Stockholm, June 1980, pp. 20–1 and OSCOM VI/8/1.

93. Done at Paris, 4 June 1974, Cmnd 5803 (1974), entered into force 6 May 1978. There are fourteen signatory states, seven of which have not ratified it, namely: Austria, Belgium, FRG, Iceland, Luxembourg, Spain, Switzerland (NB the two land-locked signatories have not ratified). The EC has adhered to it; ICES has observer status. It has been ratified by Denmark, France, Netherlands, Norway, Portugal, Sweden, UK.

94. Annexe A (banned pollutants) can be amended differently, i.e. by a three-quarters vote, following which the Commission submits the amendments to contracting governments for approval. Those which cannot accept must notify the depositary (France); if no such notification is received, the amendment enters into force for all parties 230 days after the Commission's vote.

95. See articles 6 (2) and 10.

96. The Interim Commission established pending entry into force of the convention accepted this interpretation; some parties initially wanted to limit the term to artificial islands.

97. PARCOM has recommended that discharges resulting directly from sea-bed operations must be free of hydrocarbons with minor exceptions; Second Meeting of Paris Commission, Stockholm, 16–18 June 1980, PARCOM ll/11/1-E p. 2, paras. 7–9. Significant discharges must be reported to PARCOM; the GDP considers implementation of the guidelines. A provisional standard for the proportion of oil in platform discharges of 40 p.p.m. has been adopted by PARCOM and sampling and other techniques prescribed, etc.

98. A PARCOM paper concluded that discharge 'of drainage water' was covered

by both conventions; older platforms combined the different waste stream before discharge; MARPOL's standard of 15 p.p.m. would have to be complied with in 'special areas' whereas PARCOM permits 40 p.p.m. concentrations of oil in water. Newer platforms have separate outflows for drainage water so the problem is avoided.

99. Delegations are meanwhile to send to the secretariat views on methods of establishing a common evaluation standard for comparing the equivalence of results of the methods. Ibid. pp. 5–6, para. 20.

100. 'Agreement for Co-operation in Dealing with Pollution of the North Sea; done at Bonn, June 9, 1969; ll *New Directions in the Law of the Sea*, p. 632. See also our *North Sea* study, pp. 130–1.

101. 'Nordic Agreement for Co-operation in Taking Measures against Pollution of the Sea by Oil, 1971', II *New Directions in the Law of the Sea*, pp. 637–40. The parties are Norway, Denmark, Finland, Sweden.

102. By 1981 it had held 6 meetings—the 5th in London October 1980; the 6th in the Hague, February 1981—and made progress in devising an operational structure. It is now considering scientific and technical problems, leading to reassessment of dispersant and recovery techniques and further research programmes.

103. For details of the North Sea continental shelf sectors see our *North Sea* study, appendix i, pp. 247–9. The Bonn boundaries are based on geographical criteria; most zones are allocated to one state only, but the UK, France, and Belgium share one; the UK and France another.

104. On a voluntary basis until the agreement can be amended by exchange of diplomatic notes.

105. Belgium, Denmark, FRG, France, Ireland, Netherlands, Norway, Sweden, UK, Canada, Italy: the IMO, ILO, EC and Oslo and Paris Commissions (represented jointly by their secretariat) have observer status.

106. WG i's (which interpreted its remit as to elicit the information necessary for designing structures that will withstand the environment, not the effect of structures *on* the environment) report and recommendations on oceanographic and meteorological matters was approved and implemented; WG ii has reported on construction and use off offshore facilities and though no direct action has been taken, certification societies have no doubt taken note of it; WG iii continues to examine personnel safety and was instructed to report in 1979 (now 1982) taking into account the work of all relevant international organizations (e.g. the recent ILO report on the subject).

107. Second Joint Meeting of the Oslo and Paris Commissions, Stockholm, 1980, OSPAR ll/11/1-E, paras, 19–24; OSPAR ll/3/l; OSPAR ll33/2.

108. Press Release, 'Conference on Safety and Pollution in the Development of Offshore Mineral Resources', The Hague, 13–17 November 1977; see also report loc. cit. n. 107, pp. 13–15, paras. 57–65 where the time-tabling difficulties of ICES, EC, and OSPARCOM for meetings and working groups are mentioned.

109. Information on the working groups was supplied in a letter to Miss Sibthorp from A. D. Read, Department of Energy, Petroleum Engineering Division, dated 5 March 1981.

110. Carson, W. G., in *The Other Price of Britain's Oil*, Martin Robertson, 1981, is

highly critical of the way the UK offshore regulatory regime has developed on this subject, but makes no mention of the need for international or regional harmonisation of laws nor of the progress of this North-West European Conference.

111. E.g. *Report from the Commission of Inquiry into the Uncontrolled Blow-out on Ekofisk Bravo, 22 April 1977* (preliminary edition), Oslo 1977; Norges Offentlige Utredninger, *Alexander L. Keilland*, Ulykken, November 1981; 11 Oslo, Universitetsforleget, 1981 (English Summary pp. 207–16); see also Carson, op. cit. n. 110.

112. Done at London, 17 December 1976; open for signature 1 May 1977–30 April 1978; it was signed by all twelve states participating in the negotiations. None has ratified it. It is open on terms (all parties must agree), however, to other states bordering the North Sea, Baltic Sea, or North Atlantic Ocean North of 36° North. The limits of liability proved difficult to negotiate (some states, e.g. Ireland and Norway, sought higher limits than proposed by the UK; Norway would prefer no limit) and though limits are provided, parties retain the national option to raise limits above these or to provide for non-discriminatory unlimited liability.

113. For a detailed description and analysis of its terms, see Henderson op. cit. n. 78, p. 1.0051. The Convention's definitions and terms limit liability in a variety of ways; see for example 'pollution damage' (undefined); 'contamination' (undefined;) claimant's need to establish actual loss to recover; the three exceptions to liability.

114. *North Sea*, appendix i, pp. 247–9.

115. Agreement relating to the Exploitation of the Frigg Field Reservoir and the Transmission of Gas Therefrom to the United Kingdom, London, 10 May 1976; in force 22 July 1977; Cmnd. 6491, 1976.

116. Agreement relating to the Exploitation of the Statfjord Field Reservoir and the Offtake of Petroleum Therefrom, Oslo, 16 October 1979, Cmnd. 7813, (1980).

117. Agreement Relating to the Exploitation of the Murchison Field Reservoir and the Offtake of Petroleum Therefrom, Oslo, 16 October 1979, Cmnd. 7814 (1980).

118. Pipeline Agreement to Carry Petroleum from the Norwegian Continental Shelf to the United Kingdom, signed and effective 22 May 1973; Cmnd. 5423 (1973), 13 *ILM* (1974) pp. 26–30; iv *New Directions*, pp. 137–44; xiii *ILM*, p. 26–30. The agreement avoids the need for the pipeline to cross the deep Norwegian Trough. Its route requires the approval of both governments.

119. Norwegian and British inspectors are granted mutual rights of access to each state's installations; one state's inspector can invite the other's to exercise his powers. Any inspector can order cessation of any activity if, in his judgement, this is necessary to avert or minimize an accident involving danger to life.

120. Information supplied orally by Department of Energy. UK departments concerned include Trade, Employment, Environment, Inland Revenue, Customs and Excise, Foreign Office, Health and Safety Executive.

121. A. Morrison, Chief Constable, Grampian Region, UK 'Policing and Enforcement', unpublished paper, Conference on Fishing in European Waters, Edinburgh, UK, October, 1978. Aberdeen is frequently the 'port of

operations' nominated by the operator and therefore responsible for policing his installations. The Frigg Field, however, is entirely physically operated and serviced from Norway. Four installations in the UK sector, close to the median line, and two in Norway's are linked by walkways: the agreement secures free movement of persons and materials. Moreover, continental shelf laws cannot be enforced on the high seas even against vessels engaged in oil-related activities such as pipe-laying from barges or support and supply services.

122. If a dispute is not settled by the Consultative Committee or by inter-governmental negotiations—and so far all have been—an arbitral tribunal of three persons (one from each state party and a third chosen by them) must be established, at the request of either government.

123. OPOL, pub. Offshore Pollution Liability Association Ltd., London, UK, 1976; vi *New Directions*, p. 515. The agreement is revised from time to time. For details see Henderson op. cit. n. 78, pp. 1.0056–1.0058.

124. 'Pollution damage' is defined as 'direct loss or damage; other than to the designated offshore facility concerned, by 'a contamination which results in a discharge of oil'.

125. 'Remedial measures' are defined to include any reasonable measures taken by a party from whose offshore facility the oil discharge emanates and by any public authority to clean up and control the oil.

126. E.g. to raise liability limits; to extend its scope (it was originally confined to the UK sector); to enlarge its definition of public authorities compensatable to exclude gas facilities.

127. Fisheries and Offshore Oil Consultation Group, *Progress Report 1975*, pub. Department of Agriculture and Fisheries Scotland. See also Grant, J., 'The Conflict between the fishing and the oil industries in the North Sea: A Case Study', 4 *Ocean Management*, 1978, pp. 137–50.

128. 'Fishermen accuse oil firms' *The Times*, 11 March 1982, p. 8. The Shetland Fishermen's Association seeks revision of the 1974 agreement; demands compensation for lost grounds, and regards the sums paid into the fund as 'totally insufficient'. Companies involved in the laying and burying of the Brent and Ninian field oil pipelines were accused of negligence in leaving large quantities of debris on the sea-bed.

129. Original agreement in viii *ILM* 1969, pp. 497–501; amended version obtainable from International Tanker Owners Pollution Federation Ltd. See also *North Sea*, p. 133.

130. Original contract in x *ILM* 1971, pp. 137–44. It was to lapse 120 days after the Fund Convention became effective. See also *North Sea*, p. 133.

131. See particularly ACOPS Annual Reports; contrast the size and scope of the 1973 and 1979–1981 Reports which summarize not only ACOPS' own expanded activities, but those of all relevant marine pollution bodies, national, regional and international, as well as major oil pollution incidents. ACOPS also promotes development of new UK legislation, and conducts an annual survey of oil pollution off the UK coasts. It has forged links with several similar international bodies.

132. See Mason, C. (ed), *The Effective Management of Resources: International Politics of the North Sea*, Frances Pinter, 1979. The Industry endeavours,

often belatedly, to adapt to changing needs. For example, following the Ekofisk Bravo blow-out and criticism of the resultant muddle, the companies adopted a 'Fire-Brigade Pact', dividing the North Sea into five zones (not corresponding to any other zones) of responsibility for fire fighting and co-ordination procedures.

133. See also 'Review of Discharges from Offshore Production Platforms into the Marine Environment', the Oil Industry International Exploration and Production Forum, March 1979, which analyses the shortcomings of present analytical methods and reviews the discharge regime as a whole. The E & P Forum strongly supports setting discharge standards in terms of Environmental Quality Objectives.

134. For detailed information, see the EEB's annual reports, esp. 1981 report.

135. de Bièvre, A., *Memorandum on Shipping and the Environment*, European Environment Bureau, December 1981.

136. On a Community Information System and an Advisory Committee for Preventing Oil Pollution; for a Directive on the Authority of the Port of Call.

137. de Bièvre, op. cit. n. 135, conclusions, pp. 40–9.

138. Hannequart, J. P. and Roncerel, A., *The Control of Disposal of Wastes at Sea*, EEB, 1981; see also Hannequart and Verbrugge, G., *Travaux Relatifs à L'Environment Effectives dans Divers Instances International et la Politique de la Communauté Européene*, EEB, 1981.

XII

Conclusions and Recommendations

We were surprised to find, during the course of the researches on which the present study is based, that there has been little or no work carried out at either an academic or official level, whether national or intergovernmental, on the existing range of bodies currently concerned with the various aspects of the numerous uses of the north-west European waters as a whole, still less on the multifaceted interrelationships which our study has brought to light. However, in formulating these conclusions and recommendations it might be useful to examine how far the recommendations proposed in our North Sea study, published in 1975, have had any influence on subsequent developments. In fact, few if any of the proposals which were then made have even been considered, although had they been adopted they could have made a substantial contribution to the better co-ordination of the rules and regulations governing the wider regional area now under consideration.

One difficulty which international law appears to have is keeping up with the ever increasing rapidity of technological change. In such an area of rapid flux, international conventions tend to become out of date even before they have been generally adopted. Moreover, even if concluded within a reasonable time at the global level, they frequently have to resort to general or ambiguous language in order to achieve the compromises necessary to attract wide ratification. This leads to the establishment of numerous *ad hoc* regional bodies to deal with details and conflicts, which are unco-ordinated at the international level, thus often leading to 'confusion worse confounded'. The chief points of conflict of interests remain as before: the control of fisheries—even though there is now a Common Fisheries Policy and in theory the EC has powers of enforcement, in practice there is no detailed agreement on how it should be implemented; the effects of the extraction of sand and gravel as contributing to the erosion of the coast and to the possible alteration of inshore currents and the disturbance of established spawning grounds; the control of pollution both as a run-off from the land and from disposal from ships; the use of the seas as a disposal area for toxic and nuclear waste; the control of navigation; the improvement of hydrography—as was demonstrated when the *Amoco Cadiz* ran aground, for that portion of the coast of Brittany was unmapped; the possible discrepancies as between defence requirements, oil extraction and exploration, fishing, and amenity, although so far this has not given rise to any serious conflicts in the area. In addition, there are the problems raised by the use of flags of convenience, the discharge of oily deposits by tankers on the high seas outside territorial limits, and the thorny questions of insurance and compensation. It is particularly important to minimize the use of sub-standard ships in north-west European waters. With regard to navigation, one of the difficulties experienced by the UK is that until very recently the bulk of the shipping round its coasts was UK-owned since, until the Second World War, it was the leading maritime nation. However, today some 77 per cent of the shipping in the North Sea and English Channel is foreign-owned, posing an obvious threat to navigation, with problems of communication and insufficiently trained crews. The development of a universally understood language, such as Seaspeak, would help further to improve this situation.

It is still doubtful how many states will be prepared to sign or ratify the new UNCLOS Convention since this means accepting also the International Sea-bed Authority controlling the extraction of minerals from the deep sea-bed. However, many of the provisions codify or extend already existing international law or accepted marine practice of states and, to that extent, it will be operative whether ratified or not. Other provisions are also likely to be brought into effect by states' practice as part of customary law. However, the Reagan proclamation on 10 March 1983 of US sovereign rights in a 200-mile Exclusive Economic Zone in terms which differ from the LOS Convention, though it may be only a straw in the wind, illustrates the regrettable likelihood of considerable variation in states' claims, since it was not based on the detailed text of the LOS Convention.

One of the salient facts to be taken into account, as emerged clearly from our earlier study, is that, as already mentioned, there are an ever-increasing number of organizations concerned with aspects of the management of the resources of the north-west European seas, a far larger number than was the case when our former study appeared. The situation is infinitely more complex now, as emerges clearly from chapters X and XI. Moreover, the organs which existed in 1975 have increasingly involved themselves in such matters as the protection of the marine environment, especially from vessel-source pollution. The growing concern for the environment has produced a 'way in' to expand their activities.

The original proposals we put forward had been that, in the first place, some overarching body was required to prevent regionalism becoming 'disguised unilateralism'. Such a regional body might lay down internationally agreed rules and standards, but provide for more stringent action, in both applying and enforcing them, regionally. We examined existing organizations in this light, found none of them fully suited to a central controlling or co-ordinating role, decided that a new organization would be unacceptable, and concluded that creation of a new co-ordinating machinery would be the best option. We proposed, *inter alia*, that a new regime treating the North Sea as a single unit should be established, the fundamental problem of involving existing bodies in such a strategy being overcome by linking them to a Standing Conference of North Sea States in which the EC and the Council of Europe could be separate participants.

Neither this nor the more detailed recommendations have been implemented, though some progress has been made in particular areas, especially in moves towards greater port state control. But in general the proposals have not even been seriously debated, in spite of the obviously growing need for better co-ordination and development of laws, policies, and administration at the regional level. It is important, therefore now to look again at our earlier conclusions in the context of the developments surveyed in the previous chapters, in regional, as well as global, organizations.

Our original proposals were:

A. (1) A Standing Conference of North Sea States should be created by international agreement between them; the EEC and the Council of Europe could also be separate parties, or have corporate participation.

(2) The aims of the Conference should be expressed to be:

- (a) to act as a channel of communications between governments, parliaments, scientists, and technicians;
- (b) to collect information and build up a body of knowledge on North Sea activities and particularly the use of its resources, in the air, waters and sea-bed, and the resulting problems;
- (c) to further co-operation and harmonization of practice between States in research and development, resource use and management, and legislative policy;
- (d) to provide means of co-ordination of the relevant work of existing organizations, governmental and non-governmental, national and international.

(3) The sphere of operations of the Conference should include fisheries; conservation and management of sea-bed resources and other marine resources; control and elimination of pollution; sea transport; and air transport in so far as it affects the North Sea.

(4) The Standing Conference might itself meet at ministerial level every two or three years, but it should, in general, function through committees or working groups, and the greatest possible use should be made of existing organizations, as indicated in paragraph 2 (d) above. It must be emphasized that the Conference is *not* to be regarded as a new international body, with executive powers, but a medium of co-ordination, an 'umbrella' organization. It would need to be serviced by a bureau or secretariat, which could be administratively incorporated in the EEC or the Council of Europe.

(5) The meetings of the Standing Conference, and those organized through it, should take different forms according to their objects and the matters to be dealt

with. The periodic meetings of the Standing Conference itself should deal with broad issues of policy in the light of developments since the last meeting and of future needs. Meetings would also be organized, for example:

(a) at Ministerial level for such matters as fisheries and sea-bed resource management;
(b) at the scientific level for questions involving, e.g., marine biology, pollution standards, climatic change;
(c) at the technical level for mining techniques and navigation (separation of traffic, etc.);

Care should be taken, however, that at the meetings of the Conference and in the activities of all committees, working groups, and other bodies, there is representation of all the requisite kinds of expertise, including legal. Further, the participation of parliamentarians should be encouraged as far as practicable.

(6) In the United Kingdom it would be desirable to set up a Permanent Committee and one or more Parliamentary Committees, covering various aspects of the uses of the North Sea, with 'feedback' from and to the Standing Conference. These should be supported by interdepartmental committees. Parliamentary Committees would ensure exchanges of information, cross-fertilization of ideas and more effective public control of governmental and industrial policies.

(7) The territorial scope of the Standing Conference should be the North Sea basin. The area covered by the North-East Atlantic Fisheries Commission and ICES is much wider, but it would be desirable that the Commission and ICES, in pursuing their normal activities, should, as far as the North Sea basin is concerned, collaborate with the Standing Conference.

B. Each North Sea State should enact legislation requiring that, before *any* project involving activity in or under the North Sea is licensed or initiated, an environmental impact statement should be prepared and published. This statement should be subject to full investigation, with free public participation at the scientific level, and the Standing Conference should have an opportunity through a working group to advise the government or governments concerned before a decision on the project is taken.

C. There should be machinery established for checking and co-ordinating the enforcement of existing and future international conventions or other agreements governing uses of the North Sea.

The present situation with regard to pollution is highly unsatisfactory. There is no generally agreed procedure for inspection for infringement of pollution regulations by ships outside territorial waters and there are legal and practical difficulties in enforcing these regulations against ships flying the flag of States outside the region. However, nothing would prevent coastal States from exercising jurisdiction to the full in respect of breaches of pollution regulations (including regulations about construction of ships and methods of handling pollutants) committed within their territorial or internal waters. Secondly, since, with certain exceptions already noted, States are free to prohibit access to their ports and internal waters, the coastal State could always refuse to grant access to a ship which could be shown to have violated the relevant regulations on the high seas. These may well be a useful deterrent since, in general, ships do not enter the North Sea unless they intend to put into port there. Prohibiting unloading and/or sale of cargo is a further possibility.

A further and a more effective way of coping with these problems would be for the navies of North Sea States to be given the power, by a treaty in which all the flag States also participated, to inspect ships for violations on the high seas and possibly to punish them as well. In such a case it might be best for these powers to be exercised by a joint policing unit rather than by individual navies (see below). But, politically, the likelihood of flag States' assenting to such an extension of coastal State jurisdiction seems, at any rate for the moment, somewhat remote.

In the event of such agreement in principle, it would remain to establish means of effective control of ships breaking agreed laws and regulations on fishing, polluting, and dumping prohibited chemicals. In the absence of such agreement, control might be exercised by the application of economic sanctions by:

(a) prohibiting access to ports;
(b) prohibiting unloading of cargoes.

An International Economic Committee to study the economic aspects of the problems could be set up by the Standing Conference.

It is therefore recommended that:

(1) A general level at which enforcement measures become operative should be established.
(2) Serious and deliberate pollution should be held to be analogous to piracy and be subject to similar enforcement measures.
(3) There should be a right of arrest of offenders on the high seas.[1]
(4) It should be possible to recover damages, or apply criminal law, when a ship is caught polluting on the high seas.
(5) Where coastal pollution from industrial plants is concerned, in the case of persistent offenders, and in the last resort, there should be power to order the closure of the plant.[2]
(6) Discharge or escape of oil from oil rigs or installations should be subject to the same penalties as those which apply to discharge of oil from ships.

D. The creation of a joint North Sea Policing Service is proposed. There would seem to be two alternative methods open:

(1) to organize an international civil policing force based on existing Coastguard units with adequate vessels equipped with the latest electronic devices. The service would require an air arm, possibly of helicopters; or
(2) to assign the task to a joint naval force, assisted by a joint air force unit. This would probably imply seconding vessels and men to a special naval enforcement unit. The policing force could well operate under the control of the North Sea Standing Conference.

E. *At the United Kingdom National level*, it is further recommended:

(1) That further research into the problems raised by the optimum use of the resources of the North Sea should be urgently undertaken.

(2) That such research should be co-ordinated in order to avoid wasteful overlapping and duplication. This requires the creation of a body with responsibility for interdepartment collaboration at Cabinet Office level.

(3) That information should be more readily accessible to government departments, interested organizations, and the general public, whose welfare is intimately involved. The factor of confidentiality of reports should be reduced to the lowest possible level.

(4) That communication between the government and the public at large should be greatly improved.

As can be seen from the above, most of the detailed recommendations are still valid. One topic which has been the subject of some recent debate is that of a United Kingdom Offshore Policing Service which links directly with suggestion D in our original proposals. It has been suggested that a Policing Service should be set up to implement the regulations covering the area of safety and rescue, since it is now becoming obvious that the number and complexity of such regulations are growing and will continue to do so, thus increasing the demands upon the supervising authority. Moreover, the extent of the area to be controlled has also grown in the recent past and bids fair to continue to expand as states claim more extensive national jurisdiction. The aim would be to divide the responsibility for the maintenance of sovereignty, the safeguarding of security, and the upholding of national jurisdiction in the enforcement of regulations governing the uses of the seas. It is further suggested that such a division of responsibility might also assist in avoiding possible disputes arising within the NATO alliance.

A further recommendation under the scheme would be that close co-operation would obtain between the proposed civil authority and the Royal Navy and that to this end there should be cross-posting between the services for training.

On the other hand, it has been stressed that there would be a number of drawbacks to such a division of responsibility since, in the last resort, if the proposed Offshore Policing Service could not cope, the Armed Services would inevitably have to be called in. Moreover, the probability would be that the provision of separate forces to carry out the tasks now performed by the services might well result in yet another command and control organization entailing more rather than fewer committees wih the concomittant bureaucracy. Considerably more research would necessarily, therefore, have to be done before the scheme could be accepted if it were to be deemed viable.

A Final Recommendation

In the light of the enlargement of the number of bodies dealing with aspects of the problems in north-west European waters, and the almost certain failure of any effort to set up an overriding organization to co-ordinate and control their activities, we feel that our formal proposal for the establishment of a Conference of North-West European States is now inappropriate. What is now required is a body to facilitate co-ordination which would survey the work of all the organizations affecting the area. It would gather and make freely available to all concerned:

(a) Information on the composition of the international and national bodies active in the region.
(b) Information on the activities of these bodies.
(c) Information on the developing legal situation, international and national.
(d) Information on the technical and scientific developments affecting activities in the region.
(e) Information on the current state of control of pollution, fishing, navigation, shipping, oil extraction and further exploration, sand and gravel extraction, and deep sea mining.
(f) Information on the probable effects of major projects such as the Waddensee enclosures, the Severn barrage, and the erection of artificial islands on the immediate area concerned.
(g) Information on the needs of defence where these conflict with other uses.

It is considered that such an organization should be strictly non-governmental in composition, thus avoiding the danger of political conflicts, particularly in the field of national priorities, providing an impartial assessment of the situation in the various fields and setting out clearly what the real difficulties are, what solutions would be best, and what are probably attainable. It should be composed of experts in the subjects involved and it would liaise closely with the international and national bodies working in the field. It would have a small secretariat and would be free to institute individual research if and where this was considered to be necessary. It would advise governments and organizations either on request as a consultancy or acting independently, where it was felt that improvements or alterations to working methods involved were clearly desirable, but it would have no executive or coercive powers. It would be for the governments or organizations concerned to accept its proposals for changes if they considered them desirable. Such recommendations could be particularly effective in the case of clashes of procedure as in navigation, or of vested interests as in fishing, oil exploration, and so forth.

The organization (possibly to be called the Sea Use Studies Institute) would require an influential head of high international reputation, an effective fund raiser, and a small secretariat chosen from the countries concerned. The funds raised should not be governmental; they could possibly come from interested industries or foundations or both, although in the case of foundations such funds are usually given for a special study. over a given period of time. The essential point is that the organization should be a *permanent* body—this, together with its independent status, would be its main value.

Index